PLACE IN RETURN BOX to remove this checkout from your record.
TO AVOID FINES return on or before date due.

DATE DUE	DATE DUE	DATE DUE
MAR 1 3 1995 237	FEB 22 2009 03	
OCT 3 1 2004 0 3 0 7 0		

The Nature and Ontogenesis
of Meaning

The Jean Piaget Symposium Series
Available from LEA

SIGEL, I. E., BRODZINSKY, D. M., & GOLINKOFF, R. M. (Eds.) • New Directions in Piagetian Theory and Practice

OVERTON, W. F. (Ed.) • The Relationship Between Social and Cognitive Development

LIBEN, L. S. (Ed.) • Piaget and the Foundations of Knowledge

SCHOLNICK, E. K. (Ed.) • New Trends in Conceptual Representation: Challenges to Piaget's Theory?

NEIMARK, E. D., De LISI, R., & NEWMAN, J. L. (Eds.) • Moderators of Competence

BEARISON, D. J., & ZIMILES, H. (Eds.) • Thought and Emotion: Developmental Perspectives

LIBEN, L. S. (Ed.) • Development and Learning: Conflict or Congruence?

FORMAN, G., & PUFALL, P. B. (Eds.) • Constructivism in the Computer Age

OVERTON, W. F. (Ed.) • Reasoning, Necessity, and Logic: Developmental Perspectives

KEATING, D. P., & ROSEN, H. (Eds.) • Constructivist Perspectives on Developmental Psychopathology and Atypical Development

CAREY, S., & GELMAN, R. (Eds.) • The Epigenesis of Mind: Essays on Biology and Cognition

BEILIN, H., & PUFALL, P. (Eds.) • Piaget's Theory: Prospects and Possibilities

WOZNIAK, R. H., & FISCHER, K. W. (Eds.) • Development in Context: Acting and Thinking in Specific Environments

OVERTON, W. F., & PALERMO, D. S. (Eds.) • The Nature and Ontogenesis of Meaning

The Nature and Ontogenesis
of Meaning

Edited by

Willis F. Overton
Temple University

David S. Palermo
Pennsylvania State University

LEA LAWRENCE ERLBAUM ASSOCIATES, PUBLISHERS
1994   Hillsdale, New Jersey   Hove, UK

Lawrence Erlbaum Associates, Inc., Publishers
365 Broadway
Hillsdale, New Jersey, 07642

Library of Congress Cataloging-in-Publication Data

The nature and ontogenesis of meaning / edited by Willis F. Overton
  and David S. Palermo.
      p.   cm.
  Includes bibliographical references and indexes.
  ISBN-0-8058-1211-3
  1. Meaning (Psychology) 2. Meaning (Philosophy) I. Overton,
Willis F. II. Palermo, David Stuart, 1929–
BF463.M4N38 1994
121′.68—dc20   94-9726
                                                             CIP

Books published by Lawrence Erlbaum Associates are printed on acid-free
paper, and their bindings are chosen for strength and durability.

Printed in the United States of America
10 9 8 7 6 5 4 3 2 1

We dedicate this book to our wives

Carol and Marion

with love and appreciation.

Contents

List of Contributors

Professor Willis F. Overton—Department of Psychology, Temple University, Philadelphia, PA 19147

Professor Kenneth J. Gergen—Department of Psychology, Swarthmore College, Swarthmore, PA 19081

Professor George Lakoff—Department of Linguistics, University of California, Berkeley, CA 94720

Professor Mark Turner—English Department, 1125 Taliaferro Hall, University of Maryland, College Park, MD 20742

Professor Ellin Kofsky Scholnick (with Kelly Cookson)—Department of Psychology, University of Maryland, College Park, MD 20742

Professor Ray Jackendoff—Program in Linguistics & Cognitive Science, Brandeis University, Waltham, MA 02154

Professor John Macnamara—Department of Psychology, McGill University, 1205 Dr. Penfield Ave, Montreal, Quebec H3A 1B1 Canada

Dr. Terrance Brown—3530 N. Lake Shore Drive, 12-A, Chicago, IL 60657

Professor Jonas Langer—Department of Psychology, University of California, Berkeley, CA 94720

Professor Lois Bloom, Box 5, Columbia University Teachers College, 525 W. 120th St., New York, NY 10027

Professor Kathy Hirsh-Pasek (with Professor Roberta Michnick Golinkoff, University of Delaware, & Lauretta Reeves, Temple University)— Department of Psychology, Temple University, Philadelphia, PA 19122

Dr. Carol Feldman (with Professor Jerome Bruner, David Kalmar, Bobbi Renderer)—New York University, Fuchsberg Hall, 249 Sullivan St., New York, NY 10012

Professor Richard F. Kitchener—Department of Philosophy, Colorado State University, Fort Collins, CO 80523

Preface

Piaget's theory, throughout its evolution, has placed meaning at the center of all attempts to understand the nature and development of knowing. The continuity of this project is evident from early works, such as the *Origins of Intelligence*, where Piaget repeatedly describes assimilation (i.e., the act of meaning making) as the fundamental process of all intelligent activity, to his last writings, such as *Toward a Logic of Meanings*, where acts of meaning describe the foundation for the development of logical deductive systems. For Piaget all knowing, whether sensorimotor, representational, or reasoned, and whether directed toward successful problem solutions or toward general understanding, is necessarily a construction and this construction arises out of meaning-making activity.

It was in the context of this centrality of the concept of meaning that the editors of this volume approached the board of directors of the Jean Piaget Society with a proposal to organize its 1991 annual symposium around the topic of the nature and development of meaning. In forming this symposium, and in moving from symposium to integrated text, we wanted to insure both a breadth and depth to the analysis of the topic. Meaning making arises in social, affective, cognitive, as well as linguistic contexts. Consequently, one of our aims was to insure that the symposium and this text reflected each of these contexts rather than being limited to a specifically linguistic context. To this end we invited Ken Gergen, a social psychologist, to discuss the social interdependency of individuals in the creation of meaning (chapter 2). Terry Brown brought a psychiatric background to the task and explores affective dimensions in the creation of meaning (chapter 7). And Jonas Langer (chapter 8) examines the developmental movement from instrumental or sensorimotor meaning making to symbolic or representational meaning making, from a comparative cognitive perspective.

George Lakoff sets the linguistic context with his presentation of cognitive semantics and his exploration of the nature of conceptual systems (chapter 3). Lakoff's position, consistent with many other participants, is that rather than being located in language per se, meaning is located in the activity of mind and may be transmitted through words or gestures. Ellin Kofsky Scholnick and Kelly Cookson (chapter 5) expand on this theme and discuss critical developmental issues in the elaboration of cognitive semantics. Mark Turner (chapter 4) describes several issues in the theory of mind that are central to cognitive semantics.

Lois Bloom's developmental approach to semantic development (chapter 9) expands and elaborates the perspective that infants acquire language in the effort to express and articulate mentally constructed personal, private meanings so as to make them public. Carol Feldman, Jerry Bruner, and their colleagues (chapter 11) explore the construction of linguistic narratives as a vehicle for the construction of meaning during childhood, adolescence, and the adult years.

While the constructivist thesis that meaning making is initially grounded in the general cognitive/affective activities of the organism is salient throughout the text, several participants introduce cautionary notes. Ray Jackendoff (chapter 6) begins from a discussion of the Piaget (constructivism)–Chomsky (nativism) debate. In that context he examines word meaning and argues the need for understanding conceptual structure as emerging from an innate combinatorial system. Kathy Hirsh-Pasek and her colleagues (chapter 10) argue that a successful understanding of the acquisition of semantics requires the postulation of innate mental language-specific biases. And John Macnamara (chapter 12), in considering the place of logic, argues for an objectivist stance that takes reference seriously, as opposed to either a constructivist or nativist cognitivist position. In a similar fashion, Richard Kitchener (chapter 13) presents a philosophical taxonomy of semantic theories and concludes by arguing for naturalized meaning by accepting an "external" point of view (realism) and abandoning an "internal" point of view (cognitivism).

Along with offering a wide range of approaches and rich depth of analysis, the text addresses major issues that constitute the foundation for dialogues that continue to frame theoretical and empirical investigations into the development of meaning. In an integrative overview, Overton (chapter 1) identifies and elaborates on the impact of several of these issues. These include alternative conceptions regarding the theory of mind (e.g., Lakoff's concept of the embodied mind and Jackendoff's concept of the computational mind) and alternative views on the locus of meaning making (e.g., the Lakoff, Jackendoff, Langer, Bloom et al. perspective of active mind as the agent of meaning making and the Gergen, Macnamara, and Kitchener perspective of the social and objective locus of meaning).

ACKNOWLEDGMENTS

We extend our thanks to the officers and board of directors of the Jean Piaget Society for their continuous support from the inception of this project through the symposium that brought the authors together to share their observations, ideas, and intuitions about the development of meaning, and finally through the process of the production of this text. A special thanks also to Ellin Kofsky Scholnick, who, as series editor of the Jean Piaget Society symposium series, was most helpful in advancing this text during the publication process.

Willis F. Overton
David S. Palermo

1

Contexts of Meaning: The Computational and the Embodied Mind

Willis F. Overton
Temple University

The formulation and description of the nature and place of the concept of meaning in any psychological theory, and particularly in a psychological theory of cognitive development, is made exceptionally difficult by the multidimensional character of this concept. The task is rendered particularly difficult by the fact that meaning, like so many other fundamental concepts, is intensely relational in nature. "I mean"/"it means" constitutes the relational matrix from which all issues of meaning are generated. When we focus on the "I mean" pole of this relationship, we focus on the contribution of the person to meaning. The "it means" pole focuses us on the contribution of the manifest world of common sense. The "I mean"/"it means" relational matrix becomes elaborated across domains of inquiry and across levels of analysis as issues of intension and extension, sense and reference, connotation and denotation, semantics and syntactics, hermeneutics and realism. Regardless, however, of domain and level, the background problem that must be satisfied always remains how most productively to understand the underlying relational matrix. When the question "What is the nature of meaning, and how does meaning develop for the child?" is raised, the answer emerges from the way we choose to formulate the relational "I mean"/"it means" matrix.

In this chapter I examine the nature of meaning and its ontogenesis by first exploring ontological and epistemological strategies that function as background to a broad understanding of the concept of meaning. In essence, the argument is that different ontological and epistemological strategies—here referred to as isolationist and systems strategies—for how to approach the "I mean"/"it means" matrix lead to different understandings of the fundamental nature of meaning. Further, it is argued that these strategies lead to alternative theories of mind; specifically the computational and the embodied mind. These alternative theories of mind in their turn then establish the conceptual base from which investigators explore issues concerning the nature and ontogenesis of psychological meaning.

ISOLATIONIST AND SYSTEMS STRATEGIES FOR UNDERSTANDING MEANING

Upon reflection, it is easy to see that there are two fundamental alternative strategies for understanding the "I mean"/"it means" or any relational matrix. The first strategy can be called an *isolationist* or *splitting strategy*, and the second, a *systems strategy*. The isolationist strategy divides or splits the relational matrix into isolated, inherently unconnected pieces and then searches for a kind of glue that can mend the split. The glue is traditionally some causal network. Here, one disconnected piece is assigned the role of cause, and the other piece the role of effect. From this strategic perspective, for example, it might be held that "it means" is fundamental and the cause of the "I mean." In this example meaning is formulated primarily as an entity that is lodged in an objective, natural world. The interpretative task of inquiry here is to deal with the remaining problem of how this world has generated the subjective world of "I mean." Scholnick and Cookson (chapter 5 of this volume) capture the developmental instantiation of this particular strategy when they note that today one popular approach to understanding development is to treat it as a knowledge-storing process. "It means" in this example constitutes the real, and generates "I mean."

A cardinal feature of the isolationist strategy is the linear either/or stance that it presents. Either the subjective intentional "I mean" constitutes the foundational real and generates the objective "it means," or the objective constitutes the real and generates the subjective. Here an ontological choice is demanded between the one or the other. Kitchener's description of efforts at naturalizing semantics (chapter 13 of this volume) illustrates this stance where naturalism asserts the fundamental ontological priority of the objective "it means." Kitchener's own conclusion that the task for psychology is to build a "naturalist psychological semantics: a theory of (psychological) meaning that continuances only naturalistic entities knowable by naturalistic methods" represents a further elaboration of this same strategy.[1] This position is further expanded by Macnamara's (chapter 7 of this volume) attempt to develop an objectivist cognitive psychology.

The either/or stance of the isolationist strategy is illustrated in a more subtle fashion by Gergen. Although Gergen (chapter 2 of this volume) argues for a relational communal approach to meaning, his argument resolves itself into a

---

[1]For a detailed critique of efforts to naturalize meaning, see Katz (1990).

critique of approaches that focus on the individual as subject and a celebration of approaches that shift toward the social dyad. The primacy of the dyad over the individual becomes foundational and privileged for Gergen. Relational is identified with dyad and stands in ontological opposition to the individual from this perspective. However, even the dyad in Gergen's approach constitutes two inherently isolated pieces that must be brought together to forge consensus. As with other isolationist strategies "I mean" evolves out of "it means," but in this case "it means" is explicitly social. As Gergen says, "lone utterances [and presumably lone actions] begin to acquire meaning when another (or others) . . . add some form of supplementary action."

The second strategy for understanding the "I mean"/"it means" relational matrix involves treating the matrix as a unified whole or self-organizing system that comes to differentiate itself into these contrasting features of "I" and "it." From this perspective neither "I mean" nor "it means" is given ontological priority at any level of analysis or for any domain. "I mean" and "it means" become bipolar features that emerge from an organized activity matrix. Each feature of the matrix defines and is defined by the other.[2] Here, no glue of associations or causes is needed to paste isolated unities together into a relationship. Instead, the relational matrix itself is primary and part-systems of "I mean" and "it means" become articulated through activity that results in these differentiations and further reintegration.

The systems strategy, then, accords no ontological priority to either subject or object. In taking this stance, the systems strategy describes a fundamentally monistic world. This is in contrast to objectivist or naturalist perspectives that proclaim themselves monistic but, in fact, simply suppress one term of a subject–object dualism. Naturalism attempts to be monistic by denying the subjective or, what amounts to the same thing, reducing the subjective to the objective. The systems perspective is monistic from the start. By taking a truly monistic stance the systems perspective can grant that meaning or knowledge is cultural in nature. Of course, it can also grant that meaning or knowledge is individualistic in nature.

As the systems perspective asserts a fundamental monism, paradoxes arise, including this paradox that meaning is entirely cultural in nature and yet meaning is entirely individual in nature. The systems stance accepts the fact that all understanding involves paradox, and therefore, self-reference and contradiction. In fact, the systems stance argues precisely against attempts at resolving such paradoxes at the level of analysis at which they occur. Such attempts at resolution necessarily involve splitting the relational matrix into independent parts and then deciding which one is really basic or basically real. The problem is that this attempt at paradox resolution is precisely the reintroduction of the isolationist alternative and, thus, a dualism.

---

[2] For an elaboration of the ontological and epistemological dimensions of the systems strategy, see Overton (1991a, 1991b, in press).

The major danger for the systems strategy is that if there were no way at all of resolving circularity and paradox, then thinking about a domain of interest—here, meaning—would become confused and muddled. If meaning is entirely cultural, and at the same time meaning is entirely individual, it is difficult to see how one could avoid vagueness and ambiguity or could arrive at any precise conclusions. The situation is not unlike a rather famous Calvin and Hobbes cartoon in which the little boy Calvin, following an argument with his father over a matter of right and wrong, discovers the neo-cubist world of unlimited perspectives. Although this world is liberating in insight, it paralyzes action. Calvin is saved only when he breaks out from this neo-cubist ontology and, imposing a single perspective, ends up telling his father that he is still wrong. In fact, the systems methodology for dealing with paradox and circularity is similar to Calvin's. When faced with paradox, the systems methodology is to move to a more inclusive level of interpretation and examine the paradox in that frame or context.[3]

Moving to a more inclusive level of interpretation is an epistemological strategy. Thus, although there are no ontological priorities, the systems perspective adopts specific epistemological priorities for purposes of analysis and inquiry. As a consequence, in order to develop a line of analysis and inquiry, the systems perspective assigns a functional priority to either the subjective or the objective pole of the relational matrix. This is analogous to the physicist Niels Bohr's solution to the paradox that light appeared to be both wavelike and particlelike in character. Bohr accepted that both views are correct and asserted the principle of complementarity according to which either perspective could be taken for purposes of a particular line of inquiry.

Consider the application of this epistemological device to the development of a system of knowledge about human activity. A psychological theory is a theory of the psyche. It is a theory of the individual. From a systems ontology, of course, individual and group are features of a relational matrix and so there can be no individual self without the group and no group without the individual self. From a systems epistemology, however, if we wish to understand the functioning of the individual, then the theory constructed will necessarily make the subjective pole of this matrix the focus of inquiry. The result will be a theory that describes individual processes and organizations such as Piaget's theory, or Chomsky's theory.

Concepts such as "organization" and "assimilation/accommodation" are concepts that describe the epistemic human agent and primarily articulate the sphere of "I mean." There is no magic here and no imperialism. It is simply that if you set out to understand the epistemic individual, the individual will be the focus of inquiry, although the objective pole will not be omitted. The obverse holds as well. A sociological theory is a description of the social-cultural world. If explanation of this world is the goal of inquiry, then the objective pole will

---

[3]See Overton (1991a) for an extensive discussion of this strategy.

become the focus of inquiry. Here, a theory like James Gibson's presents concepts such as "affordances" that describe an environment, not an individual. As a consequence, Gibson's theory primarily articulates the sphere of "it means." From this vantage point, taking a perspective from the subjective pole, or from the objective pole, is not an either/or struggle for a correct or a best approach to meaning as it seems to be for Gergen, Macnamara, and Kitchener (chapters 2, 7, and 13 of this volume, respectively). The choice here is a functional one that is relative to purposes of inquiry.[4]

The systems strategy can, as a whole, be summarized by the paradox that the child creates meaning, but meaning is waiting there to be created. The systems strategy accepts this paradox and enters into inquiry by formulating psychologically oriented theories that explore systems that create meaning and sociologically oriented theories that explore meaning waiting to be created.

The fundamental distinction between an isolation strategy and a systems strategy points to novel ways of directing inquiry to a number of issues involving meaning. For example, questions about the origin of intersubjectivity of meaning represent a classical problem (see Gergen, chapter 2 of this volume).[5] From an isolationist perspective, shared meaning develops either from the individual or from the group or from some additive combination of the two. From a systems perspective intersubjectivity is the basic ground from which individual and group, self and other, differentiate. Thus, the primary question is not which one of the two is primary, or even how much each contributes to meaning. The primary question for investigation is how both individual processes and social processes lead to the kind of differentiations that continue and elaborate shared meaning.

The relation of constructivist theories and social constructivist theories is another classical problem that benefits from the isolationist/systems distinction. From the isolationist perspective one or the other of these types of theories must be correct or must contribute explanation of "greater amounts of variance" to understanding. From the systems viewpoint individual construction and social construction are two sides of the same ontological coin. Which is selected depends on the aims of inquiry. It is possible to ask from the systems epistemology vantage point how the individual constructs its world of meaning, and it is possible to ask how the social world operates to fashion the opportunities. For a fully adequate understanding of constructivism, specific readings of individual theories become critical. Both isolationist and systems perspectives use the term *constructivism*. However, the differing contexts lead to very different implications. G. H. Mead's theory is most often put forth as a prototype of social

---

[4]This is not to suggest that the systems perspective is a kind of relativism in which "anything goes." Theory choice is based on interlocking sets of criteria that can be articulated and, thus, evaluated (see Overton, 1991a, in press).

[5]See Overton and Horowitz (1991) for an expanded discussion concerning a systems analysis of intersubjectivity and intrasubjectivity.

constructivist explanation. However, on virtually any reading, Mead's theory is based on an isolationist strategy that offers a behaviorist ontology as fundamental. That is, Mead's theory splits the subject–object relational matrix and offers the social or object as the ultimate source of meaning. Vygotsky is also—particularly in contemporary contextualist readings—often understood as offering a similar position. This becomes particularly the case when Vygotsky is presented as an either/or alternative to Piaget,[6] or as one who in some way explains individual development better than Piaget. On the other hand, there are readings of Piaget and Vygotsky that offer these theories as a paradigmatic example of the systems strategy. In this latter reading both deny an ontological subject–object split. Piaget is read as focusing on the individual while respecting the social; Vygotsky focuses on the social while respecting the individual.[7]

The issue of an individual mind and a group mind is yet another domain that benefits from an awareness of isolationist and systems approaches to meaning. Isolationist perspectives understand mind as either an individual subjectivity or a communally generated set of standards of action (see Gergen, chapter 2 of this volume). Systems perspectives understand mind ontologically as both. Historically, theories of mind have been offered as accounts (i.e., epistemological devices) of the organization and processes of human agency. From a systems perspective, the answer to the question Can there be an individual mind? is, of course there can. The individual mind, like the group mind, is an analytic device created to further the effort at knowledge building. That is, the individual mind is a set of concepts designed to frame a psychological theory. The systems strategy focus on individual mind does not represent an attempt to impose a kind of autistic or—to acknowledge the postmodern distaste for the role of the author as a device of control—*authori*tarian theory of meaning. A focus on individual mind is just that, a focus that permits the elaboration of a knowledge system called the psychological.

Contemporary theories of psychological meaning are, in fact, all formulated within the framework of broader theories of the nature of the individual mind. The type of theory of individual mind that gets formulated, thus, becomes critical to understanding the nature and development of psychological meaning. To state this in a slightly different way, the focus on the individual mind as a context for the understanding of psychological meaning does not necessarily implicate an isolationist strategy. However, some theories of individual mind are isolationist in conception, whereas others are systems defined. In order to examine some specific issues concerning the nature and development of psychological meaning we, therefore, turn attention to isolationist and systems approaches to theories of mind.

---

[6]An example of this ideological position is found in Rogoff and Morelli (1989) who claimed that Vygotsky's stress on the inseparability of development from social and cultural activity "contrasts with the image of the solitary little scientist provided by Piaget's theory" (p. 345).

[7]Bidell (1988) provided an excellent account of this dialectical reading of the relationship of Vygotsky and Piaget.

THE COMPUTATIONAL MIND
AND THE EMBODIED MIND

Until recently, the only well-formulated and explicitly articulated theory of mind available to investigators was the computational theory of mind. This theory represents an unqualified isolationist approach that is replete with splits among its various components including mind and brain, self and other, intension and extension, semantics and syntactics. More recently, however, an alternative theory of mind, termed *embodiment theory*, has received increasing attention as a coherent alternative to the computational perspective. Embodiment theory rests on a systems approach and asserts that each of the features understood as independent components from the computational view, are more adequately, and productively understood as differentiations that emerge from a fundamental activity matrix.

The computational theory of mind draws on the analogy of the brain as a digital computer, and the mind as a computer program. Embodied theory understands the brain as a living, self-organizing system and the mind as a specific developmental emergent organization of this system. The computational mind has served, until recent challenges, as the conceptual foundation for that brand of cognitive science called *cognitivism*. The embodied mind has long been a fundamental feature—although only implicitly articulated as a theory of mind—of the cognitive developmental theories of Heinz Werner and Jean Piaget. It has recently received increasing articulation in cognitive science by investigators such as Johnson (1987), Lakoff (1987; see also chapter 3 of this volume), and Mark Turner (chapter 4 of this volume); in biology by Edelman (1992), and Varela, Thompson, and Rosch (1991); and in philosophy by Searle (1992) and Taylor (1991).[8]

BRAIN AND MIND

A first important isolationist strategic split that cognitivism introduces simply echoes the split between body or brain and mind originally introduced by Descartes.[9] If brain is conceived as computer and mind as program, then it is possible, and indeed reasonable, to study mind as an entity that is independent of brain

---

[8]Not all authors listed agree on all points concerning embodiment theory. For example, although Searle (1992) rejected philosophical objectivism, he argued in favor of metaphysical realism, and argued that mind is ultimately physical. The present version of embodiment is based on a thoroughgoing interpretationism (see Overton, in press). For a sympathetic review of Searle which, however, is critical of his stance on metaphysical realism, see Feldman (1991). For a sympathetic review of Searle which, however, is critical on his stance concerning physicalism, see Nagel (1993).

[9]It was, of course, Descartes who created the dualism that defines the isolationist strategy and is responsible for all of the described splits.

processes or embodied action as a whole (see Turner, chapter 4 of this volume). The justification for this approach lies in the recognition that the realization of any software program is independent of the particular hardware on which it is run. All that is required of the machine, of whatever type—whether it be the most advanced digital computer or a series of cogs and levers of an old-fashioned calculator—is the achievement of the computational descriptions where the zeros and ones of the program get appropriately assigned. From the cognitivist perspective this split is not problematic. It simply derives from the underlying functionalism that forms an integral part of contemporary cognitivism.[10]

Embodiment theory asserts that mind and brain constitute a unified whole, a brain/mind relational matrix. Here, there is no attempt to reduce one pole to the other or to deny one of the poles. Both, in their interrelationship, are necessary to an understanding of cognitive phenomena. As Edelman (1992) suggested, for embodiment theory, "thought is not transcendent but depends critically on the body and the brain. This position is exactly opposite to that of functionalism . . . The mind is embodied, it is necessarily the case that certain dictates of the body must be followed" (p. 239). Rorty (1991) captured this fundamental characteristic of embodiment theory as it affirms the necessary nonreducible relationship between mind and body when he described mind as a web of beliefs, desires, and intentions that find their root in "habits of action" (p. 60). For embodiment theory, these habits are not, however, the contingent randomly emitted responses favored by behaviorists. They are brain-behavior self-organizing systems that transform and become transformed as they operate.

The assertion by embodiment theory that mind is rooted in systems of action is familiar to developmentalists who have attended to Heinz Werner's and Jean Piaget's organismic visions of cognitive development. The lesson is sometimes forgotten, however, by even sympathetic cognitive scientists who, although eschewing the functionalist position, still tend to isolate mind and meaning primarily to the realm of symbol manipulation and linguistic phenomena (see Lakoff, chapter 3 of this volume; Turner, chapter 4 of this volume). Scholnick and Cookson (chapter 5 of this volume) offer an extended critique of the problems and issues associated with this tendency to encapsulate meaning in the symbolic system. They also describe possible developmental remedies.

Langer (chapter 9 of this volume), supplements Scholnick's critique with empirical evidence supporting the developmental assertion that meaning is not limited to symbol manipulation. He also demonstrates—using comparative evidence—that the embodied organization of the action systems offers constraints on the meanings ultimately created. Langer begins from the Wernerian and Piagetian

---

[10]Jackendoff (1989), a major proponent of the computational mind, stated, "Just as we need not deal with the actual wiring of the computer when writing our programs, so we can investigate the information processed by the brain and the computational process the brain performs on this information, independent of questions of neurological implementation. This approach is often called *functionalism*" (p. 15).

position that all living systems produce meaning through their embodied sensory and physical activity and through resistances that this activity meets. For Piaget, meaning construction and meaning development are grounded in the relational embodied activity of the assimilation/accommodation process. From the subject "I mean" perspective, assimilation is the primary process that creates meaning.

Assimilation is the act of interpretation or meaning construction whether, as Langer points out, the resulting form of meaning is the embodied act of instrumental meaning, the embodied symbol of representational meaning, or the embodied symbol system of reasoned meaning. When viewed from the "I mean" perspective, accommodation is secondary to assimilation. It is embodied activity that is dependent on the resistances that assimilation meets. Accommodation is the act of differentiation. Although assimilation imposes necessity by projecting outward, accommodation opens possibilities through the partial failures of these projections as they are reflected inward. Thus, changes in the embodied system proceed by partial successes and partial failures of embodied activity. The progressive equilibration of assimilation/accommodation and reflective abstraction, in turn, explains the developmental movement from instrumental, to representational, to reasoned systems of meaning.

This developmental analysis of meaning construction is isomorphic with Lakoff's account (chapter 3 of this volume) of the nature of conceptual systems. Lakoff's theory includes two fundamental concepts: *image schema* and *conceptual metaphor*. These are designed to understand conceptual systems from an embodied mind rather than a computational mind orientation. Image schema describes the embodied organization of the individual. However, Lakoff, given his focus on the explanation of concepts, concentrates on the representational-symbolic level of this organization. But when image schema is shorn of its representational and symbolic trappings, and cast in a more generic frame, it is identical with Piaget's concept of *action scheme*. Action schemes describe the initial psychological organization that forms the base for the projection of the instrumental meanings that Langer describes. In Lakoff's terminology it can be said that action schemes structure image schemata, and in turn "conventional images are structured by image schemata" (Lakoff, chapter 3 of this volume).

With image schemata and conventional images as an organismic base for the construction of concepts, metaphor, for Lakoff, comes to describe the process of projecting these organizations and, thus, forming *cross-domain mappings*. Again, however, if this understanding of metaphor is cast into a more generic and less representational frame, metaphor becomes identical with Piaget's *assimilation*. In addition, a recognition that assimilation is always, in fact, assimilation/accommodation serves to solve an important problem for Lakoff. When Glucksberg claims that metaphor is simply categorization (Lakoff, chapter 3 of this volume), the appropriate reply is that it can never be simply categorization because ever present accommodation assures that novelty constantly enters the system in the sense of opening new possibilities. Indeed, in general, Lakoff's theory would be strengthened significantly by an explicit recognition that the progressive equilibrations of cross-domain mappings offers a powerful explanatory tool for understanding the movement from action schemes to image-based reasoning to abstract reasoning.

A similar analysis of processes underlying meaning development also appears in Bloom's (chapter 10 of this volume) presentation of evidence for the thesis that the child moves from personal, private, mentally constructed meaning to conventionally constructed language. Bloom argues that this progression is explained by what she identifies as the principle of discrepancy and the principle of elaboration. According to the principle of discrepancy, progress occurs as constructed meanings become increasingly discrepant from the data of perception. This situation, however, is exactly the case of assimilation (i.e., a current meaning) meeting resistance (i.e., a partial failure or discrepant perception) and leading to accommodation. Further, as resistance leads to accommodation, accommodations are understood as elaborations or differentiations of the initial meaning. And it is this differentiation that constitutes Bloom's principle of elaboration.

To sum up to this point, a fundamental split introduced by the cognitivist computational model is that between mind and body or brain. This split isolates the role of body and brain from the formation and ongoing functioning of mind. For cognitivism, brain is not ignored in every proposal. For example, Jackendoff (chapter 6 of this volume)—from a computational mind stance—mentions the possibility of concepts being instantiated by neurons in the brain. However, this is clearly a distinctly separate problem that is isolated from the primary computational concern about "the properties of the combinational space available to the brain." From the computational perspective, brain is not, and cannot be, an integral part of the formation and functioning mind/brain matrix. From the embodied perspective, it is and must be such a feature.

MIND AND OBJECT

Following from the body–mind split, a second fundamental split that computational theory introduces into the study of mind is the split between mind and object. As body and brain are isolated from mind in the computer model approach, so also is the individual's world of social-cultural-physical objects isolated from mind. This ontological split of mind from the world of common sense has two critical implications for understanding the nature of meaning. First and foremost, by isolating the cultural context from mind, culture—like brain in the mind-brain split—plays no formative role in the development of mind.

Mind and Culture

In this mind–object relation we again have the image of two disconnected pieces. To join these pieces, form is divorced from content, and culture is treated as the source of the contents of mind. Thus, although the formation and, therefore, the structure of mind are disconnected from and impervious to the commonsense world, the contents of mind are understood as the reflection of this world. It is this split that has led information-processing approaches to maintain that the only thing that develops in development is world knowledge or object meaning. Mind does not develop in the sense of becoming transformed through activity operating in a cultural context. Mind is a storehouse with a built-in apparatus for moving items from place to place. Reflections of culture and physical objects are the source of the items stored (i.e., what we know), but they are not the source of the creation of the operating structures (i.e., how we know). According to this perspective, "it means" is taken as foundational, and the ultimate source of "I mean." Mind participates in this process only through the manipulation (including encoding, storing, retrieving, etc.) of symbolic representations of the social-cultural-object world.

The claim of embodied mind theory with respect to the social-cultural-object world extends the stance it assumes for body and brain. Here, as in the general case where no ontological distinction is made between subject and object, mind is necessarily located as a systems relational concept. Ontologically, mind is neither a disengaged subjective concept emerging from an isolated and reified biology, nor a set of equally disengaged cultural and linguistic norms. To borrow a term from Charles Taylor (1991), mind is *dialogical* in character. Mind includes both body and other, as self and other are themselves bipolar systems concepts. The isolationist computational model is *monological* or a split representationalist picture of the human agent. It describes mind primarily as a subject of symbolic representations that parallel an objectivist mind-independent world. In the dialogic understanding, mind emerges out of embodied practices that both constitute and are constituted by the manifest world of common sense. Thus, the central core of embodiment theory is the claim that the web called mind is most coherently explained as a directional evolution that differentiates from the activity matrix termed the *biocultural field*. It is within this embodied frame that Bruner (1990) described the relation of mind and cultural in the co-construction of personal meanings called narratives; and it is within this frame that Bruner and his colleagues (Feldman, Bruner, Kalmar, & Renderer, chapter 12 of this volume) present developmental observations supporting the significance of narrative models in our understanding of cognitive development.

Syntax and Semantics

A second implication that follows from the ontological disconnection of mind and experienced world entails the forced split between syntax and semantics that cognitivism adopts (see Turner, chapter 4 of this volume). Semantics is, of course, the province of meaning. However, the computational mind is a syntactical machine that is limited to manipulating its own internal symbols. Cognition or knowing is defined within this framework as the manipulation of symbols. Computations are operations on, or manipulations of, symbols and these are governed by a system of rules that constitute syntax. Cognitivism also asserts the claim that the rule system is a prewired feature of the human mind, just as the rule system that governs the computer program is part and parcel of that program. When Jackendoff (chapter 6 of this volume) refers to "states of a combinatorial system instantiated . . . in a system of symbols," he is referring to just such a rule system.

Meaning or semantics becomes related to this syntactical system through the glue of *representation*. The symbol is taken to be both a physical code and a mental representation of something other than itself. As mental representations, symbols "reference" or are "about" (i.e., mean) something concerning an assumed mind-independent world. Thus, meaning is a symbol-to-object correspondence. Representations as mental states are intentional states and they include states of beliefs and desires as well as intentions per se. However, these states are not drawn directly from the posited mind-independent object world. Instead, cognitivism maintains these semantic states mirror, or parallel, syntax. By assuming this position, cognitivism is able to offer both a nativism and a naturalism or objectivism. The mind, even at the representational level, is prewired; however, semantic representations accurately *correspond* to objects and categories of the mind-independent (i.e., objectivist) world. The strongest form of this stance was introduced by Fodor (see Jackendoff, chapter 6 of this volume) and it proposes that all mental activity is a prewired language of thought called "mentalese."

Varela et al. (1991) succinctly described the functioning of the glue of representations as cognitivism uses representations: "We assume that the world is pregiven, that its features can be specified prior to any cognitive activity. Then to explain the relation between this cognitive activity and a pregiven world, we hypothesize the existence of mental representations inside the cognitive system" (p. 135). They further illustrated this isolationist process through the metaphor of a cognitive agent who is parachuted into a pregiven but completely foreign world. The agent can survive only if it is endowed with a map, and learns to act on this map. The map is the language of thought, and the task of development is to learn to use this map.

Jackendoff (chapter 6 of this volume) illustrates a cognitivist theoretical argument applied to word meaning. The combinatorial system, as the defining feature of mind, is the universal frame within which word meaning is explained. As already noted, this is the computational program, universal grammar, or syntactical system. The particular subsystem of this program relevant to word meaning Jackendoff terms *conceptual structure*. Word meaning is conceived as states of this subsystem instantiated in a system of symbols. A specific conceptual structure, in turn, derives from "conceptual well-formedness rules." These are composed of sets of primitives and principles of combination. Thus, it is conceptual well-formedness rules that constitute the innate base for the generation of conceptual structure and conceptual structure, in turn, is fundamental to word meaning. Specific word meanings are fragments of conceptual structure that are linked to language, to perceptual and motor representations; and to other conceptual structures.

In Jackendoff's argument, the combinatorial system is treated as background, "the only reasonable way anyone has been able to conceive of a word meaning within cognitive theory is in terms of states of a combinatorial system." However, although the nature of primitives discussed by Jackendoff is itself a basic issue, it is exactly the combinatorial system that is the core issue in the debate between advocates of the computational mind and advocates of the embodied mind. Does the combinatorial system best characterize the nature and origin of mind, or is the combinatorial system itself the outgrowth of a directional development? Is the syntactical system fundamental or are syntactical and semantic systems differentiations that arise from a fundamental activity matrix. Langer's (chapter 9 of this volume) discussion of the development of meaning from instrumental act to representational symbolic meaning suggests that both the primitives described by Jackendoff, and the combinatorial system itself, find their origin in early action meaning systems.

Bloom's (chapter 10 of this volume) argument that both word meaning (semantics) and the structure of language (syntax) arise from a more primitive action defined meaning system also supports the embodied mind perspective. Further, Bloom's debate with Hirsh-Pasek, Golinkoff, and Reeves (chapter 11 of this volume) is an extension of the core debate between embodiment and computational theories over the nature of meaning and meaning development. Bloom understands symbolic representational language meaning to be constructed from presymbolic mental organization. Arising from acts of interpretation (i.e., Piaget's activity of assimilation), the child constructs intentional states and later representations within these states. Embodied representations, thus, constitute the personal and private meanings that underlie acts of expression and form the base for language acquisition. Hirsh-Pasek et al. argue, on the other hand, that the child must necessarily be prewired with language-specific lexical and grammatical biases in order for language acquisition to proceed.

For both Hirsh-Pasek et al. and Jackendoff—as well as for other cognitivists— acceptance of the categories of the computational framework render even the possibility of fundamental transformational change inconceivable. Although computer programs can additively rearrange pieces in a nearly infinite number of ways, programs do not change their identity. Emerging novelty in the sense of a metamorphosis from one form to a novel form is simply not a fundamental category of the computer or the computer program. Cognitivism's need to find an identity of elements across development is a direct logical consequence of the categories it asserts as defining the human agent. When cognitivists study language development, they necessarily—not empirically—discover some language specific features available from the outset of development. When cognitivists study conceptual development, they necessarily—not empirically— discover some symbolic, representational capacities available from the outset of development. Empirical evidence may increase or decrease the plausibility of these logical discoveries. It will not be foundational to the discoveries themselves.

As the cognitivist's vision is constrained by categories of the computational frame, embodiment theorists adopt constraining categories that are identified with self-organizing systems. Chief among these are the categories of differentiation, integration, and emergent levels of organization. From this epistemological stance, an initial organized whole that ontologically constitutes the biocultural field differentiates through activity into a body-mind-object system. Mind is an emergent organization just as water is an emergent organization of hydrogen and oxygen molecules.[11] Mind as an emergent organized activity matrix initially lacks substantial psychological differentiation. It is characterized by the system properties of instrumentality and affectivity (see Brown, chapter 8 of this volume). As this system acts (i.e., assimilates, integrates, projects, constructs action meanings) and meets resistances that lead to differentiations (i.e., accommodations) these differentiations come to be characterized, as Brown suggests, as intentions and values. At some point in the self-organizing process, mind as action system becomes reorganized and representational mind appears as a new level of emergent organization. Representational mind does not lose its ontological underpinnings, but as an emergent organization it is characterized by the system property of symbolization. Here, as the child earlier constructed the world, in the context of a world waiting to be constructed, the child now constructs representations and language, in the context of a language system waiting to be constructed. At this level, as at the earlier level, and at later levels of reflective representation, progressive differentiations and reintegration operate through processes such as Lakoff's metaphorical projection (and the resistance it meets) and Bloom's principles of discrepancy and elaboration.

To this point the discussion has centered around two fundamental ontological splits that are introduced when the categories of the computational mind are affirmed. The first split isolates body and brain from the formation and functioning of mind. The second isolates mind from social-cultural-object world of commonsense experience. The categories of the embodied mind represent an alternative stance to these splits; a stance that understands body-mind-object as differentiations that arise from a self-organizing activity matrix. These alternative visions of the nature of mind impact in diverse ways on our understanding of the nature and development of meaning. A third and final fundamental ontological split that the cognitivist computational model introduces is the split between various spheres of mind itself. This is the mind-mind split.

---

[11]This position is neither a substance dualism nor a property dualism as all forms of ontological dualism are rejected in this position. The idea of emergent systems follows Edelman (1992) and Searle (1992). As Searle noted, "Consciousness is a higher-level or emergent property of the brain in the utterly harmless sense of 'higher-level' or 'emergent' in which solidity is a higher level emergent property of H_2O molecules when they are in a lattice structure (ice)" (p. 14).

THE INFERENTIAL MIND AND
THE IMAGINATIVE MIND

For computational theory, mind constitutes a single uniform sphere of activity, the linear combinatorial sphere of computations. This is a sphere where linear logic not only reigns supreme, it defines the territory. This seemingly monistic position, however, hides a dualism, because it suppresses other spheres of activity known to commonsense but not accounted for by the conjunctions, disjunctions, negations, and propositions built from these atomic elements. The realm of mind in which there are no negatives, in which categories flow one into the other, in which affectivity as feeling is unframed by linear logic is just such a suppressed, and thus isolated, sphere for the computational mind. That this sphere is a necessary part of that web of intentions, desires, and beliefs called mind, and that this sphere contributes to meaning, has long been affirmed by philosophy and explored by those psychologists who have been centrally concerned with meaning making.

In Hegel's (1807) vision, mind is a differentiation into two dialectically related moments of consciousness, the subjective moment and the objective moment. Within the subjective moment, Hegel saw mind as a further differentiation into two primary relational modes or spheres of knowing—The Reason (*Vernunft*) and The Understanding (*Verstand*). *Verstand* is the analog of the computational mind. It operates in terms of exclusive either . . . or categories. Every question put to *Verstand* is answered in terms of "either . . . or." Either the phenomena involved are different and thus they are not identical, or they are identical, in which case they are not different. In this mode categories are static and fixed. In *Verstand* opposites are mutually exclusive and absolutely cut off from each other. The Aristotelian law of identity holds absolutely: $A = A$ and it is never the case that $A = not\ A$. Both identities and differences are considered, but each is taken separately. As a consequence, concepts are either identical ($A = A$), or they are different ($not\ [A = B]$).

Vernunft or reason, on the other hand, is the mode of knowing that asserts the principle of the identity of opposites ($A = not\ A$). Here categories break up and flow into each other. Both modes consider identity and difference, but *Vernunft* rejects the exclusive nonrelational "either . . . or," and considers identity and difference simultaneously. In *Vernunft* what is identical is also different, and what is different is also identical. Categories in *Vernunft* are both identical and distinct.

Contemporary philosophy—excepting analytic philosophy, which like cognitivism suppresses *vernunft*—has retained the distinction and describes these relational spheres of mind as the sphere of imagination (*Vernunft*) and the sphere of inference or inquiry (*Verstand*). Turner (chapter 4 of this volume) discusses the sphere of imagination as it impacts on meaning at representational and reasoned levels of construction. These relational spheres of mind have also been contrasted as the aesthetic and the theoretic; and the intuitive and the analytic.

When psychoanalytically oriented and object relations personality theorists have pursued their investigations into affective-conative-cognitive meaning constructions (see Brown, chapter 8 of this volume; Bloom, chapter 10 of this volume) they have found these relational spheres of imagination and inference to be indispensable descriptions of the process of meaning making. Freud characterized the spheres as primary and secondary processes; Melanie Klein described them as paranoid-schizoid and depressive positions; Harry Stack Sullivan discussed them in terms of prototaxic-parataxic and syntaxic modes; and Donald Winnicott termed them object relations and object use. Each initial term in the bipolar pair of each conceptualization is understood as the sphere of the nonlinear, where action, affect, and impulse are minimally regulated, consciousness is unmediated, categories have permeable boundaries and flow one into the other, and a dialectical organization prevails. The latter term of each pair constitutes the sphere of linear regulated understanding described by the rules of inductive and deductive logic. From a systems perspective each sphere is a necessary part of the whole, and from a psychological perspective, the isolation of one sphere from another constitutes pathology.[12]

Jackendoff (1989) has recognized—from his cognitivist viewpoint—that the computational mind is itself inadequate to account for a number of events that from a commonsense perspective would count as mind relevant distinctions. Jackendoff's solution to this problem is to postulate a separate mind, the phenomenological mind. Having then created a dualist mind–mind problem, Jackendoff's proposed solution to this additional problem is to glue the pieces back together. This is done by accepting the computational mind as fundamental and understanding the phenomenological mind as "caused by/supported by/projected from" (p. 24) computational distinctions. Embodiment theory, on the other hand, rejects this split, as it rejects other splits, and claims that (a) awareness or consciousness is a systemic property of mind as a whole; (b) computational distinctions are characteristics of the inferential sphere of mental functioning; and (c) the inferential sphere and the imaginative sphere simultaneously arise from an original relatively undifferentiated activity matrix termed the biocultural matrix.

Ontogenetically, embodiment theory proposes that mind initially differentiates through its activity and resistances into a subject pole and an object pole of consciousness. This is the psychological relational field of "me" and "not me" and, thus, the psychological basis for "I mean" and "it means." It is also this differentiation that simultaneously establishes the embodied basis for the formation of a protologic. This protologic signals the beginning of a linear sphere of mind. Here the fundamental laws of linear logic (i.e., Law of Identity: $A = A$; Law of Contradiction: *not* $[A = not\ A]$; Law of Excluded Middle: $[A$ must be either A or *not* $A]$) become established as an extension of the instrumental

[12]See Overton and Horowitz (1991) for an extended discussion of these spheres of mind in relation to developmental psychopathology.

understanding of "me" (*A*) and "not me" (*not A*). In essence then, the differentiation into subject pole and object pole proceeds simultaneously with a differentiation of the subject pole into a sphere of Inference and a sphere of Imagination.[13] Each of these differentiations, of course, occur at the instrumental level. With sufficient progress this self-organizing system will create novel symbolic and reflective symbolic levels of functioning and at each of these levels parallel differentiations and reintegrations will operate.

In conclusion, the answer to the question, "What is the nature of meaning, and how does meaning develop for the child?" emerges from how we choose to formulate the relational "I mean"/"it means" matrix. If our strategy is to split the matrix into fundamentally disconnected pieces, then the resulting theory of mind describes a computational field in which mind is split from body, from culture, and from mind itself. In this context, little develops and meaning resides in the glue of symbolic representations that are designed to attach an isolated computational mind to an isolated objective mind-independent world. If, alternatively, our strategy is to maintain the matrix as a self-organizing relational system and to disavow any disconnected splits, then the resulting theory of mind describes a mind that arises as a series of differentiations from the organized activity matrix termed the biocultural field. From this embodied mind perspective, meaning is the interpretative activity of mind. In this context, meaning is present in ontogeny from the outset, but it becomes modified and transformed from its instrumental origins, through representational and reasoned levels, according to the organism's active encounters and the resistances that these encounters face.

ACKNOWLEDGMENTS

I would like to express my appreciation to Carol Groves, Ulrich Muller, Nora Newcombe, and Mary Winn for their careful reading of earlier drafts and for their helpful comments.

REFERENCES

Bidell, T. (1988). Vygotsky, Piaget and the dialectic of development. *Human Development, 31*, 329–348.

Bruner, J. (1990). *Acts of meaning.* Cambridge, MA: Harvard University Press.

Edelman, G. M. (1992). *Bright air, brilliant fire: On the matter of the mind.* New York: Basic.

Feldman, C. F. (1991). Intentionality, narrativity, and interpretation: The new image of man. In E. Lepore & R. van Gulick (Eds.), *John Searle and his critics* (pp. 323–333). Cambridge, MA: Blackwell.

Hegel, G. W. F. (1807). *Phenomenology of spirit.* New York: Oxford University Press.

Jackendoff, R. (1989). *Consciousness and the computational mind.* Cambridge, MA: MIT Press.

---

[13]These multiple differentiations and reintegrations are discussed at length in Overton (in press).

Johnson, M. (1987). *The body in the mind.* Chicago: University of Chicago Press.

Katz, J. J. (1990). *The metaphysics of meaning.* Cambridge, MA: MIT Press.

Lakoff, G. (1987). *Women, fire, and dangerous things. What categories reveal about the mind.* Chicago: University of Chicago Press.

Nagel, T. (1993, March 4). The mind wins! *New York Review of Books*, pp. 37–41.

Overton, W. F. (1991a). Metaphor, recursive systems, and paradox in science and developmental theory. In H. W. Reese (Ed.), *Advances in child development and behavior* (Vol. 23, pp. 59–71). New York: Academic.

Overton, W. F. (1991b). The structure of developmental theory. In H. W. Reese (Ed.), *Advances in child development and behavior* (Vol. 23, pp. 1–37). New York: Academic.

Overton, W. F. (in press). The arrow of time and cycles of time: Concepts of change, cognition, and embodiment. *Psychological Inquiry.*

Overton, W. F., & Horowitz, H. (1991). Developmental psychopathology: Differentiations and integrations. In D. Cicchetti & S. Toth (Eds.), *Rochester symposium on developmental psychopathology* (Vol. 3, pp. 1–41). Rochester, NY: University of Rochester Press.

Rogoff, B., & Morelli, G. (1989). Perspectives on children's development from cultural psychology. *American Psychologist, 44,* 343–348.

Rorty, R. (1991). Inquiry as recontextualization: An anti-dualist account of interpretation. In D. R. Hiley, J. F. Bohman, & R. Shusterman (Eds.), *The interpretive turn: Philosophy, science, culture* (pp. 59–80). Ithaca, NY: Cornell University Press.

Searle, J. (1992). *The rediscovery of the mind.* Cambridge, MA: MIT Press.

Taylor, C. (1991). The dialogical self. In D. R. Hiley, J. F. Bohman, & R. Shusterman (Eds.), *The interpretive turn: Philosophy, science, culture* (pp. 304–314). Ithaca, NY: Cornell University Press.

Varela, F. J., Thompson, E., & Rosch, E. (1991). *The embodied mind: Cognitive science and human experience.* Cambridge, MA: MIT Press.

2

The Communal Creation of Meaning

Kenneth J. Gergen
Swarthmore College

Scholarly problems are invariably wedded to particular perspectives—languages for framing them as "problems" and demanding something we call "solutions." Likewise, the way in which problems are articulated simultaneously circumscribes the range of possible outcomes. A problem stated within a given system of understanding will limit itself to solutions born of that system; assertions from alternative systems will fail to be recognized as proper candidates for solution. In large measure, the problem of meaning within the human sciences has largely been framed within a particular tradition of Western epistemology (see Overton, 1991). It is a venerable tradition to which Piaget's work represents an esteemed contribution. Yet, in my view, this very tradition so frames the issue of meaning as to preclude a viable answer; the tools of the tradition are ill formed to solve the question as posed. As I hope to demonstrate in what follows, if the problem is structured by an alternative system of suppositions, we gain purchase not only in terms of intellectual comprehension, but in terms of research practices and broad societal promise.

Although the concept of "meaning" is a promontory in a variety of intellectual landscapes, for many scholars—psychologists included—it is preeminently defined in terms of *individual signification*—or the internal symbolization (representation, conceptualization) of the external world. Scholars derive from this grounding concern not simply one "problem of meaning," but a set of interrelated and profoundly challenging enigmas. Among the more prominent, how is it that the external world comes to have meaning for the individual (the problem of epistemology), how can we account for what appear to be differences among people in the meaning of events (cultural psychology), and how does individual meaning come to be expressed in language (psycholinguistics)? Yet, it is to none of these daunting problems and the centuries of accumulated rumination that I direct my present remarks. Rather, I raise a derivative but equally significant issue, namely that of *meaning with others*. Here the chief question is how can we apprehend each other's meanings, successfully communicate, or understand each other? For whatever solutions are offered to the plaguing questions of individualized symbolization, they must finally be responsible for an account of meaning with others. Any theory of individual meaning that cannot be squared with the possibility of shared meaning would leave us not only with the unsatisfactory conclusion that social understanding is impossible. It would additionally leave us with the unhappy paradox that we could not understand the theory itself.

If we focus, then, on the problem of meaning with others, we may distinguish two orientations, one of rich tradition and the other of recent and more humble origin. I first consider the initial orientation, partly because of its stronger intuitive appeal, its regnant command over contemporary psychology, and its congeniality with the Piagetian framework. Further, as the inadequacy of this outlook is made clear, we open the way for serious consideration of the alternative. The traditional orientation in this case derives from a fundamental belief in individual signification—the phenomenal "I," or process of subjective agency or symbolization. It is "I" who can mean, and it is the "I" who conveys meaning—although crudely and unevenly—by words and deeds. To "know another's meanings" from this perspective is to gain access to the other's subjectivity or symbol system. It is to press past the visible surface to the other's interior, to comprehend what he or she "meant" by words and deeds. If we are to communicate successfully, from this standpoint, we must acquire a state of intersubjective transparency.

The problem of intersubjective understanding has had an uneven history over the past century. For 19th-century German scholars the problem was critical for separating the natural sciences (*Naturwissenschaften*)—concerned with understanding the physical world—from the human sciences (*Geisteswissenschaften*), focally concerned with the meaningful activity of human beings. As it was often argued, the processes necessary for understanding physical objects (nonmeaningful entities) must necessarily differ from those involved in understanding intentional agents. In Dilthey's (1914/1984) terms:

> In the human studies ... [t]he nexus of psychic life constitutes the originally primitive and fundamental datum. We explain nature, but we understand psychic life ... Just as the system of culture—economy, law, religion, art and science—and the external organization of society in the ties of family, community, church and state, arise from the living nexus of the human mind (*Menschenseele*), so can they be understood only by reference to it. (p. 76)

Although such concerns continued into the present century within sectors of social and personality psychology, the hegemony of American behaviorism largely cast such issues to the margins of interest. From the behaviorist standpoint, there simply is no problem of intersubjectivity. It was not until the cognitive movement gradually reinstantiated the domain of mental life that the problem of intersubjectivity again entered the scholarly agenda. However, as Bruner (1990) argued in his recent volume, *Acts of Meaning*, the dominant metaphor of the individual as "information processor" has continued to obscure the problem. The cognitive movement has yet to confront the issue of social meaning—meaning with others—in a direct and forthright manner.

It is appropriate that the issue meaning with others should be confronted at the meetings of the Jean Piaget Society. For indeed, unlike modern cognitivists, Piaget was concerned with how meaning can be transmitted from one subjectivity to another. It is in the following passage from Piaget's (1955) *The Language and Thought of the Child*, that we find the clearest framing of the issue from the standpoint of individual signification:

> [U]nderstanding between children occurs only in so far as there is contact between two identical mental schemas already existing in each child. In other words, when the explainer and his listener have had . . . common preoccupations and ideas, then each word of the explainer is understood, because it fits into a schema already existing and well defined within the listener's mind. (p. 133)

Yet, in spite of the importance of this work and the richness of the tradition that it represents, I fear that its elaboration can only end in impasse. So long as the problem of interpersonal meaning is derived from a belief in the individual as the center of meaning, it will remain recalcitrant to solution. In effect, to begin with assumption of meaning as individual signification will lead us to the untenable conclusion that interpersonal understanding is impossible. Thus, now to extend, embroider, or elaborate on the Piagetian view—even if enlightened by contemporary cognitive formulations—is unfortuitous. Let me fortify this conclusion with two troublesome lines of argument, and then consider what, to me, is the more promising alternative.

THE HERMENEUTIC IMPASSE

There are many grounds for suspicion of the intersubjective view of human meaning, some as old as the tradition itself. For it is a view that grows from the soil of dualism—from distinguishing a mind (logos, soul, consciousness) separated from material, a "within here" from an "out there." And it has long been nettlesome that if we begin with human consciousness (an "in here"), we have no way of being certain of an external reality—which also includes the possible existence of other minds. We have no means of transcending subjectivity, of locating a vantage point from which we can view the relation between the subjective and the objective, or between two isolated subjectivities, to determine when and how the one is related to the other. These were Piaget's problems as well, as he attempted to compensate for the debilitating consequences of his rationalist commitment with large doses of pragmatism and functionalism. So severe are the problems of dualist epistemology that materialists, phenomenologists, and Wittgensteinians alike have since opted (albeit on differing grounds) for an abandonment of dualist metaphysics.

Although these and other problems of epistemology have long plagued the dualist tradition, it is to other arguments that I turn in what follows. These are discussions of more recent vintage and are more distinctly tied to issues of human meaning. The first derives from the context of hermeneutic theory, and more specifically theories concerning the proper or valid interpretation of texts. Hermeneutic theory is pivotal to the issue of human meaning, for a proper theory of textual interpretation should, by traditional standards, furnish insight into the means by which intersubjectivity is achieved. That is, hermeneutic theory should elucidate the means by which one can press past the phonemic surface to intentional impulse. And if hermeneutic theory cannot answer this challenge, we have reason to suspect the very concept of intersubjective synchrony.

There are at least two important strands of hermeneutic thought within the past century that lend strong support to the intersubjective account of human meaning. On the one hand, romanticist hermeneutics, reaching its apex within the preceding century, was centrally concerned with the means by which the individual can "inhabit" or "ingest" the experience of the other. To understand another is to experience in some manner the other's subjectivity. It is in this vein, for example, that Dilthey proposed a process of *Verstehen* by which the individual prereflexively transposes him or herself into the other, empathizing with or apprehending some aspect of the "lived experience" of the other. Yet, in spite of their romantic appeal, such views of shared subjectivities could not be sustained. This is so in part because theorists could not render a compelling account of how a process such as *Verstehen* could take place. By what faculty does such mental transposition take place; how does mind grasp the experience of the other; how can accuracy be determined? The answers to such questions remain clouded in mystery.

With the 20th-century transition of scholarship from a romanticist to a modernist base, belief in the empathic grasping of others' subjectivity was pushed aside in favor of the concepts of reason and observation. Emblematic of modernist hermeneutics is the work of E. D. Hirsch. In his widely debated *Validity in Interpretation*, Hirsch (1967) proposed that authors are privileged with respect to the meaning of their words; in effect, they know what they mean. Thus, readers or interpreting agents must properly deploy processes of systematic examination of the text, combined with logical inference, to move from the text as given to increasingly more accurate interpretations of the author's intent. Understanding, then, remains a matter of the individual mind attempting to make contact with the otherwise isolated mind of the author.

Yet, modernist views of hypothesis testing are infrequently voiced in contemporary debate, and at least one significant reason for their demise is the extension of Heideggerian arguments by his disciple, Hans-Georg Gadamer. As Gadamer (1975) proposed, we confront the text (and by analogy, each other) with an array of prejudgments or prejudices, questions that we put to the text and assumptions concerning the array of possible answers. This array of prejudices is historically contingent, its character evolving over the course of time and circumstance. In effect, we approach the text with a given *horizon of understanding* that will influence the way in which we interpret the meaning of the text. Thus, for Gadamer there is no meaning in itself, an authorial impulse that we must necessarily plumb in order to derive the correct interpretation of the text.

Although compelling, such a conclusion propels Gadamer (1975) into a new problem, that of solipsism. Does the reader simply recapitulate his or her own biases with each new confrontation with a text? How would the horizon then change across time? How could one ever escape the prison of prejudice? To answer, Gadamer proposed that one's horizons may be expanded by joining with the text in a dialogic relationship. The text is thus allowed to influence one's prejudices while its meaning is simultaneously influenced by these prejudices. This *fusion of horizons* is achieved when the voice of the text is allowed to ask questions of the reader, and thereby enables him or her to gain consciousness of his or her array of prejudgments. Interpretation, on this account, does not take place in the head of the reader, but grows out of the dialogic interplay between text and prejudices. Or, as Gadamer would have it, the fusion of horizons takes place between reader and text; the result is not thereby a correct or accurate reading, but one that represents a fusion of historical eras.

Yet, in my view Gadamer (1975) did not fully succeed in this elaboration in solving either his self-imposed problem of solipsism or the more general problem of social meaning. For if the individual can only understand in terms of a system of meaning brought to a text, there is no obvious means by which he or she can stand outside this system to allow the text to place its own questions, to generate a consciousness of one's own biases. How would the "questions of the text" now be understood if the forestructure is bracketed? In an attempt to avoid this problem Gadamer took final refuge in the halls of human nature. That is, because of the universal similarity of human beings, and because all those within a culture share similar experiences, the cultural heritage in which the text is embedded will ensure transcendence of the contemporary horizon and invite the interpreter into new forms of understanding. Such a conclusion fails to be compelling, for not only does it subtly reintroduce the presumption of intersubjective similarity (e.g., "I understand you because our experience is the same."), but it fails to account for understandings at variance with such grounding and that change over the course of human history. Thus, although raising significant questions with the assumption of intersubjective connection, I do not believe Gadamer's theory provides sufficient replacement.

Piaget (1955) himself labored with the hermeneutic problem. As he puzzled in *The Language and Thought of the Child*, how is he to be certain that his own mental structures correspond with those of his subjects. "It is impossible," he admitted, "by direct observation to be sure whether they [the children] are understanding each other. The child has a hundred and one ways of pretending to understand, and often complicates things still further by pretending not to understand" (p. 93). Piaget never solved the problem, and for my own part, I believe there are principled difficulties underlying the intersubjectivist attempt to establish validity in interpretation. The problem commences when one treats the text (or other social action) as opaque, and presumes a second level (an internal language) that must be located in order to render the overt transparent. All we have at our disposal in the process of understanding is a domain of public discourse (or action). We imagine there is a domain of private discourse to which this must be attached. Yet, we possess access neither to the private discourse itself nor to the rules by which it is translated into the public domain. It follows that any attempt to translate (or locate meaning) must be based on an a priori array of suppositions, and must thereby draw conclusions both limited to and determined by definition. In effect, readings or translations can proceed through a circular process of self-verification (a "hermeneutic circularity").

We would face a similar problem if we assumed that all cloud formations were symbols of God's thoughts. Such thoughts could be read if we could but crack the code of how God's thoughts were transformed into nimbus as opposed to cirrus clouds, to thunderstorms and tornadoes. If such presumptions were made, what hope would we have of discovering through observation the impulses of God? All readings would inevitably be the result, first of an imaginary vernacular of the Holy One (e.g., God is a being who "wishes," "desires," "wills," etc.), and a second set of imaginary translation rules (e.g., when God is "angry" the sky is dark). Once developed, such vehicles would indeed render God's thoughts transparent. However they would do so only by virtue of the imaginary system of definitions constructed to carry out the task. If there is no "inner voice" to which one can gain access, then all attempts to interpret the "inner" by virtue of the "outer" must be inherently circular. It is in this same vein that Charles Taylor (1971) concluded,

> making sense . . . [of another's actions] cannot but move in a hermeneutical circle. Our conviction that an account makes sense is contingent on our reading of action and situation. But these readings cannot be explained or justified except by reference to other such readings, and their relation to the whole. If an interlocutor does not understand this kind of reading, or will not accept it as valid, there is nowhere else the argument can go. (p. 127)

FROM INTERPRETATION TO TEXTUALITY

Let us consider a second and related line of discussion, in this case focused on literary criticism. Literary theory of the past two decades represents a major disjunction with its preceding history, and the unfolding dialogue is of critical relevance to the conception of human meaning. A central concern within the literary domain is with standards for textual criticism. On what grounds or by what criteria is a literary rendering to be judged; or resonating with hermeneutic concerns, are there any rational or foundational standards for preferring or privileging certain interpretations over others? Traditionally, literary criticism had shared in the Western commitment to an intersubjective view of communication. One's concern was to locate the "inner meaning" of the literary work, that is, the meaning that the author was attempting to express in language. However, with the advent of the New Criticism in the 1950s, authorial intention began to wane in significance. For, as the new critics compellingly argued, a literary work is a unity unto itself. Interpretation should properly focus on its structure, internal workings, coherence, and the like. What the author him or herself happened to think or feel about the work was slowly reduced to irrelevance.

With the waning of authorial standpoint in the modernist period, the stage was set for the more radical move of the postmodern. Consider the recently emerging romance with reader response (Suleiman & Crosman, 1980). Reflecting Gadamer's (1975) concerns with the reader's disposition to generate meaning, theorists in this case focus on the presumptions, heuristics, ideologies, or cognitive dispositions that determine the reader's interpretation of texts. As reader dispositions dominate the meaning derived from the text, authorial intention or subjectivity recedes into further insignificance. There is an important sense in which reader response theorists such as Fish (1980) also began to furnish an alternative to the subjectivism that continued to haunt and ultimately subvert the Gadamerian orientation. For Gadamer, the reader brought to the text a horizon or forestructure of understanding that could, without intervention, wholly appropriate the text. For Fish this individualized sensitivity is replaced by a *community of interpreters.* It is the standards of interpretation embedded within the community that determine the interpretive dispositions of the individual agent. Although Fish, along with most reader response analysts, stops short of a fully social account (imbuing the reader, as he did, with processes of reason, intention and the like), it would be but a short step to eradicate the individual mind altogether. One could account for the actions of the individual reader without recourse to his or her "mind" and simply place the full explanatory weight on the communally generated criteria. In this sense, the individual mind of the interpreter would join the subjectivity of the author in vanishing from the spectrum of analysis. We return to this possibility shortly.

Yet, even with this more extended departure from intersubjectivist assumptions, in my view reader response accounts fail to take us far enough. For in the end we are left without a viable account of human meaning. Rather, in place of the impenetrable isolation of the intersubjectivist account, we are left with a form of social solipsism. Each community of readers shares its standards of interpretation through which texts are appropriated. Encountered texts themselves fail to alter or transform the local standards of interpretation. This is to say that the content of the encountered text would never be comprehended on its own terms. Few would be satisfied with such a view of human meaning.

More radical in its subversion of the intersubjectivist account of communication is deconstructionist literary theory. The chief villain in Derrida's writings (1976) is essentially the *logocentric* view of human functioning, the view that individual actors possess reasoning powers capable of fixing meaning and generating language. In effect, his goal was the eradication of individual subjectivity in the process of communication. In part this end is accomplished by demonstrating the fatal incoherence of texts that sustain the logocentric tradition. More critically, however, Derrida demonstrated the futility of the search for the signified—the meaning behind or within the text. We have traditionally proceeded as if others present us with spoken or written language (an array of *signifiers* in Derrida's terms), and that this language informs us about the state of one's mind (e.g., intentions, meanings) and of the world (objects, structures, etc.)—that is, realms of the *signified*. However, as we probe the domain of the signifiers to locate the signified, we find that each signifier in itself lies empty. In itself, it tells us nothing; its meaning (or signified) is displaced. For clarification, we are led to other signifiers—those that inform us of the precise nature of what is signified. Yet, this deferral of meaning is again but temporary, for the signifiers purporting to clarify or elucidate the signified are found on closer inspection to lie empty—unless supplemented by still further signifiers. Ultimately, then, meaning cannot be fixed, each choice point leaves us in a state of indecision. The realms of the signified are lost, and we are left, in Derrida's terms, with "nothing outside of text."

Yet, if there is nothing outside of text, how are we to understand the process by which humans relate with words? In what manner does one enter the array of signifiers? Why are certain interpretations preferred over others? Why does the endless search for the signified ever come to a conclusion? If all attempts at interpretation are principally undecidable, why are we not forever at the choice point? At present, deconstruction theorists fail to furnish answers to such questions. Of course, the deconstructionist could reply at this point by questioning the concept of human meaning altogether. That is, from the deconstructionist standpoint, theories of meaning are not about the world; they are essentially arrays of signifiers within a body of interrelated texts. Their meaning is not derived from their relationship to an actual process of meaningful interchange (even the term *actual* is defeasible), but from their relationship to other signifiers. In this sense, we are invited to abandon the present theoretical quest as simply one more textually determined (or merely academic) exercise.

Yet, even by deconstructionist standards, one is also free to reject such an invitation—not for any reason (merely another textual gesture, from the deconstructionist standpoint), but merely as an ungrounded action in itself. I select to do so, in part, however, because I fail to be entirely convinced by the deconstructionist argument itself. In particular, if signifiers can refer to other signifiers, or carry their historical traces into a text, then there is nothing to prevent what we call "actions" or "objects" to be reintroduced as constituents of texts (i.e., as signifiers). There is nothing about the concept of "texts," in effect, that limits them to linguistic signifiers, or nothing about the concept of signifier that limits it to sounds or markings. In a Wittgensteinian sense, this is to argue that language games (or the plays of signifiers) are, after all, embedded within forms of life—patterns of human action within what we call "material" contexts. And if this is so, we might usefully work toward the development of a viable theory of meaning, not because the term *meaning* is a reflection of the world, but because such a theory may be used by persons to alter or sustain particular forms of life. It is toward this end that the remainder of this chapter is devoted.

MEANING IN RELATIONSHIP

As we find, recent developments in hermeneutic and literary theory leave us in the following condition: The traditional view that meaning originates within the individual mind, is expressed within words (and other actions), and is deciphered within the minds of other agents, is deeply problematic. If meaning was preeminently an individual matter, we should be unable to communicate. There appear to be no means of inferentially or intuitively moving past another's words (or actions) to the subjective source, nor of translating another's words (or actions) into a system of understanding that is not already at one's disposal. Or in short, to begin the problem of human meaning with the assumption of individual subjectivity leaves no means by which it can be solved.

Yet, as I indicated in my introductory remarks, we need not frame the question of meaning within the individualist tradition. There is an alternative way of approaching the issue of social meaning, and by not taking the individual as its starting point, it opens a range of promising possibilities. Rather than commencing with individual subjectivity and working toward an account of human understanding through language, we may begin our analysis at the level of the human relationship as it generates both language and understanding. Such an approach is given impetus, for one, by the semiotics movement pioneered by Pierce and Saussure and significantly extended by Barthes, Eco, Greimas, and many others.[1]

---

[1]The present analysis also finds roots in the sociological tradition, Vygotskian developmental theory, and structuralist anthropology. However, although indebted to these traditions, this analysis demonstrates distinct differences. It should also be noted that Piaget was fully aware of the possibility of a social invasion of the mental. In *The Psychology of the Child*, he and Inhelder (1969) warn of the threat posed by the "sociological school of Durkheim" and the argument that "language constitutes not only an essential . . . factor in the learning of logic, . . . but is in fact the source of all logic for the whole of humanity" (p. 87). Evidence is then put forward to dispute this possibility and reinstantiate the individualist conclusion that "language does not constitute the source of logic, but is, on the contrary, structured by it" (p. 90). However, the evidence in this case depends on hermeneutic assumptions that are not only unworkable, as argued in the present chapter, but also virtually guarantee the conclusion.

In this case one begins not with subjectivity but with the system of language or signs common to a given culture. Social understanding is generated from participation within the common system. In this sense, it is not the individual who preexists the relationship and initiates the process of signification, but patterns of relationship and their embedded meanings that preexist the individual.

In important respects, literary theory of the kind just discussed is congenial with, or draws heavily from, the semiotic tradition. Reader response theory abandons the problem of meaning within the mind of the author, and concentrates instead on the shared sign systems of the interpretive community. In effect, the community generates the meaning of the text by absorbing it into its system of signs. Similarly, for Derrida the meaning of any given signifier is both evanescent and contingent, for meaning is ever deferred to other signifiers, and ultimately diffused throughout the entire system of signification. Yet, as we have also seen, in their present form such theories fail to provide a satisfactory account of the means by which humans generate or sustain meaning. Nor within the semiotic tradition more generally are there unequivocal accounts of this process. As one commentator (Sless, 1986) observed, "Nowhere in semiotics is the sense of uncertainty more obvious and profound than in relation to meaning" (p. 88).

It would be cavalier at this juncture to attempt a fully articulated account of social meaning from a relational perspective. However, for present purposes it is useful to lay out the rudiments of such an account and explore their implications. I make use of the semiological tradition and its near relatives, but with one major departure. The chief focus of the tradition is on language (and more typically, the text); the production of meaning is attributed to linguistic (or textual) patterning. However, this focus is to obscure the location from which meaning derives. Words (or texts) within themselves bear no meaning; they fail to communicate. They only appear to generate meaning by virtue of their place within the realm of human interaction. I replace textuality with communality. This shift allows us to restructure much that has been said about meaning within texts as a commentary on forms of relatedness. At the same time it allows me to draw from additional resources in literary, rhetorical, ethnomethodological, and social constructionist writings, and to extend some of my previous work (Gergen, 1988, 1990). I offer, then, the following rudiments for a relational account of human meaning:

An Individual's Utterances in Themselves Possess No Meaning. If we begin our account of meaning with individual subjectivity, the mind of the individual serves as an originary source of meaning. Meaning is generated within the mind and transmitted via words or gestures. However, in the relational case, there is no proper beginning, no originary source, no specific region in which meaning takes wing. For we are always already in a relational context, a condition in which we are positioned vis a vis others and the world. Therefore to speak of origins we must generate a hypothetical space in which there is an utterance (marking, gesture, etc.) without relational embedding. Granting this idealized case, we find that the single utterance of an individual in itself fails to possess meaning. This is most obvious in the case of uttering any selected morpheme (e.g., *the*, *ed*, *too*). Standing alone, the morpheme fails to be anything but itself. It operates, as in the textual case, as a freestanding signifier, opaque and indeterminate. (One may generate a variety of apparent exceptions to this initial assumption—e.g., a shout of "help" on a dark night; or more extended word sequences, such as "Eat at Joe's"—but the communicative value of such exceptions proves, on closer inspection, to depend on an implied context.) Even by placing the morphemic arrangement within a specific environmental setting does not grant meaning to the utterance. Consider the sound "woo," issuing from the lips of a damsel in a nearby glade. Although the utterance drips with significatory potential, it remains ultimately opaque. The sounds, even in context, remain "untranslatable."

The Potential for Meaning Is Realized Through Supplementary Action.
Lone utterances begin to acquire meaning when another (or others) coordinate themselves to the utterance, that is, when they add some form of supplementary action (whether linguistic or otherwise). The supplement may be as simple as an affirmation (e.g., "yes" or "right") that indeed the initial utterance has succeeded in communicating. It may take the form of an action, for example, shifting the line of gaze upon hearing the word, "look!" Or it may extend the utterance in some way, for example, when "the" uttered by one interlocutor is followed by "end!" uttered by a second. In the case of the damsel, meaning is generated when we hear a voice that responds to "Woo" with, "Yes, dear," now furnishing the sound with its meaning as the calling of a name.

We thus find that an individual alone can never "mean"; another is required to supplement the action, and thus furnish it with a form of meaning (see also Shotter, 1980, on "joint action"). To communicate is thus to be granted by others a privilege of meaning. If others do not treat one's utterances as communication, if they fail to coordinate themselves around the offering, one's utterance is reduced to nonsense. In this regard, virtually any form of utterance may be granted the privilege of being meaningful, or conversely, serves as a candidate for nonsense. (Jerzey Kozinsky's *Being There* furnishes numerous puckish examples of how the words of an idiot may be turned into profundity by surrounding believers. Garfinkel's [1967] exercises in questioning the routine grounds of everyday conversation—for example, "what do you mean exactly by 'flat tire'?"—demonstrate the possibility of aborting even the most obvious and the most sophisticated candidates for meaning.)

In semiotic terms, the present attempt is to remove meaning from the impersonal structure of the text and to place it within the structure of relationship. For many semioticians, the fundamental unit of meaning is contained in the relationship between signifier and signified; it is not located within either unit individually, but within the linkage between the two. In the present case, however, this linkage is removed from its textual location and placed within the social realm. Thus, we may view an individual's actions as a primitive "signified," whereas the responses of another person may serve the place of the "signifier." This "sign" relationship, signifier-linked-to-signified in semiotic terms, is now replaced by action-and-supplement. It is only by virtue of adding supplementing signifiers that actions gain their capacity as signifieds, and it is only within the relationship of action-and-supplement that meaning is to be located at all.

Supplements Act Both to Create and Constrain Meaning. The initial action (utterance, gesture, etc.) of the individual does not, in the hypothetical space developed thus far, demand any particular form of supplementation. In Pearce and Cronen's (1980) terms, in itself it possesses no *logical force*. The act of supplementation thus operates in two opposing ways. First, it grants a *specific potential* to the meaning of the utterance. It treats it as meaning *this* and not *that*, as requiring one form of action as opposed to another, as having a particular logical force as opposed to some other. Thus, if you come to me and say, "Do you have a light," I can, in the first instance, stare at you in puzzlement (thus negating what you have said as meaningful action). Or, conversely, I can react in a variety of different ways, each bestowing a different meaning on the utterance. For example, I can busily search through my pockets and answer "no," I can answer "yes" and walk away, I can tell you "I am not serving beer," I can ask you what it is you really want, or I can even shriek and fall into a fetal position.

If I create your meaning in one of these various ways, I simultaneously act to constrain it in many others. Because your words do mean *this*, they cannot mean *that*. In this sense, although I invite you into being, I also act so as to negate your potential. From the enormous array of possibilities, I thus create direction and temporarily narrow the possibilities of your being.

Any Supplement (or Action-and-Supplement) Is a Candidate for Further Supplementation. The social supplement, once executed, now comes to stand in the same position as the initial action or utterance. It is open to further specification, clarification, or obliteration through subsequent actions of the initial actor (or others). Its function as supplement, then, is transient and contingent on what follows. Thus, the supplement does not finally affix meaning, but serves as a temporary and defeasible functionary. At the simplest level, the supplement in its signifying capacity, comes to serve secondarily as a new form of the signified—an action that has no meaning until clarified by further supplementation. However, because the supplement is more typically viewed by the participants within the context of the initial action, it is the relationship between action and supplement (the "sign" in semiotic terms) that becomes subject to future revision and clarification. Thus, for example, if you ask me if I have a light, and I say "yes" and walk away, we have formed a unit that stands to be resignified by you. If you stare after me in amazement, you fail to grant to our interchange (action-and-supplement) the status of a meaningful interchange. If, however, you hurl an oath in the direction of my retreat, you affirm that the action and supplement had meaning (in this case, my supplement serving as a calloused and spiteful gesture). In the same way, you may stand puzzled at my comments on serving beer, thus negating the act-and-supplement as communication; or you may react with a laugh (granting it allusionary significance to recent light beer commercials), and thereby restore the interchange to the status of meaningful interchange.

Simultaneous with the instigation of the second-order supplement, the relationship between the interlocutors has again been expanded in its potential and again constrained. Of all possible meanings that might be made of your question and my response in terms of serving beer, your laughter constitutes us as having brought off a joke together. In this sense, your laughter grants us a particular form of potential, one that would not be furnished through, for example, a scowl or curt rejoinder. And as it invites one pattern of coordinated action, it reduces the possibility of others.

Meanings Are Subject to Continuous Reconstitution Via the Expanding Sea of Supplementation. In light of the aforementioned considerations we find that whether meaningful communication occurs, and what is communicated among persons, is inherently undecidable. That is, "the fact of meaning" stands as an open possibility, subject to the continuous accretion in supplementary significations. All that is fixed and settled in one instance, may be cast into ambiguity or undone in the next. Sarah and Sam may find themselves frequently laughing together, until Sam announces that Sarah's laughter is "unnatural and forced," just her attempt to present herself as an "easygoing person" (in which case the definition of what had been communicated would be altered). Or Sarah announces, "You are so superficial, Sam, that we really don't communicate" (thus negating the interchange altogether as a form of meaningful activity). At the same time, these latter moves within the ongoing sequence are subject to negation ("Sam, that's a crazy statement."), and alteration ("You are only saying that, Sarah, because you find Bill so attractive."). Such instances of negation and alteration may be far removed temporally from the interchange itself (e.g., consider a divorcing pair who retrospectively redefine their entire marital trajectory), and are subject to continuous change through interaction with and among others (e.g., friends, relatives, therapists, the media, etc.).

It is also this fundamentally open character of "what is meant," that lends itself to inquiries into the ongoing processes by which participants manage meaning within a relationship. Garfinkel's (1967) early work on the indexicality of meaning and the ad hoc character of making sense within a relationship are classic contributions to this domain. Studies of the ways in which communities of scientists work out mutually acceptable views of "the facts" (Latour & Woolgar, 1979), psychologists collectively hammer out a vision of the human subject (Danziger, 1990), families establish mutually acceptable views of the past (Middleton & Edwards, 1990), acquaintances structure each other's identities (Shotter, 1984), and political figures renegotiate the meaning of their public speeches (Edwards & Potter, 1992), all serve to fill out the picture of meaning in the making.

Yet, to focus on the face-to-face relationship may ultimately be delimited. For we find that whether I make sense is not under my control, nor is it ultimately under the control of the dyad in which the potential for meaning initially struggles toward realization. Rather, meaningful communication in any given situation ultimately depends on a protracted array of relationships, not only "right here, right now," but how it is that you and I are related to a variety of other persons, and they to still others—and ultimately, one might say, to the relational conditions of society as a whole. We are all in this way interdependently interlinked—without the capacity to mean anything, to possess an "I"—except for the existence of a potentially assenting world of relationships.

As Linguistic Relationships Become Coordinated (Ordered), So Do Ontologies and Their Instantiations Develop.   There is a close relationship between meaning and order. If the interchange between two individuals is random—such that any action on the part of one can serve as the prelude to any reaction of another—we would scarcely be able to say that the interchange is meaningful. It is only as our actions together come to develop order, such that the range of contingencies is constrained, that we move toward meaning.[2] If I throw you a ball and you cast it away, I throw you another and you place it in your pocket, and I throw you another and you crush it under foot, we have generally failed by common standards to generate meaning. However, if I throw you a ball and you throw it back, and on each succeeding throw you do the same, then you have given my throw the meaning of an invitation for you to return the throw, and vice versa. Actions thus come to have meaning within relatively structured sequences. If we are to move toward meaning we must move toward mutual constraint.[3]

The direction and form of any ordering is also critically determined by the other social orderings in which one is engaged. For example, within recent history we of the cultural West have tended to view our orderings in terms of "purposes," "functions," or "goals." Thus, in newly developing contexts of relationship, the ordering of relationships will typically be rationalized and directed by these understandings. We order our relationships in ways that we can index as "functional" within these preexisting relationships, and these orderings will tend toward recursion. If a hungry American tourist and the owner of a Kyoto noodle

---

[2] To put it another way, this is to say that one demonstrates what we call understanding in a relationship not by accessing the other's subjectivity, but by carrying out an appropriate action within an established sequence. For an illustration in terms of understanding others' emotions, see Gergen and Gergen, 1988.

[3] Although the present analysis may suggest considerable latitude in one's capacity to create and constrain meaning, the existence of longstanding patterns of interchange within the culture virtually ensures that not "everything goes"—nor is everything denied.

shop manage to coordinate their gestures so that food is sold (on the one side) and hunger is reduced (on the other), these gestures will be rapidly replicated on future visits to the shop.

To put the matter in discursive terms, participants in a relationship will tend to develop a *positive ontology*, or a series of mutually shared "callings," that enable interaction to proceed unproblematically. Thus, researchers in astrophysics do not shift their theoretical vocabulary from moment to moment, for to do so would mean the destruction of the group's capacity to achieve what they term productive research results. The effective functioning of the group depends on maintaining a relatively stable system of discourse. In other terms, the positive ontology becomes the culture's array of sedimented or commonsense understandings. It is precisely this sedimentation that enables scholars to treat the language system as a fixed structure, with logical implicature, and/or governed by rules.

As Consensus Is Established, So Are the Grounds for Both Understanding and Misunderstanding. In the preceding, I have layed out rudimentary grounds for understanding the communal generation of meaning. As the argument has unfolded, we find relationships tending toward ordered and recursive sequences in which meaning is transparent for the various participants. Yet, these suppositions in themselves leave us with no account of mis-meaning, that is, instances in which persons claim they do not understand, or fail to comprehend each other. Given the preceding analysis, it is clear that problems of incomprehension are not to be solved by recourse to individual subjectivities. However, the social orientation to the question "why misunderstanding," does engender three different but related answers. First and most simply, there are multiple contexts in which relationships are formed and local ontologies develop. Participation in one such set of coordinated activities is no necessary preparation for others. The most obvious illustration is when one visits a culture without any knowledge of the local language.

Misunderstandings are also generated within the same general culture. In these cases people employ a common language, but find the process of understanding to be fraught with difficulty. Such disharmonies may be understood in part because of the continuously unfolding nature of human relatedness. As persons move through life, the domain of relationships typically expands and the context of any given relationship typically changes. In effect, we are continuously confronted with some degree of novelty—new contexts and new challenges. Yet, our actions in such circumstances will necessarily represent some simulacre of the past; we borrow, reformulate, and patch together various pieces of preceding relationships in order to achieve local coordination of the moment. Figuratively put, in each new action one becomes a metaphor of one's past identity—a translocation of the self from a previous (or literal) context, a reformation of self but for different purposes. In this sense, every cultural implement for engendering meaning (words, gestures, pictures, etc.) is subject to multiple recontextualization. Each term in the language becomes polysymous, multiply meaningful. This places us in the following condition: Each move within a coordinated sequence is simultaneously a move in other possible sequences. Each action is thus a possible invitation to a multiplicity of intelligible sequences; each meaning is potentially some other, and the potential for misunderstanding permanently and pervasively at hand.

There is a third major source of misunderstanding within a given culture, and to me the most interesting. The Russian literary theorist Mikael Bakhtin recognized two major tendencies in the linguistic patterns of a culture, the one *centripetal* (or moving toward a centralization or unification) and the other *centrifugal* (decentering and unsettling the existing unity). Thus, forces toward stabilization were forever competing with opposing linguistic tendencies. "Every utterance participates in the 'unitary language' . . . and at the same time partakes of social and historical heteroglossia" (Bakhtin, 1981, p. 272). In the present context we may frame this oppositional dynamic in terms of the necessary discursive domain established by and at the margins of the positive ontology. That is, as the positive ontology is constituted, so does it generate the grounds for the negative—or oppositional—ontology. The existence of the *negative ontology* has significant implications for subsequent patterns of relationship. For the nuclear group confronts the lingering possibility of negation—that their premises may be replaced by their opposition—and thus the possibility of relational extermination. As communities sustain themselves by virtue of concepts such as God, democracy, equality, and so on, they must be forever watchful of negating discourses (e.g., atheism, fascism, racism). This antagonistic posture would not exist save for the initial articulation of the positive ontology. Or to put it otherwise, the development of meaning within a community establishes the grounds for a domain of countermeaning that forever poses a threat to meaning itself.

Of course, there is ample reason within a dominant culture for such continued suspicion of the unspoken. The negative ontology always stands open to development and enrichment. For any marginalized or mistreated subculture, the negative ontology is ready-made as a language for coordinating new forms of community—or more precisely, countercommunities. If there is a "necessity for war," a peace movement is invited; if there are prohibitions against abortion, there is an opportunity for a language of "choice"; and if there is a celebration of free expression, the way is paved for a critique of "political correctness." Further, as communities coalesce around the opposing argots, as they elaborate, enrich, and adorn the opposing discourses, the ground is prepared for nothing less than *systematic misunderstanding*. Each community is now dependent on a positive ontology, the very sustenance of which is dependent on maintaining its opposition. The communities seek each other's destruction, but simultaneously must ensure a continued existence. "To understand," that is, to coordinate one's actions with those of the opposition, would be to lose one's sense of the real and the right. Discussions seeking "mutual understanding" will often lurch toward failure, for participants will ensure that the other is not understood—otherwise both sides of the essential antinomy would give way.[4]

WHITHER COGNITION AND HUMAN DEVELOPMENT?

By weaving together and extending various lines of recent inquiry, I have tried to fashion the rudiments of a communal theory of meaning. The formulation envisions the generation of meaning as a constantly shifting, dynamic social process. "Successful" communication may be achieved under local circumstances through coordinated and interdependent actions of the participants. However, each localized coordination is dependent on the vicissitudes of broader social processes in which it is embedded—and thus vulnerable to reconstitution as a failed project. My sense of understanding you is not thus my possession, but ours, and ours only by virtue of the cultural processes in which we are embedded. Further, each achievement of meaning within a group sets in motion forces that will work toward destabilization and misunderstanding. In effect, we find a close, interdependent relationship between consensus and conflict: To generate social understanding lays the groundwork for its potential dissolution. It remains now to explore the implications of this analysis for the future study of both cognition and human development.

In my view, the present analysis strongly circumscribes the cognitive venture. As we found, the presumption of minds as possessions of independent individuals generates a set of intractable problems regarding social understanding. By commencing with communal coordination rather than individual subjectivity we avoid the critiques posed by hermeneutics, reader response, and textual indeterminacy. Yet, one may respond, in the same way that the traditional account leaves the individual unable to escape into relationship, so does the communal approach leave one with the problem of how the sociolinguistic system gains entry into the realm of cognition. In effect, have we not created yet another intellectual challenge of some gravity? For the question of how the social becomes personal was indeed Saussure's problem; it was also Vygotsky's, and it remains robust today. Consider, for example, the major problematic of Katherine Nelson's (1985) volume, *Making Sense, the Acquisition of Shared Meaning*: "The study of the development of meaning ... depends upon determining how internal systematicity emerges from the external experience of meaning in context" (p. 9). In spite of the brilliance of this work, my own view is that, indeed, the

---

[4]It should not be therefore concluded that we are locked into more or less permanent and necessarily conflicting systems of meaning. Change and synthesis is surely possible, and it remains a challenge for the further development of the present theory to demonstrate how this is so.

problem of how the "outer" seeps its way into the "inner" is equally as intractable as the companionate enigma of how the inner is communicated to others. Both problems fall out of a individualist tradition, and neither is soluble in principle.[5]

At the same time, this problem is not a natural heir to the communal orientation to social understanding. It is only a valid question if one already accepts the reality of cognitive processes and their centrality in human affairs. Yet, if one steps into the communal framework, the descriptive and explanatory vocabularies should, if fully expanded, furnish a full account of human action. "Doesn't *something* happen within the individual when exposed to other's actions," the critic may rejoin, "and isn't this something vital in determining what the person does?" To be sure, something does happen, but a uniquely cognitive account of this something is no more essential than a neurological account, or even an account in terms of atomic physics. But why are any of these accounts essential? A description of the "inner essence" seems no more necessary for getting on with social understanding (or relational accounts of such understanding) than knowing the atomic properties of a tennis ball is to winning at Wimbledon.

This is not to foreclose on all future "psychologizing." Psychological accounts are essential to Western cultural life, not because of their descriptive accuracy, but because they are constitutive features of relational patterns. If I cannot speak of "my thoughts, hopes, feelings, desires" and the like, there are many forms of cultural life in which I can scarcely participate. As I argued in *The Saturated Self* (Gergen, 1991), the profession of psychology is—for good or ill—a major contributor to this repository of symbolic resources. Further, there may be a place for a specifically "cognitive" vocabulary within the relational framework outlined earlier. In particular, with a reconceptualization of cognition, such terms could be used to account for *implicit social actions*, that is private rehearsal, play, or anticipatory activity that otherwise gains its meaning and significance from its placement within relational sequences.

This leads us, at last, to exploring the implications of a relational approach to meaning for developmental theory and research. Three issues are of special significance. First, the present arguments press strongly toward relational accounts of human development. That is, rather than viewing development either in terms of ontogenetic unfolding (heredity), or in terms of environmental impact (environment), analysis may profitably center on relational units and processes. Neither formal nor efficient causality are necessary for explanatory purposes in such cases: All elements within the relational process are related as pieces in a puzzle or instruments in a string quartet. There are, of course, related and significant departures already at hand within the developmental sphere. Works by Kurtines and Gewirtz (1987) on social dimensions of moral development, Rogoff (1989) on child apprenticeship, Youniss and Smoller (1985) on adolescent relations, Corsaro (1985) on friendship in the early years, and Hinde (1988) on

---

[5]For further expansion of this argument, see Gergen, 1989.

relationships within families are among the most visible. The recent renaissance of Vygotskian theory is also testimony to the "shift toward the social." However, in my view, most of this work remains timidly poised at the entry to the relational domain. For in most such instances, the concern for the social is secondary to the individual. The social world is said to influence the cognitive or emotional development of the individual child, and/or vice versa, but the psyche of the individual child remains in the pivotal position. So long as individual functioning continues to be the grounds for understanding relationships, then relationships will remain secondary and synthetic.

Closely related to this initial invitation is a second: Inquiry in human development may usefully be expanded to the broader spheres of sociality. The mother–child relationship is surely a significant one, but it tends to have the same engulfing quality as "the mind of the infant." And it is not simply that attentions might usefully shift to the full set of family relationships of which the child is a part, or to friends and community. Rather, human development may be fruitfully considered a constitutive feature of broadscale social process—fully enmeshed in the economic, political, educational, technological, and other practices of the culture. It is not simply that the conception of child development may wax and wane as changes take place within various cultural institutions (see Gergen, Gloger-Tippelt, & Glickman, 1990), but as patterns of parent–child relations are changed so may they alter forms of institutional life. An adolescent's exercises in moral decision making, for example, are not thus possessions of the adolescent; they may usefully be viewed as outcomes of an extended pattern of relationships. In the broadest sense, we all contribute to actions that are parochially viewed as local. Again, scattered works within the field do attempt to generate historical and cultural consciousness of the developmental process (e.g., Borstelman, 1983; Henriques, Hollway, Venn, Walkerdine, & Urwin, 1984; Kessen, 1979; van den Berg, 1961). However, the present arguments opt for a significant expansion of such inquiries.

Finally, the present account invites professional self-reflection. The arguments extend the implications of Wittgenstein's arguments of linguistic meaning as a product of social use. As such, they also call attention to the contingent character of professional language, the manner in which theory and research are embedded within patterns of relationship. Of special importance, developmental theory often leaps the boundaries of professional circles and enters into the broader practices of the society. (Consider, e.g., the insinuation of Piagetian theory into educational practices and childrearing manuals.) And finally, such an orientation has the advantage of giving priority to human relatedness as opposed to isolation. It is a matter of serious ethical and social importance, then, to consider how we in the profession chose to characterize human lives. In this respect, developmental theories for which the explanatory fulcrum is the psyche of the individual continue to foster a view of persons as fundamentally isolated and self-contained. Encouraged are practices based on a view of persons as separated, alone, and inherently competitive. In contrast, the present view brings into focus the reality of relatedness. One is never, on this account "unrelated" or independent; all that we call "individual subjectivity" is indeed premised on a prior relatedness. If today's theories become the commonsense realities of tomorrow, I find special promise in elaborating the matrix of relationship.

REFERENCES

Bakhtin, M. (1981). *The dialogic imagination.* Austin: University of Texas Press.

Billig, M. (1987). *Arguing and thinking: A rhetorical approach to social psychology.* Cambridge, England: Cambridge University Press.

Borstelman, L. J. (1983). Children before psychology: Ideas about children from antiquity to the late 1800's. In P. H. Mussen (Ed.), *Handbook of child psychology* (Vol. 1, pp. 67–107). New York: Wiley.

Bruner, J. (1990). *Acts of meaning.* Cambridge, MA: Harvard University Press.

Corsaro, W. A. (1985). *Friendship and peer culture in the early years.* Norwood, NJ: Ablex.

Danziger, K. (1990). *Constructing the subject: Historical origins of psychological research.* Cambridge, England: Cambridge University Press.

Derrida, J. (1976). *Of grammatology.* Baltimore: Johns Hopkins University Press.

Dilthey, W. (1984). *Selected writings.* Cambridge, England: Cambridge University Press. (Original work published 1914)

Edwards, D., & Potter, J. (1992). *Discursive psychology.* London: Sage.

Fish, S. (1980). *Is there a text in this class? The authority of interpretive communities.* Cambridge, MA: Harvard University Press.

Gadamer, H. G. (1975). *Truth and method.* New York: Seabury.

Garfinkel, H. (1967). *Studies in ethnomethodology.* Englewood Cliffs, NJ: Prentice-Hall.

Gergen, K. J. (1988). If persons are texts. In S. B. Messer, L. A. Sass, & R. L. Woolfolk (Eds.), *Hermeneutics and psychological theory* (pp. 28–51). New Brunswick, NJ: Rutgers University Press.

Gergen, K. J. (1989). Social psychology and the wrong revolution. *European Journal of Social Psychology, 19,* 463–484.

Gergen, K. J. (1990). Social understanding and the inscription of self. In J. W. Stigler, R. A. Shweder, & G. Herdt (Eds.), *Cultural psychology* (pp. 569–606). Cambridge, England: Cambridge University Press.

Gergen, K. J. (1991). *The saturated self: Dilemmas of identity in contemporary life.* New York: Basic.

Gergen, K. J., & Gergen, M. M. (1988). Narrative and the self as relationship. In L. Berkowitz (Ed.), *Advances in experimental social psychology* (Vol. 21, pp. 17–56). New York: Academic.

Gergen, K. J., Gloger-Tippelt, G., & Glickman, P. (1990). Everyday conceptions of the developing child. In G. Semin & K. J. Gergen (Eds.), *Everyday understanding: Social and scientific implications* (pp. 108–129). London: Sage.

Henriques, J., Hollway, W., Venn, C., Walkerdine, V., & Urwin, C. (1984). *Changing the subject: Psychology, social regulation and subjectivity.* London: Methuen.

Hinde, R. A. (1988). *Relationships within families.* New York: Oxford University Press.

Hirsch, E. D. (1967). *Validity in interpretation.* New Haven, CT: Yale University Press.

Kessen, W. (1979). The American child and other cultural inventions. *American Psychologist, 34,* 815–820.

Kurtines, W. M., & Gewirtz, J. L. (Eds.). (1987). *Social interaction and sociomoral development.* New York: Wiley.

Latour, L., & Woolgar, S. (1979). *Laboratory life: The social construction of scientific facts.* Beverly Hills, CA: Sage.

Middleton, D., & Edwards, D. (1990). *Collective remembering.* London: Sage.

Nelson, K. (1985). *Making sense: The acquisition of shared meaning.* New York: Academic.

Overton, W. E. (1991). The structure of developmental theory. In P. van Geert & L. P. Mos (Eds.), *Annals of theoretical psychology* (Vol. 7, pp. 191–235). New York: Plenum.

Pearce, W. B., & Cronen, V. (1980). *Communication, action and meaning.* New York: Praeger.

Piaget, J. (1955). *The language and thought of the child.* New York: Meridian.

Piaget, J., & Inhelder, B. (1969). *The psychology of the child.* New York: Basic.

Rogoff, B. (1989). *Apprenticeship in thinking.* New York: Oxford University Press.

Shotter, J. (1980). Action, joint action, and intentionality. In M. Brenner (Ed.), *The structure of action* (pp. 31–43). Oxford, England: Blackwell.

Shotter, J. (1984). *Social accountability and selfhood.* Oxford, England: Blackwell.

Sless, D. (1986). *In search of semiotics.* Totowa, NJ: Barnes & Noble.

Suleiman, S. R., & Crosman, I. (1980). *The reader in the text.* Princeton, NJ: Princeton University Press.

Taylor, C. (1971). Interpretation and the sciences of man. *The Review of Metaphysics, 25,* No. 1.

van den Berg, J. H. (1961). *The changing nature of man.* New York: Dell.

Youniss, J., & Smoller, J. (1985). *Adolescent relations with mothers, fathers, and friends.* Chicago: University of Chicago Press.

3
What Is a Conceptual System?

George Lakoff
University of California at Berkeley

The study of how a child's conceptual system develops assumes that one knows what the final product is, what an adult conceptual system is like. If there is a radical change in the idea of what an adult conceptual system is, then research on conceptual development must pay attention if researchers are to know what to study the development of.

During the 1980s, research in the cognitive sciences, especially in cognitive linguistics, has produced a radically new idea of what a conceptual system is. Many of these results were surveyed in *Women, Fire, and Dangerous Things* (Lakoff, 1987). The fundamental notions in conceptual system research in cognitive linguistics are relatively new to the tradition of child development research, notions like frame semantics, radial categories, basic-level categories, types of metonymic prototypes, image schemas, mental spaces, and perhaps the most radical of all, conceptual metaphor.

To those brought up in the Piagetian paradigm, such a rapid expansion of adult conceptual system research may seem daunting. It should also be exciting. If adult conceptual systems are radically different than they were thought to be, then there is a world of new research to be done on conceptual development.

I believe that it is important to bring together research on adult conceptual systems with conceptual development research. Each needs the other. The purpose of this chapter is to help bridge the gap between research on adult conceptual systems and research on child development—to provide an introduction for researchers in child development to the most elaborate and conceptually radical

41

branch of contemporary conceptual system research—the study of systems of conventional conceptual metaphor.

Before we proceed with details, it is well worth noting that, however new much of this research is, it does confirm certain of Piaget's fundamental insights—especially the insight that conceptual structure has everything to do with one's body and with how one interacts as part of one's physical environment. Though I do not stress that here, Mark Johnson's (1987) *The Body in the Mind* makes the case overwhelmingly. This research strongly disconfirms the idea that concepts are disembodied abstractions whose only interesting properties are formal properties—an idea common to all versions of formal semantics, from classical deductive logic to model-theoretic semantics in the Montague tradition to Jerry Fodor's language of thought and Noam Chomsky's logical forms.

If there is a major moral of metaphor system research, it is that abstract concepts are understood in terms of concrete physical and interpersonal experience. As we see, notions as abstract as time, event, state, cause, purpose, means, and action are metaphorical—fundamentally understood in terms of physical experience. Metaphor is not just a poetic device; it is the major mechanism we have for comprehending most domains of our experience. We have a vast conventional system of conceptual metaphor whose job is to allow us to use our everyday concrete experience to understand other aspects of our experience.

THE CLASSICAL AND THE CONTEMPORARY THEORIES

Do not go gentle into that good night.
—Dylan Thomas
Death is the mother of beauty . . .
—Wallace Stevens, "Sunday Morning"

These famous lines by Thomas and Stevens are examples of what classical theorists, at least since Aristotle, have referred to as metaphor: instances of novel poetic language in which words like *mother*, *go*, and *night* are not used in their normal everyday senses. In classical theories of language, metaphor was seen as a matter of language, not thought. Metaphorical expressions were assumed to be mutually exclusive with the realm of ordinary everyday language: Everyday language had no metaphor, and metaphor used mechanisms outside the realm of everyday conventional language.

The classical theory was taken so much for granted over the centuries that many people did not realize that it was just a theory. The theory was not merely taken to be true, but came to be taken as definitional. The word *metaphor* was defined as a novel or poetic linguistic expression where one or more words for a concept are used outside of its normal conventional meaning to express a similar concept.

But such issues are not matters for definitions; they are empirical questions. As a cognitive scientist and a linguist, one asks: What are the generalizations governing the linguistic expressions referred to classically as *poetic metaphors*? When this question is answered rigorously, the classical theory turns out to be false. The generalizations governing poetic metaphorical expressions are not in language, but in thought: They are general mappings across conceptual domains. Moreover, these general principles, which take the form of conceptual mappings, apply not just to novel poetic expressions but to much of ordinary everyday language.

In short, the locus of metaphor is not in language at all, but in the way we conceptualize one mental domain in terms of another. The general theory of metaphor is given by characterizing such cross-domain mappings. And in the process, everyday abstract concepts like time, states, change, causation, and purpose also turn out to be metaphorical.

The result is that metaphor (i.e., cross-domain mapping) is absolutely central to ordinary natural language semantics, and that the study of literary metaphor is an extension of the study of everyday metaphor. Everyday metaphor is characterized by a huge system of thousands of cross-domain mappings, and this system is made use of in novel metaphor.

Because of these empirical results, the word *metaphor* has come to be used differently in contemporary metaphor research. The word *metaphor* has come to mean "a cross-domain mapping in the conceptual system." The term *metaphorical expression* refers to a linguistic expression (a word, phrase, or sentence) that is the surface realization of such a cross-domain mapping (this is what the word *metaphor* referred to in the old theory). I adopt the contemporary usage throughout this chapter.

Experimental results demonstrating the cognitive reality of the extensive system of metaphorical mappings are discussed by Gibbs (1990, 1994). Mark Turner's 1987 book, *Death Is the Mother of Beauty*, whose title comes from Stevens' great line, demonstrates in detail how that line uses the ordinary system of everyday mappings. For further examples of how literary metaphor makes use of the ordinary metaphor system, see *More Than Cool Reason: A Field Guide to Poetic Metaphor*, by Lakoff and Turner (1989) and *Reading Minds: The Study of English in the Age of Cognitive Science*, by Turner (1991).

Beyond the Old Literal–Figurative Distinction

A major assumption that is challenged by contemporary research is the traditional division between literal and figurative language, with metaphor as a kind of figurative language. This entails, by definition, that: What is literal is not metaphorical. In fact, the word *literal* has traditionally been defined in terms of a set of assumptions that have since proved to be false:

1. All everyday conventional language is literal, and none is metaphorical.

2. All subject matter can be comprehended literally, without metaphor.
3. Only literal language can be contingently true or false.
4. All definitions given in the lexicon of a language are literal, not metaphorical.
5. The concepts used in the grammar of a language are all literal; none is metaphorical.

The big difference between the contemporary theory and traditional views of metaphor lies in this set of assumptions. The reason for the difference is that, in the intervening years, a huge system of everyday, conventional, conceptual metaphors has been discovered. It is a system of metaphor that structures our everyday conceptual system, including most abstract concepts, and that lies behind much of everyday language. The discovery of this enormous metaphor system has destroyed the traditional literal–figurative distinction, because the term literal, as used in defining the traditional distinction, carries with it all those false assumptions.

A major difference between the contemporary theory and the classical one is based on the old literal–figurative distinction. Given that distinction, one might think that one "arrives at" a metaphorical interpretation of a sentence by "starting" with the literal meaning and applying some algorithmic process to it (see Searle, in Ortony, 1993). Though there do exist cases where something like this happens, this is not in general how metaphor works, as we shall see shortly.

What Is Not Metaphorical

Although the old literal–metaphorical distinction was based on assumptions that have proved to be false, one can make a different sort of literal–metaphorical distinction: Those concepts that are not comprehended via conceptual metaphor might be called literal. Thus, although I argue that a great many common concepts like causation and purpose are metaphorical, there is nonetheless an extensive range of nonmetaphorical concepts. Thus, a sentence like "The balloon went up" is not metaphorical; nor is the old philosopher's favorite "The cat is on the mat." But as soon as one gets away from concrete physical experience and starts talking about abstractions or emotions, metaphorical understanding is the norm.

THE CONTEMPORARY THEORY: SOME EXAMPLES

Let us now turn to some examples that are illustrative of contemporary metaphor research. They come mostly from the domain of everyday conventional metaphor, because that has been the main focus of the research. I turn to the discussion of poetic metaphor only after I discuss the conventional system, because knowledge of the conventional system is needed to make sense of most of the poetic cases.

The evidence for the existence of a system of conventional conceptual metaphors is of five types:

1. Generalizations governing polysemy, that is, the use of words with a number of related meanings.
2. Generalizations governing inference patterns, that is, cases where a pattern of inferences from one conceptual domain is used in another domain.
3. Generalizations governing novel metaphorical language (see Lakoff & Turner, 1989).
4. Generalizations governing patterns of semantic change (see Sweetser, 1990).
5. Psycholinguistic experiments (see Gibbs, 1990, 1994).

We discuss primarily the first three of these sources of evidence, because they are the most robust.

Conceptual Metaphor

Imagine a love relationship described as follows: Our relationship has hit *a dead-end street.* Here love is being conceptualized as a journey, with the implication that the relationship is *stalled*, that the lovers cannot *keep going the way they've been going*, that they must *turn back*, or abandon the relationship altogether. This is not an isolated case. English has many everyday expressions that are based on a conceptualization of love as a journey, and they are used not just for talking about love, but for reasoning about it as well. Some are necessarily about love; others can be understood that way: Look *how far we've come.* It's been *a long, bumpy road.* We can't *turn back* now. We're at a *crossroads.* We may have to *go our separate ways.* The relationship isn't *going anywhere.* We're *spinning our wheels.* Our relationship is *off the track.* The marriage is *on the rocks.* We may have to *bail out* of this relationship. These are ordinary, everyday English expressions. They are not poetic, nor are they necessarily used for special rhetorical effect. Those like *Look how far we've come*, which are not necessarily about love, can readily be understood as being about love.

As a linguist and a cognitive scientist, I ask two commonplace questions:

1. Is there a general principle governing how these linguistic expressions about journeys are used to characterize love?
2. Is there a general principle governing how our patterns of inference about journeys are used to reason about love when expressions such as these are used?

The answer to both is yes. Indeed, there is a single general principle that answers both questions. But it is a general principle that is neither part of the grammar of English, nor the English lexicon. Rather, it is part of the conceptual system underlying English: It is a principle for understanding the domain of love in terms of the domain of journeys.

The principle can be stated informally as a metaphorical scenario:

> The lovers are travelers on a journey together, with their common life goals seen as destinations to be reached. The relationship is their vehicle, and it allows them to pursue those common goals together. The relationship is seen as fulfilling its purpose as long as it allows them to make progress toward their common goals. The journey is not easy. There are impediments, and there are places (crossroads) where a decision has to be made about which direction to go in and whether to keep traveling together.

The metaphor involves understanding one domain of experience, love, in terms of a very different domain of experience, journeys. More technically, the metaphor can be understood as a mapping (in the mathematical sense) from a source domain (in this case, journeys) to a target domain (in this case, love). The mapping is tightly structured. There are ontological correspondences, according to which entities in the domain of love (e.g., the lovers, their common goals, their difficulties, the love relationship, etc.) correspond systematically to entities in the domain of a journey (the travelers, the vehicle, destinations, etc.).

To make it easier to remember what mappings there are in the conceptual system, Johnson and I (Lakoff & Johnson, 1980) adopted a strategy for naming such mappings, using mnemonics that suggest the mapping. Mnemonic names typically (though not always) have the form: *target-domain is source-domain*, or alternatively, *target-domain as source-domain*. In this case, the name of the mapping is *love is a journey*. When I speak of the *love is a journey* metaphor, I am using a mnemonic for a set of ontological correspondences that characterize a mapping, namely:

1. The lovers correspond to travelers.
2. The love relationship corresponds to the vehicle.
3. The lovers' common goals correspond to their common destinations on the journey.
4. Difficulties in the relationship correspond to impediments to travel.

It is a common mistake to confuse the name of the mapping, *love is a journey*, for the mapping itself. The mapping is the set of correspondences. Thus, whenever I refer to a metaphor by a mnemonic like *love is a journey*, I refer to such a set of correspondences.

If mappings are confused with names of mappings, another misunderstanding can arise. Names of mappings commonly have a propositional form, for example, *love is a journey*. But the mappings themselves are not propositions. If mappings are confused with names for mappings, one might mistakenly think that, in this theory, metaphors are propositional. They are, of course, anything but that: Metaphors are mappings, that is, sets of conceptual correspondences.

The *love-as-journey* mapping is a set of ontological correspondences that characterize epistemic correspondences by mapping knowledge about journeys onto knowledge about love. Such correspondences permit us to reason about love using the knowledge we use to reason about journeys. Let us take an example. Consider the expression, "We're stuck," said by one lover to another about their relationship. How is this expression about travel to be understood as being about their relationship?

"We're stuck" can be used of travel, and when it is, it evokes knowledge about travel. The exact knowledge may vary from person to person, but here is a typical example of the kind of knowledge evoked. The italicized expressions represent entities in the ontology of travel, that is, in the source domain of the *love is a journey* mapping given earlier:

Two *travellers* are in a *vehicle, traveling with common destinations.* The *vehicle* encounters some *impediment* and gets stuck, that is, makes it nonfunctional. If they do nothing, they will not *reach their destinations.* There are a limited number of alternatives for action:

1. They can try to get it moving again, either by fixing it or getting it past the *impediment* that stopped it.
2. They can remain in the nonfunctional *vehicle* and give up on *reaching their destinations.*
3. They can abandon the *vehicle.*

The alternative of remaining in the nonfunctional *vehicle* takes the least effort, but does not satisfy the desire to *reach their destinations.*

The ontological correspondences that constitute the *love is a journey* metaphor map the ontology of travel onto the ontology of love. In so doing they map this scenario about travel onto a corresponding love scenario in which the corresponding alternatives for action are seen. Here is the corresponding love scenario that results from applying the correspondences to this knowledge structure. The target domain entities that are mapped by the correspondences are italicized:

Two *lovers* are in a *love relationship, pursuing common life goals.* The *relationship* encounters some *difficulty,* which makes it nonfunctional. If they do nothing, they will not be able to *achieve their life goals.* There are a limited number of alternatives for action:

1. They can try to get it moving again, either by fixing it or getting it past the *difficulty.*
2. They can remain in the nonfunctional *relationship,* and give up on *achieving their life goals.*
3. They can abandon the *relationship.*

The alternative of remaining in the nonfunctional *relationship* takes the least effort, but does not satisfy the desire to *achieve life goals*.

This is an example of an inference pattern that is mapped from one domain to another. It is via such mappings that we apply knowledge about travel to love relationships.

Metaphors Are Not Mere Words

What constitutes the *love-as-journey* metaphor is not any particular word or expression. It is the ontological mapping across conceptual domains, from the source domain of journeys to the target domain of love. The metaphor is not just a matter of language, but of thought and reason. The language is secondary. The mapping is primary, in that it sanctions the use of source domain language and inference patterns for target domain concepts. The mapping is conventional; that is, it is a fixed part of our conceptual system, one of our conventional ways of conceptualizing love relationships.

This view of metaphor is thoroughly at odds with the view that metaphors are just linguistic expressions. If metaphors were merely linguistic expressions, we would expect different linguistic expressions to be different metaphors. Thus, "We've hit a dead-end street" would constitute one metaphor. "We can't turn back now" would constitute another, entirely different metaphor. "Their marriage is on the rocks" would involve still a different metaphor. And so on for dozens of examples. Yet we do not seem to have dozens of different metaphors here. We have one metaphor, in which love is conceptualized as a journey. The mapping tells us precisely how love is being conceptualized as a journey. And this unified way of conceptualizing love metaphorically is realized in many different linguistic expressions.

It should be noted that contemporary metaphor theorists commonly use the term "metaphor" to refer to the conceptual mapping, and the term "metaphorical expression" to refer to an individual linguistic expression (like *dead-end street*) that is sanctioned by a mapping. We have adopted this terminology for the following reason: Metaphor, as a phenomenon, involves both conceptual mappings and individual linguistic expressions. It is important to keep them distinct. Because it is the mappings that are primary and that state the generalizations that are our principal concern, we have reserved the term "metaphor" for the mappings, rather than for the linguistic expressions.

In the literature of the field, italics like *love is a journey* are used as mnemonics to name mappings. Thus, when we refer to the *love is a journey* metaphor, we are referring to the set of correspondences discussed earlier. The English sentence "Love is a journey," on the other hand, is a metaphorical expression that is understood via that set of correspondences.

Generalizations

The *love is a journey* metaphor is a conceptual mapping that characterizes a generalization of two kinds:

1. Polysemy generalization: A generalization over related senses of linguistic expressions, for example, *dead-end street, crossroads, stuck, spinning one's wheels, not going anywhere*, and so on.
2. Inferential generalization: A generalization over inferences across different conceptual domains.

That is, the existence of the mapping provides a general answer to two questions:

1. Why are words for travel used to describe love relationships?
2. Why are inference patterns used to reason about travel also used to reason about love relationships?

Correspondingly, from the perspective of the linguistic analyst, the existence of such cross-domain pairings of words and of inference patterns provides evidence for the existence of such mappings.

Novel Extensions of Conventional Metaphors

The fact that the *love is a journey* mapping is a fixed part of our conceptual system explains why new and imaginative uses of the mapping can be understood instantly, given the ontological correspondences and other knowledge about journeys. Take the song lyric, "We're driving in the fast lane on the freeway of love." The traveling knowledge called upon is this: When you drive in the fast lane, you go a long way in a short time and it can be exciting and dangerous. The general metaphorical mapping maps this knowledge about driving into knowledge about love relationships. The danger may be to the vehicle (the relationship may not last) or the passengers (the lovers may be hurt, emotionally). The excitement of the love-journey is sexual. Our understanding of the song lyric is a consequence of the preexisting metaphorical correspondences of the *love-as-journey* metaphor. The song lyric is instantly comprehensible to speakers of English because those metaphorical correspondences are already part of our conceptual system.

The *love-as-journey* metaphor and Reddy's (1979) *conduit metaphor* were the two examples that first convinced me that metaphor was not a figure of speech, but a mode of thought, defined by a systematic mapping from a source to a target domain. What convinced me were the three characteristics of metaphor that I have just discussed:

1. The systematicity in the linguistic correspondences.
2. The use of metaphor to govern reasoning and behavior based on that reasoning.
3. The possibility for understanding novel extensions in terms of the conventional correspondences.

Motivation

Each conventional metaphor, that is, each mapping, is a fixed pattern of conceptual correspondences across conceptual domains. As such, each mapping defines an open-ended class of potential correspondences across inference patterns. When activated, a mapping may apply to a novel source domain knowledge structure and characterize a corresponding target domain knowledge structure.

Mappings should not be thought of as processes, or as algorithms that mechanically take source domain inputs and produce target domain outputs. Each mapping should be seen instead as a fixed pattern of ontological correspondences across domains that may, or may not, be applied to a source domain knowledge structure or a source domain lexical item. Thus, lexical items that are conventional in the source domain are not always conventional in the target domain. Instead, each source domain lexical item may or may not make use of the static mapping pattern. If it does, it has an extended lexicalized sense in the target domain, where that sense is characterized by the mapping. If not, the source domain lexical item will not have a conventional sense in the target domain, but may still be actively mapped in the case of novel metaphor. Thus, the words *freeway* and *fast lane* are not conventionally used of love, but the knowledge structures associated with them are mapped by the *love is a journey* metaphor in the case of "We're driving in the fast lane on the freeway of love."

Imageable Idioms

Many of the metaphorical expressions discussed in the literature on conventional metaphor are idioms. On classical views, idioms have arbitrary meanings. But within cognitive linguistics, the possibility exists that they are not arbitrary, but rather motivated. That is, they do arise automatically by productive rules, but they fit one or more patterns present in the conceptual system. Let us look a little more closely at idioms.

An idiom like "spinning one's wheels" comes with a conventional mental image, that of the wheels of a car stuck in some substance—either in mud, sand, snow, or on ice—so that the car cannot move when the motor is engaged and the wheels turn. Part of our knowledge about that image is that a lot of energy is being used up (in spinning the wheels) without any progress being made, that the situation will not readily change of its own accord, that it will take a lot of effort on the part of the occupants to get the vehicle moving again—and that may not even be possible.

The *love-as-journey* metaphor applies to this knowledge about the image. It maps this knowledge onto knowledge about love relationships: A lot of energy is being spent without any progress toward fulfilling common goals, the situation will not change of its own accord, it will take a lot of effort on the part of the lovers to make more progress, and so on. In short, with idioms that have associated conventional images, it is common for an independently motivated conceptual metaphor to map that knowledge from the source to the target domain. For a survey of experiments verifying the existence of such images and such mappings, see Gibbs (1990, 1994).

Mappings Are at the Superordinate Level

In the *love is a journey* mapping, a love relationship corresponds to a vehicle. A vehicle is a superordinate category that includes such basic-level categories as car, train, boat, and plane. Indeed, the examples of vehicles are typically drawn from this range of basic-level categories: car (*long bumpy road, spinning our wheels*), train (*off the track*), boat (*on the rocks, foundering*), plane (*just taking off, bailing out*). This is not an accident: In general, we have found that mappings are at the superordinate rather than the basic level. Thus, we do not find fully general submappings like *a love relationship is a car*; when we find a love relationship conceptualized as a car, we also tend to find it conceptualized as a boat, a train, a plane, and so on. It is the superordinate category *vehicle* not the basic-level category *car* that is in the general mapping.

It should be no surprise that the generalization is at the superordinate level, whereas the special cases are at the basic level. After all, the basic level is the level of rich mental images and rich knowledge structure. (For a discussion of the properties of basic-level categories, see Lakoff, 1987.) A mapping at the superordinate level maximizes the possibilities for mapping rich conceptual structure in the source domain onto the target domain, because it permits many basic-level instances, each of which is information rich.

Thus, a prediction is made about conventional mappings: The categories mapped will tend to be at the superordinate rather than basic level. Thus, one tends not to find mappings like *a love relationship is a car* or *a love relationship is a boat*. Instead, one tends to find both basic-level cases (e.g., both cars and boats), which indicates that the generalization is one level higher, at the superordinate level of the vehicle. In the hundreds of cases of conventional mappings studied so far, this prediction has been borne out: It is superordinate categories that are used in mappings.

BASIC SEMANTIC CONCEPTS
THAT ARE METAPHORICAL

Most people are not too surprised to discover that emotional concepts like love and anger are understood metaphorically. What is more interesting, and I think more exciting, is the realization that many of the most basic concepts in our conceptual systems are also comprehended normally via metaphor—concepts like time, quantity, state, change, action, cause, purpose, means, modality, and even the concept of a category. These are concepts that enter normally into the grammars of languages, and if they are indeed metaphorical in nature, then metaphor becomes central to grammar.

What I suggest is that the same kinds of considerations that lead to our acceptance of the *love-as-journey* metaphor lead inevitably to the conclusion that such basic concepts are often, and perhaps always, understood via metaphor.

Categories

Classical categories are understood metaphorically in terms of bounded regions, or "containers." Thus, something can be *in* or *out* of a category; it can be *put into* a category or *removed from* a category, and so on. The logic of classical categories is the logic of containers (see Fig. 3.1): If *X* is in container A and container A is in container B, then *X* is in container B. This is true not by virtue of any logical deduction, but by virtue of the topological properties of containers. Under the *classical categories are containers* metaphor, the logical properties of categories are inherited from the logical properties of containers. One of the principal logical properties of classical categories is that the classical syllogism holds for them. The classical syllogism,

> Socrates is a man.
> All men are mortal.
> Therefore, Socrates is mortal.

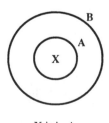

X is in A
A is in B
∴ X is in B

FIG. 3.1   The image-schematic basis of the classical syllogism.

is of the form: If X is in category A and category A is in category B, then X is in category B. Thus, the logical properties of classical categories can be seen as following from the topological properties of containers plus the metaphorical mapping from containers to categories. As long as the topological properties of containers are preserved by the mapping, this result will be true.

In other words, there is a generalization to be stated here. The language of containers applies to classical categories and the logic of containers is true of classical categories. A single metaphorical mapping ought to characterize both the linguistic and logical generalizations at once. This can be done provided that the topological properties of containers are preserved in the mapping.

The joint linguistic-and-inferential relation between containers and classical categories is not an isolated case. Let us take another example.

Quantity and Linear Scales

The concept of quantities involves at least two metaphors. The first is the well-known *more is up, less is down* metaphor as shown by a myriad of expressions like "Prices rose, Stocks skyrocketed, The market plummeted," and so on. A second is that *linear scales are paths*. We can see this in expressions like:

John is *far* more intelligent than Bill.
John's intelligence *goes way beyond* Bill's.
John is *way ahead of* Bill in intelligence.

The metaphor maps the starting point of the path onto the bottom of the scale and maps distance traveled onto quantity in general.

What is particularly interesting is that the logic of paths maps onto the logic of linear scales (see Fig. 3.2):

1. Path inference: If you are going from A to C, and you are now at an intermediate point B, then you have been at all points between A and B and not at any points between B and C. Example: If you are going from San Francisco to New York along route 80, and you are now at Chicago, then you have been to Denver but not to Pittsburgh.

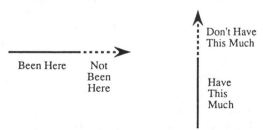

FIG. 3.2.   The image-schematic basis of linear scale inferences.

2. Linear scale inference: If you have exactly $50 in your bank account, then you have $40, $30, and so on, but not $60, $70, or any larger amount.

The form of these inferences is the same. The path inference is a consequence of the cognitive topology of paths. It will be true of any path image schema. Again, there is a linguistic-and-inferential generalization to be stated. It would be stated by the metaphor *linear scales are paths*, provided that metaphors in general preserve the cognitive topology (that is, the image-schematic structure) of the source domain.

Looking at the inferential structure alone, one might suggest a nonmetaphorical alternative in which both linear scales and paths are instances of a more general abstract schema. But when both the inferential and lexical data are considered, it becomes clear that a metaphorical solution is required. An expression like "ahead of" is from the spatial domain, not the linear scale domain: "Ahead" in its core sense is defined with respect to one's head—it is the direction in which one is facing. To say that there is no metaphorical mapping from paths to scales is to say that "ahead of" is not fundamentally spatial and characterized with respect to heads; it is to claim rather that "ahead" is very abstract, neutral between space and linear scales, and has nothing to do with heads. This would be a bizarre analysis. Similarly, for sentences like "John's intelligence goes beyond Bill's," the nonmetaphorical analysis would claim that "go" is not fundamentally a verb of motion at all, but is somehow neutral between motion and a linear relation. This would also be bizarre. In short, if one grants that "ahead of" and "go" are fundamentally spatial, then the fact that they can also be used of linear scales suggests a metaphor solution. Indeed, there could be no such neutral sense of "go" for these cases, because "go beyond" in the spatial sense involves motion, whereas in the linear scale sense, there is no motion or change, but just a point on a scale. Here the neutral case solution is not even available.

The Invariance Principle

In the examples we have just considered, the image schemata characterizing the source domains (containers, paths) are mapped onto the target domains (categories, linear scales). This observation leads to the following hypothesis, called the invariance principle: Metaphorical mappings preserve the cognitive topology (that is, the image-schema structure) of the source domain, in a way consistent with the inherent structure of the target domain. What the invariance principle does is guarantee that, for container schemata, interiors will be mapped onto interiors, exteriors onto exteriors, and boundaries onto boundaries; for path schemata, sources will be mapped onto sources, goals onto goals, trajectories onto trajectories, and so on.

To understand the invariance principle properly, it is important not to think of mappings as algorithmic processes that "start" with source domain structure and wind up with target domain structure. Such a mistaken understanding of mappings would lead to a mistaken understanding of the invariance principle; namely, that one first picks all the image-schematic structure of the source domain, then one copies it onto the target domain unless the target domain interferes.

One should instead think of the invariance principle in terms of constraints on fixed correspondences: If one looks at the existing correspondences, one will see that the invariance principle holds: Source domain interiors correspond to target domain interiors; source domain exteriors correspond to target domain exteriors; and so on. As a consequence it will turn out that the image-schematic structure of the target domain cannot be violated: One cannot find cases where a source domain interior is mapped onto a target domain exterior, or where a source domain exterior is mapped onto a target domain path. This simply does not happen.

Target Domain Overrides

A corollary of the invariance principle is that image-schema structure inherent in the target domain cannot be violated, and that inherent target domain structure limits the possibilities for mappings automatically. This general principle explains a large number of previously mysterious limitations on metaphorical mappings. For example, it explains why you can give someone a kick, even if they do not have it afterwards, and why you can give someone information, even if you do not lose it. This is just a consequence of the fact that inherent target domain structure automatically limits what can be mapped. For example, consider that part of your inherent knowledge of actions that says that actions do not continue to exist after they occur. Now consider the *actions are transfers* metaphor, in which actions are conceptualized as objects transferred from an agent to a patient, as when one gives someone a kick or a punch. We know (as part of target domain knowledge) that an action does not exist after it occurs. In the source domain, where there is a giving, the recipient possesses the object given after the giving. But this cannot be mapped onto the target domain because the inherent structure of the target domain says that no such object exists after the action is over. The target domain override in the invariance principle explains why you can give someone a kick without his having it afterward.

Abstract Inferences as Metaphorical Spatial Inferences

Spatial references are characterized by the topological structure of image-schemas. We have seen cases such as *categories are containers* and *linear scales are paths* where image-schema structure is preserved by metaphor and where abstract inferences about categories and linear scales are metaphorical versions of spatial inferences about containers and paths. The invariance principle hypothesizes that image-schema structure is always preserved by metaphor.

The invariance principle raises the possibility that a great many, if not all, abstract inferences are actually metaphorical versions of spatial inferences that are inherent in the topological structure of image schemata. What I do now is turn to other cases of basic, but abstract, concepts to see what evidence there is for the claim that such concepts are fundamentally characterized by metaphor.

Time

It has often been noted that time in English is conceptualized in terms of space. The details are rather interesting:

Ontology: Time is understood in terms of things (i.e., entities and locations) and motion.

Background condition: The present time is at the same location as a canonical observer.

Mapping:
—Times are things.
—The passing of time is motion.
—Future times are in front of the observer; past times are behind the observer.
—One thing is moving, the other is stationary; the stationary entity is the deictic center.

Entailment:
—Because motion is continuous and one-dimensional, the passage of time is continuous and one-dimensional.

Special Case 1:
—The observer is fixed; times are entities moving with respect to the observer.
—Times are oriented with their fronts in their direction of motion.

Entailments:
—If time 2 follows time 1, then time 2 is in the future relative to time 1.
—The time passing the observer is the present time.
—Time has velocity relative to the observer.

Special Case 2:
—Times are fixed locations; the observer is moving with respect to time.

Entailment:
—Time has extension, and can be measured.

—An extended time, like a spatial area, may be conceived of as a bounded region.

This metaphor, *time passing is motion*, with its two special cases, embodies a generalization that accounts for a wide range of cases where a spatial expression can also be used for time. Special Case 1, *time passing is motion of an object*, accounts for both the linguistic form and the semantic entailments of expressions like:

> The time will *come* when ... The time has long since *gone* when ... The time for action has *arrived*. That time is *here*. In the weeks *following* next Tuesday ... On the *preceding* day, ... I'm looking *ahead* to Christmas. Thanksgiving is *coming* up on us. Let's put all that *behind* us. I can't *face* the future. Time is *flying* by. The time has *passed* when ...

Thus, Special Case 1 characterizes the general principle behind the temporal use of words like *come, go, here, follow, precede, ahead, behind, fly, pass*, accounting not only for why they are used for both space and time, but why they mean what they mean.

Special Case 2, *time passing is motion over a landscape*, accounts for a different range of cases, expressions like:

> There's going to be trouble *down the road.*
> He stayed there *for* 10 years.
> He stayed there a *long* time.
> His stay in Russia *extended over* many years.
> He *passed* the time happily.
> He *arrived* on time.
> We're *coming up on* Christmas.
> We're getting *close to* Christmas.
> He'll have his degree *within* 2 years.
> I'll be there *in* a minute.

Special Case 2 maps location expressions like *down the road, for* + location, *long, over, come, close to, within, in, pass*, onto corresponding temporal expressions with their corresponding meanings. Again, Special Case 2 states a general principle relating spatial terms and inference patterns to temporal terms and inference patterns.

The details of the two special cases are rather different; indeed, they are inconsistent with one another. The existence of such special cases has an especially interesting theoretical consequence: Words mapped by both special cases will have inconsistent readings. Take, for example, the *come* of *Christmas is coming* (Special Case 1) and *We're coming up on Christmas* (Special Case 2). Both instances of *come* are temporal, but one takes a moving time as first argument and the other takes a moving observer as first argument. The same is true of *pass* in *The time has passed* (Special Case 1) and in *He passed the time* (Special Case 2).

These differences in the details of the mappings show that one cannot just say blithely that spatial expressions can be used to speak of time, without specifying details, as though there were only one correspondence between time and space. When we are explicit about stating the mappings, we discover that there are two different—and inconsistent—subcases.

The fact that time is understood metaphorically in terms of motion, entities, and locations accords with our biological knowledge. In our visual systems, we have detectors for motion and detectors for objects/locations. We do not have detectors for time (whatever that could mean). Thus, it makes good biological sense that time should be understood in terms of things and motion.

Duality

The two special cases (location and object) of *time passing is motion* metaphor is not merely an accidental feature of our understanding of time. As we see later, there are other metaphors that come in such location-object pairs. Such pairs are called *duals*, and the general phenomenon in which metaphors come in location-object pairs is referred to as *duality*.

Simultaneous Mappings

It is important to recall that metaphorical mappings are fixed correspondences that can be activated, rather than algorithmic processes that take inputs and give outputs. Thus, it is not the case that sentences containing conventional metaphors are the products of a real-time process of conversion from literal to metaphorical readings. A sentence like *The time for action has arrived* is not understood by first trying to give a literal reading to *arrive*, and then, upon failing, trying to give it a temporal reading. Instead, the metaphor *time passing is motion* is a fixed structure of existing correspondences between the space and time domains, and *arrive* has a conventional extended meaning that makes use of that fixed structure of correspondences.

Thus, it is possible for two different parts of a sentence to make use of two distinct metaphorical mappings at once. Consider a phrase like, *within the coming weeks*. Here, *within* makes uses of the metaphor of time as a stationary landscape that has extension and bounded regions, whereas *coming* makes use of the metaphor of times as moving objects. This is possible because the two metaphors for time pick out different aspects of the target domain. *The coming weeks* conceptualizes those weeks as a whole, in motion relative to the observer. *Within* looks inside that whole, conceptualizing it as a bounded region with an interior. Each mapping is used partially. Thus, although the mappings—as wholes—are inconsistent, there are cases where parts of the mappings may be consistently superimposed. The invariance principle allows such parts of the mappings to be picked out and used to characterize reasoning about different aspects of the target domain.

Simultaneous mappings are very common in poetry. Take, for example the Dylan Thomas line "Do not go gentle into that good night." Here *go* reflects *death is departure*, *gentle* reflects *life is a struggle*, with death as defeat. *Night* reflects *a lifetime is a day*, with death as night. This one line has three different metaphors for death, each mapped onto different parts of the sentence. This is possible because mappings are fixed correspondences.

There is an important lesson to be learned from this example. In mathematics, mappings are static correspondences. In computer science, it is common to represent mathematical mappings by algorithmic processes that take place in real time. Researchers in information processing psychology and cognitive science also commonly represent mappings as real-time algorithmic procedures. Some researchers from these fields have mistakenly supposed that the metaphorical mappings we are discussing should also be represented as real-time, sequential algorithmic procedures, where the input to each metaphor is a literal meaning. Any attempt to do this will fail for the simultaneous mapping cases just discussed.

EVENT STRUCTURE

I now want to turn to some research by myself and some of my students (especially Sharon Fischler, Karin Myhre, and Jane Espenson) on the metaphorical understanding of event structure in English. What we have found is that various aspects of event structure, including notions like states, changes, processes, actions, causes, purposes, and means, are characterized cognitively via metaphor in terms of space, motion, and force.

The general mapping for the *event structure metaphor* we have found goes as follows:

1. States are locations (bounded regions in space).
2. Changes are movements (into or out of bounded regions).
3. Causes are forces.
4. Actions are self-propelled movements.
5. Purposes are destinations.
6. Means are paths (to destinations).
7. Difficulties are impediments to motion.
8. Expected progress is a travel schedule; a schedule is a virtual traveler, who reaches prearranged destinations at prearranged times.
9. External events are large, moving objects.
10. Long-term, purposeful activities are journeys.

This mapping generalizes over an extremely wide range of expressions for one or more aspects of event structure. For example, take states and changes. We speak of being *in* or *out* of a state, of *going into* or *out of* it, of *entering* or *leaving* it, of getting *to* a state or emerging *from* it.

This is a rich and complex metaphor whose parts interact in complex ways. To get an idea of how it works, consider the submapping "Difficulties are impediments to motion." In the metaphor, purposive action is self-propelled motion toward a destination. A difficulty is something that impedes motion to such a destination. Metaphorical difficulties of this sort come in five types: blockages, features of the terrain, burdens, counterforces, lack of an energy source. Here are examples of each:

1. Blockages: He got *over* his divorce. He's trying to get *around* the regulations. He *went through* the trial. We *ran into a brick wall*. We've got him *boxed into a corner*.

2. Features of the terrain: He's *between a rock and a hard place*. It's been *uphill* all the way. We've been *bogged down*. We've been *hacking our way through a jungle* of regulations.

3. Burdens: He's *carrying* quite a load. He's *weighed down* by a lot of assignments. He's been trying to *shoulder* all the responsibility. Get *off my back!*

4. Counterforces: Quit *pushing* me around. She's *leading him around* by the nose. She's *holding* him *back*.

5. Lack of an energy source: I'm *out of gas*. We're *running out of steam*.

To see just how rich the event structure metaphor is, consider some of its basic entailments:

1. Manner of action is manner of motion.
2. A different means for achieving a purpose is a different path.
3. Forces affecting action are forces affecting motion.
4. The inability to act is the inability to move.
5. Progress made is distance traveled or distance from goal.

We consider examples of each of these one by one, including a number of special cases:

1. Aids to Action Are Aids to Motion: It is *smooth sailing* from here on in. It's all *downhill* from here. There's *nothing in our way*.

2. A Different Means of Achieving a Result Is a Different Path: Do it *this way*. She did it *the other way*. Do it *any way* you can. However you want to *go about* it is fine with me.

3. Manner of Action Is Manner of Motion: We are *moving/running/skipping right along*. We *slogged through* it. He is *flailing around*. He is *falling* all over himself. We are *leaping over hurdles*. He is *out of step*. He is *in step*.

4. Careful Action Is Careful Motion: I'm *walking on eggshells*. He is *treading on thin ice*. He is *walking* a fine line.

5. Speed of Action Is Speed of Movement: He *flew* through his work. He is *running* around. It is *going* swimmingly. Keep things *moving* at a good clip. Things have *slowed to* a crawl. She is *going by leaps and bounds*. I am *moving at a snail's pace*.

6. Purposeful Action is Self-Propelled Motion to a Destination: This has the following special cases:

7. Making Progress Is Forward Movement: We are *moving ahead*. Let's forge *ahead*. Let's keep *moving forward*. We made lots of *forward movement*.

8. Amount of Progress Is Distance Moved: We've *come a long way*. We've *covered lots of ground*. We've made it *this far*.

9. Undoing Progress Is Backward Movement: We are *sliding backward*. We are *backsliding*. We need to *backtrack*. It is time to *turn around* and *retrace our steps*.

10. Expected Progress Is a Travel Schedule: a Schedule Is a Virtual Traveler who reaches prearranged destinations at prearranged times: We're *behind* on the project. We got a *head start* on the project. I'm trying to *catch up*. I finally got *a little ahead*.

11. Starting an Action Is Starting Out on a Path: We are just *starting out*. We have *taken the first step*.

12. Success Is Reaching the End of the Path: We've *reached the end*. We are *seeing the light at the end of the tunnel*. We only have *a short way to go*. The end is *in sight*. The end is *a long way off*.

13. Lack of Purpose Is Lack of Direction: He is just *floating* around. He is *drifting aimlessly*. He needs some *direction*.

14. Lack of Progress Is Lack of Movement: We are at a *standstill*. We aren't *getting any place*. We aren't *going anywhere*. We are *going nowhere* with this.

15. External Events Are Large Moving Objects

16. Special Case 1: Things—How're things *going*? Things are *going with* me. Things are *going against* me these days. Things took *a turn* for the worse. Things are *going my way*.

17. Special Case 2: Fluids—You gotta *go with the flow*. I'm just trying to *keep my head above water*. The *tide* of events ... The *winds* of change ... The *flow* of history ... I'm trying to *get my bearings*. He's *up a creek without a paddle*. We're all *in the same boat*.

18. Special Case 3: Horses—Try to keep a *tight rein* on the situation. Keep a *grip* on the situation. Don't let things *get out of hand*. *Wild horses* couldn't make me go. *"Whoa!"* (said when things start to get out of hand).

Such examples provide overwhelming empirical support for the existence of the event structure metaphor. And the existence of that metaphor shows that the most common abstract concepts—*time, state, change, causation, action, purpose,* and *means*—are conceptualized via metaphor. Because such concepts are at the very center of our conceptual systems, the fact that they are conceptualized metaphorically shows that metaphor is central to ordinary abstract thought.

Inheritance Hierarchies

Metaphorical mappings do not occur isolated from one another. They are sometimes organized in hierarchical structures, in which "lower" mappings in the hierarchy inherit the structures of the "higher" mappings. Let us consider an example of a hierarchy with three levels:

Level 1: The Event Structure Metaphor
Level 2: *a purposeful life is a journey*
Level 3: *love is a journey; a career is a journey*

To refresh your memory, recall that the event structure metaphor has as its target domain events and as its source domain space, and that the general mapping goes as follows:

1. States are locations (bounded regions in space).
2. Changes are movements (into or out of bounded regions).
3. Causes are forces.
4. Actions are self-propelled movements.
5. Purposes are destinations.
6. Means are paths to destinations.
7. Difficulties are impediments to motion.
8. Expected progress is a travel schedule; a schedule is a virtual traveler, who reaches prearranged destinations at prearranged times.
9. External events are large, moving objects.
10. Long-term, purposeful activities are journeys.

In our culture, life is assumed to be purposeful, that is, we are expected to have goals in life. In the event structure metaphor, purposes are destinations and purposeful action is self-propelled motion toward a destination. A purposeful life is a long-term, purposeful activity, and hence a journey. Goals in life are destinations on the journey. The actions one takes in life are self-propelled movements, and the totality of one's actions form a path one moves along. Choosing a means to achieve a goal is choosing a path to a destination. Difficulties in life are impediments to motion. External events are large moving objects that can impede motion toward one's life goals. One's expected progress through life is charted in terms of a life schedule, which is conceptualized as a virtual traveler that one is expected to keep up with.

In short, the metaphor *a purposeful life is a journey* makes use of all the structure of the event structure metaphor, because events in a life conceptualized as purposeful are subcases of events in general:

A purposeful life is a journey
Target Domain: Life   Source Domain: Space
—The person leading a life is a traveler.
Inherits Event Structure Metaphor, with:
     Events = Significant Life Events
     Purposes = Life Goals

Thus we have expressions like: He got *a head start* in life. He's *without direction* in his life. I'm *where I want to be* in life. I'm *at a crossroads* in my life. He'll *go places* in life. He's never let anyone *get in his way*. He's *gone through* a lot in life.

Just as significant life events are special cases of events, so events in a love relationship are special cases of life events. Thus, the *love is a journey* metaphor inherits the structure of the *life is a journey* metaphor. What is special about the *love is a journey* metaphor is that there are two lovers, who are travelers, and that the love relationship is a vehicle. The rest of the mapping is a consequence of inheriting the *life is a journey* metaphor. Because the lovers are in the same vehicle, they have common destinations, that is, common life goals. Relationship difficulties are impediments to travel:

Love is a journey
Target Domain: Love   Source Domain: Space
—The lovers are travelers.
—The love relationship is a vehicle.
Inherits the *life is a journey* metaphor.

A career is another aspect of life that can be conceptualized as a journey. Here, because *status is up*, a career is actually a journey upward. Career goals are special cases of life goals:

A career is a journey
Target Domain: Career   Source Domain: Space

—A careerist is a traveler.
—Status is up.
Inherits *life is a journey*, with:
    Life Goals = Career Goals
Ideal: To go as high, far, and fast as possible.

Examples include: He *clawed* his way to the top. He's *over the hill*. She's *on the fast track*. He's *climbing* the corporate *ladder*. She's *moving up* in the ranks quickly.

This inheritance hierarchy accounts for a range of generalizations. First, there are generalizations about lexical items. Take the word *crossroads*. Its central meaning is in the domain of space. But it can be used in a metaphorical sense of any extended activity, of one's life, of a love relationship, or of a career: I'm at a *crossroads* on this project. I'm at a *crossroads* in life. We're at a *crossroads* in our relationship. I'm at a *crossroads* in my career.

The hierarchy allows one to state a general principal: that *crossroads* is extended lexically via the submetaphor of the event structure metaphor that says long-term purposeful activities are journeys, and that all its other uses are automatically generated via the inheritance hierarchy. Thus, separate senses for each level of the hierarchy are not needed.

The second generalization is inferential in character. Thus the understanding of difficulties as impediments to travel occurs not only in events in general, but also in a purposeful life, in a love relationship, and in a career. The inheritance hierarchy guarantees that this understanding of difficulties in life, love, and careers is a consequence of such an understanding of difficulties in events in general.

The hierarchy also allows us to characterize lexical items whose meanings are more restricted: Thus, *climbing the ladder* refers only to careers, not to love relationships or to life in general.

Such hierarchical organization is a very prominent feature of the metaphor system of English and other languages. So far we have found that the metaphors higher up in the hierarchy tend to be more widespread than those mappings at lower levels. Thus, the event structure metaphor is very widespread (and may even be universal), whereas the metaphors for life, love, and careers are much more restricted culturally.

Duality in the Event Structure System

In our discussion of time metaphors, we noted the existence of an object-location duality. There were two related time metaphors. In both, the passage of time was understood in terms of relative motion between an observer and a time. In the object dual, the observer is fixed and times are moving objects. In the location dual, the opposite is true. The observer moves and times are fixed locations in a landscape.

The event structure system that we have seen so far is based wholly on location. But there is another event structure system that is the dual of the one we have just discussed—a system based on objects rather than locations. In both systems, *change is motion* and *causes are forces* that control motion. The difference is this:

In the location system, change is the motion of the thing-changing to a new location or from an old one.
In the object system, the thing-changing does not necessarily move. Change is instead the motion of an object to, or away from, the thing-changing.

In addition, the object in motion is conceptualized as a possession and the thing-changing as a possessor. Change is thus seen as the acquisition or loss of an object. Causation is seen as giving or taking. Here are some examples:

1. I have a headache. (The headache is a possession.)
2. I got a headache. (Change is acquisition—motion to.)
3. My headache went away. (Change is loss—motion from.)
4. The noise gave me a headache. (Causation is giving—motion to.)
5. The aspirin took away my headache. (Causation is taking—motion from.)

We can see the duality somewhat more clearly with a word like *trouble*:

1. I'm in trouble. (Trouble is a location.)
2. I have trouble. (Trouble is an object that is possessed.)

In both cases, trouble is being attributed to me, and in both cases, trouble is metaphorically conceptualized as being in the same place as me (colocation)—in one case, because I possess the trouble object and in the other case, because I am in the trouble location. That is, attribution in both cases is conceptualized metaphorically as colocation. In "I'm in trouble," trouble is a state. A state is an attribute that is conceptualized as a location. Attributes (or properties) are like states, except that they are conceptualized as possessable objects.

Thus, *states are locations* and *attributes are possessions* are duals, because possession and location are special cases of the same thing—colocation—and because states and attributes are also special cases of the same thing—what can be attributed to someone.

Given this, we can see that there is an object version of the event structure metaphor:

1. Attributes are possessions.

2. Changes are movements (of possessions, namely, acquisitions or losses).
3. Causes are forces (controlling the movement of possessions, namely, giving or taking away).

These are the duals of:

1. States are locations.
2. Changes are movements (to or from locations).
3. Causes are forces (controlling movement to or from locations).

Similarly, *actions are self-propelled movements* (to or from locations) has as its object dual *actions are self-controlled acquisitions or losses*. Thus, there is a reason why one can "take" certain actions—you can take a shower, or take a shot at someone, or take a chance.

The submapping *purposes are destinations* also has a dual. Destinations are desired locations, and so the submapping can be rephrased as *purposes are desired locations*, and *achieving a purpose is reaching a desired location*. Replacing *location* by *object*, we get the dual *purposes are desired objects*, and *achieving a purpose is acquiring a desired object* (or ridding oneself of an undesirable one).

Here are some examples of *achieving a purpose is acquiring a desired object*: They just *handed* him the job. It's within my *grasp*. It *eluded* me. *Go for* it. It *escaped* me. It *slipped through my hands*. He is *pursuing* a goal. *Reach for/grab* all the gusto you can get. *Latch onto* a good job. *Seize* the opportunity. He *found* success.

There is also a hierarchical structure in the object version of the event structure metaphor. A special case of getting an object is getting an object to eat. Hence, *achieving a purpose is getting something to eat*: He *savored* the victory. All the good jobs have been *gobbled* up. He's *hungry* for success. The opportunity has me *drooling*. This is a *mouth-watering* opportunity. Traditional methods of getting things to eat are hunting, fishing, and agriculture. Each of these special cases can be used metaphorically to conceptualize achieving (or attempting to achieve) a purpose:

1. *Trying to achieve a purpose is hunting:* I'm *hunting* for a job. I *bagged* a promotion. The pennant is *in the bag*.

The typical way to hunt is to use projectiles (bullets, arrows, etc.): I'm *shooting* for a promotion. I'm *aiming* for a career in the movies. I'm afraid *I missed* my chance.

2. *Trying to achieve a purpose is fishing:* He's *fishing* for compliments. I *landed* a promotion. She *netted* a good job. I've *got a line out on* a good used car. It's time *to fish or cut bait*.

3. *Trying to achieve a purpose is agriculture:* It's time I *reaped* some rewards. That job is a *plum*. Those are the *fruits* of his labor. The contract is *ripe* for the *picking*.

I will not try to survey all the dualities in the English metaphor system, but it is worth mentioning a few to see how subtle and pervasive dualities are. Take, for example, the *life is a journey* metaphor, in which goals in life are destinations, that is, desired locations to be reached. Because the dual of *purposes are destinations* is *purposes are desired objects*, the dual of *life is a journey* is a metaphor in which life is an activity through which one acquires desired objects. In this culture, the principle activity of this sort is business, and hence, *life is a business* is the dual of *life is a journey*. So, for *a purposeful life is a business*: He has a *rich* life. It's an *enriching* experience. I want to *get a lot out of* life. He's going about the *business* of everyday life. It's time to *take stock* of my life.

Recall that *love is a journey* is an extension of *a purposeful life is a journey*. It happens that *love is a journey* has a dual that is an extension of the dual of *a purposeful life is a journey*, which is *a purposeful life is a business*. The dual of *love is a journey* is *love is a partnership*, that is, a two-person business. Thus, we speak of lovers as "partners"; there are marriage contracts, and in a long-term love relationship the partners are expected to do their jobs and to share in both responsibilities (what they contribute to the relationship) and benefits (what they get out of it). Long-term love relationships fail under the same conditions as businesses fail—when what the partners get out of the relationship is not worth what they put into it.

Duality is a newly discovered phenomenon. The person who first discovered it in the event structure system was Jane Espenson, a graduate student at Berkeley who stumbled upon it in the course of her research on causation metaphors. Since Espenson's discovery, other extensive dualities have been found in the English metaphor system. However, at present, it is not known just how extensive dualities are in English, or even whether they are all of the location-object type.

At this point, I leave off discussing the metaphor system of English, even though hundreds of other mappings have been described to date. The major point to take away from this discussion is that metaphor resides for the most part in this huge, highly structured, fixed system. This system is anything but "dead." Because it is conventional, it is used constantly and automatically, with neither effort nor awareness. Novel metaphor uses this system, and builds on it, but only rarely occurs independently of it. But, most interestingly, this system of metaphor seems to give rise to abstract reasoning, which appears to be based on spatial reasoning.

Invariance Again

The metaphors I have discussed primarily map three kinds of image schemata: containers, paths, and force images. Because of the complexity of the subcases and interactions, the details are intricate, to say the least. However, the invariance principle does make claims in each case as to what image schemata get mapped onto target domains. I do not go through most of the details here, but so far as I can see, the claims made about inferential structure are reasonable ones.

For example, the logic of force dynamics does seem to map, via the submapping *causes are forces*, onto the logic of causation. The following are inferences from the logic of forces inherent in force dynamics:

1. A stationary object will move only when force is applied to it; without force, it will not move.
2. The application of force requires contact; thus, the applier of the force must be in spatial contiguity with the thing it moves.
3. The application of force temporally precedes motion, because inertia must be overcome before motion can take place.

These are among the classic inferential conditions on causation: spatial contiguity, temporal precedence, and that A caused B only if B would not have happened without A.

At this point, I would like to take up the question of what else the invariance principle would buy us. I consider two cases that arose while Mark Turner and I were writing *More Than Cool Reason* (Lakoff & Turner, 1989). The first concerns image metaphors and the second, generic-level metaphors. But before I move on to those topics, I should point an important consequence of invariance.

Johnson and I argued in *Metaphors We Live By* (Lakoff & Johnson, 1980) that a complex propositional structure could be mapped by metaphor onto another domain. The main example we gave was *argument is war*. Kövecses and I, in our analysis of anger metaphors (Kövecses, 1990; Lakoff, 1987, Case Study 1), also argued that metaphors could map complex propositional structures. The invariance principle does not deny this, but it puts those claims in a very different light. Complex propositional structures involve concepts like time, states, changes, causes, purposes, quantity scales, and categories. If all of these abstract concepts are characterized metaphorically, then the invariance principle claims that what we had called propositional structure is really image-schematic structure. In other words, so-called propositional inferences arise from the inherent topological structure of the image schemata mapped by metaphor onto concepts like time, states, changes, actions, causes, purposes, means, quantity, and categories. The reason that I have taken the trouble to discuss all those abstract concepts is to demonstrate this consequence of the invariance principle; namely, that what have been seen in the past as propositional inferences are really image-based inferences. If the invariance principle is correct, it has a remarkable consequence, namely that: Abstract reasoning is a special case of image-based reasoning. Image-based reasoning is fundamental and abstract reasoning is image-based reasoning under metaphorical projections to abstract domains.

To look for independent confirmation of the invariance principle, let us turn to image metaphors.

NOVEL METAPHORS

Image Metaphors

There is a class of metaphors that function to map one conventional mental image onto another. These contrast with the metaphors I have discussed so far, each of which maps one conceptual domain onto another, often with many concepts in the source domain mapped onto many corresponding concepts in the target domain. Image metaphors, by contrast, are "one-shot" metaphors: They map only one image onto one other image.

Consider, for example, this poem from the Indian tradition:

Now women-rivers
belted with silver fish
move unhurried as women in love
at dawn after a night with their lovers
(Merwin & Masson, 1981, p. 71)

Here the image of the slow, sinuous walk of an Indian woman is mapped onto the image of the slow, sinuous, shimmering flow of a river. The shimmering of a school of fish is imagined as the shimmering of the belt.

Metaphoric image mappings work in just the same way as all other metaphoric mappings: by mapping the structure of one domain onto the structure of another. But here, the domains are conventional mental images. Take, for example, this line from André Breton: "My wife . . . whose waist is an hourglass." This is a superimposition of the image of an hourglass onto the image of a woman's waist by virtue of their common shape. As before, the metaphor is conceptual; it is not in the words themselves, but in the mental images. Here, we have a mental image of an hourglass and of a woman, and we map the middle of the hourglass onto the waist of the woman. Note that the words do not tell us which part of the hourglass to map onto the waist, or even that it is only part of the hourglass shape that corresponds to the waist. The words are prompts for us to map from one conventional image to another. Similarly, consider this line, taken from Rabelais, "The Descriptions of King Lent," translated by J. M. Cohen:

His toes were like the keyboard of a spinet.

Here too, the words do not tell us that an individual toe corresponds to an individual key on the keyboard. Again, the words are prompts for us to perform a conceptual mapping between conventional mental images. In particular, we map aspects of the part–whole structure of one image onto aspects of the part–whole structure of another. Just as individual keys are parts of the whole keyboard, so individual toes are parts of the whole foot.

Image mapping can involve more than mapping physical part–whole relationships. For example, the water line of a river may drop slowly and that slowness is part of the dynamic image, which may be mapped onto the slow removal of clothing:

> Slowly slowly rivers in autumn show
> sand banks
> bashful in first love woman
> showing thighs
> (Merwin & Masson, 1981, p. 69)

Other attributes are also mapped: the color of the sandbank onto the color of flesh, the quality of light on a wet sandbank onto the reflectiveness of skin, the light grazing of the water's touch receding down the bank onto the light grazing of the clothing along the skin. Notice that the words do not tell us that any clothing is involved. We get that from a conventional mental image. Part–whole structure is also mapped in this example. The water covers the hidden part of the bank just as the clothing covers the hidden part of the body. The proliferation of detail in the images limits image mappings to highly specific cases. That is what makes them one-shot mappings.

Such mappings of one image onto another can lead us to map knowledge about the first image onto knowledge about the second. Consider the following example from the Navaho ("War God's Horse Song I" words by Tall Kia ahni, interpreted by Louis Watchman):

> My horse with a mane made of short rainbows.

The structure of a rainbow, its band of curved lines for example, is mapped onto an arc of curved hair, and many rainbows onto many such arcs on the horse's mane. Such image mapping allows us to map our evaluation of the source domain onto the target. We know that rainbows are beautiful, special, inspiring, larger than life, almost mystic, and that seeing them makes us happy and awe-inspired. This knowledge is mapped onto what we know of the horse: It too is awe-inspiring, beautiful, larger than life, almost mystic. This line comes from a poem containing a series of such image mappings:

> My horse with a hoof like a striped agate,
> with his fetlock like a fine eagle plume:

my horse whose legs are like quick lightning
whose body is an eagle-plumed arrow:
my horse whose tail is like a trailing black cloud.

Image metaphors raise two major issues for the general theory of metaphor:

1. How do they work? What constrains the mappings? What kind of internal structures do mental images have that permit some mappings to work readily, others only with effort, and others not at all?
2. What is the general theory of metaphor that unifies image metaphors with all the conventional metaphors that map the propositional structure of one domain onto the propositional structure of another domain?

Turner and I (Lakoff & Turner, 1989) suggested that the invariance principle could be an answer to both questions. We suggested that conventional mental images are structured by image schemata and that image metaphors preserve image-schematic structure, mapping parts onto parts and wholes onto wholes, containers onto containers, paths onto paths, and so on. The generalization would be that all metaphors are invariant with respect to their cognitive topology; that is, each metaphorical mapping preserves image-schema structure.

Generic-Level Metaphors

When Turner and I were writing *More Than Cool Reason* (Lakoff & Turner, 1989), we hypothesized the existence of what we called *generic-level metaphors* to deal with two problems that we faced—first, the problem of personification and second, the problem of proverbs, which requires an understanding of analogy. I discuss each in turn.

Personification. In studying a wide variety of poems about death in English, we found that, in poem after poem, death was personified in a relatively small number of ways: drivers, coachmen, footmen; reapers, devourers, and destroyers; or opponents in a struggle or game (say, a knight or a chess opponent). The question we asked was: Why these? Why isn't death personified as a teacher or a carpenter or an ice cream salesman? Somehow, the ones that occur repeatedly seem appropriate. Why?

In studying personifications in general, we found that the overwhelming number seem to fit a single pattern: Events (like death) are understood in terms of actions by some agent (like reaping). It is that agent that is personified. We thus hypothesized a very general metaphor, *events are actions*, which combines with other, independently existing metaphors for life and death. Consider, for example, the *death is departure* metaphor. Departure is an event. If we understand this event as an action on the part of some causal agent—someone who brings about, or helps to bring about, departure—then we can account for figures like drivers, coachmen, footmen, and so on. Or take the *people are plants* metaphor. In the natural course of things, plants wither and die. But if we see that event as a causal action on the part of some agent, then that agent is a reaper. So far, so good. But why destroyers and devourers? And what about the impossible cases?

Destruction and devouring are actions in which an entity ceases to exist. The same is true of death. The overall "shape" of the event of death is similar in this respect to the overall shapes of the events of destruction and devouring. Moreover, there is a causal aspect to death: The passage of time will eventually result in death. Thus, the overall shape of the event of death has an entity that over time ceases to exist as the result of some cause. Devouring and destruction have the same overall "event shape." That is, it is the same with respect to causal structure and the persistence of entities over time.

Turner (1987) noticed a similar case in *Death Is the Mother of Beauty*, his classic work on kinship metaphor. In expressions like "Necessity is the mother of invention," or "Edward Teller was the father of the H-bomb," causation is understood in terms of giving birth or fathering—what Turner called the *causation is progeneration* metaphor. But, as he observed, this metaphor could not be used for just any instance of causation. It could only be used for cases that had the overall event shape of progeneration: Something must be created out of nothing, and the thing created must persist for a long time (as if it had a life).

Thus, for example, we can speak of Saussure as the father of modern synchronic linguistics, or of New Orleans as giving birth to jazz. But we cannot use this metaphor for a single causal action with a short-lived effect. Thus, we could not speak of Jose Canseco as the father of the home run he just hit, or of that home run as giving birth to the Oakland As' victory in the game. Though, of course, we could speak of Babe Ruth as the father of modern home-run hitting, and of the home runs giving birth to the era of baseball players as superstars. The overall event shape of the target domain limits the applicability of the metaphor.

Recalling Turner's (1987) observation about *causation is progeneration*, we therefore hypothesized that *events are actions* is constrained in the following way: The action must have the same overall event shape as the event. What is preserved across the mapping is the causal structure, the aspectual structure, and the persistence of entities. We referred to this as *generic-level structure*.

The preservation of generic-level structure explained why death is not metaphorized in terms of teaching, or filling the bathtub, or sitting on the sofa. They simply do not have the same causal and overall event structure; that is, they do not share generic-level structure.

Proverbs. In Asian figures—proverbs in the form of short poems—the question arises as to what are the limitations on the interpretation of a proverb. Some interpretations are natural; others seem impossible. Why?

Consider the following example from *Asian Figures*, translated by William Merwin (1973):

Blind
blames the ditch

To get some sense of the possible range of interpretations for such a proverb, consider the following application of the proverb:

Suppose a presidential candidate knowingly commits some personal impropriety (though not illegal and not related to political issues) and his candidacy is destroyed by the press's reporting of the impropriety. He blames the press for reporting it, rather than himself for committing it. We think he should have recognized the realities of political press coverage when he chose to commit the impropriety. We express our judgment by saying, "Blind / blames the ditch."

Turner and I (Lakoff & Turner, 1989) observed that the knowledge structure used in comprehending the case of the candidate's impropriety shared certain things with the knowledge structure used in comprehending the literal interpretation of "Blind / blames the ditch." That knowledge structure is the following:

1. There is a person with an incapacity, namely, blindness.
2. He encounters a situation, namely a ditch, in which his incapacity, namely his inability to see the ditch, results in a negative consequence, namely, his falling into the ditch.
3. He blames the situation, rather than his own incapacity.
4. He should have held himself responsible, not the situation.

This specific knowledge schema about the blind man and the ditch is an instance of a general knowledge schema, in which specific information about the blindness and ditch are absent. Let us refer to it as the *generic-level schema* that structures our knowledge of the proverb. That generic-level knowledge schema is:

1. There is a person with an incapacity.
2. He encounters a situation in which his incapacity results in a negative consequence.
3. He blames the situation rather than his own incapacity.
4. He should have held himself responsible, not the situation.

This is a very general schema characterizing an open-ended category of situations. We can think of it as a variable template that can be filled in in many ways. As it happened, Turner and I were studying this at the time of the Gary Hart scandal, when Hart, a presidential candidate, committed certain sexual improprieties during a campaign, had his candidacy dashed, and then blamed the press for his downfall. "Blind / blames the ditch" fits this situation. Here's how:

1. The person is the presidential candidate.
2. His incapacity is his inability to understand the consequences of his personal improprieties.
3. The context he encounters is his knowingly committing an impropriety and the press's reporting it.
4. The consequence is having his candidacy dashed.
5. He blames the press.
6. We judge him as being foolish for blaming the press instead of himself.

If we view the generic-level schema as mediating between the proverb "Blind / blames the ditch" and the story of the candidate's impropriety, we get the following correspondence:

1. The blind person corresponds to the presidential candidate.
2. His blindness corresponds to his inability to understand the consequences of his personal improprieties.
3. Falling into the ditch corresponds to his committing the impropriety and having it reported.
4. Being in the ditch corresponds to being out of the running as a candidate.
5. Blaming the ditch corresponds to blaming the press coverage.
6. Judging the blind man as foolish for blaming the ditch corresponds to judging the candidate as foolish for blaming the press coverage.

This correspondence defines the metaphorical interpretation of the proverb as applied to the candidate's impropriety. Moreover, the class of possible ways of filling in the generic-level schema of the proverb corresponds to the class of possible interpretations of the proverb. Thus, we can explain why "Blind / blames the ditch" does not mean "I took a bath" or "My aunt is sitting on the sofa" or any of the myriad of things the proverb cannot mean.

All of the proverbs that Turner and I (Lakoff & Turner, 1989) studied turned out to involve this sort of generic-level schema. And the kinds of things that turned up in such schemata seemed to be pretty much the same in case after case. They include: (a) causal structure, (b) temporal structure, (c) event shape; that is, instantaneous or repeated, completed or open-ended, single or repeating, having fixed stages or not, preserving the existence of entities or not, and so on, (d) purpose structure, (e) modal structure, and (f) linear scales. This is not an exhaustive list. But what it includes are most of the major elements of generic-level structure that we discovered. What is striking to us about this list is that everything on it is, under the invariance principle, an aspect of image-schematic structure. In short, if the invariance principle is correct, the way to arrive at a generic-level schema for some knowledge structure is to extract its image-schematic structure.

The metaphoric interpretation of such discourse forms as proverbs, fables, allegories, and so on seems to depend on our ability to extract generic-level structure. Turner and I (Lakoff & Turner, 1989) called the relation between a specific knowledge structure and its generic-level structure the *generic is specific* metaphor. It is an extremely common mechanism for comprehending the general in terms of the specific.

If the invariance principle is correct, then the *generic is specific* metaphor is a minimal metaphor that maps what the invariance principle requires it to and nothing more. Should it turn out to be the case that generic-level structure is exactly image-schematic structure, then the invariance principle would have enormous explanatory value. It would obviate the need for a separate characterization of generic-level structure. Instead, it would itself characterize generic-level struc-ture—explaining possible personifications and the possible interpretations for proverbs.

Analogy.   The *generic is specific* metaphor is used for more than just the interpretation of proverbs. Turner (1991) suggested that it is also the general mechanism at work in analogic reasoning, and that the invariance principle characterizes the class of possible analogies. We can see how this works with the Gary Hart example cited earlier. We can convert that example into an analogy with the following sentence: "Gary Hart was like a blind man who fell into a ditch and blamed the ditch." The mechanism for understanding this analogy makes use of: (a) a knowledge schema for the blind man and the ditch, (b) a knowledge schema concerning Gary Hart, and (c) the *generic is specific* metaphor. The *generic is specific* metaphor maps the knowledge schema for the blind man and the ditch into its generic-level schema. The generic-level schema defines an open-ended category of knowledge schemas. The Gary Hart schema is a member of that category, because it fits the generic-level schema given the correspond-ences stated previously.

It appears at present that such analogies use this metaphorical mechanism. But it is common for analogies to use other metaphorical mechanisms as well, for instance, the great chain metaphor and the full range of conventional mappings in the conceptual system. Sentences like "John is a wolf" or "Harry is a pig" use the great chain metaphor (see Lakoff & Turner, 1989).

A good example of how the rest of the metaphor system interacts with *generic is specific* is the well-known example of Glucksberg and Keysar (Ortony, 1993).

"My job is a jail." First, the knowledge schema for a jail includes the knowledge that a jail imposes extreme physical constraints on a prisoner's movements. The *generic is specific* metaphor preserves the image-schematic structure of the knowledge schema, factoring out the specific details of the prisoner and the jail: X imposes extreme physical constraints on Y's movements. But now two additional conventional metaphors apply to this generic-level schema: the event structure metaphor, with the submetaphor *actions are self-propelled movements*, and *psychological force is physical force*. These metaphors map "X imposes extreme physical constraints on Y's movements" into "X imposes extreme psychological constraints on Y's actions." The statement "My job is a jail" imposes an interpretation in which X = my job and Y = me, and hence yields the knowledge that "My job imposes extreme psychological constraints on my actions." Thus, the mechanism for understanding "My job is a jail" uses very common, independently existing metaphors: *generic is specific*, *psychological force is physical force*, and the event structure metaphor.

The Glucksberg–Keysar Claim. I mention this example because of the claim by Glucksberg and Keysar (Ortony, 1993) that metaphor is simply a matter of categorization. However, in personal correspondence Glucksberg has written, "We assume that people can judge and can also infer that certain basic level entities, such as 'jails' typify or are emblematic of a metaphoric attributive category such as 'situations that are confining, unpleasant, etc.' " Glucksberg and Keysar give no theory of how it is possible to have such a "metaphoric attributive category"—that is, how it is possible for one kind of thing (a general situation) to be metaphorically categorized in terms of a fundamentally spatial notion like 'confining.' Because Glucksberg is not in the business of describing the nature of conceptual systems, he does not see it as his job to give such an account. I have argued in this chapter that the general principle governing such cases is the event structure metaphor. If such a metaphor exists in our conceptual system, then Glucksberg's "jail" example is accounted for automatically and his categorization theory is not needed. Indeed, the category he needs—"situations that are confining, unpleasant, etc."—is a "metaphoric attributive category." That is, to get the appropriate categories in his categorization theory of metaphor he needs an account of metaphor. But given such an account of metaphor, his metaphor-as-categorization theory becomes unnecessary.

Even worse for the Glucksberg–Keysar theory (Ortony, 1993), it cannot account for either everyday conceptual metaphor of the sort we have been discussing or for really rich poetic metaphor, such as one finds in the works of, say, Dylan Thomas, or for image metaphor of the sort common in the examples cited earlier from the Sanskrit, Navaho, and surrealist traditions. Because it does not even attempt to deal with most of the data covered by the contemporary theory of metaphor, it cannot account for "how metaphor works."

More on Novel Metaphor

As common as novel metaphor is, its occurrence is rare by comparison with conventional metaphor, which occurs in most of the sentences we utter. Our everyday metaphor system, which we use to understand concepts as commonplace as *time, state, change, causation, purpose,* and so on, is constantly active, and is used maximally in interpreting novel metaphorical uses of language. The problem with all the older research on novel metaphor is that it completely missed the major contribution played by the conventional system.

As Turner and I discussed in detail (Lakoff & Turner, 1989), there are three basic mechanisms for interpreting linguistic expressions as novel metaphors: extensions of conventional metaphors, generic-level metaphors, image metaphors. Most interesting poetic metaphor uses all of these superimposed on one another. Let us begin with examples of extensions of conventional metaphors.

Dante begins the *Divine Comedy*:

In the middle of life's road
I found myself in a dark wood.

"Life's road" evokes the domain of life and the domain of travel, and hence the conventional *life is a journey* metaphor that links them. "I found myself in a dark wood" evokes the knowledge that if it is dark you cannot see which way to go. This evokes the domain of seeing, and thus the conventional metaphor that *knowing is seeing,* as in expressions like "I see what you're getting at," "His claims aren't clear," "The passage is opaque," and so forth. This entails that the speaker does not know which way to go. Because the *life is a journey* metaphor specifies destinations are life goals, it is entailed that the speaker does not know what life goals to pursue; that is, he is without direction in his life. All of this uses nothing but the system of conventional metaphor, ordinary knowledge structure evoked by the conventional meaning of the sentence, and metaphorical inferences based on that knowledge structure.

Another equally simple case of the use of the conventional system is Robert Frost's:

Two roads diverged in a wood, and I—
I took the one less traveled by,
And that has made all the difference.

Because Frost's language often does not overtly signal that the poem is to be taken metaphorically, incompetent English teachers occasionally teach Frost as if he were a nature poet, simply describing scenes. (I have actually had students whose high school teachers taught them that!) Thus, this passage could be read nonmetaphorically as being just about a trip on which one encounters a crossroads. There is nothing in the sentences themselves that forces one to a metaphorical interpretation. But, because it is about travel and encountering crossroads, it evokes a knowledge of journeys. This activates the system of conventional metaphor we have just discussed, in which long-term, purposeful activities are understood as journeys, and further, how life and careers can also be understood as one-person journeys (love relationships, involving two travelers, are ruled out here). The poem is typically taken as being about life and a choice of life goals, though it might also be interpreted as being about careers and career paths, or about some long-term, purposeful activity. All that is needed to get the requisite range of interpretations is the structure of conventional metaphors discussed earlier, and the knowledge structure evoked by the poem. The conventional mapping will apply to the knowledge structure yielding the appropriate inferences. No special mechanisms are needed.

Searle's Theory

At this point I leave off discussion of other more complex poetic examples, because they require lengthy discussion and because such discussion can be found in Lakoff and Turner (1989), Turner (1987), and Turner (1991). Instead, I confine myself to discussing three examples from John Searle's theory of metaphor (Ortony, 1993). Consider first Disraeli's remark, "I have climbed to the top of the greasy pole."

Certainly, this could be taken nonmetaphorically, but its most likely metaphorical interpretation is via the *career is a journey* metaphor. This metaphor is evoked jointly by source domain knowledge about pole climbing (which is effortful, self-propelled, destination-oriented motion upward) and knowledge that the metaphor involves effortful, self-propelled, destination-oriented motion upward. Part of the knowledge evoked is that the speaker is as high as he can get on that particular pole, that the pole was difficult to climb, that the climb probably involved backwards motion, that it is difficult for someone to stay at the top of a greasy pole, and that he will most likely slide down again. The *career is a journey* metaphor maps this knowledge onto corresponding knowledge about the speaker's career: The speaker has as much status as he or she can get in that particular career, that it was difficult to get to that point in the career, that it probably involved some temporary loss of status along the way, that it is difficult to maintain this position, and that he or she will probably lose status before long. All this follows with nothing more than the conventional career-as-journey mapping, which we all share as part of our metaphorical systems, plus knowledge about climbing greasy poles.

The second example of Searle's (Ortony, 1993) I consider is "Sally is a block of ice." Here there is a conventional metaphor that *affection is warmth*, as in ordinary sentences like "She's a warm person," "He was cool to me," and so on. "A block of ice" evokes the domain of temperature, and, because it is predicated of a person, it also evokes knowledge of what a person can be. Jointly, both kinds of knowledge activate *affection is warmth*. Because "a block of ice" is something that is very cold and not able to become warm quickly or easily, this knowledge is mapped onto Sally's being very unaffectionate and not being able to become affectionate quickly or easily. Again, common knowledge and a conventional metaphor that we all have is all that is needed.

Finally, Searle (Ortony, 1993) discussed "The hours crept by as we waited for the plane." Here we have a verb of motion predicated of a time expression; the former activates the knowledge about motion through space and the latter activates the time domain. Jointly, they activate the time-as-moving-object mapping. Again the meaning of the sentence follows only from everyday knowledge and the everyday system of metaphorical mappings.

Searle (Ortony, 1993) accounted for such cases by his Principle 4, which says that "we just do perceive a connection" that is the basis of the interpretation. This is vague and does not say what the perceived connection is or why we "just do" perceive it. When we spell out the details of all such "perceived connections," they turn out to be the system of conceptual metaphors that I have been describing. But given that system, Searle's theory and his principles become unnecessary.

In addition, Searle's (Ortony, 1993) account of literal meaning makes most of the usual false assumptions that accompany that term. Searle assumed that all everyday, conventional language is literal and not metaphorical. He would thus rule out every example of conventional metaphor that is described not only in this article, but in the whole literature of the field.

The study of the metaphorical subsystem of our conceptual system is a central part of synchronic linguistics. The reason is that much of our semantic system, that is, our system of concepts, is metaphorical, as we saw earlier.

THE EXPERIENTIAL BASIS OF METAPHOR

The conceptual system underlying a language contains thousands of conceptual metaphors—conventional mappings from one domain to another, such as the event structure metaphor. The novel metaphors of a language are, except for image metaphors, extensions of this large conventional system.

Perhaps the deepest question that any theory of metaphor must answer is this: Why do we have the conventional metaphors that we have? Or alternatively: Is there any reason why conceptual systems contain one set of metaphorical mappings rather than another? There do appear to be answers to these questions for many of the mappings found so far, though they are in the realm of plausible accounts, rather than in the realm of scientific results.

Take a simple case: the *more is up* metaphor, as seen in expressions like: Prices *rose*. His income *went down*. Unemployment is *up*. Exports are *down*. The number of homeless people is *very high*.

There are other languages in which *more is up* and *less is down*, but none in which the reverse is true, where *more is down* and *less is up*. Why not? The answer given in the contemporary theory is that the *more is up* metaphor is *grounded in experience*—in the common experiences of pouring more fluid into a container and seeing the level go up, or adding more things to a pile and seeing the pile get higher. These are thoroughly pervasive experiences; we experience them every day of our lives. They are experiences with a structure—a correspondence between the conceptual domain of quantity and the conceptual domain of verticality: *more* corresponds in such experiences to *up* and *less* corresponds to *down*. These correspondences in real experience form the basis for the correspondence in the metaphorical cases, which go beyond the cases in real experience: In "Prices rose" there is no correspondence in real experience between quantity and verticality, but understanding quantity in terms of verticality makes sense because of the existence of a regular correspondence in so many other cases.

Consider another case: What is the basis of the widespread *knowing is seeing* metaphor, as in expressions like: I see what your saying. His answer was clear. This paragraph is murky. He was so blinded by ambition that he never noticed his limitations. The experiential basis, in this case, is the fact that most of what we know comes through vision, and that in the overwhelming majority of cases, if we see something, then we know it is true.

Consider still another case: Why, in the event structure metaphor, is achieving a purpose understood as reaching a destination (in the location subsystem) and as acquiring a desired object (in the object subsystem)? The answer again seems to be correspondences in everyday experience. To achieve most of our everyday purposes, we either have to move to some destination or acquire some object. If you want a drink of water, you have to go to the water fountain. If you want to be in the sunshine, you have to move to where the sunshine is. And if you want to write down a note, you have to get a pen or pencil. The correspondences between achieving purposes and either reaching destinations or acquiring objects is so utterly common in our everyday existence that the resulting metaphor is completely natural.

But what about the experiential basis of *a purposeful life is a journey*? Recall that that mapping is in an inheritance hierarchy, where life goals are special cases of purposes, which are destinations in the event structure metaphor. Thus, *a purposeful life is a journey* inherits the experiential basis of *purposes are destinations*. Thus, inheritance hierarchies provide *indirect experiential bases*, in that a metaphorical mapping lower in a hierarchy can inherit its experiential basis indirectly from a mapping higher in the hierarchy.

Experiential bases motivate metaphors, they do not predict them. Thus, not every language has a *more is up* metaphor, though all human beings experience a correspondence between *more* and *up* in their experience. What this experiential basis does predict is that no language will have the opposite metaphor *less is up.* It also predicts that a speaker of language that does not have that metaphor will be able to learn that metaphor much more easily than the opposite metaphor.

Realizations of Metaphor

Consider objects like thermometers and stock market graphs, where increases in temperature and prices are represented as being *up* and decreases as being *down.* These are real man-made objects created to accord with the *more is up* metaphor. They are objects in which there is a correlation between *more* and *up.* Such objects are a lot easier to read and understand than if they contradicted the metaphor; say, if increases were represented as down and decreases as up.

Such objects are ways in which metaphors impose a structure on real life, through the creation of new correspondences in experience. And of course, once such real objects are created in one generation, those objects serve as an experiential basis for that metaphor in the next generation.

There are a great many ways in which conventional metaphors can be made real. Metaphors can be realized in obvious imaginative products such as cartoons, literary works, dreams, visions, and myths. But metaphors can be made real in less obvious ways as well, in physical symptoms, social institutions, social practices, laws, and even foreign policy and forms of discourse and of history. Let us consider some examples:

1. Cartoons: Conventional metaphors are made real in cartoons. A common example is the realization of the *anger is a hot fluid in a container* metaphor, in which one can be "boiling mad" or "letting off steam." In cartoons, anger is commonly depicted by having steam coming out of the character's ears. Similarly, social clumsiness is indicated by having a cartoon character "fall on his face."

2. Literary works: It is common for the plot of a novel to be a realization of the *purposeful life is a journey* metaphor, where the course of a life takes the form of an actual journey. *Pilgrim's Progress* is a classical example.

3. Rituals: Consider the cultural ritual in which a newborn baby is carried upstairs to ensure his or her success. The metaphor realized in this ritual is *status is up*, exemplified by sentences such as: He clawed his way *to the top.* He *climbed the ladder* of success. You'll *rise* in the world.

4. Dream Interpretation: Conceptual metaphors constitute the vocabulary of dream interpretation. It is the collection of our everyday conceptual metaphors that make dream interpretations possible. Consider one of the most celebrated of all dream interpretations: Joseph's interpretation of Pharaoh's dream from Genesis. In Pharaoh's dream, he is standing on the river bank, when seven fat cows come out of the river, followed by seven lean cows that eat the seven fat ones and still remain lean. Then Pharoah dreams again. This time he sees seven "full and good" ears of corn growing, and then seven withered ears growing after them. The withered ears devour the good ears. Joseph interprets the two

dreams as a single dream. The seven fat cows and full ears are good years and the seven lean cows and withered ears are famine years that follow the good years. The famine years "devour" what the good years produce. This interpretation makes sense to us because of a collection of conceptual metaphors in our conceptual system—metaphors that have been with us since biblical times. The first metaphor used is: *times are moving entities*. A river is a common metaphor for the flow of time; the cows are individual entities (years) emerging from the flow of time and moving past the observer; the ears of corn are also entities that come into the scene. The second metaphor used is *achieving a purpose is eating*, where being fat indicates success and being lean indicates failure. This metaphor is combined with the most common of metonymies: *a part stands for the whole*. Because cows and corn were typical of meat and grain eaten, each single cow stands for all the cows raised in a year and each ear of corn for all the corn grown in a year. The final metaphor used is: *resources are food*, where using up resources is eating food. The devouring of the good years by the famine years is interpreted as indicating that all the surplus resources of the good years will be used up by the famine years. The interpretation of the whole dream is thus a composition of three conventional metaphors and one metonymy. The metaphoric and metonymic sources are combined to form the reality of the dream.

5. Myths: In the event structure metaphor, there is a submapping *external events are large, moving objects* that can exert a force upon you and thereby effect whether you achieve your goals. In English the special cases of such objects are "things," fluids, and horses. Pamela Morgan (personal communication) observed that in Greek mythology, Poseidon is the god of the sea, earthquakes, horses, and bulls. The list might seem arbitrary, but Morgan observed that these are all large moving objects that can exert a force on you. Morgan surmised that this is not an obvious list. The sea, earthquakes, horses, and bulls are all large moving objects that can exert a significant force. Poseidon, she surmised, should really be seen as the god of external events.

6. Physical Symptoms: The unconscious mind makes use of our unconscious system of conventional metaphor, sometimes to express psychological states in terms of physical symptoms. For example, in the event structure metaphor, there is a submapping *difficulties are impediments to motion* which has, as a special case, *difficulties are burdens*. It is fairly common for someone encountering difficulties to walk with his shoulders stooped, as if "carrying a heavy weight" that is "burdening" him.

7. Social Institutions: We have a *time is money* metaphor, shown by expressions like: He's *wasting* time. I have to *budget* my time. This will *save* you time. I've *invested* a lot of time in that. He doesn't *use* his time *profitably*. This metaphor came into English about the time of the Industrial Revolution, when people started to be paid for work by the amount of time they worked. Thus, the factory led to the institutional pairing of periods of time with amounts

of money, which formed the experiential basis of this metaphor. Since then, the metaphor has been realized in many other ways. The budgeting of time has spread throughout American culture.

8. Social Practices: There is conceptual metaphor that *seeing is touching*, where the eyes are limbs and vision is achieved when the object seen is "touched." Examples are: My eyes *picked out* every detail of the pattern. He *ran* his eyes over the walls. He couldn't *take* his eyes *off* of her. Their eyes *met*. His eyes are *glued* to the TV. The metaphor is made real in the social practice of avoiding eye "contact" on the street, and in the social prohibition against "undressing someone with your eyes."

9. Laws: Law is major area where metaphor is made real. For example, *corporations are persons* is a tenet of American law, which not only enables corporations to be "harmed" and assigned "responsibility" so that they can be sued when liable, but also gives corporations certain First Amendment rights.

10. Foreign Policy: *A state is a person* is one of the major metaphors underlying foreign policy concepts. Thus, there are "friendly" states, "hostile" states, and so on. Health for a state is economic health and strength is military strength. Thus a threat to economic "health" can be seen as a death threat, as when Iraq was seen to have a "stranglehold" on the "economic lifeline" of the United States. Strong states are seen as male, and weak states as female, so that an attack by a strong state on a weak state can be seen as a "rape," as in the rape of Kuwait by Iraq. A "just war" is conceptualized as a fairy tale with villain, victim, and hero, where the villain attacks the victim and the hero rescues the victim. Thus, the United States in the Gulf War was portrayed as having "rescued" Kuwait. As President Bush said in his address to Congress, "The issues couldn't have been clearer: Iraq was the villain and Kuwait, the victim."

11. Forms of discourse: Common metaphors are often made real in discourse forms. Consider three common academic discourse forms: the guided tour, the heroic battle, and the heroic quest. The guided tour is based on the metaphor that *thought is motion*, where ideas are locations and one reasons "step-by-step," "reaches conclusions," or you fail to reach a conclusion if you are engaged in "circular reasoning." Communication in this metaphor is giving someone a guided tour of some rational argument or of some "intellectual terrain." The present chapter is an example of such a guided tour, where I, the author, am the tour guide who is assumed to be thoroughly familiar with the terrain, and where the terrain surveyed is taken as objectively real. The discourse form of the heroic battle is based on the metaphor that *argument is war*. The author's theory is the hero, the opposing theory is the villain, and words are weapons. The battle is in the form of an argument defending the hero's position and demolishing the villain's position. The heroic quest discourse form is based on the metaphor that knowledge is a valuable but elusive object that can be "discovered" if one perseveres. The scientist is the hero on a quest for knowledge, and the discourse

form is an account of his difficult journey of discovery. What is "discovered" is, of course, a real entity.

What makes all of these cases realizations of metaphors is that in each case there is something real structured by conventional metaphor, and that is made comprehensible, or even natural, by those everyday metaphors. What is real differs in each case: an object like a thermometer or graph, an experience like a dream, an action like a ritual, a form of discourse, and so forth. What these examples reveal is that a lot of what is real in a society or in the experience of an individual is structured and made sense of via conventional metaphor.

Experiential bases and realizations of metaphors are two sides of the same coin: They are both correlations in real experience that have the same structure as the correlations in metaphors. The difference is that experiential bases precede, ground, and make sense of conventional metaphorical mappings, whereas realizations follow, and are made sense of, via the conventional metaphors. And as we noted earlier, one generation's realizations of a metaphor can become part of the next generation's experiential basis for that metaphor.

SUMMARY OF RESULTS

As we have seen, the contemporary theory of metaphor is revolutionary in many respects. To give you some idea how revolutionary, here is a list of the basic results that differ from most previous accounts.

The Nature of Metaphor

1. Metaphor is the main mechanism through which we comprehend abstract concepts and perform abstract reasoning.
2. Much subject matter, from the most mundane to the most abstruse scientific theories, can only be comprehended via metaphor.
3. Metaphor is fundamentally conceptual, not linguistic, in nature.
4. Metaphorical language is a surface manifestation of conceptual metaphor.
5. Though much of our conceptual system is metaphorical, a significant part of it is nonmetaphorical. Metaphorical understanding is grounded in nonmetaphorical understanding.
6. Metaphor allows us to understand a relatively abstract or inherently unstructured subject matter in terms of a more concrete, or at least a more highly structured subject matter.

The Structure of Metaphor

1. Metaphors are mappings across conceptual domains.
2. Such mappings are asymmetric and partial.

3. Each mapping is a fixed set of ontological correspondences between entities in a source domain and entities in a target domain.

4. When those fixed correspondences are activated, mappings can project source domain inference patterns onto target domain inference patterns.

5. Metaphorical mappings obey the invariance principle: The image-schema structure of the source domain is projected onto the target domain in a way that is consistent with inherent target domain structure.

6. Mappings are not arbitrary, but grounded in the body and in everyday experience and knowledge.

7. A conceptual system contains thousands of conventional metaphorical mappings, which form a highly structured subsystem of the conceptual system.

8. There are two types of mappings: conceptual mappings and image mappings; both obey the invariance principle.

Some Aspects of Metaphor

1. The system of conventional conceptual metaphor is mostly unconscious, automatic, and is used with no noticeable effort, just like our linguistic system and the rest of our conceptual system.

2. Our system of conventional metaphor is "alive" in the same sense that our system of grammatical and phonological rules is alive; namely, it is constantly in use, automatically and below the level of consciousness.

3. Our metaphor system is central to our understanding of experience and to the way we act on that understanding.

4. Conventional mappings are static correspondences, and are not, in themselves, algorithmic in nature. However, this by no means rules out the possibility that such static correspondences might be used in language processing that involves sequential steps.

5. Metaphor is mostly based on correspondences in our experiences, rather than on similarity.

6. The metaphor system plays a major role in both the grammar and lexicon of a language.

7. Metaphorical mappings vary in universality; some seem to be universal, others are widespread, and some seem to be culture-specific.

8. Poetic metaphor is, for the most part, an extension of our everyday, conventional system of metaphorical thought.

These are the conclusions that best fit the empirical studies of metaphor conducted over the past decade or so. Though much of it is inconsistent with traditional views, it is by no means all new, and some ideas—for example, that abstract concepts are comprehended in terms of concrete concepts—have a long history.

CONCLUDING REMARKS

The evidence supporting the contemporary theory of metaphor is voluminous and grows larger each year as more research in the field is done. The evidence, as we saw previously, comes from five domains: (a) generalizations over polysemy, (b) generalization over inference patterns, (c) generalizations over extensions to poetic cases, (d) generalizations over semantic change, and (e) psycholinguistic experiments. I have discussed only a handful of examples of the first three of these, hopefully enough to make the reader curious about the field.

But evidence is convincing only if it can count as evidence. When does evidence fail to be evidence? Unfortunately, all too often. It is commonly the case that certain fields of inquiry are defined by assumptions that rule out the possibility of counterevidence. When a defining assumption of a field comes up against evidence, the evidence usually loses: The practitioners of the field must ignore the evidence if they want to keep the assumptions that define the field they are committed to.

Part of what makes the contemporary theory of metaphor so interesting is that the evidence for it contradicts the defining assumptions of so many academic disciplines. In my opinion, this should make one doubt the defining assumptions of all those disciplines. The reason is this: The defining assumptions of the contemporary theory of metaphor are minimal. There are only two:

1. The generalization commitment: To seek generalizations in all areas of language, including polysemy, patterns of inference, novel metaphor, and semantic change.
2. The cognitive commitment: To take experimental evidence seriously.

But these are nothing more than commitments to the scientific study of language and the mind. No initial commitment is made as to the form of an answer to the question of what is metaphor.

However, the defining assumptions of other fields do often entail a commitment about the form of an answer to that question. It is useful, in an interdisciplinary volume of this sort, to spell out exactly what those defining assumptions are, because they will often explain why different authors reach such different conclusions about the nature of metaphor.

Literal Meaning Commitments

I started this chapter with a list of the false assumptions about literal meaning that are commonly made. These assumptions are, of course, false only relative to the kinds of evidence that supports the contemporary theory of metaphor. If one ignores all such evidence, then the assumptions can be maintained without contradiction.

Assumptions about literality are the locus of many of the contradictions between the contemporary theory of metaphor and various academic disciplines. Let us review those assumptions. In the discussion of literal meaning given earlier, I observed that it is taken as definitional that: What is literal is not metaphorical. The false assumptions and conclusions that usually accompany the word *literal* are:

1. All everyday conventional language is literal, and none is metaphorical.
2. All subject matter can be comprehended literally, without metaphor.
3. Only literal language can be contingently true or false.
4. All definitions given in the lexicon of a language are literal, not metaphorical.
5. The concepts used in the grammar of a language are all literal; none is metaphorical.

We begin with the philosophy of language. The generalization commitment and the cognitive commitment are not definitional to the philosophy of language. Indeed, most philosophers of language would feel no need to abide by them, for a very good reason. The philosophy of language is typically not seen as an empirical discipline, constrained by empirical results, such as those that arise by the application of the generalization and cognitive commitments. Instead, the philosophy of language is usually seen as an a priori discipline, one that can be pursued using the tools of philosophical analysis alone, rather than the tools of empirical research. Therefore, all the evidence that has been brought forth for the contemporary theory of metaphor simply will not matter for most philosophers of language.

In addition, the philosophy of language comes with its own set of defining assumptions, which entail many of the false assumptions usually associated with the word *literal*. Most practitioners of the philosophy of language usually make one or more of the following assumptions:

1. They use the correspondence theory of truth.
2. Meaning is defined in terms of reference and truth.
3. Natural language semantics is to be characterized by the mechanisms of mathematical logic, including model theory.

These assumptions entail the traditional false assumptions associated with the word *literal*. Thus the very field of philosophy of language comes with defining assumptions that contradict the main conclusions of the contemporary theory of metaphor.

Consequently, we can see why most philosophers of language have the range of views on metaphor that they have: They accept the traditional literal–figurative distinction. They may say that there is no metaphorical meaning and that most metaphorical utterances are either trivially true or trivially false. Or, like Grice (1989) and Searle (Ortony, 1993), they will assume that metaphor is in the realm of pragmatics; that is, that a metaphorical meaning is no more than the literal meaning of some other sentence that can be arrived at by some pragmatic principle. This is required, because the only real meaning for them is literal meaning, and pragmatic principles are those principles that allow one to say one thing (with a literal meaning) and mean something else (with a different, but nonetheless literal, meaning).

Much of generative linguistics accepts one or more of these assumptions from the philosophy of language. The field of formal semantics accepts them all, and thus formal semantics, by its defining assumptions, is at odds with the contemporary theory of metaphor. Formal semantics simply does not see it as its job to account for the generalizations discussed in this chapter. From the perspective of formal semantics, the phenomena that the contemporary theory of metaphor is concerned with are either nonexistent or uninteresting, because they lie outside the purview of the discipline. Anyone who accepts mathematical logic as the correct approach to natural language semantics must see metaphor as being outside of semantics proper and, therefore, must also reject the entire enterprise of the contemporary theory of metaphor.

Chomsky's theory of government and binding also accepts crucial assumptions from the philosophy of language that are inconsistent with the contemporary theory of metaphor. Government and binding, following my early theory of generative semantics, assumes that semantics is to be represented in terms of logical form. Government and binding, like generative semantics, thus rules out the very possibility that metaphor might be part of natural language semantics as it enters into grammar. Because of this defining assumption, I would not expect Chomskyan theorists to become concerned with the phenomena covered by the contemporary theory of metaphor, because it is inconsistent with their theoretical assumptions.

Interestingly, much of continental philosophy and deconstructionism is also characterized by defining assumptions that are at odds with the contemporary theory of metaphor. Nietzsche (see, Johnson, 1981) held that all language is metaphorical, which is at odds with those results that indicate that a significant amount of everyday language is not metaphorical. Much of continental philosophy, observing that conceptual systems change through time, assumes that conceptual systems are purely historically contingent—that there are no conceptual universals. Though conceptual systems do change through time, there do, however, appear to be universal, or at least very widespread, conceptual metaphors. The event structure metaphor is my present candidate for a metaphorical universal.

Continental philosophy also comes with a distinction between the study of the physical world, which can be scientific, and the study of human beings, which it says cannot be scientific. This is very much at odds with the conceptual theory of metaphor, which is very much a scientific enterprise.

Finally, the contemporary theory of metaphor is at odds with certain traditions in symbolic artificial intelligence and information-processing psychology. Those fields assume that thought is a matter of algorithmic symbol manipulation, of the sort done by a traditional computer program. This defining assumption puts it at odds with the contemporary theory of metaphor in two respects: First, the contemporary theory has an image-schematic basis: The invariance hypothesis applies both to image metaphors and characterizes constraints on novel metaphor. Because symbol-manipulation systems cannot handle image schemata, they cannot deal with image metaphors or imagable idioms. Second, those traditions must characterize metaphorical mapping as an algorithmic process, which typically takes literal meanings as input and gives a metaphorical reading as output. This is at odds with cases where there are multiple, overlapping metaphors in a single sentence, and that require the simultaneous activation of a number of metaphorical mappings.

I mention all this because it is important for researchers in conceptual development to be aware of the often hidden theoretical assumptions that lie behind disciplines like generative linguistics and formal logic, as well as both Anglo-American and continental philosophical approaches to language. Those theoretical assumptions can blind one to the most interesting and extensive contemporary research on adult conceptual systems.

Research Questions

The examples given in this chapter are just a tiny sample of the vast and highly structured system of conceptual metaphor that lies at the heart of our conceptual systems. The existence of metaphor systems raises a large number of questions for the study of child development:

1. How does this system develop?
2. Could any conceptual metaphors be learned before children acquire the language to express them? If so, how could one tell?
3. Which metaphors, if any, are universal?
4. Are metaphors that are universal (or widespread across cultures) learned earlier than metaphors that are culture-specific?
5. Does the inheritance hierarchy in the metaphor system define a set of stages such that metaphors higher in the hierarchy are always learned before metaphors lower in the hierarchy?

6. Are metaphorical duals learned at the same time?

7. Which conceptual metaphors are learned relatively late, say, between 8 and 12 years of age?

8. Which conceptual metaphors are learned automatically, effortlessly, and unconsciously, and which have to be taught?

9. Are some metaphors harder to learn than others, and if so, why?

10. Do children acquire conceptual metaphors that are not in the adult system?

ACKNOWLEDGMENTS

This research was supported in part by grants from the Sloan Foundation and the National Science Foundation (IRI-8703202) to the University of California at Berkeley.

The following colleagues and students helped with this article in a variety of ways, from useful comments to allowing me to cite their research: Ken Baldwin, Claudia Brugman, Jane Espenson, Sharon Fischler, Ray Gibbs, Adele Goldberg, Mark Johnson, Karin Myhre, Alan Schwartz, Eve Sweetser, and Mark Turner.

REFERENCES

Gibbs, R. W., Jr. (1990). Psycholinguistics studies on the conceptual basis of idiomaticity. *Cognitive Linguistics, 1*(4), 417–462.

Gibbs, R. W., Jr. (1994). *The poetics of mind.* Cambridge: Cambridge University Press.

Grice, P. (1989). *Studies in the way of words.* Cambridge, MA: Harvard University Press.

Johnson, M. (1981). *Philosophical perspectives on metaphor.* Minneapolis: University of Minnesota Press.

Johnson, M. (1987). *The body in the mind: The bodily basis of meaning, reason and imagination.* Chicago: University of Chicago Press.

Kövecses, Z. (1990). *Emotion concepts.* New York: Springer-Verlag.

Lakoff, G. (1987). *Women, fire, and dangerous things: What categories reveal about the mind.* Chicago: University of Chicago Press.

Lakoff, G., & Johnson, M. (1980). *Metaphors we live by.* Chicago: University of Chicago Press.

Lakoff, G., & Turner, M. (1989). *More than cool reason: A field guide to poetic metaphor.* Chicago: University of Chicago Press.

Merwin, W. S. (1973). *Asian figures.* New York: Atheneum.

Merwin, W. S., & Masson, J. M. (Trans.). (1981). *The peacock's egg.* San Francisco: North Point Press.

Ortony, A. (1993). *Metaphor and thought* (2nd ed.). Cambridge, England: Cambridge University Press.

Reddy, M. (1979). The conduit metaphor. In A. Ortony (Ed.), *Metaphor and thought* (1st, ed., pp. 284–324). Cambridge, England: Cambridge University Press.

Sweetser, E. (1990). *From etymology to pragmatics: The mind-as-body metaphor in semantic structure and semantic change.* Cambridge, England: Cambridge University Press.

Turner, M. (1987). *Death is the mother of beauty: Mind, metaphor, criticism.* Chicago: University of Chicago Press.

Turner, M. (1991). *Reading minds: The study of English in the age of cognitive science.* Princeton, NJ: Princeton University Press.

4

Design for a Theory of Meaning

Mark Turner
University of Maryland

Πάντων μέτρον ἄνθρωπος
—Πρωταγορας

BACK TO PROTAGORAS

In the fifth century B.C., when the Attic philosopher Protagoras proposed that man is the measure of all things, he offered a design for a theory of meaning. The distinctive character of any theory of meaning congruent with this design is its conception of meaning not as a static property external to human beings but rather as an aspect of dynamic human thought grounded in human nature.

Because Protagoras's epistemology is known to us principally from dubious and hostile summaries in Plato's *Theaetetus,* we have no reliable idea of the specific character of his own specific theory of meaning. It is clear that he lost the epistemological contest of his age, and of ours. Socrates, Plato, and Aristotle rejected his fundamental stand, as did most later theorists of meaning. Our present century stands out as a particularly abysmal time for the premise of Protagoras, in which prominent theorists have attempted to explain the nature of meaning as quite independent of the human person. Reference theories of meaning tell us, for example, that the light is on and it does not matter whether anybody is home: Meaning is conceived of in such theories as essentially anchored in states of affairs in an objective reality, with the consequence that the meaning of an utterance must be the reality to which it refers. This leaves the human person out of the loop altogether: A semantic express train shoots straight from the linguistic symbols to an objective reality without passing through the human brain, let alone stopping in the human brain, let alone taking its entire journey there.

Other contemporary theories, such as formalist theories of meaning, do make a stop in the human brain, but it is only a courtesy stop, which consists of acknowledging that the human brain is the site in which meaning is attributed but viewing this fact as incidental, a matter of mere implementational detail. For example, artificial intelligence theories commonly regard mind as a formal engine that performs formal computation over meaningless symbols that remain meaningless as they undergo manipulation but that receive a separate interpretation from some register of fixed interpretations. The combined competence of the formal engine and the fixed interpretations is called an interpreted formal system, otherwise known as a *semantic* engine. The formal, syntactic engine does all the work while the rules of interpretation go along for the syntactic ride, and the result is meaning. Meaning is thus a precipitate of a lot of formal computation, and the real job of a theory of meaning is to discover the nature of this formal computation. This view has its roots in the work of Alan Turing. It is familiar from the work of Alan Newell and Herbert Simon, who saw intelligence as an aspect of a physical symbol system, which is to say, as the result of manipulating symbols by means of formal rules. The tradition behind Newell and Simon stretches back through Alfred North Whitehead, Bertrand Russell, Gottlob Frege, the Wittgenstein of the *Tractatus,* Hobbes, Leibniz, and Descartes. Although numerous objections have been laid against the premises of this approach, including that formal syntactic work plus fixed interpretation is insufficient to generate semantics, that the world is not like a computer tape, and that the brain is not a Turing machine, nonetheless over the last several decades many thinkers have concluded that the brain simply must be a type of interpreted formal system, or at least that there is no plausible alternative hypothesis. (For a summary, see Edelman, 1989.)

In practice, these traditions work from the largely unargued assumption that it is merely incidental that the interpreted formal system happens to be instantiated in a human brain or a human body. The human being is not the measure of all things; the interpreted formal system is. No accommodation is required in the theory or in the fact for the humanness of the brain and the humanness of the body in which the system happens to have been implemented. The human being is the platform on which a portable utility is installed. Questions about human nature are peripheral. Protagoras would not have approved.

Protagoras seems today to have come in for a revival, by which I mean that certain cognitive investigations of the nature of meaning appear to be taking as fundamental rather than incidental the fact that meaning is attributed by a human brain in a human body. (For surveys of these cognitive investigations, see, e.g., Edelman, 1987, 1989, 1992; Johnson, 1987; Lakoff, 1987; Lakoff & Turner,

1989; Turner, 1987, 1991; see also chapter 3 of this volume). A staggering mistake was made two and a half millennia ago in trivializing the premise of Protagoras, and we are only beginning to get over it. Of course, we will need to perform some crucial updating of its technical details. Whatever concept of the human person Protagoras had in mind, a modern concept would view the human person as patterns of dynamic activity in a human brain that has evolved to serve the human body of which it is a part. Culture, society, language, and the rest of human life are patterns in brains. Meaning is patterns in human brains.

If we embrace an updated version of the premise of Protagoras to view meaning as an aspect of neural activity in a brain that is structured in accord with the body it serves, the cost is high: We must cross off our list of conceptual instruments for building theories of meaning most of what has historically proved indispensable. The first thing to cross off our list is the partitioning of meaning into objective and subjective.

OBJECTIVE MEANING VERSUS SUBJECTIVE MEANING

Objective meaning is meaning that exists independently of any human agency in conceiving that meaning. On the premise of Protagoras, we must regard objective meaning as an oxymoron, because no meaning exists independently of its attribution by the human brain.

The premise of Protagoras does not require us to discard everything associated with the concept of objective meaning. It allows us, for example, to keep the sense that certain capacities for attributing meaning are virtually indispensable and not open to choice. Some parts of our human system for attributing meaning are directly susceptible to pressures of fitness. For example, it seems to be a very fit part of brain activity to: (a) attribute a vertical up–down gradient to the environment; (b) distinguish between the interior and the exterior of one's body, with the skin as boundary; (c) partition the world into objects and actions; (d) understand certain objects as agents; and (e) attribute purposes to agents.

Inabilities to attribute meaning in these ways would count as fundamental deficits in the organism: Someone lacking them would die. It is hard even to imagine that someone lacking them could count as a human being. Evolution is likely to be extremely conservative in regard to such features. On the other hand, pressures of fitness seem virtually indifferent to other capacities, such as synaesthesia in the form of connecting certain colors to certain sounds. (For a discussion of differential evolutionary pressures, see Wimsatt, 1986.)

Our ways of attributing meanings, and the actual meanings we attribute, are thus not undifferentiated. They are differentiated both by the degree to which they are susceptible to pressures of fitness and by the degree of fitness they in fact have. The premise of Protagoras forbids us from talking about objective meaning as part of a theory of meaning, but it allows us to talk about the fitness of a conceptual system, and even about the extremely high fitness of some of its components. We can therefore feel perfectly respectable in believing that certain meanings and patterns of meaning are just indispensable, which is not to say objective. Fitness is not a measure of correspondence to objective reality but rather a measure of success. By inference, fitness is a measure of capacity, provided good and bad luck average out for large numbers of cases. In principle, two unlike conceptual systems for attributing meaning could be equally fit.

Protagoras seems to have suggested that we view things in exactly this way. It is a weak citation, but in Plato's *Theaetetus*, we find Plato's Socrates trying to imagine what the ghost of Protagoras might say on this point. The conjured ghost of Protagoras, as invented by Socrates and then remembered by Plato, argues that although it is beside the point to say that some understandings are truer than others, it is surely the case that some are simply practically better than others. A sick person may find food distasteful (or, I suppose, see the visual field in an odd way, or find something warm to be cold, or be unable to distinguish up from down, and so on). Although it is beside the point to say that the sick person's understanding of the world is untrue, it is obvious that the sick person is messed up and is not going to do very well. We want to avoid saying that the healthy person has true ideas, but we surely want to say that he has better ideas of what is going on. He will do a lot better. The case is the same, so this ghostly Protagoras argues, with respect to education: The teacher leads the student not from false to true concepts, but from unsound to sound concepts. Sound concepts are those that make us more competent.

More subtly, the premise of Protagoras does not require us to abandon the view that extremely fit concepts are true reflections of objective reality; it merely asks us to take this view as itself fit rather than true. We can thus keep the most commonsensical part of the objectivist view. Some ways of attributing meaning are virtually indispensable and not open to choice. To lack them is to suffer, perhaps fatally. Viewing reality as objective and objectively knowable is a fit habit, however embarrassing as a tenet of a theory of meaning.

Although Protagoras asks us to discard from any theory of meaning the notion of objective meaning, the alternative is not to embrace the notion of subjective meaning—meaning that is private to the individual and essentially arbitrary. Protagoras was much attacked on just this point. He was dismissed as a radical relativist.

If meaning is attributed by human brains, then the concept of subjective meaning is as mistaken as the concept of objective meaning. Human capacities for attributing meaning show regularities that keep them from being radically private or arbitrary not because they are grounded in objective meaning but because the human brain develops under what we might call necessary biology and necessary experience.

Necessary Biology and Necessary Experience

For phylogenetic reasons, we all share a certain neurobiological endowment. We share not only gross anatomical structure in the brain but also dispositions of neuroembryology (Churchland, 1986; Edelman, 1987, 1989, 1992). This brain, endowed with necessary biology, develops under what we might call necessary experience. Given the standard neurobiological endowment, it is not possible for an infant to fail to have early experience of the gravity vector, of force dynamics, of image-schemas such as the source-path-goal schema, and so on. This necessary neurobiological endowment and this necessary early experience, common to all, work to develop a brain that attributes meaning in certain ways.[1] Although those ways belong to the individual, they are not appropriately to be called subjective, because they are common to all of us.

For example, we all recognize the 11 basic color categories and their central members; the neurobiological basis of this has been discovered. This capacity for attributing meaning comes exclusively from the individual brain—therefore it is not objective—but nothing about it is private or arbitrary—therefore it is not subjective. One can lack part of this capacity by being color-blind, but that is clearly a lack of what everybody else has (Berlin & Kay, 1969; Calvin, 1989; DeValois & Jacobs, 1968; Gregory, 1990; Lakoff, 1987).

To take another example, the human brain knows the bilateral symmetry of our body and of our experience with the world. Our bodies are bilaterally symmetric as a consequence of our ancestors' having had necessary experience over our phylogenetic history, in which they experienced our environment in a certain way, namely, as asymmetric in two dimensions but symmetric in the third. Our environments are asymmetric up–down (by virtue of gravity) and forward–back (by virtue of our directed movement forward), but they are symmetric right–left. What can happen from the right can happen from the left and conversely. What we can do to the right we can do to the left and conversely. We are endowed phylogenetically to recognize and exploit right–left symmetry in our environments. This experience is incorporated in our genetic endowment not by Lamarckian mechanisms but by mechanisms of selection for fitness: Those organisms that are bilaterally symmetric and are endowed to recognize bilateral symmetry are fitter; their differential replication is higher, indeed so much higher that they are the only members of the species to survive.

Our biology carries the experience of our ancestors by means of the survival of some genes and the disappearance of others. Each of us is guided by the

---

[1]The interaction of phylogenetic endowment and ontogenetic experience is not modeled in connectionist neural nets that lack analogues of genetically provided neuroembryological dispositions. "Structured connectionism" might attend to ways in which these dispositions contribute to the structure of knowledge and consciousness as they develop under ontogenetic experience. Unstructured connectionism—the training of random nets—stands open to objections laid traditionally against associationism.

successes and failures of our ancestors through encoding in the gene pool by means of selection for fitness. Recognizing bilateral symmetry is part of this necessary phylogenetic biology that we all share. It is also part of necessary individual ontogenetic experience that we all share. We all have early experience of balance. We develop the capacity to attribute meaning according to this right–left symmetry, to see some things as in balance or in equilibrium. This has proven to be an extremely fit capacity, with the result that we all share this specific capacity for attributing meaning to our world and ourselves. It is just the wrong question to ask whether this meaning is objective or subjective. The capacity and the disposition to attribute meaning in this way are extremely fit and universal parts of our conceptual apparatus. They come from necessary biology and necessary experience.

The Metaphoric Basis of the Objective Versus Subjective Distinction

The distinction between objective and subjective meaning, which the updated premise of Protagoras asks us to cross off our list, seems to derive from a conceptual metaphor in which we understand mind in terms of a container. In this basic metaphor, meaning is an object. Objective meaning is, metaphorically, located outside the mind-container. Metaphorically, we can have inside the mind-container a copy of this external objective meaning. If the copy is good, then we know objective meanings. We can all have copies, connected by virtue of their all having an external referent. In this metaphor, these internal copies cannot be connected to each other directly. They can be connected only through the intermediary of the objective referent, which is located outside the brain, and which is independent of the copies, and which has priority over the copies.

Under an updated version of the premise of Protagoras, this metaphor and its implications are swept aside. Meaning lies in patterns in human brains. Meaning lies inside the brain in a nonmetaphoric sense. No meaning lies outside the human brain. Meanings in different brains are connected not as copies of an external meaning, but because the brains share a biological and functional similarity in the activities of attributing meaning. We share genetic dispositions and we share universal early individual experience. As a result, we share ways of attributing meaning. We all have bodies asymmetric top to bottom and we all experience the gravity vector. We all have retinas and lateral geniculate nuclei that are structured neurobiologically in similar ways and we all experience the visible spectrum of light. We all have bodies that are right–left symmetric and we all experience moments of physical equilibrium. We all have bodies that bleed when their skin is punctured and we all have a great deal of early experience with objects going into or out of the body. And so on. By virtue of our shared phylogenetic past and our similar ontogenetic experiences, we share some fundamental ways of attributing meaning. It is merely misleading and confusing to ask whether the meaning, as attributed by these capacities, is objective or subjective. It is neither.

It is interesting to note that nothing is lost when we delete the distinction between objective meaning and subjective meaning from our list of useful conceptual instruments. Given the tenacity with which this distinction has been held, one would think that it does some profound conceptual work. On the contrary, if instead of thinking of a concept, idea, or model as the one that is objectively "most true," we think of it as merely the one that is "most fit," no functional capacity will be lost. There will be no consequence for our practical or scientific behavior. We will still inquire in the same way into the nature of things and still have the same standards for experiment, discovery, and belief. We will still be motivated to find the fittest ways of making sense of the world. True, our abandoning the distinction of objective versus subjective may change some of our metaphysical sense of our existence, but it will rob us of none of our knowledge or our practice.

THE MIND VERSUS THE BODY

The next conceptual instrument to cross off our list under the guidance of Protagoras is an ancient distinction that lives with us strongly in the present, the distinction between the mind and the body. This distinction comes in two avatars. The first, in which the body is viewed as a machine inhabited by an incorporeal ghost called the mind, belonged to Plato, Boethius, and Descartes, but is no longer taken seriously.

The second avatar is fundamental to the dominant theories of meaning from Plato to current artificial intelligence approaches. It is doubtful that Protagoras would have had any sympathy with it. In this view, the workings of the mind are disembodied; the brain is of course connected at its far margins to sensory receptors and motor neurons, but if we shave off this negligible surface, then we are left with the essence of mind: a structural and relational conceptual arena in which thought is configured, essentially free of the lowly body. Different theories take different views as to what is configured within this arena, but the usual candidates include varieties of formalism, such as recursive function theory, geometrical thinking, predicate calculus, logic of some stripe, or certainly something that is assumed to transcend the body and its experience.

This view of meaning as disembodied is contradicted by the growing neurobiological and cognitive research that suggests that the human mind is very deeply constrained, structured, and limited by the human body in which it resides and the human environment in which it lives (Edelman, 1987, 1989, 1992; Johnson, 1987; see also chapter 3 of this volume). The human body incorporates the experience over time of the human species within its highly specific environment. This specificity structures the brain, constraining and guiding mental operations. A surgically removed brain in a vat may lack its fleshy house but is not disembodied, for the brain carries in its structure and operation the nature of the body it serves. The sensory sheets of the central nervous system, for example, do not stop at the surface periphery of the brain. Rather, they are projected with topological integrity deep into the brain. An attempt to remove them would destroy the most inward reaches of the brain. The pure mind depends on the daily body. As Patricia Churchland (1986) writes in *Neurophilosophy*:

> One of the most promising and puzzling discoveries about the organization of nervous systems is that many structures abide by a principle of topographic mapping, whereby neighborhood relations of cells at one periphery are preserved in the arrangement of cells at other locations in the projection system. If we think of the neurons at the sensory periphery as forming a receptor sheet, then deformed versions of that sheet are represented in a large number of CNS [central nervous system] regions. Whatever the functional principle served, it must be served successfully, since wide areas of the cerebral cortex as well as other structures abound in such maps, and new research is turning up more all the time. (pp. 119–120)

The brain is not an unconstrained general-purpose machine. It has some highly specific purposes and values and corresponding structure (Edelman, 1992). As an example of this specificity, consider that everyone has a right–left symmetric environment, a right–left symmetric body, and a right–left symmetric brain, with the result that having a human body means having a human brain that is disposed to attribute meaning according to its understanding of balance and equilibrium. Such bodily understanding is available to be projected metaphorically to impart structure and meaning to more abstract concepts, such as our concept of justice. Although different societies can have different concepts, conceptual categories, and ways of naming, nonetheless the image-schemas of balance and equilibrium are to be found at work in the structuring of concepts wherever one cares to look. For example, our concept of balance in a line of poetry is a metaphoric projection from our supposedly low-level embodied knowledge of balance and force-dynamics (Johnson, 1987; Turner, 1991).

The premise of Protagoras would suggest that some patterns in the brain are inherently meaningful to human beings with human bodies because those patterns correspond to human bodily situations.[2] Patterns in the brain not inherently

---

[2]The immediate question arises, by what exact process might patterns of brain activity come into being that correspond to patterns in experience? See, for example, Cowan and Sharp, 1988:

> The Boltzmann machine learning process is autoassociative or unsupervised, depends only on correlations between pairs of units, and creates in the set of connection weights a distributed representation of the correlations that exist in and between members of the set of stimulus patterns. To put it another way, a Boltzmann machine can form a representation that eventually reproduces relations between classes of events in its environment. It therefore provides a possible solution to Marr's problem of how to construct such representations *ab initio* in the granule cells of the hippocampus and the neocortex. More generally, it provides a way in which distributed representations of abstract symbols can be formed and therefore permits the investigation by means of adaptive neural nets of symbolic reasoning. (p. 102)

meaningful would derive their meaning through links to patterns that are inherently meaningful. In other words, patterns that are inherently meaningful could be present in other concepts, such as abstract concepts, so that even the most refined parts of our conceptual apparatus for attributing meaning could be ineradicably embodied.

CULTURE VERSUS BIOLOGY

A view of the nature and ontogenesis of meaning as ineradicably embodied would blur in two profound ways the distinction between culture and biology, requiring us to cross this distinction off our list of respectable conceptual instruments. The first blurring is now apparent: If meaning is structured and guided by the mapping of the body in the brain, then it is not possible to separate human culture from human bodies. Culture is patterns of activity in brains; brains are structured in accord with their bodies; therefore culture, which is activity in brains, is structured in accord with the bodies in which it resides. Conversely, brains are in various ways developed under cultural experience, such as experience of language. A certain amount of our actual neurobiology is inseparable from culture.

The second blurring is equally evident, having to do not with the mapping of the body in the brain but simply with the fact that the instantiation of culture can only be neurobiological. Meanings reside in the brain. Imagine you are microscopic and inside a brain, gazing about, trying to distinguish between biology and culture. You could not meaningfully point to one synapse and say, "see that, that's biology," and then point to a different synapse and say, "see that, that's culture." It's an absurd and untenable distinction. To the extent that there is culture, it just is neurobiology; it just consists of neurobiological events and structures. If, while you are in miniature and touring the brain, you observed some neurobiological activity involved in, say, language, you could not say in a meaningful fashion, "see that, it's just biology, culture is not involved." At the level of what exists, as opposed to the level of metaphysics, culture cannot be distinguished from neurobiology.

INNATE VERSUS ACQUIRED

Among the largest and most influential concepts to be crossed off our list of instruments for constructing a theory of meaning is the distinction between innate and acquired. The innate versus acquired distinction lines up with some related distinctions: innate is internal, genetic, fundamental, manifested early, and so on; acquired is external, experiential, relatively optional, late in development, and so on.

The distinction of innate versus acquired derives from a metaphoric view of the mind as a medium to which the world can add. In specific metaphors, this medium is specified as a wax tablet of a certain nature, upon which the world imprints, or as a sheet of paper bearing certain innate inscriptions and upon which the world additionally writes, or as an engine of certain capacities that are augmented by the world through experience and learning.

What is missing from the distinction of innate versus acquired is the recognition of how regular our experience is. Is there necessary experience? The answer is clearly yes. Some of our experience is so constant and universal that it must count as innate, in a certain sense. Capacities that are absolutely indispensable to the phenotype do not have to be carried by the genotype, or at least not exclusively by the genotype, provided that they arise from experience that can be absolutely counted upon. For example, consider our capacity to use the image-schema of a path from a source to a goal. We use this image-schema to attribute meaning to many things, from the street we live on to the direction of an argument. A human being who lacked this image-schema of *source-path-goal* would be so incapacitated as to seem fundamentally deficient. Now imagine that the *source-path-goal* schema arises only through early experience. This would present no problem, because it is a matter of necessary early experience. Conceivably, severe sensory deprivation of a developing child could prevent it from "acquiring" the *source-path-goal* schema. But this would not mean that, because the schema is acquired, it is therefore optional or exterior to the organism or anything but fundamental to the organism.

What is fundamental, criterial, or indispensable to the organism need not be carried genetically, or at least not exclusively so, provided that it is carried by necessary experience. A great deal of the development of the brain as a system for attributing meaning depends on early experience, but much of this early experience counts as predictable nourishment rather than as optional acquisition. Our fitness in attributing meaning is a matter not just of genetic endowment, but of the regularity of the environment we encounter.

One student of evolutionary biology, William Wimsatt (1986), recently proposed that we replace the distinction of innate versus acquired with an alternative concept that saves what is useful about the distinction but discards what is specious. Instead of disputing whether a capacity is innate or acquired, we should consider its degree of "generative entrenchment." A feature or capacity is more generatively entrenched the more other features or capacities depend on it. Evolution is likely to be extremely conservative for capacities that are deeply generatively entrenched, and less so for capacities that have low generative entrenchment. Deeply generatively entrenched capacities are, on average, likely to appear earlier in development. But deeply generatively entrenched capacities need not be innate, in the sense of interior to the organism, or independent of experience, or carried exclusively by genetic material. They can equally come from the stability of the environment. Wimsatt writes of the imprinting of the greylag goose upon its mother:

[N]ot only is the imprinting mechanism of the greylag goose at birth "innate" (as on the standard ethological accounts), but the object of imprinting is also "innate." When the infant goose extricates itself from its shell, it imprints upon and follows any moving object. . . . In their natural environment, however, there is a very high probability that the young goose will properly imprint on its mother and will, in short order, learn to distinguish her cries and her appearance from that of other female greylag geese nearby. The family structure and behavior of the mother greylag goose at the time of birth makes it almost a certainty that the baby geese will imprint properly. . . . Thus the correct information (that a close moving object first detected at birth is mother) is reliably present in the environment. (pp. 200–201)

In short, this capacity of the greylag goose for operating in its world is innate but comes from experience. In this sense, necessary experience of a regular environment is innate and acquired. The distinction of innate versus acquired fails.

To eliminate the distinction of innate versus acquired might prove particularly unsettling at the present stage of inquiries into the nature of human thought and language because eliminating the distinction necessarily impeaches the hypothesis that human beings are born with an innate language module whose operation is independent of experience and autonomous from other cognitive capacities. Were we to grant for the sake of discussion that some of our linguistic capacities are fundamental, universal, interior to the organism, and incapable of being developed through the ontogenetic experience of the individual alone, this would not entail that these linguistic capacities must be carried exclusively or even largely by genetic material. The manifestation of these capacities could perfectly well depend on experience, provided that the experience was necessary, which is to say, that it came from stable parts of our interaction with the environment, such as the experience of bounded interiors, of the gravity vector, of balance and equilibrium, of force dynamics, of image-schemas like *source-path-goal*, and so on.

GENETICS VERSUS EXPERIENCE

The distinction between innate and acquired is usually correlated with the distinction between genetics and experience, but this is misleading, because most of what is carried genetically is present because of experience. Through mechanisms of selection, genetic material embodies the history of the experience of its ancestors. The gene pool reflects bad experience by lacking the genetic material that disposed its phenotypes to bad experience; it reflects successful experience by carrying the genetic material that disposed its phenotypes to successful experience. We still have the sense of smell because our ancestors had certain kinds of experience as a result of having the sense of smell. In this way, the phylogenetic endowment reflects the differential experience of evolutionarily prior organisms. Our genes, for example, carry the instructions for constructing a body that is bilaterally symmetric because our ancestors in the phylogenetic tree experienced the world as right–left symmetric. Those organisms best adapted to this right–left symmetry were selected for. Bilaterally symmetric bodies have been selected for through the interaction of our ancestors and their environments. In this sense, our genetic material, and our bodies, reflect the experience of our species. Our bodies incorporate the history of our species with the environment. The genes that build these bodies incorporate the history of our species with the environment.

Blurring the distinction between genetics and experience will require us to reconceive in a second way the hypothesis that human beings are born with an innate language module whose operation is independent of experience and autonomous from other cognitive capacities. Even if such a language module exists, and even if it is carried entirely in genetic material, in such a way that universal capacities of language are not in the least developed under the influence of ontogenetic experience, nonetheless those linguistic capacities would still be, in a fundamental sense, the result of experience, the experience of the individual organisms in the phylogenetic tree behind us. The genetic material disposing us to the possession of a language module would have been subject to selection. The mechanism of this selection, natural and sexual, would have been exactly the experiential interaction between the organism and its environment.

The dispute over the extent to which language is innate versus acquired is likely to be with us for a very long time, first because the distinction itself is conceptually confused and so prevents us from thinking clearly about the issue, but second because we have failed to take into account the regularity of human experience. To the extent that universal linguistic capacity could depend on individual ontogenetic experience, that ontogenetic experience would have to be universal. Experience that is ontogenetically universal for us is virtually certain to have been ontogenetically universal for our ancestors. This sharing of universal experience between ourselves and our ancestors leads to a difficulty in analyzing the origins of linguistic capacities: The genetic basis that could lie behind these capacities and the individual experiential basis that could lie behind these capacities just are equivalent. For a great many basic things, the average experience of ancestors, as represented in the genome, will be exactly the same experience to be had by the individual developing organism, and not just one such developing organism, but every such developing organism. We see the particular human linguistic capacity, but it will be hard to deduce its source, because the genetic basis it could have and the experiential basis it could have are not distinguishable. Do you have a capacity because you developed it in response to certain experience, or do you have it because every one of your ancestors had that experience and so evolution, through differential selection of capacity, developed it genetically for you and placed it into your genes? Or is it a combination of both? Logically, any of the three answers is possible, and the actual answer about the genesis of a specific capacity can only come, then, from empirical work, much of it necessarily in the sciences of genetics, neuroembryology, and developmental neurobiology. In consequence, the debate over the source of linguistic capacity in human beings cannot be resolved through "in principle" reasoning. A great deal of practical, empirical work lies before us, and it will simply have to be done.

It is important to realize that the question of whether a linguistic capacity is autonomous from other capacities—such as our capacities for seeing, for hearing, for understanding force dynamics, for understanding spatial relations, and so on—is not a question of innate versus acquired or of genetics versus experience. There is no reason to conclude that a linguistic capacity to which our genes might dispose us must be autonomous from nonlinguistic capacities. The phylogenetic development of linguistic capacity could depend on nonlinguistic capacities; the ontogenetic development of linguistic capacity could depend on nonlinguistic capacity; and the actual operation of linguistic capacity in the individual could involve or depend on nonlinguistic capacity. Evolution the tinker seems always to work with and build upon what it has. My own guess—and it can count only as a guess at this stage in our research—is that various capacities for attributing meaning to the world must have been in place before the development of a linguistic capacity, and that the linguistic capacity depends on them to some considerable extent. These capacities include image-schematic, visual, tactile, auditory, proprioceptive, sensorimotor, and other capacities (Edelman, 1992). I think it just improbable that whatever genetic endowment we have for a linguistic capacity was not constructed in part by borrowing strength from these prior capacities, but only empirical work can tell. The argument from the paucity of linguistic data in the early life of the individual to the assertion of an innate, autonomous language module does not follow. In this argument, it is asserted that children do not have sufficiently rich linguistic experience to allow them to develop the rich linguistic capacity they in fact do develop, and therefore that this linguistic competence must be carried genetically. What is missing from this argument is a consideration of the possible contribution to linguistic development of nonlinguistic experience. The brain may well draw on nonlinguistic capacities, as reflected in the genome or as developed through early experience, in arriving at a linguistic competence.

If we were to grant that the linguistic capacity is innate, it would not follow that it is independent of ontogenetic experience: The capacity of the greylag goose to recognize its mother is innate and depends absolutely on reliable ontogenetic experience, predictable from the regularity of the environment. Nor would it follow that the linguistic capacity would be autonomous of nonlinguistic capacities: It may well have arisen genetically by drawing upon nonlinguistic capacities as they are carried in genetic material.

BACK TO THE IMAGINATIVE MIND

Under Protagoras's design for a theory of meaning, any capacity of mind has a claim to be respected within theories of meaning. But under objectivist designs, only mental capacities imagined as leading to so-called objective meaning have any claim on our respect. The appallingly influential objectivist design to be found in Descartes's (1637) *Discours de la Méthode Pour bien conduire sa raison, et chercher la verité dans les sciences,* for example, views mind as dramatically separate from anything bodily, and considers the recognition of meaning as the exclusive province of the conscious mind and its supposed arsenal of capacities for objective knowledge (Wilkes, 1988). In such an objectivist design, imaginative human mental capacities we associate with poetry are effectively dismissed from playing any role in theories of meaning. They are instead to be studied within the branches of rhetoric and poetics, and viewed as peripheral, optional, decorative, and secondary to the science of mind. As a pedagogical consequence, it is assumed that their study can be safely eliminated from the curriculum of those concerned with entailment and class inclusion, syntax and reference. The study of the theory of meaning in our century has largely ignored these rhetorical, figural, and narrative capacities of mind, at least until roughly the last decade.

If we look back to classical antiquity and its discussion of meaning and language, we see many marvelous claims. Someone like Demetrius (1932), for example, feels comfortable explaining in his work *On Style* that:

1. Everyday language is widely and ineradicably metaphoric.[3]
2. The conceptual metaphoric mappings we see manifested in language are asymmetric.[4]
3. Metaphoric conceptions can be as true as any others.[5]

---

[3]"Usage, which is our teacher everywhere, is so particularly in regard to metaphors. Usage, in fact, clothes almost all conceptions in metaphor, and that with such a sure touch that we are hardly conscious of it. It calls a voice 'silvery,' a man 'keen,' a character 'rugged,' a speaker 'long,' and so on with metaphors in general" (Demetrius, 1932, p. 359). The Greek word ἡ συνήθεια, here translated as "usage," means "everyday language," "habit," "common usage"; etymologically, it means "that which we live by."

[4]"Homer could call the lower slope of Ida its 'foot,' but he could not go further and call a man's foot his 'slope' " (Demetrius, 1932, p. 353).

[5]"Some things are, however, expressed with greater clearness and precision by means of metaphors than by means of the precise terms themselves: as 'the battle shuddered.' No change of phrase could, by the employment of precise terms, convey the meaning with greater truth or clearness" (Demetrius, 1932, p. 355). The word *truth* here is not a mistranslation. The original is ἀληθέστερον, comparative of ἀληθῶς, "truly," adverbial form of ἀληθής, "true, real, actual."

4. We understand linguistic constructions to some extent in terms of what we might now call image-schemas.[6]

In Longinus (1932), we can find the view that figural understanding is all the more powerful when it is so automatic that we do not recognize its figural nature.[7]

This view that our conceptual system and our consequent languages are fundamentally and ineradicably dependent on rhetorical or poetic capacities sounds new because it is new to us. Education has split the scientific study of the mind, meaning, and language off from the rhetorical and literary study of the imaginative mind; it has done this on the pretext that it is safe to do so, because rhetorical and poetic capacities of mind are merely acquired extras, subjective, optional, and peripheral to any study of meaning: Certainly they cannot be innate; certainly they cannot be fundamental to the capacity of the organism. The study of meaning has been prosecuted as the study of literal meaning, on the view that objective meaning is literal. Figural meaning has been characterized as unimportant.

But if we adopt the updated premise of Protagoras, we must abandon this split between the scientific study of mind and the rhetorical study of mind. The human mind attributes meaning. We should look at how it actually manages to do so, without preconceptions about how it ought to do so. When we begin that investigation, we find something quite interesting. Rhetorical powers of mind, such as the figural and the narrative, are not peripheral. Indeed, they appear to be fundamental, ineradicable, and indispensable to the organism. They appear to be ubiquitous in the meanings we do attribute. They appear in fact to play a dominant role in capacities that were once thought to be where all the action is: categorization, deduction, reasoning, argument. These rhetorical powers of mind have a claim as good as any to be called literal and innate, in the sense that they are basic, ineradicable, and indispensable to the normal functioning of the human organism.

I have sketched the outlines of such a cognitive rhetorical inquiry into the nature and ontogenesis of meaning in *Reading Minds: The Study of English in*

---

[6]Demetrius (1932) talks of linguistic constructions being "rounded," "disjointed," "hastening towards a definite goal as runners do when they leave the starting-place," "circular," "tense," "periodic," and so on. He points out that thought comes with part–whole structure that can be mirrored in the linguistic construction (pp. 295–297). We would now refer to this mirroring as iconic syntax. He writes, "The form of the oratorical period is tense and circular; it needs a neatly rounded mouth and a hand which follows closely each movement of the rhythm" (p. 311). He comments on the experiential or image-schematic basis of our reaction to syntactic constructions, as in, "Long journeys are shortened by a succession of inns, while desolate paths, even when the distances are short, give the impression of length. Precisely the same principle will apply also in the case of members [linguistic constructions]" (p. 331).

[7]"So we find that a figure is always most effective when it conceals the very fact of its being a figure" (Longinus, 1932, p. 185).

the Age of Cognitive Science (Turner, 1991). Cognitive rhetoric is compatible with the premise of Protagoras in viewing the human person as the measure of all things. The human person has a human brain in a human body in a human environment that it must find meaningful if it is to survive. In consequence, the human person finds certain patterned experience inherently meaningful. The human person also has certain fundamental conceptual capacities for attributing meaning, such as the metaphoric, the metonymic, and the narrative. Far from trivial or peripheral, these capacities appear to be indispensable to the organism; they necessarily evolve ontogenetically according to necessary biology and necessary experience. Our job, as theorists of meaning, is to discover how they evolve and how they work.

REINVENTING THE UNIVERSITY

The premise of Protagoras is a design for a theory of meaning, and, as such, it is a design for the invention of the university, or at least that part of the university that considers human beings, the brain, and meaning. On this design, it would be best to bring together as one division of the university all those studies concerned with the way in which the human brain attributes meaning. This would include cognitive linguistics and cognitive psychology, rhetoric and neurobiology, indeed any field of study concerned with the interpretive or creative mind. Under the premise of Protagoras, this division would be called "the humanities," because it would concern whatever belongs to human beings, the measure of all things.

Such a definition of the humanities may seem strange to us now, but it would not have seemed strange when the humanities were originally carved out as the study of what belongs to human beings, by contrast with the study of divinity, which was already established as the study of what belonged to divine beings. Under the premise of Protagoras, the study of the human brain is part of the humanities, as is the study of human language, human psychology, human development, and human neuroscience. If calling this organization "the humanities" seems objectionable, we can give it another name. But if the intellectual organization itself seems conceptually strange rather than merely unfamiliar, then we have some rethinking to do. The university as we know it is organized according to a rejection of the premise of Protagoras. If that premise manages, in the next age, to come back into its own, it will mean a changed view not only of what belongs to a theory of meaning, but also of how a university should be organized. It is just such a reorganization, I think, that is most likely to lead us to the discovery of the nature and ontogenesis of meaning.

REFERENCES

Berlin, B., & Kay, P. (1969). *Basic color terms: Their universality and evolutions.* Berkeley: University of California Press.
Calvin, W. H. (1989). *The cerebral symphony: Seashore reflections on the structure of consciousness.* New York: Bantam.

Churchland, P. (1986). *Neurophilosophy: Toward a unified science of the mind/brain.* Cambridge, MA: MIT Press.

Cowan, J. D., & Sharp, D. H. (1988). Neural nets and artificial intelligence. In S. R. Graubard (Ed.), *The artificial intelligence debate: False starts, real foundations* (pp. 85–121). Cambridge, MA: MIT Press.

Demetrius (1932). *On style* (W. R. Roberts, Trans.). Cambridge, MA: Harvard University Press.

Descartes, R. (1953). Discours de la Méthode. In André Bridoux (Ed.), *Œuvres et lettres* (pp. 126–179). Paris: Gallimard. (Original work published 1637)

DeValois, R. L., & Jacobs, G. H. (1968). Primate color vision. *Science, 162,* 533–540.

Edelman, G. (1987). *Neural Darwinism: The theory of neuronal group selection.* New York: Basic.

Edelman, G. (1989). *The remembered present: A biological theory of consciousness.* New York: Basic.

Edelman, G. (1992). *Bright air, brilliant fire.* New York: Basic.

Gregory, R. (1990). *Eye and brain: The psychology of seeing* (4th ed.). Princeton, NJ: Princeton University Press.

Johnson, M. (1987). *The body in the mind.* Chicago: University of Chicago Press.

Lakoff, G. (1987). *Women, fire, and dangerous things: What categories reveal about the mind.* Chicago: University of Chicago Press.

Lakoff, G., & Turner, M. (1989). *More than cool reason: A field guide to poetic metaphor.* Chicago: University of Chicago Press.

Longinus (1932). *On the sublime* (W. H. Fyfe, Trans.). Cambridge, MA: Harvard University Press.

Turner, M. (1987). *Death is the mother of beauty: Mind, metaphor, criticism.* Chicago: University of Chicago Press.

Turner, M. (1991). *Reading minds: The study of English in the age of cognitive science.* Princeton, NJ: Princeton University Press.

Wilkes, K. V. (1988). —, yìshì, duh, um, and consciousness. In A. J. Marcel & E. Bisiach (Eds.), *Consciousness in contemporary science* (pp. 16–41). Oxford, England: Clarendon.

Wimsatt, W. C. (1986). Developmental constraints, generative entrenchment, and the innate–acquired distinction. In W. Bechtel (Ed.), *Integrating scientific disciplines* (pp. 185–208). Dordrecht, Netherlands: Martinus Nijhoff.

5

A Developmental Analysis of Cognitive Semantics: What Is the Role of Metaphor in the Construction of Knowledge and Reasoning?

Ellin Kofsky Scholnick
Kelly Cookson
University of Maryland, College Park

We have a fantasy of writing an intellectual history of psychology by examining changes in the meaning of its key concepts and terminology. It would trace how and why one concept was transformed into another and how and why a once popular concept disappeared and then suddenly resurfaced. That imaginary history might track the concept of development, which has been converted into learning, and then report how learning became the processing system by which information is acquired and stored. In its latest metamorphosis, the concept of development has been reinterpreted to refer to the knowledge that is stored and the prime developmental questions are those that motivated this book. What is the nature of knowledge? How is it organized, used, and extended?

One recycled concept worthy of a case study is analogy because of its role in explaining the construction and extension of meaning. In an analogy, a well-known domain, the source, is used to understand some aspect of a less familiar or less organized domain, the target. Analogies reflect the insight that in some way the target domain works like the source domain. For example, in describing the mind as a computer, we assume both process information in the same way.

The study of analogy initially intrigued psychologists interested in scientific and artistic creativity. Analogies can be used to build new scientific models, such as the explanation of the symptoms of disease in terms of defense mechanisms (Johnson, 1987). In one of its guises, metaphor,[1] analogy is a literary device as

---

[1]Analogy and metaphor are used interchangeably because metaphors are rich and often carry with them a set of implications about a knowledge domain. However, it remains to be proven that the two involve identical cognitive processes.

well. Both scientific analogies and literary metaphors require recognizing and mapping commonalities between the system of relations existing in the source and the system of relations in the target field (Holyoak & Thagard, 1989). The fate of research on analogy was to become decontextualized so as to isolate recognition and mapping. The study of recognition of commonalities was narrowed to research on transfer. Transfer of training was predicted on the basis of the number of identical elements shared by the source and target domains (Brown, 1990). Scrutiny of mapping was relegated to assessing performance on proportional analogies such as those found in intelligence tests (Sternberg & Nigro, 1980). Eventually research on analogy passed out of fashion.

Lately interest in analogy has resurfaced. It is reputed to be one of the five indispensable processes of cognitive change (Siegler, 1989), a universal, general problem-solving skill (Anderson & Thompson, 1989), and the foundation of our system of meaning (Lakoff & Johnson, 1980; Lakoff & Turner, 1989). Transformations and recyclings are often correlated. When early theories of a phenomenon are transformed, old material is assimilated to fit the new paradigm (Kuhn, 1962). The transformation of development into the acquisition of knowledge may be one reason why our interest in analogy has been reawakened. If development is defined as skill in deploying already acquired meanings to acquire new meanings, then analogy is a prime instrument for gaining knowledge. The study of analogical reasoning becomes the study of the acquisition process. Conversely, analogy, which is the extension of knowledge, depends on having knowledge to extend. The study of analogical thinking leads to an examination of the nature of knowledge itself.

Both the redefinition of development and the reevaluation of the importance of analogy are reflections of a shift in how we define cognitive development. In this new perspective, development is the acquisition of knowledge that automatically leads to its use. But knowledge is not acquired evenly across different domains and early acquisition of knowledge does not guarantee its deployment. People do not automatically integrate and use their knowledge. There are unresolved problems in current theories of cognitive development, and the same unresolved issues bedevil our attempts to explain analogy. Knowledge-based theories of development are approaching an impasse because we lack a theory of the nature of knowledge and a theory of knowledge use. This chapter is a first step at realizing an imagined plan for analyzing current theories of development by examining current work on the development of analogical reasoning.

Our discussion proceeds as follows. It begins with a summary of research on analogical reasoning in children in order to illustrate why current conceptualizations of the nature of knowledge and its use are unsatisfactory. We then critically examine how cognitive semantics could remedy those problems by providing a theory of meaning and analogical extension. We then argue that this theory currently lacks a strong developmental framework, and use recent Piagetian theory to suggest how the study of development and analogical reasoning might get back on course.

ANALOGICAL REASONING IN CHILDREN

The history of research on children's analogical reasoning reveals shifting interpretations of its necessary prerequisites (see Brown, 1989; Goswami, 1991). Analogical reasoning has often been assessed by proportional analogies that have the form $A : B :: C : D$. For example, *cat* is to *dog* as *tiger* is to *?*. The missing term lies at the intersect of two sets of classes: (a) cat and tiger are both felines, whereas dog and the missing term are both canines; (b) cats and dogs are tame, but tigers and the missing item are both wild. Thus, the missing term is a wild canine, such as a wolf. The failure of 8-year-olds on these tasks was initially attributed to their inability to map the intersect of the two classes.

That interpretation was soon qualified because young children can map certain commonalities but not others. In order to explain which analogies are accessible to young children, Gentner (1988, 1989) postulated a hierarchy of similarities differing in salience and in age of access. Surface similarities, such as color and form, are easy to detect and map, but categorical and causal relations are harder because they require more complex semantic representations. Thus younger children are likely to detect single perceptual similarities but not webs of conceptual relations.

Recently Brown (1989, 1990) argued differences in knowledge account for the purported perceptual to relational shift. We do not have to know much about objects to note that they are similar in color or shape. In contrast, considerable information about cats and tigers is required to categorize them as felines. Structural analogies that are based on causal links between elements may be the hardest to produce because they require understanding the workings of a domain. Thus, substituting *sun* : *planets* :: *proton* : *?* for the wild canine analogy increases task difficulty because the analogy is carried by an $A : B$ and $C : D$ relation of center to periphery without sun and proton having much in common. Solving the analogy requires understanding two complex and disparate relational fields.

Brown (1989, 1990) also contested the existence of a general relational shift or point at which the child has acquired enough knowledge about every domain to detect its structure and to use that structure in mapping. She argued that at best the shift is local, reflecting the status of the child's theory about specific content areas. Theories about familiar fields ought to be relatively sophisticated because the child has become expert in them. Brown made an even more radical claim, that the preference for perceptual mappings is merely a fall-back strategy when children have no other information. Children always search for causal mechanisms in building and mapping conceptual structures.

In support of this view, Brown (1990; Goswami & Brown, 1989) demonstrated that even 3-year-olds can perform pictorial proportional analogies tasks when the material taps familiar content and familiar relations such as whole versus broken. In a simplified analogical transfer task, 17- to 36-month-olds, who were taught to rake in a toy with a particular tool, picked a new instrument that preserved the necessary functional properties of a rake and ignored useless tools of the same color or size. Brown noted that preschoolers can be adept analogical reasoners, but they lack rich and well-organized knowledge about certain fields, like astronomy, that would enable them to detect certain relations and map them. They also lack metacognitive competence. They are slower to realize that analogical reasoning is useful.

Thus, performance on analogies fits a common explanation of the failure of young children on a myriad of problem-solving tasks. They are universal novices who lack properly organized knowledge bases that would enable them to represent problem spaces appropriately. Given extensive exposure to a field, their knowledge becomes appropriately organized and they learn how and when to use their knowledge in problem solving (Brown, 1989).

But this explanation is insufficient. It shifts the problem of deployment of knowledge to yet another kind of knowledge base, of metaprocedural skills, without describing that knowledge base or the means by which it is acquired. Moreover, we are slowly converting the study of cognition into the study of meaning without any consensus on an acceptable theory of meaning. A good theory should define precisely what constitutes a domain and should specify a priori the domains where the child first gains familiarity, the realms likely to be mastered later, and the factors that govern the expansion of knowledge within and across domains. A theory of meaning must define what knowledge is. We have a new metaphor of children as cognitive imperialists who explore new content areas and add them to their empire. But there is no map of either the starting point or the course of these explorations (Keil, 1990). We are in danger of having multiple specific theories of tiny contents based on content-specific principles, operating on unique timetables. Instead of being the product of development, like the spatial maps of bees and homing pigeons, human knowledge is characterized as the product of innate "domain specific organizing structures that direct attention to the data that bear on the concepts and facts relevant to a particular domain" (Gelman, 1990, p. 5).

Which knowledge is likely to reflect domain-specific organizing devices? Brown (1989, 1990) nominated one privileged domain. Human survival depends on distinguishing between physical objects and biological life, so children first gain the knowledge of the causal mechanisms underlying each category. This explanation omits how we make further specifications of these two general categories and gain knowledge of other categories. We need a more elaborate theory of meaning.

COGNITIVE SEMANTICS

Image Schemata

Cognitive semantics[2] may provide the theory of the nature of meaning and the course of its extension that developmental psychologists lack. We summarize that theory before evaluating whether this account is consistent with current research on children's thinking. The basic theme of cognitive semantics is captured by the title of Johnson's (1987) book, *The Body in the Mind*. Babies initially construct meaning from their understanding of their body, of the space in which the body resides, the movements of bodies in space, and the forces that operate on bodies. Because the body is a container, it structures ideas about "in" and "out," "empty" and "full." We and some of the objects around us move in space, so we detect paths as movements from an initial to a final location. We understand how forces work because we are subject to them and initiate them. Our bilateral symmetry creates ideas about balance (Turner, 1991).

These universal experiences that arise from our embodiment are encoded as *image schemata*. We experience our own body, our caretaker's body, the shape of a purse and of a bottle. We do not just notice their distinct contours; we also extract a single abstract image of containment in which the outline of a circle represents the closed boundary between an interior and its exterior. Hence we are born with very powerful capacities for abstraction and we are predisposed to coalesce experiences at this generic image-schematic level.

Image schemata are powerful because they have a gestalt organization (Johnson, 1987; Lakoff & Johnson, 1980; see also chapter 3 of this volume). For example, the container-schema entails a relation between a boundary and its exterior and interior. The path schema implies continuous movement in a particular direction and a metric that describes the distance from starting point to goal. Each schema is a rich dynamic system with a characteristic *event shape* (Lakoff & Johnson, 1980; Turner, 1991).

These basic image schemata are the preconscious foundation for our concepts. Our concept of closed shapes is based on our intuitive understanding of containment. Our concept of journey reflects our understanding of paths, and so on. Because many concepts are based on image schemata, they, too, are relational systems permitting a variety of inferences.

---

[2] For purposes of exposition, we treat the three major proponents of cognitive semantics as similar, though they differ in explanations of the derivations of logic and in the disciplines they wish to explain.

Metaphorical Extension

Abstract Domains. Basic image schemata give the knower an entry into understanding certain aspects of life. But not all of our concepts are directly derived from universal physical experiences. One way we extend embodied meanings is by using image schemata as metaphorical models to structure abstract domains (Lakoff & Johnson, 1980). The image schema becomes a source domain to structure abstract target domains. We are so accustomed to using our basic image schemata to interpret events, that we automatically map them onto new domains and extract the range of implications the image schemata afford. We use the familiar model of a path of travel to understand the abstract idea of purpose. The start of a purpose is a wish; its final realization is the goal. We employ the image schema of symmetry, that encodes a balance between opposing forces, to formulate ideas about justice.

Certain principles guide the choice of the appropriate image schema to structure abstract domains. The target concept must fit with the source image schema. We are unlikely to map containers onto paths because they lack a similar event shape or relational underpinning. Experiential correlations also shape metaphorical extensions (Lakoff & Johnson, 1980). When we want something, we have to travel to get it. Purposes and paths coincide. Pouring more water into a glass raises the level of the liquid. In stacking coins, each addition increases the height of the column. More is correlated with up. Anger is accompanied by physiological signs such as "increased body heat, increased internal pressure" (Lakoff, 1987, p. 381) that influence our view of emotions. So anger is understood as the heat of a fluid in a container and emotions as physical forces that build up psychological as well as physiological pressure. Cultures also use certain metaphors to interpret events, seeing arguments as war, or as linear paths.

Generic Categories and Metaphors. Meaning is also constructed by creating generic categories and metaphors from basic ones (Lakoff, 1987). Lakoff drew on Rosch's (Mervis & Rosch, 1981) theory to claim that there is a basic level at which we categorize the world because that level tends to maximize the similarity of exemplars within a class while providing manageable distinctiveness between the class and other contrasting categories. Early analogies are formed between basic-level categories. However, these basic categories need to be organized and linked so as to permit easy retrieval, mapping, and extension of knowledge. One important organizational device is a taxonomic hierarchy. Turner (1991) claimed that this taxonomic organization is, itself, a product of metaphor. The relational structure of the known basic category is extended to create a new superordinate category. We employ a metaphorical principle that the generic category works like the specific category. For example, each specific animal metaphor draws on the same properties—spontaneous movement, instinctual behavior, and biological functioning—so each can be used to create a generic animal category (Turner, 1987).

The creation of generic categories enables the construction of metaphorical relations between them, such as EVENTS ARE ACTIONS (Turner, 1991). For example, we metaphorically map time, an event, onto the act of traveling. Next, because actions are caused by agents, we have a basis for personification (Time becomes a traveler), which can be used to organize existent metaphorical extensions and to understand new abstract ideas and unfamiliar events.

Deductive Logic.   Knowledge is extended in yet another way, by deduction. The most challenging move in cognitive semantics is the attempt to generate abstract, disembodied, syntactic rules of reasoning (extensional logic) from embodied meaning. Some revealing examples are reasoning about categories (Johnson, 1987; Lakoff, 1987; Turner, 1991) and physical (Johnson, 1987) and psychological causation (Turner, 1987).

Understanding of categorical logic is explained through the metaphorical mapping of physical spaces onto conceptual spaces (Lakoff, 1987). We map the image of a bounded space, with an interior and exterior, onto our understanding of a class. We delimit members falling within the boundaries of a category from nonmembers that fall outside (Johnson, 1987; Lakoff, 1987). At a more symbolic level, we can use the container-schema to envision the interior of a category as a proposition, p, and the exterior space as *not-p*.

The image of containers also structures our understanding of class inclusion. The superordinate class is a container, and the subsets are its contents. This image supports the deduction that the container superordinate class is at least as large as any of the subsets contained within it. The image of several containers nested within each other is the basis for transitive logic. If canister A contains canister B, and canister B contains canister C, then A also contains C, and A is a more inclusive class than C. These "inferential patterns arise from our bodily experience of containment. Their use in abstract reasoning is a matter of metaphorical projection upon the CONTAINER schemata in which the inferential structure is preserved by the metaphorical mapping" (Johnson, 1987, p. 40).

Class inclusion can also be understood in terms of another body image, of parts, such as the features of the face, and wholes. We map part–whole relations metaphorically onto subset–set relations (Lakoff, 1987). The part–whole image schema implies that subordinate classes are necessarily smaller in extension than superordinate classes because the former are parts or subdivisions of the latter, higher order classes.

Causal Inference.   Causality has also been explained in metaphorical terms. Johnson (1987) derived causation from a set of FORCE image schemata. We are often subject to compelling external forces such as wind or the crush of a crowd. We form an image schema of a force of a given intensity moving on a straight line path toward some object that is moved further along that force vector until the movement is blocked. This image of compulsion enables us to understand the modal verb *must* and the logic of necessity.

Metaphorically we understand our own potential movements as acting like a compelling force because we have a capacity (that is not always realized) to create a directed movement that has an impact on other objects (Johnson, 1987; Lakoff & Johnson, 1980). The realization of that potential in direct action is the basis for our understanding of the properties of human causation, such as the possession of a purpose that guides movement. And the result of movement is the transferral of force by contact onto some object that visibly changes. Potential force or enablement also underlies our notions of possibility.

Because these FORCE schemata do not explain the origin of ideas and qualitative change, Turner (1987, 1991) postulated a birth or progeneration metaphor. By this metaphor, we explain certain facets of conceptual life, such as the sudden bursting forth of new ideas after a single act of "creation," and the unpredictability of the particular product we will flesh out once we gain insight.

Summary of Cognitive Semantics

Lakoff (1987) called the collective approach to cognitive semantics *experiential realism*. The program unites the two case studies of the change of meanings that led to a dilemma for developmental psychology. If cognition is the acquisition of knowledge, what is the knowledge we acquire? Of all the things we could know, where do we begin to acquire concepts? Experiential realism argues that we begin with the experience of our body in a terrestrial world of space and time. Having bodies that are subject to physical forces and that are situated in space and time necessarily exposes us to a common set of repetitive experiences that we use to construct and organize our system of meaning. We first extract preconscious image schemata that capture experiential regularities. We then use those schemata to structure conceptual models. These early conceptual models are the source domains that we map analogically onto experiences that are less closely linked to our physical experience and are the basis for formal reasoning. Analogy is important because it extends knowledge and creates tools for knowledge acquisition. The relations, such as causation, that we use to construct a new area of knowledge were themselves often created analogically. The inductive inferences we make in new fields stem from analogies. Thus experiential realism defines the initial construals the baby has and the putative routes by which the child translates those initial insights into a mature system of knowledge and reasoning.

DEVELOPMENTAL COGNITIVE SEMANTICS

Experiential realism could provide a model unifying current work on infant cognition, preschool semantic understanding, and the emergence of reasoning skills if it drew upon research in cognitive development. Currently, cognitive semantics is derived from analyses of adult speech and literary works. These are the products of already constructed meaning systems. Experiential realists use as their instruments of examination their own highly developed literary sensibilities. Consequently, the theory lacks detail on the process of structuring of a source domain and its later use. The theory goes beyond current analyses of cognitive development by providing a beginning as well as an end point of development. We wish to discuss transition states. Observations of children suggest that embodiment develops; the grasp of relations encoded in image schemata also develops, and the mapping of preconceptual construals into conceptual models and deductive logic is a delicate, intricate, and extended process.

Embodiment

The body we map onto our mind develops. The baby is charged by experiential realists with the daunting task of extracting invariant relations such as force, containment, and symmetry, and even simple relations like in and out, front and behind, center and periphery. Meanwhile the baby's body size, brain, and muscular control change dramatically. Adults (Turner, 1991) may see humans as symmetrical creatures, but infants are developing some symmetries such as focusing both eyes on the same object, while concurrently developing the asymmetry that underlies speech processing and handedness. Gravity has a different meaning for neonates who lack the muscular control to raise the head, 6-month-olds who can sit, and 14-month-olds who are struggling with the postural adjustments in walking. Gravity may have a different meaning for the child who cannot voluntarily release an object than for the child who can. We have to adjust our body-schemata as our powers change.

Until we understand the implications of those changes for the child's meaning system, we will not know which processes and experiences produce an embodied image schema and what the developmental course of embodiment is. The exact role of embodiment in the construction of knowledge is complicated. The history of psychology has witnessed debates about the source of the gestaltlike perceptual organization that characterizes image schemata. Competing claims have attributed the origin of perception of form and space (and the image schemata representing them) to motor experience, increasing acquaintance with environmental regularities, inherent organizational principles, and to perceptual biases to attend to the movement of three-dimensional surfaces (Spelke, 1988, 1990, 1991).

Constructing a Schema. The CONTAINER schema illustrates why embodiment is a complicated process. Infants experience being contained in the womb, in clothes, and in cribs. They, themselves, are containers for nutrients and body organs. These cumulative experiences would seem to be a firm basis for the notion of containment. But babies also have many contradictory experiences because their hands, a means to create containment, are not under voluntary control. Which experiences and which cues do they use to construct a prototype of containment? Until 4 months babies lack motor control so they do not anticipate the shape of an object they wish to hold as they reach for it. There are additional problems for older infants who do not gain the ability to release objects voluntarily until the latter part of the first year. When an object is put in a transparent container or behind a transparent wall, 5-month-olds must know that the object is inside the container because they will not reach toward an empty box. But they have difficulty getting the toy. Because of their poor aim, during the course of reaching for the toy, babies may touch the edge of the box, and a set of reflex avoidance responses produces withdrawal. Alternatively, they may grasp the edge of the box rather than the edge of the toy (Diamond, 1991). Even though 7-month-old children can reach accurately inside a box to extract a toy, if they have to change the direction of their movements, they become derailed. The immaturity of their frontal cortex hampers the coordination of sequences of movements (Diamond, 1991). The infants trying to extricate an object from a container understand the difference between "in" and "out," but their body sends contradictory messages. There are daily frustrations in trying to reach objects, and yet babies understand containment. If bodily movements were the only direct source of our image schemata, the infant's knowledge would be sorely restricted.

Embodiment is built on the experience of a changing body. Often movement cues must be ignored until they come under voluntary control and motor input becomes congruent with other sources of data. In other cases, such as understanding the impact of body contact on objects, kinesthetic input is veridical from its onset. The significance of specific actions for constructing meaning may vary across concepts and over time. Often embodiment develops piece by piece. The course of the coordination of embodied input and its consequences for the child's conceptual organization is a current research endeavor for cognitive developmentalists that may enrich the field of cognitive semantics.

Research on infants also suggests that there are age differences in the salience of perceptual inputs. Many image schemata depict either a bounded object or a path of movement. Spelke and her colleagues (1988, 1990, 1991) investigated how and when infants construct form boundaries. Before 4.5 months, infants appear to rely on object movement and depth cues. When one object occludes a portion of another object, babies perceive that the two pieces appearing behind the occluding object are part of the same whole only if the two exposed parts move in synchrony. Infants do not use static form cues, like identical surface pattern or good form continuation, to infer that the exposed parts represent a whole object. Even for a meaningful pattern, the face, when a horizontal strip hides the nose and cheeks, babies do not conclude that the exposed mouth-chin area and eye-hair area belong to the same face.

Spelke (1990, 1991) speculated that a bias to attend to common movements of a surface in space is the basis for the construction of contours. These surfaces are then coordinated to produce objects. This preliminary organization is later enriched by experiences with objects that lead to the piecemeal construction and application of gestalt principles of organization. Thus developmental data may provide a detailed and much needed analysis of the construction of image schemata.

Timetables for Construction. Spelke's (1988, 1990, 1991) research also suggests that some image schemata emerge later than others. Gravity and inertia are incorporated into several image schemata. For example, one image of force depicts its blockage by an obstacle (Johnson, 1987). Balance and symmetry are explained in terms of gravitational pull (Johnson, 1987; Turner, 1991). Three-month-olds seem to understand that objects move in a continuous path (Baillargeon, 1987), but neither they nor 6-month-olds understand much about gravity or inertia. They are not amazed when a support is removed from under a ball and the ball remains in midair. They are not fazed when a ball rolled behind a screen stops dead before reaching a barrier. They do not realize that hitting a barrier will deflect the course of an object's trajectory (Spelke, 1991). Even the 10-month-old infant understands limited aspects of gravity and inertia in a limited set of situations. Few adults have an accurate working model of inertia. It is important to know which schemata emerge early, why these emerge early, and whether developmental precedence is in any way correlated with later ease of application. How does the construction of one image schema influence the construction of other schemata? The step from developing brain and experience to construction of the source domain for a metaphor is actually a leap that justifies the need for a developmental cognitive semantics.

When Is a Schema a Schema? Another claim of experiential realism is that image schemata are organized gestalts that permit a wide range of inferences. Developmental data do not always support this claim. For adults, the container schema implies that movement of a container changes the location of its contents. Suppose a toy is put in a bucket. The bucket is first hidden behind a screen and then moved to a second screened location. Contrast this scenario with one where the toy is put in front of the bucket. Again a screen is lowered, hiding the two objects. Afterwards the bucket moves to a new hiding place. In each case, where is the toy? Adults infer that when the toy is within the bucket, the toy's location is determined by the bucket's movements. If the toy is outside the container, the movement of that container does not affect the location of the toy. So in the scenario where there was containment, the toy is behind the second screen. When the toy is outside the container, despite the movement of the bucket, the toy remains at its original hiding place. Nine-month-olds do not make this inference. They assume that if the bucket moves, the toy moves, too, even if the toy was outside the bucket (DeLoache & Bryant, 1991).

What does it mean to say a child possesses a schema if the child cannot make inferences appropriate to the schema? Can inferences based on the schema change without the schema itself changing? What kind of change allows a child to make new inferences? Is the change in the schema, or in some integrative or inferential capacity?

From Image and Concept to Metaphor

The same developmental concerns apply to claims of cognitive semantics about the origin of the tools of reasoning and abstract ideas. Lakoff (1987) admitted that the move to account for syntactic functioning by experiential semantics is risky. The rules of logic admit no exceptions, but semantic categories are fuzzy, particularly when they are created by metaphorical extension. Moreover, in discussing image schemata, he noted ". . . The fact that reasoning can be done with them does not prove that reasoning is done with them" (p. 459).

We can give Lakoff's (1987) caveat another construal. Even though metaphors can be used to construct abstract concepts and tools of thought, that neither proves that abstract concepts are constructed metaphorically or that the metaphors chosen by experiential realists are the child's first entry into particular abstract domains. In addition, the translation of meaningful images into formal rules requires a more detailed theory of the detection of similarities and mapping relations than cognitive semantics currently provides.

We use developmental research on children's knowledge of taxonomies to argue that knowledge of containers and part–whole relations may be insufficient to derive the formal logic of class inclusion. Because children do not exploit the full implications of the container schema we question whether it structures category formation or simply bolsters already present category knowledge. We also evaluate whether the part–whole schema is sufficient for understanding inclusion.

A Class as a Container.   We begin with the analogy between containers and categories as enclosures for instances that share some commonality. We argue that if the container schema structures our knowledge of categories, a body of implications should be present very early. The child should know that a category delimits objects belonging to a class from those that do not. But research on formation of classes shows a piecemeal emergence of this insight. During manipulative play, 12-month-olds sometimes touch similar objects in sequence. But they do not touch every similar item. When given a group containing one dissimilar toy, most 12- and 18-month-olds do not eliminate the offending exemplar. Even when these children form a class of similar objects (e.g., red), they do not immediately grasp that this class implies a complement (e.g., not red). It is not until a year later that most children systematically divide items into two contrasting categories (Sugarman, 1982). Yet another reason for doubting an image schema underlies understanding is that toddlers only group together items that are practically identical, as opposed to members of basic categories. The slow mastery of sorting skills does not suggest that the child's performance is automatically guided by a coherent theory of category extension based on some underlying schema. Perhaps the structure is there, but the child has difficulty mapping it.

Does containment help in forming categories? It does in a peculiar way. When asked to sort objects, young children are seduced by the manipulative potential of blocks and they create designs rather than categories. They fare much better when they sort items into bags (Markman, Cox, & Machida, 1981). Using an actual container focuses the child on the task of collection rather than the self-imposed task of design construction. Whether metaphorical containment plays the same role is dubious. Containers depict class boundaries, or class extension, without providing the intensional rule that sets the boundary by defining what is in the class. A jar may contain a heterogeneous mixture, but not an equivalence class.

Taxonomies as Part–Whole Structures. The fit of the part–whole metaphor and the container metaphor to class inclusion (Lakoff, 1987) is even less straightforward and the developmental course of application of the metaphor may not be linear. There are many kinds of part–whole relations. A pie can be sliced; a forest contains trees; a superordinate category has subclasses. Slices, trees, and subcategories are each parts. But cutting a pie into pieces destroys the totality, whereas acknowledging that oaks are trees may not have a similar impact. Young children sometimes fail class inclusion because they use the "pie" part–whole relation instead of the logical one (Inhelder & Piaget, 1964). A tree is part of a collective forest; it maintains its distinctive identity even when it is part of the total forest. The forest remains if a tree is cut down. The metaphorical structuring of subclasses as "members of a crowd" helps the 5-year-old to segregate the parts while maintaining the cohesion of the whole (Markman & Seibert, 1976). It might lead the child to envision the third variant on the relations of parts to wholes, abstract subcategories belonging to a more inclusive class, but the child will fall into logical error if the child thinks that the tree–forest relation is the same as the oak–tree relation. You can make inferences about an oak from your knowledge of trees. Do not try the same strategy with forests and trees. Thus the child has to figure out which part–whole image applies. The wrong interpretation would hamper the child, and only the conceptual part–whole one will enable the child to understand that class inclusion integrates both intensional and extensional relations.

Which aspect of a metaphor is relevant or generative? Lakoff (see, e.g., 1987) suggested that reasoner may not be constrained by one metaphor because part–whole, parent–child, and container schemata all apply to class inclusion. But in each case, only certain facets of the relation hold for inclusion relations, whereas others are irrelevant. Which does the child choose? There are several nonmetaphorical strategies for understanding inclusion, too (see Scholnick, 1983). For example, Johnson-Laird (1983) proposed a very direct means of computing categorical relations that relies on a conceptual model of intensional relations. There are multiple redundant ways of structuring the implications of taxonomic relations. Perhaps early in development, the child takes advantage of any or all of them to build category logic. Some of these metaphors will then prove to be more productive than others and the child must sort out the appropriate strategies for particular tasks. There is an intriguing story yet to be told about how these strategies are chosen, combined, and maybe even discarded during the course of development and during the solution of particular tasks.

Taxonomies as Containers.   Using a container as a metaphor for conceptualizing class inclusion raises another concern, the order of precedence. Which comes first, the understanding of the source or the target domain? Courses in logic teach us to convert class inclusion problems into spatial problems. Using nested and intersecting circles is a handy prop for solving categorical syllogisms. But the imposition of those schematic diagrams is an art for those who are verbal rather than spatial in their problem-solving strategies; the symbolism of sets is far from transparent. Perhaps, an intuitive grasp of category structure must exist before using the container metaphor; then the use of the metaphor further refines knowledge of categorical relations. Containers clarify the relative extension of the superordinate and subordinate classes. Fitting containers to class intension may require modification of the metaphor.

Are Abstract Domains Structured Metaphorically?   In the preceding section, we argued that it is not always clear that a familiar image schema initially structures reasoning. Similarly, some abstract domains may already be structured before the metaphor arises that might strengthen that structure. A case in point is the use of family relations and birth to structure ideas about causality, categorization, and mental life. Children's confusion about kinship relations (Piaget, 1991) makes it unlikely that they initially import that relation to understand taxonomies. Whether children use the knowledge of progeneration to understand mental causation is also somewhat problematical (Turner, 1987). By 4 years of age, children seem to be working on a theory of mind that links the outside world to thought and action (Astington, Harris, & Olson, 1988). But at the same age, their knowledge of the birth process is limited. They may not have an image schema of birth as a sudden bursting of something from nothing. They may be ignorant of the range of possible genetic combinations the act of conception could produce. Thus, whether and how they apply the model of birth to understanding the mind, indeterminacy, and qualitative change is hard to know. Again we suspect there is a reciprocal process in which growing knowledge of the source domain (birth) influences the choice of targets (mental life and qualitative change). As knowledge of both domains increases, a richer mapping occurs that elaborates each domain in ways consistent with their overlapping structure.

This developmental story suggests that the relative impact of knowledge and analogical reasoning differ during different phases of conceptual growth. It differs from cognitive semantics in invoking a fuller range of methods of knowledge acquisition in the initial structuring of certain domains. We have probably exaggerated the cognitive semantic position because we have been intrigued by their demonstrations of the ways in which abstract domains could be structured metaphorically. A weaker characterization of their theory is consistent with our approach. Analogies create new knowledge as well as bolster existing knowledge. The million dollar question is: "How do analogical reasoning and knowledge constrain and restructure each other during the course of conceptual development?"

ANOTHER ROUTE TO CONSTRUCTION
OF MEANING AND METAPHOR

Constructivism and Experiential Realism

Cognitive semantics is grounded in a particular form of constructivism. There is no objective reality. Instead, we construct models based on our meaningful embodied experiences. We then use the models to construct formal reasoning through such devices as metaphor. Logic is a product of imagination, not a product of progressive abstraction of form from content. The task for the child is finding the right metaphor. Currently, cognitive semantics presents lists of basic metaphors. Its model of the process by which those metaphors are accessed is considerably less detailed. The most prevalent explanation is that the process occurs by pattern matching and experiential covariation (Turner, 1991; see also chapter 3 of this volume). Little thought seems to have been given to the possibility that the mechanisms for detecting patterns and correlation might undergo development. Formal logic enters into cognitive semantics as a nuisance. We do not really need some parts of it to understand the world. Besides, if we needed logic to pass some required college courses, we could understand it best by evoking imaginative metaphors. Abstractions do occur but they occur through the accumulation of knowledge about basic categories that are then made more cohesive by the metaphorical creation of higher order ones. The givens of cognitive semantics are powerful cognitive tools for abstraction and extension and a lack of concern for form.

Our critique of cognitive semantics reflects a different, but not necessarily incompatible, philosophical stance. We in no way reject embodiment as a starting point for knowledge. We simply argue that embodiment and the tools for deriving and applying it develop. A theory of meaning must address not only the nature of core meanings but must address meaning as a developmental process from its origin. Nor can a theory of meaning be divorced entirely from a theory of application and processing of knowledge, each of which also has developmental components. Cognitive semantics implies inbuilt powerful engines for deriving, coordinating, and mapping knowledge. We are proposing instead something closer to what Falmagne (1990) called semantic bootstrapping in which meaning and form develop reciprocally, perhaps in some central domains of experience.

These concerns are most powerfully articulated by Piaget (1991; Piaget & Garcia, 1991) whose recent writings reveal the same constructivist agenda as cognitive semantics, the use of meaningful embodied action schemes to derive logic. Piaget (Piaget & Garcia, 1991) even used the same bodily experiences, inserting objects into the mouth, as the origin of category relations. However, he maintained that the construction of form is fundamental to knowledge. In his view, there are classical categories and invariant transformations with necessary consequences. It is no accident that Piaget tested his theory by having children explore and explain mathematical puzzles and the workings of mechanical apparatuses. These are the very content areas where formal classes and tools of reasoning exist. Because this is the case, the path from meaningful action to logical competence is not forged solely by imaginative projection but also by abstraction. The logic the child derives is not a frill but essential to developing understanding, because logic organizes understanding. Characteristically, Piaget argued forcefully that the instruments for the construction of meaning themselves have to be constructed.

What Is Meaning?

This is not the place to argue about the psychological reality of formal rules or the sufficiency of semantic analyses for accounting for cognitive growth (Overton, 1991; Scholnick, 1991). Instead, we wish to use some of Piaget's ideas to enrich the agenda of those who wish to study the development of meaning. Some of Piaget's ideas about the nature of meaning are implicit in cognitive semantics. The inspiration for some of the developmental concerns we have raised should also be apparent. The key issues are: What is it that we become knowledgeable about and how do we become knowledgeable?

Something is missing from cognitive semantics: the answer to the questions, Why does the child extract a particular image schema? What gives the image schema meaning? Piaget called the missing element *significant implication* (Inhelder & de Caprona, 1990; Overton, 1990). Meaning is understanding how an action changes (transforms) the world. Significant implication constructs the action-result regularities that image schemata represent. Thus, in order to understand the logic of action, the baby must first build contingencies based on the inference that certain actions rather than others produce specific results. The logic is based on discovery of a linking mechanism (note the similarity to Brown,

1990). Having a skin does not produce containment, but crossing a threshold into an enclosed space that limits further visual and motor exploration does. Children must first recognize that entrance has inevitable consequences, and eventually they must understand the reasons for those consequences stemming from the nature of barriers. Piaget proposed an extended timetable for the development of understanding of reasons, whereas cognitive semantics assumes rapid detection and understanding of regularities. We suspect that the construction of some image schemata may take longer than others and many image schemata are constantly reworked.

Transformation of Meaning and Morphisms

Second, understanding significant implication on the level of practical action does not constitute a mature conceptual space. Piaget suggested that when infants begin to grasp that actions have necessary consequences, they also infer that each action-consequent sequence is related to others. Inserting implies its inverse, extricating. But the implications are often local and fragmented. In order for the relations so derived to be accessible and cohesive, they have to be "lifted" to another plane of representation that allows more conscious reflection and more compiling and coordination of insight. Unlike the cognitive semantics approach, Piaget claimed that the translation of actions into signs and symbols is a qualitative change. Moreover, the implications of a give experience may not be automatically and unconsciously accessible for other cognitive tasks. Piaget and cognitive semanticists are perhaps extremes on a continuum between those who claim that analogy is powerful at the onset versus those who claim its power is constructed. The truth may lie in between these positions. Perhaps cognitive development is discovering the power of metaphors and cognitive developmentalists will learn much from observing how children make those discoveries.

The third Piagetian theme grows out of the second. The development of tools for abstraction, for organizing knowledge, and for analogical transfer are intermeshed. Meaning consists of actions on objects in the world. The transfer of those meaning schemes is limited by what the child knows about an object and about the causal mechanisms that affect the impact of actions. Growth in understanding the criteria by which objects can be substituted for others without violating an implicational schema permits wider transfer of knowledge. Nelson (1983) described the process as discovering first which objects can fill different slots and then inferring what the slot fillers have in common. Through experience with objects the child must learn to extract or "variablize" the essential form of the object (see similar comments by Anderson & Thompson, 1989). But the abstraction is limited by the child's grasp of the set of transformations the object can undergo and still remain itself. A familiar example is conservation. The first step in conservation is an awareness that one piece of clay can take many shapes. This leads to the insight that its amount remains invariant because the clay has merely been rearranged. That insight remains localized until children can substitute objects in the rearrangement scheme, such as milk poured into different beakers, or cubes rearranged into different towers. Even then, it may not be obvious that all the conservations are analogous because each is a product of a system of necessarily interconnected transformations. The state of knowledge, its abstraction, and use are intermeshed.

CONCLUSIONS

Current theory often equates development with knowledge. Babies are born equipped with powerful constraints that focus their attention on the relevant mechanisms that structure privileged domains. They are also born with the means to extract and apply that knowledge. But those theories are problematical because we lack a persuasive reason to claim that specific domains are privileged and that specific constraints organize the child's knowledge. There are no constraints on constraints. The claim that children rapidly develop intuitive theories of the world runs counter to data that suggest their knowledge is often localized and insufficiently detailed. To account for children's inadequacies we have invented a second kind of knowledge explanation: Children know, but they do not know that what they know is useful. Alternatively we reduce the gains of adulthood and claim mature individuals operate as imperfectly as children. Only true experts have cohesive, transportable knowledge. We eradicate development and eliminate learning.

Cognitive semantics accounts for the origin and growth of meaning. The theory is rooted in embodiment and metaphorical projection of embodied image schemata. This account specifies the privileged domains, the principles organizing the structure of knowledge for those domains, and the means of extending knowledge. But the story is based on an adult perspective.

In this chapter, we have suggested how to put development back into the story. Not all embodied relations are readymade, and the implications of embodied image schemata are not always obvious. The tools for abstracting meaning, analogy, and abstraction, and the meanings that result, are intermeshed. A satisfactory history of the interplay of meaning, analogy, and abstraction has yet to be written.

ACKNOWLEDGMENT

We wish to thank Kathleen Wallner, who shares our interest in these topics.

REFERENCES

Anderson, J. R., & Thompson, R. (1989). Use of analogy in a production system architecture. In S. Vosniadou & A. Ortony (Eds.), *Similarity and analogical reasoning* (pp. 267–297). Cambridge, MA: Cambridge University Press.

Astington, J. W., Harris, P. L., & Olson, D. R. (1988). *Developing theories of mind.* Cambridge, England: Cambridge University Press.

Baillargeon, R. (1987). Object permanence in 3.5- and 4.5-month-old infants. *Developmental Psychology, 23,* 655–664.

Brown, A. L. (1989). Analogical learning and transfer: What develops? In S. Vosniadou & A. Ortony (Eds.), *Similarity and analogical reasoning* (pp. 369–412). Cambridge, MA: Cambridge University Press.

Brown, A. L. (1990). Domain specific principles affect learning and transfer in children. *Cognitive Science, 14,* 107–133.

DeLoache, J., & Bryant, P. (1991). *In or out: Infants' understanding of containment.* Paper presented at the biennial meeting of the Society for Research in Child Development, Seattle.

Diamond, A. (1991). Neuropsychological insights into the meaning of object concept development. In S. Carey & R. Gelman (Eds.), *The epigenesis of mind: Essays on biology and cognition* (pp. 67–110). Hillsdale, NJ: Lawrence Erlbaum Associates.

Falmagne, R. (1990). Language and the acquisition of logical knowledge. In W. F. Overton (Ed.), *Reasoning, necessity, and knowledge: Developmental perspectives* (pp. 111–134). Hillsdale, NJ: Lawrence Erlbaum Associates.

Gelman, R. (1990). Structural constraints on cognitive development. *Cognitive Science, 3,* 3–10.

Gentner, D. (1988). Metaphor and structure mapping: The relational shift. *Child Development, 59,* 47–59.

Gentner, D. (1989). The mechanisms of analogical learning. In S. Vosniadou & A. Ortony (Eds.), *Similarity and analogical reasoning* (pp. 199–241). Cambridge, MA: Cambridge University Press.

Goswami, U. (1991). Analogical reasoning: What develops. A review of research and theory. *Child Development, 62,* 1–22.

Goswami, U., & Brown, A. L. (1989). Melting chocolate and melting snowmen: Analogical reasoning and causal relations. *Cognition, 35,* 69–95.

Holyoak, K. J., & Thagard, P. R. (1989). A computational model of analogical problem solving. In S. Vosniadou & A. Ortony (Eds.), *Similarity and analogical reasoning* (pp. 242–266). Cambridge, MA: Cambridge University Press.

Inhelder, B., & de Caprona, D. (1990). The role and meaning of structures in genetic epistemology. In W. F. Overton (Ed.), *Reasoning, necessity, and knowledge: Developmental perspectives* (pp. 33–44). Hillsdale, NJ: Lawrence Erlbaum Associates.

Inhelder, B., & Piaget, J. (1964). *The early growth of logic in the child.* New York: Norton.

Johnson, M. (1987). *The body in the mind.* Chicago: University of Chicago Press.

Johnson-Laird, P. N. (1983). *Mental models: Towards a cognitive science of language, inference, and consciousness.* Cambridge, MA: Harvard University Press.

Keil, F. (1990). Constraints on constraints: Surveying the epigenetic landscape. *Cognitive Science, 14,* 135–168.

Kuhn, T. S. (1962). *The structure of scientific revolutions.* Chicago: University of Chicago Press.

Lakoff, G. (1987). *Women, fire and dangerous things: What categories reveal about the mind.* Chicago: University of Chicago Press.

Lakoff, G., & Johnson, M. (1980). *Metaphors we live by.* Chicago: University of Chicago Press.

Lakoff, G., & Turner, M. (1989). *More than cool reason: A field guide to poetic metaphor.* Chicago: University of Chicago Press.

Markman, E. M., Cox, B., & Machida, S. (1981). The standard object sorting task as a measure of conceptual organization. *Developmental Psychology, 17,* 115–117.

Markman, E. M., & Seibert, J. (1976). Classes and collections: Internal organization and resulting holistic properties. *Cognitive Psychology, 8,* 561–577.

Mervis, C., & Rosch, E. (1981). Categorization of natural objects. *Annual Review of Psychology, 32,* 89–115.

Nelson, K. (1983). The derivation of concepts and categories from event representations. In E. K. Scholnick (Ed.), *New trends in conceptual representation: Challenges to Piaget's theory?* (pp. 41–70). Hillsdale, NJ: Lawrence Erlbaum Associates.

Overton, W. F. (1990). Competence and procedures; constraints on the development of logical reasoning. In W. F. Overton (Ed.), *Reasoning, necessity, and knowledge: Developmental perspectives* (pp. 1–32). Hillsdale, NJ: Lawrence Erlbaum Associates.

Overton, W. F. (1991). The structure of developmental theory. In H. W. Reese (Ed.), *Advances in child development and behavior* (Vol. 23, pp. 1–37). San Diego: Academic.

Piaget, J. (1991). *Morphisms and categories.* Hillsdale, NJ: Lawrence Erlbaum Associates.

Piaget, J., & Garcia, R. (1991). *Toward a logic of meanings.* Hillsdale, NJ: Lawrence Erlbaum Associates.

Scholnick, E. K. (1983). Why are new trends in conceptual representation a challenge to Piaget's theory? In E. K. Scholnick (Ed.), *New trends in conceptual representation: Challenges to Piaget's theory?* (pp. 41–70). Hillsdale, NJ: Lawrence Erlbaum Associates.

Scholnick, E. K. (1991). The development of world views: Towards future synthesis. In H. W. Reese (Ed.), *Advances in child development and behavior* (Vol. 23, pp. 49–58). San Diego: Academic.

Siegler, R. (1989). Mechanisms of cognitive development. *Annual Review of Psychology, 40,* 353–379.

Spelke, E. E. (1988). Where perceiving ends and thinking begins: The apprehension of objects in infancy. In A. Yonas (Ed.), *Perceptual development in infancy. Minnesota symposia on child psychology* (Vol. 20, pp. 191–234). Hillsdale, NJ: Lawrence Erlbaum Associates.

Spelke, E. E. (1990). Principles of object perception. *Cognitive Science, 14,* 57–78.

Spelke, E. E. (1991). Physical knowledge in infancy: Reflections on Piaget's theory. In S. Carey & R. Gelman (Eds.), *The epigenesis of mind: Essays on biology and cognition* (pp. 133–169). Hillsdale, NJ: Lawrence Erlbaum Associates.

Sternberg, R. J., & Nigro, G. (1980). Developmental patterns in the solution of verbal analogies. *Child Development, 51,* 27–38.

Sugarman, S. (1982). Developmental change in early representational intelligence: Evidence from spatial classification strategies and related verbal expressions. *Cognitive Psychology, 14,* 410–449.

Turner, M. (1987). *Death is the mother of beauty: Mind, metaphor and criticism.* Chicago: University of Chicago Press.

Turner, M. (1991). *Reading minds: The study of English in the age of cognitive science.* Princeton, NJ: Princeton University Press.

6

Word Meanings and What It Takes to Learn Them: Reflections on the Piaget–Chomsky Debate

Ray Jackendoff
Brandeis University

Many years after the fact, I finally got around to reading Piattelli-Palmerini (1980), the chronicle of the 1975 debate between Jean Piaget and Noam Chomsky, with the participation of many other interested parties. Being a deeply committed Chomskian, though not an altogether orthodox one, I was surprised by the vehemence of the debate. After all, Piaget and Chomsky have a great deal in common. Both believe in complex unconscious mental processing. Both believe that the structure of the world we experience is in large part determined by internal mental constructs of potentially great abstraction. Both are firmly opposed to behaviorism.

As far as I can determine, the major difference between the Piagetian and Chomskian traditions concerns what it takes to learn. Not a small part of the problem in the debate was that Chomsky's argument focused almost exclusively on complex details of the learning of syntax, about which Piaget had virtually nothing to say; likewise, Piaget's ground for argument was conceptual learning, about which Chomsky had virtually nothing to say. So the debate was not carried on in common territory, which led to a certain amount of the mutual misunderstanding and rancor.

Here I try to simplify the problem of learning presented by Chomsky and Fodor in the course of debate, and see where the main point of disagreement lies. Furthermore, I do it on a ground more recognizable by Piagetians, in the domain of concept learning, as revealed by the child's learning of word meanings. In order to do so, however, I have to present a rather lengthy excursus on what I think concepts and word meanings are.

THE REPERTOIRE OF CONCEPTS

How do I conceive of a word meaning? The only reasonable way anyone has been able to conceive of a word meaning within a cognitive theory is in terms of states of a combinatorial system, instantiated either in a system of symbols, or in a system of neurons, or in a system of neuronesque elements such as a connectionist network. Furthermore, the combination of word meanings into phrase and sentence meanings has to be governed by a combinatorial system that in some way more or less parallels the combinatorial properties of the syntax in which the phrases and sentences are expressed. This much has to be essentially unexceptionable.

To make this only slightly more concrete, I think of word meanings as instantiated in large part in a particular subsystem of the brain's combinatorial organization that I call *conceptual structure*. The relation of conceptual structure to mental organization as a whole is diagrammed in Fig. 6.1.

In order to alleviate potential misunderstanding, I should start by saying that the arrows in this figure do not stand for psychological processes that take place over time, but just for formal relations of *constraint* among different combinatorial structures. This notion of constraint becomes clearer shortly.

The full class of humanly possible concepts (or conceptual structures) is determined by the combinatorial principles of the conceptual well-formedness rules. That is, the conceptual well-formedness rules characterize the space of possible conceptual states—the resources available in the brain for forming concepts. The set of concepts attained by any particular person will be some subset of these. I am not concerned here with how concepts are instantiated by neurons in the brain; crucial as it is, I do not think we have any useful understanding of this issue at the moment. Rather, I want to keep stressing, I am interested in the properties of the combinatorial space available to the brain—what possibilities exist, and what concepts are related to what other concepts in what dimensions. This way of looking at things so far ought to be fairly comfortable to the Piagetian as well as to the Chomskian tradition.

What about the other three components in Fig. 6.1? First look at the inference rules. These are relations among conceptual structures, specifying how to pass from one concept to another. So, for instance, if you believe that X caused Y to take place, you can infer that Y took place; whereas by contrast if you believe that X **tried** to cause Y to take place, you cannot tell whether Y took place. These differences have to be expressed by the interaction between conceptual structures and the *rules of inference*. Incidentally, I include under the term rules of inference principles of pragmatics and heuristics; by contrast with much of the philosophical tradition, I do not think there is any serious difference between these and rules of logical inference (see Jackendoff, 1983, for discussion).

In addition, conceptual structures of course have to be linked by a principled set of *correspondence rules* to the mental representations that serve language: Conceptual structures are by hypothesis the form in which the meanings of

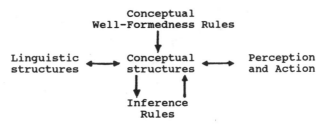

FIG. 6.1. The relation of conceptual structure to mental organization as a whole.

linguistic expressions must be couched internally. Finally, conceptual structures have to be linked by a different set of correspondence rules to the representations for perception and action, so that perceptual experience can be encoded in a form suitable for linguistic expression.

I should also point out that a combinatorial form like conceptual structure is necessary even for nonlinguistic cognition. For example, there is nothing in a perceptual representation as such that can encode the difference between, say, a particular dog Rover and a generic or stereotypical dog. That is, the difference between a token (or known individual) and a type (or category) is not a perceptual difference, but a conceptual one (see Jackendoff, 1983, chapter 5 and Jackendoff, 1987, chapter 10 for extended discussion). Therefore, I conceive of conceptual structure as a meeting ground between concrete perceptual and motor representations and abstract concepts, whether or not they are expressed linguistically.

In short, conceptual structures form a combinatorial space whose possibilities are determined by the well-formedness rules; a particular subset of conceptual structure is linked to language; different, possibly overlapping subsets are linked to perceptual and motor representations; and in addition, conceptual structures are linked to one another by rules of inference.

HOW WORDS MEAN

What is a word meaning, then? Under this view, a word meaning is a fragment of conceptual structure that is linked in long-term memory with a phonological structure (its pronunciation) and a syntactic structure (its part of speech and other syntactic properties such as grammatical gender and case-marking characteristics). That is, the words one knows consist of stored concepts linked with stored elements of linguistic expression.

So far there should be no great surprises. In particular, I have not ruled out the possibility that word meanings contain stereotypes, lexical extensions, citations of familiar instances, or a host of other possibilities suggested in the literature. All that is required is that if such phenomena are part of word meanings, the conceptual well-formedness rules must make them possible. That is, the expressive possibilities for word meanings, whatever they are, must be encompassed in the well-formedness rules.

In this story, a number of factors combine to make a word mean what it does. First is the connection of the concept expressed by the word to perception and action. If the word names an object, for instance, this connection links the concept to what the object looks like, tastes like, sounds like, and what actions can be performed on it; if the word names an action, this connection specifies what the action looks like, what it is like to perform the action, and so forth. This connection, then, is the present theory's counterpart of what the philosophical tradition calls the *reference* of the word. However, it concerns not the real-world counterpart of the concept but the *mental representations* linked to the concept in the perceptual and motor modalities. Note that not all words, nor all aspects of any particular word, are linked to perceptual or motor components. Many words and parts of word meanings are purely abstract, for instance the token-type distinction just mentioned, which has no perceptual counterpart. So referential linkage is clearly not all there is to word meanings.

A second crucial aspect of word meaning is its interaction with the inference rules. What makes the verb *approach* differ from the verb *reach*, for example? If you approach an object, you are going toward it, but you do not necessarily get there. By contrast, if you reach an object, you have been going toward it, and you have gotten there. This difference in inference, like the difference between causing and trying described previously, follows from a feature of "completive-ness" or "boundedness" in conceptual structure interacting with an inference rule that depends on the value of that feature. *Approach* and *try* are noncompletive or unbounded actions, so one cannot infer the final state of the action; whereas *reach* and *cause* are completive or bounded actions, so one can infer the final goal. (See Jackendoff, 1991, for a more precise description.)

A third factor contributing to a word's meaning is its relationship to the rest of the lexicon. For instance, consider the taxonomic relations between *dog* and *animal* in one direction and between *dog* and *poodle* in the other direction. These links within the lexicon form concepts into hierarchies, and they are an important part of our conceptual knowledge; again, they often cannot be specified perceptually. In addition, a well-known phenomenon within these intralexical relations is the tendency of the sisters in a taxonomy to expand their range of applicability to fill gaps between them. For instance, whatever the class of focal color words in a language, each focal color word can be applied to any other colors sufficiently near to the focal color and sufficiently distant from the others (Berlin & Kay, 1969; Miller & Johnson-Laird, 1976). What this means is that in a language with more focal color words, each of the focal color words automatically has a narrower range of application. This does not follow from any perceptual facts or from any inference rules—it follows from the taxonomic structure of the lexicon.

A fourth aspect of word meanings concerns the interaction of the word with the grammatical patterns of the language. For instance, a number of people (e.g., Anderson, 1971; Pinker, 1989; Rappaport & Levin, 1985; Tenny, 1987) have noted that certain verbs vary in completiveness depending on the syntactic pattern in which they appear. A well-known example is the verb *to load*. If I *load a truck with furniture*, the implication is that the truck is full of furniture at the end—that is, the sentence is completive. But if I express a similar action as *loading furniture onto a truck*, there is no necessary implication that the truck is full at the end. A similar alternation occurs with a wide range of verbs, suggesting that the grammatical pattern itself is carrying an element of meaning that interacts with the meaning of the verb to make the inference possible.

In short, each of the components that constrains conceptual structure—the well-formedness rules, the inference rules, and the connections to grammatical expression and to nonlinguistic modalities, as well as the repertoire of related words in the lexicon—has an effect on the meaning of a word, and on how it is used and understood in linguistic and nonlinguistic contexts.

LEARNED AND INNATE COMPONENTS
OF WORD MEANING

What does this have to do with the debate between Piaget and Chomsky? As I said earlier, the major issue that separates them, I think, is the nature of learning. In order for me to address this issue, I have to ask: In the present approach to word meanings, what is entailed in a child (or an adult) learning a new word meaning?

Very abstractly, we have to think of the child selecting a conceptual structure for the word and linking it with a linguistic expression (i.e., with a phonological and a syntactic structure). At the same time, if the concept is completely or partially concrete (i.e., has perceptual or motor counterparts), those linkages too must be established in order to achieve competence at using the word.

But what determines the possible concepts that the learner can consider? At bottom, the possibilities are constrained by the conceptual well-formedness rules, which are by hypothesis the resources that make possible all humanly attainable concepts. Now the point that is crucial to notice here, and the place in the argument where many people get caught, is the question of where the conceptual well-formedness rules come from. The point is that they cannot be learned: They are the foundation on which learning is based. This is an argument that in its modern form is due to Jerry Fodor (1975), but its basic idea goes back probably to Kant. What does this mean? In essence, it means that the conceptual well-formedness rules have to be innate—part of the wiring of the brain. If you like, the conceptual well-formedness rules specify what kind of a computer the part of the brain is that deals with conceptual structure. In turn, this wiring must be determined by some as yet unknown combination of genetic structure and the principles of neural growth, about which no one has anything useful to say at the moment, as far as I know.

By using the word *innate* I undoubtedly have raised some readers' hackles. Many people, for various reasons, have a strong objection to the idea that brain structure (and therefore mental structure) could be to any significant degree innate. And of course it is Chomsky's contentions about innateness that have enamored—and enraged—different segments of the psychological and philosophical communities. But again, so far I have not said very much that should be controversial. As Fodor (1975) points out, everyone believes in *some* degree of innateness. For the most extreme case, suppose you are an unreconstructed associationist. Then, within this way of describing things, you believe in effect that the conceptual well-formedness rules encompass the space of possibilities provided by sense data, plus the combination of elements of that space by the principle of association. But children do not learn to have sense data and they do not learn to form associations; these have to be given as the innate substrate from which learning can proceed.

So the real issue has to be not: Is the space of possible concepts constrained by a set of innate principles? because everyone turns out to believe that it is. Rather, the issue is: How specific and detailed is the set of innate principles, and what are the specifics and details? So it is a matter of degree, not one of absolutes, and one can find positions all along the spectrum. At one end, perhaps, fall the unreconstructed associationists. Perhaps at the other end is Jerry Fodor himself, who at least in some of his incarnations (Fodor, 1975, 1981; Fodor, Garrett, Walker, & Parkes, 1980) believes that all word meanings are innate in complete detail, and there is no such thing as word learning. That is, for Fodor, the conceptual well-formedness rules in effect contain a vast *list* of complete word meanings.

I, for one, find Fodor's position untenable. All serious research on lexical organization confirms common sense in suggesting that word meanings are composite—that they are built up from some set of conceptual primitives and principles of combination. On this view, then, learning a word meaning is to be viewed as *constructing* some structured combination out of the primitives and principles of combination available in the conceptual well-formedness rules. Word learning is therefore conceived of as an active constructive process, not just a passive process of association—a conception shared by the Piagetian school.

But, on the other side of the coin, one must bear in mind that the child cannot learn the primitives themselves. Put differently, one cannot simultaneously claim both that something is a primitive and that it is learned, for learning entails construction from primitives. If I were to claim that some conceptual unit is a primitive, and it turned out to be learned, I would have no choice but to change my claim and to look for a deeper or more primitive set of basic units from which my unit could be constructed. This is a simple point of the logic of combinatorial systems.

In particular—and this too just follows from the logic of combinatorial systems—a particular set of primitives and principles of combination creates a space of possible concepts. This space is perhaps infinite, but it will have a certain number of inherent dimensions or degrees of freedom that follow from the innate basis (or the axioms, if you like) out of which it is generated. If one wants to add a new degree of freedom to the space, one has to add a new primitive to the innate basis. There is logically no way around this.

So an important empirical issue is: What is a plausible set of innate primitives and principles of combination that on one hand creates the space of concepts possible for adults, and that on the other hand makes this space of concepts learnable for the child?

One of the important hypotheses of Piaget is that children acquire their repertoire of concepts in a certain order, starting with basic sensorimotor concepts and gradually progressing from them to more abstract domains, eventually arriving at the most abstract concepts of pure logic. Piaget (1970), as I understand him, claimed that this progression or "passage from one stage to another" is a product of a construction or invention that is ultimately based on the original sensorimotor concepts. It is not based on anything "innate," but is just "the result of development" (p. 47). He contested the view of the "nativist or apriorist [who] maintains that the forms of knowledge are predetermined inside the subject and thus . . . , strictly speaking, there can be no novelty" (p. 77).

Notice, by the way, that Piaget (1970) somewhat overstated the nativist position, outside of the extreme Fodorian view that all word meanings are innate in toto. If what is innate is a set of conceptual well-formedness rules, that is, a set of primitives and principles of combination, then this set provides an infinite number of possible concepts, only some finite number of which is attained by any particular human being. This means that within the system there are always new concepts to be constructed that no one has had before. That is, there can be a great amount of novelty in concepts, even if there is none in the potential expressive power of the system.

Interestingly, a view similar to Piaget's (1970) has been espoused recently in the work of George Lakoff (Lakoff, 1987, 1990; Lakoff & Turner, 1989; see also chapter 3 of this volume), who claims that abstract concepts are constructed by means of a process of "metaphor" from a basis of concrete perceptual concepts. Lakoff too rejects the need for positing any innate basis for abstract concepts themselves. Although Lakoff does not as far as I know cite Piaget, his theory of metaphor is easily interpreted as one realization of Piaget's theory of genetic epistemology (see chapter 5 of this volume). For example, just like Piaget (1966), Lakoff has argued (1987) that mathematical concepts arise from basic sensori-motor or "embodied" operations, and he argues that the process bringing about this evolution is metaphor. So this issue is not confined to the Piagetian school.

I believe Piaget is correct in seeing a connection between sensorimotor concepts and abstract ones (Jackendoff, 1976, 1983). On the other hand, I believe that Piaget, and with him Lakoff, have not examined the process of extension quite closely enough, and that a crucial logical part of the process is being missed.

To illustrate this point, I want to look at a particular case in which there is a relation of spatial concepts to another domain, and I want to pick apart very carefully what can be learned and what has to be innate. I argue that in this case an extension of spatial concepts to this new domain cannot take place unless some aspects of the domain are already made available by the primitives of conceptual structure; that is, that they are innate. Therefore, even if Piaget and Lakoff are correct in thinking that abstract concepts are built by extending perceptual concepts, they are not correct in claiming that the abstract concepts therefore need no innate basis.

A TEST CASE: CONCEPTS OF OWNERSHIP

That is where the argument is going. To motivate it, we have to look at some facts. The domain we examine is concepts of *ownership* and especially *change of ownership*. Example 1 gives some expressions in this domain:

Example 1
a. Bill gave a book *to* Harry.
   Harry donated the book *to* the library.
b. Harry received/got a book *from* Bill.
c. The book was a present/gift *from* Bill *to* Harry.
d. Harry gave the book *back* to Bill.
   Bill got the book *back* from Harry.
e. Bill gave the book *away*.

Notice that the italicized words in Example 1 also appear in sentences about spatial motion, as in Example 2:

Example 2
a. Bill went *to* the store.
   Bill threw the ball *to* Harry.
b. Harry came *from* the store.
   Bill brought a newspaper *from* the store.
c. We were on a train *from* Boston *to* Philadelphia.
d. Then we went *back* to Boston.
   We came *back* from Philadelphia.
e. Bill pushed the food *away*.

In both cases, there is an entity that undergoes change: In the sentences in Example 1, the book changes possession; in Example 2, a variety of things change location. In both cases, the object of the preposition *to* is associated with the final state of the change: the possessor at the end of the events described in Example 1, the final location of the motions described in Example 2. Similarly, the object of the preposition *from* is associated with the initial state of the change: the possessor at the beginning of the events described in Example 1, the starting point of motion in the events described in Example 2. The use of the adverb *back* in both cases suggests that the change actually involves a return to an earlier starting point that precedes the described event, either the previous possessor in Example 1 or the previous location in Example 2. Finally, the use of *away* indicates a change whose initial point is either possession by the subject of sentence 1e or location at or near the subject of sentence 2e and whose final point is some other unspecified possessor or location.

The parallelism goes a little further. We can use the verb *go* not only to describe physical motion in space, but under certain circumstances change of possession, as in Example 3:

Example 3
The inheritance went to Philip.

The verb *keep* can be used to describe either causing something to stay in a physical location over a period of time, as in Example 4a, or deliberate possession over a period of time, as in Example 4b:

Example 4
a. Harry kept the book on the shelf.
b. Harry kept the book.

The verb *be* can be used to indicate either spatial position (Example 5a) or possession (Example 5b):

Example 5
a. Harry *is* in Camden.
b. The book *is* Harry's.

In many languages, for example French, this last parallelism is even stronger, in that even the same preposition is used, as in Example 6:

Example 6
a. Harry *est à* Camden.
b. Le livre *est à* Harry.

What do we make of this linguistic parallelism? It is duplicated in language after language, so it does not look like just a sheer accident of English grammar or of the history of English. Rather, as many different people have suggested, the grammatical parallelism we observe here is a reflection of a parallelism in the conceptual structure underlying these expressions. The conceptual parallelism proceeds like this:

X is in physical location Y therefore	parallels	X belongs to Y
Change in physical location of X	parallels	Change in possessor of X
Initial location of X	parallels	Initial possessor of X
Final location of X	parallels	Final possessor of X
Return to previous location of X	parallels	Return to previous possessor of X
Unspecified different location of X	parallels	Unspecified different possessor of X
Caused stasis in X's location	parallels	Caused stasis in X's owner

That is, the initial conceptual parallelism induces a whole system of parallelisms, which show themselves linguistically as parallelism in use of various verbs, prepositions, and adverbs.

Suppose, then, that there is this conceptual parallelism that accounts for the linguistic parallelism. But what accounts for the conceptual parallelism? To start with, observe that spatial location goes roughly under the rubric of a sensorimotor concept, but ownership definitely does not: There is no general way of telling who an object belongs to by looking at it and at its context. That is, ownership is surely an abstract concept. Therefore, according to Piagetian genetic epistemology, one would guess that the child learns the system of concepts surrounding ownership and change in ownership by some suitable extension or abstraction or progression from the understanding of location and motion in space. Similarly, I assume that Lakoff would want to claim that the domain of spatial location and motion constitutes a metaphor for possession and change of possession. In either case, the idea is that the child, having understood spatial concepts, becomes capable of constructing possessional concepts from spatial concepts by some process of conceptual extension. But possessional concepts are not themselves innate.

Under this assumption, let us (artificially) suppose that a child's learning goes in two stages: At Stage 1 the child has acquired spatial concepts but not possessional concepts, and at Stage 2 possessional concepts are present as well. How does the child get from Stage 1 to Stage 2?

Let us suppose further that the child can observe the grammatical parallelisms in the expression of spatial and possessional concepts. Then when he or she hears a sentence like *Give the doll to Harry*, not knowing the possessional sense of the word *give*, he or she may guess from the use of the preposition *to* that the speaker wishes him or her to cause the doll to move spatially so that its final position is next to Harry. However, this knowledge will not enable the child to guess that he or she necessarily is supposed to let go of the doll or relinquish control of it, which is part of the meaning conveyed by *give*. (Compare *Give the doll to Harry* to a truly spatial sentence like *Take the doll over to the sofa*, which carries no implications of relinquishing control.) Furthermore, about the only possible concept available to the child in the spatial domain for *The doll is mine* is that the doll is in spatial proximity to me.

Now it is true that spatial proximity is often a physical cue for ownership: *My* clothes are usually on *me*, and *yours* are on *you*, for example. How will the child get the idea that ownership is something different from spatial proximity? Perhaps someone says: *Put the doll down, it's mine, not yours*. The child can infer that his or her own spatial proximity to the doll is not sufficient for ownership; that is, that the concept of ownership is not spatial.

What next? With what concept shall the child replace the incorrect spatial interpretation of ownership? Suppose, following Piaget and Lakoff, that no abstract concepts are innate. In the terms that I have stated the problem, this means that the conceptual well-formedness rules provide no possibilities for abstract concepts. Then the child is in a pickle, for there is no way he or she can ever achieve the concept of possession: The space of possibilities simply does not contain a notion of ownership—it cannot be constructed from any combination of spatial primitives.[1]

One might try a different explanation: that what is innate is completely general and unstructured, and that possession falls out as a reasonable possibility when spatial location is rejected. There are two problems with this: First, what does "completely general" mean? If possession is not a primitive, out of what completely general primitives is it constructed? Are we back to association again, which we know is inadequate? And second, of all the millions of possible concepts putatively available in a "completely general" system, how does the child manage to pick possession?

Let us see how difficult this concept would be to pick out of a "completely general" system, even if one could state one. Very roughly, if *X* owns *Y*, three things follow:

1. *X* has a right to use *Y*.
2. Nobody else has a right to use *Y* without *X*'s permission.
3. *X* and only *X* has the right to assign rights 1 and 2 to another individual, at which point *X* does not have these rights to *Y* anymore.

---

[1]Lakoff (personal communication, at the conference) suggested that the relevant physical basis for possession is not spatial proximity but rather holding or grasping, and that the notion of physical control generalizes or extends to social control, of which possession is one particular form. But the very same problem arises: Social control simply is not physical control; some new abstract notion must be introduced that makes this concept available. In addition, the grammatical expressions of holding and grasping do not display the parallels to possession seen in Example 2, so the child would have no grammatical basis for a "metaphorical" extension, as is possible in the present analysis.

The child must discover a concept with these very inferences, from a space of millions of possibilities that by hypothesis has no innate organization. But consider the content of these inferences: The notions of rights and of permission—and of the right to assign rights—are incredibly abstract, and do not follow at all from the spatial parallel. How is the child supposed to discover them in an unstructured class of possibilities, just by using extension or metaphor?

In addition, the parallels between physical space and possession are very strictly limited. Physical space is of course three-dimensional, so an object can move *up*, *down*, *frontwards*, *backward*, and *sideways*. By contrast, the possessional parallel has no dimensions: You cannot *give* something *upwards* or *frontwards*. Physical space is continuous: If something moves from Point A to Point B, it occupies all the intermediate positions between A and B along the way. By contrast, the possessional parallel is discontinuous: There are no intermediate positions that an object traverses between being owned by X and being owned by Y. One can *move* a book *toward* or even *partway toward* Bill; but you cannot *give* a book *toward*, much less *partway toward* Bill.

If the notion of possession is constructed simply by extending spatial concepts, why are there these striking differences? And if it is constructed by a "general-purpose" system, how does the child happen to construct this particular possibility, with these particular inferences, out of the millions of algebraic possibilities, given that there is no definitive sensory input that picks out this choice?

I would like to suggest an alternative, which flows from what has been called (for reasons that need not concern us here) the Thematic Relations Hypothesis (Jackendoff, 1976, 1983). This hypothesis claims that the parallelism between spatial and possessional concepts is the result of three independent factors. The first is the conception of physical space and of objects being located in it; this is presumably fairly hard-wired and connected to the perceptual system. (It is not clear that Piaget would have accepted even this as innate, but never mind; contemporary developmental evidence—e.g., Spelke, 1983—suggests that at least a lot of it is.) The second factor is the notion of possession—a relation between a possessed object and a person, the possessor. We discuss shortly to what degree this might be innate, but fundamentally I think some version of it has to be.

The third and crucial factor involved in the parallelism is an innate abstract organizing system for concepts that elaborates a simple stative relation into a full system of concepts for change over time, beginning points, ending points, stasis, and so forth. This abstract system admits of different realizations, among which are the conceptual systems for space and for possession. This theory is compared very schematically with the theory of spatial extension or spatial metaphor in Fig. 6.2.

Let us see how on this story a child might progress from Stage 1, knowing only spatial language, to Stage 2, knowing possessional language as well. At Stage 1, the child understands, for instance, that the object of *from* indicates the initial point of motion and that the object of *to* indicates the final point of motion.

Piaget/Lakoff

spatial concepts ──▶ possessional concepts

Thematic Relations Hypothesis

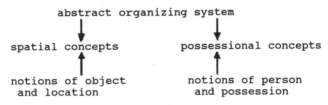

FIG. 6.2. The extension of spatial concepts to possessional concepts: Piaget/Lakoff versus the thematic relations hypothesis.

The child has presumably constructed this linkage by associating spatial language with perceivable events of location and motion. Now, recall the crucial point when the child receives evidence that *give the doll to Harry* implies something other than spatial movement. At this point, the conceptual well-formedness rules provide a salient alternative for the relation in question, namely possession. Furthermore, once the child has "discovered" the notion of possession among the innate stock of primitives, the abstract organizing system immediately tells the child how to use known grammatical structures to organize this system, for instance that the object of *from* indicates an initial possessor and the object of *to* indicates a final possessor. That is, given the initial innate "germ" for the system of possession, the spatial parallel permits the child to immediately induce the meaning of the grammatical expressions for possessional concepts.

On the other hand, the child would not expect a full parallelism with spatial expressions, because the notion of location in physical space ranges over three continuous orthogonal degrees of freedom, whereas what we might call "possessional space" ranges over the discontinuous unstructured set of individuals.

In short, although at first glance it looks as if the child is learning by a process of "metaphor," this is not actually the case; the parallelism between the two fields plays a somewhat different role in learning. And, as I have tried to show, the child cannot use the parallel to construct a new field unless the well-formedness rules make the germ of the new field available.

On the other hand, Piaget may well be right that the child has to understand spatial language before possessional language. Why? The reason is that the referential status of spatial terms allows the child to associate the grammatical patterns of the language with the abstract organizing system, and without this association there is no way to get into the organization of the abstract possessional concepts, where nothing can be observed directly. More generally, this is why sensorimotor concepts provide the anchor for the learning of abstract concepts.

Looking at possession a little more closely, I certainly do not want to claim that the American or European notions of ownership are totally innate; there are certainly wide cultural variations. However, as far as I know, all cultures have a concept of ownership or property rights that can be seen as a variation of ours, varying in what kinds of things you can own, what that entitles you to, and some variants in the exact details of the inferences (e.g., whether you have the right to give away your land). I think these variations can probably be learned from observation or instruction. But, as I am continuing to emphasize, the fundamental relation of possession and the fundamental notion of a right cannot be learned from observation or instruction—they have to be available innately in the conceptual well-formedness rules in order to be on one hand culturally universal and on the other hand culturally modulated.

Some people may find themselves incredulous at the idea that a concept as abstract and eccentric as possession is innate—hard-wired in the brain. We can understand how a hard-wired set of spatial concepts could have evolved to solve longstanding problems of navigation, but the evolution of a notion of possession seems less inherently plausible. I have three lines of reply. First, the formal analysis of combinatorial systems, which this chapter began with, shows that possessional concepts cannot be derived from spatial concepts alone, without adding something else. Second, the way evolution typically works is by innovating some weird little eccentric device, not by innovating big general-purpose systems. So the evolution of an eccentric domain of possession is on evolutionary grounds more plausible than that of a totally general-purpose problem solver, which is in any event likely to be inadequate to the task of learning the notion of possession. Third, the notion of possession is tremendously fundamental to human culture—this abstraction and its inferences is one of a very small number of major issues around which each culture constructs its equivalent of a legal system. It is hard even to imagine what a society would be like in which this concept was fundamentally altered—you might even say that Karl Marx tried to imagine such a society, and in practice it did not exactly work out. So, eccentric and abstract as the concept of possession may be, there are a lot of independent reasons to think it is a basic part of human nature.

CONCLUSIONS

This ends my story about the relation of spatial location and possession. The larger point I want to make from this is that the very same story has to be true for *any* kind of concept learning. In order for a child to acquire concepts in a new domain, this domain must be within the space of possibilities provided by the conceptual well-formedness rules. In other words, we must understand Piaget's theory of genetic epistemology via conceptual extension, as well as Lakoff's theory of conceptual learning via metaphorical extension, in a somewhat different way. We have to think of the child as applying an abstract combinatorial system, evoked by the original field, to a previously specified and probably innate "germ" concept for the new field. The process of abstracting away from the original field thus amounts to pulling the combinatorial system off so it can be applied elsewhere. (See Jackendoff & Aaron, 1991, for further discussion of Lakoff's theory of metaphor and its relation to the Thematic Relations Hypothesis.)

Still more generally, I think this is the point Chomsky and Fodor were trying to make in the Piaget–Chomsky debate. Whatever mental processes generalize to new domains, be they association, assimilation and accommodation, inference patterns, or symbolic structure, the domain these processes generalize to cannot be created out of whole cloth. Rather, one should think in terms of a new domain being, if you like, "discovered": A previously unsalient or unnoticed possible germ concept is evoked and instantiated in the system of actual concepts, then the existing abstract organizing system is applied to it to construct the entire conceptual domain.

This seems to me a reasonably realistic way to view learning, and one congenial with the overall Piagetian outlook. In particular, like the Piagetian view, it considers conceptual innovation as constructive and even creative. The only part possibly not congenial is the issue of innateness; but much of what I think Piaget objected to in innateness has been drained out. In particular, if we think of conceptual structure as constructed from an innate combinatorial system, a great deal of novelty is indeed possible, because the system provides an infinite number of possibilities, only one small fragment of which are actually realized by any single human being.

To recapitulate, then, I want to stress that the issue ought not to be: How can we account for learning without falling back on innateness? but rather the less prejudged question: How can we account for learning at all, and how much of it relies on an innate basis? From such a standpoint, our competing schools of thought can see potential disagreements not as incontestable matters of faith but as matters of degree, hence negotiable. Perhaps this can lead to making some progress together.

ACKNOWLEDGMENTS

This chapter has appeared also in my collection *Languages of the Mind* (MIT Press, 1992), and is reproduced in slightly different form here by permission. I am grateful to John Macnamara for extensive discussion of the issues, and to David Palermo and George Lakoff for useful comments on the version presented at the conference.

REFERENCES

Anderson, S. (1971). On the role of deep structure in semantic interpretation. *Foundations of Language, 6*, 387–396.

Berlin, B., & Kay, P. (1969). *Basic color terms: Their universality and evolution*. Berkeley: University of California Press.

Fodor, J. (1975). *The language of thought.* Cambridge, MA: Harvard University Press.

Fodor, J. (1981). The present status of the innateness controversy. In J. Fodor (Ed.), *Representations* (pp. 257–316). Cambridge, MA: Bradford/MIT Press.

Fodor, J., Garrett, M., Walker, E., & Parkes, C. (1980). Against definitions. *Cognition, 8,* 263–367.

Jackendoff, R. (1976). Toward an explanatory semantic representation. *Linguistic Inquiry, 7*(1), 89–150.

Jackendoff, R. (1983). *Semantics and cognition.* Cambridge, MA: MIT Press.

Jackendoff, R. (1987). *Consciousness and the computational mind.* Cambridge, MA: MIT Press.

Jackendoff, R. (1991). Parts and boundaries. *Cognition, 41,* 9–45.

Jackendoff, R., & Aaron, D. (1991). Review of Lakoff and Turner (1989). *Language, 67*(2), 320–338.

Lakoff, G. (1987). *Women, fire, and dangerous things.* Chicago: University of Chicago Press.

Lakoff, G. (1990). The invariance hypothesis: Is abstract reasoning based on image-schemas? *Cognitive Linguistics, 1*(1), 39–74.

Lakoff, G., & Turner, M. (1989). *More than cool reason: A field guide to poetic metaphor.* Chicago: University of Chicago Press.

Miller, G., & Johnson-Laird, P. (1976). *Language and perception.* Cambridge, MA: Harvard University Press.

Piaget, J. (1966). *Psychology of intelligence.* Totowa, NJ: Littlefield, Adams.

Piaget, J. (1970). *Genetic epistemology.* New York: Columbia University Press.

Piattelli-Palmerini, M. (Ed.). (1980). *Language and learning: The debate between Jean Piaget and Noam Chomsky.* Cambridge, MA: Harvard University Press.

Pinker, S. (1989). *Learnability and cognition: The acquisition of argument structure.* Cambridge, MA: Bradford/MIT Press.

Rappaport, M., & Levin, B. (1985). *The locative alternation: A case study in lexical analysis.* Unpublished manuscript, MIT, Center for Cognitive Science, Cambridge, MA.

Spelke, E. (1983). Perception of unity, persistence, and identity: Thoughts on infants' conceptions of objects. In J. Mehler (Ed.), *Infant and neonate cognition.* Hillsdale, NJ: Lawrence Erlbaum Associates.

Tenny, C. (1987). *Grammaticalizing aspect and affectedness.* Unpublished doctoral dissertation, MIT, Cambridge, MA.

7

The Foundations of Logic and the Foundations of Cognition

John Macnamara
McGill University

Jean Piaget stands almost alone among modern psychologists in his use of logic. Logic is the language in which he expressed his theory of cognition and the tool he uses to explore cognition more deeply—see, for example, Piaget (1953) and Inhelder and Piaget (1958). True, there were problems with his particular choice of logic and the use he made of it—see Ennis (1977). Nevertheless, he took logic seriously and in this he was fully justified. This chapter is an attempt to explore further the relations between the foundations of logic and the foundations of cognition. I hope to show that Piaget's intuition can be carried further than he imagined and that in carrying it further the foundations of both cognitive psychology and logic are greatly illuminated. All of the ideas of this chapter were developed in close collaboration with Gonzalo and Marie Reyes, and I would like to acknowledge their contribution at the outset.

The plan of the chapter is as follows. After an introductory section on the relations between logic and psychology I offer a little historical background to my theme: that logic is to cognitive psychology as calculus is to dynamics. In developing the theme, I briefly present the argument of Macnamara (1986) that logic is highly relevant to cognitive psychology. I then go on to argue that logic will be enriched by application to cognitive psychology, just as mathematics was enriched by applications in dynamics. I then go on to explain that my position is not psychologistic—the logic envisaged does not describe mental states, nor are the logic's principles justified by appeal to cognitive psychology. The approach I advocate supplements traditional approaches and so I go on to describe the additional sources of evidence. Throughout, I try to relate my thinking to cognitive development in children and to language learning in childhood. The chapter ends with a statement that places the diverse elements of the chapter in perspective.

Over the broad expanse of psychology the received position is that logic and psychology have little or nothing to do with one another. This position, adopted at the turn of the last century, is the result of two events. One was the divorce between philosophy and psychology. In the settlement after the divorce the test of specifying standards of correct inference went to philosophy, whereas to psychology went what were viewed as the facts of mental life. In other words logic was viewed as the property of philosophy, not of psychology.

The second event was the close of the psychologism debate. That was the debate about the proper relation between logic and psychology. One side maintained that the foundations of logic rest on a psychological basis; that the truth of logical claims and the soundness of logical inference rules are guaranteed by the facts of psychology. This position in its full strength seems to originate with Jakob Fries (1783–1844) and Friedrich Beneke (1798–1854) and was shared by many 19th century logicians including John Stuart Mill. The debate was settled to most people's satisfaction by the appearance of two books: Gottlob Frege (1884/1959), *The Foundations of Arithmetic*; Edmund Husserl (1900/1970), *Logical Investigations*. These books argued that:

1. Logic does not derive its basic principles from psychology.
2. Logic does not describe psychological states and events.

Elliott Sober (1978) captured something of the atmosphere of the times when he said, "While the psychologists were leaving, philosophers were slamming the door behind them." This shows up in a third position, which Susan Haack (1978) attributed to Frege:

3. "Logic has nothing to do with mental processes" (p. 238).

Although Frege certainly argued that logic had nothing to learn from psychology, it is not at all clear that he denied that psychology could learn from logic, as Notturno (1984) pointed out.

For all that, the third statement describes well how psychologists regard logic. A search through some of the better known handbooks of psychology and cognitive science reveals either a total neglect of logic or the attitude that at best logic is a quarry from which to wrest hypotheses for experimental investigation of human thought processes. An exception already mentioned is the work of Jean Piaget, though he frequently attributed to children illogical schemata and inference rules, thus rendering the emergence of logically sound ones totally mysterious. One of the few psychologists to write about the psychologism debate is George

Humphrey. In his influential book *Thinking* (1951), he claimed that Husserl's polemic against psychologism had "freed psychology from the shackles of logic" (p. 78). George Miller (1951) in the same year put the relation between the two disciplines as follows: "The fact is that logic is a formal system, just as arithmetic is a formal system, and to expect untrained subjects to think logically is much the same as to expect preschool children to know the multiplication table" (p. 806).

As we see later, not all psychologists agree with Miller. At the same time no psychology department, so far as I know, insists that its students study logic. The only formal tool insisted on for psychology students is statistics, which curiously does not enter the theory of psychology. The only formal tool insisted on for philosophy students is logic, where logic frequently plays an essential role in the theory. Philosophers seem to think that logic is useful for exploring and expressing certain standards of perfection that apply to human reasoning. Because psychologists by and large have eschewed such standards, they see little need for an education in logic.

My thesis is that logic and psychology mutually constrain each other in something like the way mathematics and physics constrain each other. Calculus, for example, was invented to express and handle concepts that are required in the study of physical forces and the movement of physical bodies. For all that calculus is an analysis of mathematical continua; not of physical bodies or their movement in physical space. Calculus, then, has a mathematical life of its own apart from mechanics. At the same time calculus is essential to the theory of mechanics in two ways: It is the principle language in which to express the theory (witness Hamilton's equations and Schrödinger's equations); it is the main conceptual tool that constrains the construction and testing of theory. Similarly, I hope to show, logic is an essential constituent of the theory of cognition; it supplies the appropriate mathematical language in which to express cognitive properties and processes and the appropriate mathematical instrument with which to explore them further. The properties and processes in question involve the ability to interpret symbols and to grasp the implicational relations among sentences. For all that, logic has a mathematical life of its own. Logic is no more cognition than calculus is mechanics. This, although logic is set up to express and handle the interpretation of symbols and the implications among sentences. In short, logic and cognition constrain each other as calculus and mechanics do. We can express this insight dramatically by

$$\frac{\text{Logic}}{\text{Cognitive Psychology}} = \frac{\text{Calculus}}{\text{Dynamics}}$$

This position is rather different from that of either Lakoff or Jackendoff (see chapters 3 and 6 of this volume, respectively). The main difference is that we take reference seriously and explore attentively models for natural language expressions and for the cognitive states that are expressed through them. Lakoff, in contrast, is a nominalist who takes a word like *dog* as picking out "an ˅aginative projection" (see Lakoff, 1988, p. 121). In other words a basic-level ˅like *dog* is a fiction. Even more, the similarities among dogs that nominalists ˅ so much on are for him psychological, not objective: "what defines the ˅l is not present in the external world; the determinants of the basic ˅ɔ do with human bodies and minds" (p. 134). Naturally, this approach ˅ɑt a tenuous relation to ours, which is a full-blooded model-theoretic ˅ɔach to kinds.

We have much more in common with Jackendoff whose fine-grained analysis of syntactic properties we find very useful and suggestive. Where we part company is that we do not interpret natural-language expressions and the cognitive states they express into conceptual structures. We interpret them into kinds, their members and their properties. We feel obliged to explore the mathematical properties of the models proposed precisely because we regard them as objective. Although we look to syntax for certain basic clues to semantics, our exploration of models is more independent of syntax than Jackendoff's ever is.

HISTORICAL NOTE ON THE DIVISION OF LABOR BETWEEN PHILOSOPHY AND PSYCHOLOGY

I suspect that psychology turned its back on standards of perfection and on ideals when Thomas Hobbes adopted Galileo's kinematics as the model for psychology—see Macnamara (1990). Certainly physics (kinematics included) idealizes— to point centers of mass, to force-free spaces, to ideal gases. But the ideals are in the theory, not in the physical world described by the theory. A psychology that apes physics will also assume that the ideals are in theories about the mind rather than in mental reality. An example of a psychological ideal is the notion of an individual's true IQ, as the mean score obtained by the individual in an infinite series of intelligence tests without learning. In such a psychology, however, the ideals are not in the mind but in the theory; they are conveniences that aid the development of theory.

The older approach is still to be found in Descartes and Leibniz. The third set of objections to Descartes's *Meditations*, written by Hobbes, and Descartes's reply to them already presage the disappearance of ideals from the subject matter of psychology. Let one example stand for all. In the fifth of the *Meditations*, Descartes (1641/1968) spoke of imagining a triangle that "although there may nowhere in the world be such a figure outside my thought, has nevertheless a determinate nature" (p. 180). Obviously, Descartes is speaking about a figure on an idealized plane bounded by three idealized lines (which having no thickness are necessarily invisible). To Hobbes the notion is incomprehensible: "If the triangle exists nowhere at all, I do not understand how it can have any nature; . . . The triangle in the mind comes from the triangle we have seen" (Third set of objections to the *Meditations*; Objection 14; Vol. 2, p. 76). The point I make is this: If one denies any objective reality to ideals one can, as Hobbes did, forget about any idealizing capacity in the mind. It seems as if this is what happened in the psychology that, in the wake of Hobbes, modeled itself on physics.

But ideals are too important to be abandoned altogether. A division of labor, well entrenched by Kant's time, assigns them to philosophy whereas assigning to psychology the facts of mental life—as though the ideals had no reality in mental life. In the following passage from Kant's *Logic* (1800/1974), we see the division of labor in full flower:

> Some logicians presuppose psychological principles in logic. But to bring such principles into logic is as absurd as taking morality from life. If we took the principles from psychology, i.e., from observations about our understanding, we would merely see *how* thinking occurs and *how it is* under manifold hindrances and conditions; this would therefore lead to the cognition of merely *contingent* laws. In logic, however, the question is not one of contingent but of *necessary* rules, not how we think but how we ought to think. The rules of logic, therefore, must be taken not from the *contingent* but from the necessary use of the understanding, which one finds, without any psychology, in oneself. (p. 16)

So the logician looks after the standards of perfect reasoning; the psychologist looks after the actual processes. As far as I know, the first important voice to be raised against this view of things is that of Noam Chomsky, albeit mainly in the domain of syntax. Later, Piaget and Garcia (1989) threw their weight on the same side. Is there not, however, a certain tortion in the distinction Kant wished to maintain? If we have standards of perfection for our actual mental processes, and if psychology occupies itself with actual mental processes, why should psychology be debarred from attempting to incorporate such standards in its scope and attempting to account for them? Is there any understanding the mind in its logical aspects without access to the mind's logical standards? Is there any explaining people's satisfaction and dissatisfaction with particular arguments and their willingness to backtrack when logical error is pointed out to them? Indeed, is there any understanding their ability to recognize logical error in their own reasoning processes? Chomsky has resisted the settlement that linguists should concern themselves with linguistic competence (standards of linguistic perfection) and that psychologists should concern them-selves with linguistic performance. In this, I believe, he is fully justified. By parity of reasoning we should resist the corresponding division of labor in the area of logic. But I am getting ahead of myself.

It is frequently said that logic is a normative science, whereas psychology is not. Notice that Kant (1800/1974), in the passage cited, said that logic is not about "how we think but how we ought to think." One also speaks about the *laws* of logic. This is alright, provided we realize that the laws in question have only to do with the desire to achieve truth. The law of contradiction, for example, is to be respected in thinking not because it is a law but because it is true. Being normative, then, is not opposed to being true, to being a fact.

LOGIC RELEVANT TO COGNITIVE PSYCHOLOGY

At the same time, there are some philosophers and psychologists who are uneasy with the orthodox position on how logic and cognition are related. Witness in particular Cohen (1981) and the numerous comments that accompany that article. In the same spirit are Henle (1962), Pylyshyn (1972), Braine (1978, 1993), Sober (1978), Rips (1984), and Macnamara (1986), to whom, as we have seen, should be added Piaget.

At its bleakest, logic elucidates certain uses of the connectives *not*, *and*, and *or*, certain uses of the words *all* and *some*, as well as certain uses of logic's key words *true* and *false*. It is obvious that any psychologist interested in explaining how children come to understand those uses of those expressions or how they enter into the mental lives of adults will want to learn what logicians have been able to discover about their interpretation. Indeed Quine (1970), Davidson (1980), and Smedslund (1990) all said that there is no interpreting anyone who has a deviant logic of such expressions. Among the people we must interpret are logicians. It follows, on the view of the authors we are discussing, that we must interpret them as exploring certain ordinary language uses of the expressions in question. Moreover, because the logicians explore the logical properties of these expressions more deeply than the rest of us, psychologists must turn to the logicians for a fuller understanding of these expressions, if they are to give an account of how those expressions (in those uses) are learned or how they are later deployed.

A less bleak logic will encompass proper names, count nouns, mass nouns, indexicals, predicables (mainly adjectival and verb phrases), the modal operators *necessary* and *possible*, and a host of others. By a logic of such expressions, I mean an account of how they contribute to the truth conditions of sentences in which they occur. That is the most accessible element in their interpretation. In *A Border Dispute* (Macnamara, 1986), I made an effort to spell all this out and to point in some detail to the psychological implications of the relevant logic. At the same time, I was careful to maintain the distinction between logic and psychology and avoid a psychologistic position. It seemed to me that logic stood little danger of being swallowed up in psychology if for its purposes psychology borrowed logical insights.

In *A Border Dispute* (Macnamara, 1986), however, I argued that classical logic is ill equipped to handle the logic of ordinary discourse precisely because classical logic derives mainly from an analysis of arithmetical sentences. Arithmetic is an unusual domain of discourse because (a) the objects in the domain are eternal and unchanging. All their properties are necessary ones. And (b) only a single basic count noun is required in arithmetical sentences: *number* or *set* depending on the level of one's work. Any other count noun can be defined as a subset of numbers or sets—for example, *prime number*, *finite set*.

Note that (a) most of ordinary discourse in contrast deals with ephemeral and changing objects, and (b) it is quite improbable that the kinds of such discourse—dogs, ideas, molecules, and so on—can be reduced to a single kind or defined as subsets of a single kind. More of this in the sequel. It follows that classical logic needs to be substantially enriched if it is to be extended to parts of ordinary discourse that elude classical logic.

My general thesis is practically a tautology. It is that one guide to how to construct a logic richer than classical logic is the manner in which we interpret the expressions of ordinary language and the manner in which we grasp implications among ordinary language sentences. These, however, are matters of psychological fact. It follows that psychological facts can guide the construction of logic. The logic so constructed is a mathematical object with a mathematical life of its own. It is not psychology. But in its construction it is constrained by certain cognitive states and events. Although the thesis seems patently obvious it has not, so far as I know, been considered as seriously as it deserves in either the philosophical or psychological literature. The reason, I suspect, is fear of psychologism—a heresy so terrible that at the mention of the word, as Brentano (1874/1973) said, "many a pious philosopher . . . crosses himself as though the devil himself were in it" (p. 306). The fear is quite ungrounded, as we see later when we have conceptualized the relation between the two disciplines more fully.

RELEVANCE OF COGNITIVE PSYCHOLOGY TO LOGIC

My strategy is to present a series of psychological claims related to the interpretation of expressions and show how these claims were employed to constrain "the logic of kinds." By that I mean the category-theoretic semantics for a range of natural-language expressions developed by Gonzalo Reyes, working in close collaboration with Marie La Palme Reyes and myself. I have so picked the psychological claims that they permit a thumbnail sketch of the logic of kinds. It is not my purpose to defend that logic here. That would be to miss the point. My excuse for selecting certain psychological claims is my belief that the logic of kinds is interesting in itself. The logic has some points of contact with the work of Peter Geach (1957, 1961, 1962, 1972), Aldo Bressan (1972), David Wiggins (1980), and Anil Gupta (1980). Further details of the logic are to be found in Macnamara and Reyes (1994a). The motivation for the logic is most fully spelled out in the article by La Palme Reyes, Macnamara, and Reyes (1994).

Each psychological claim is to the effect that we can understand P or that we cannot understand Q. The claim that we can understand P is followed by the claim that there is a logic underlying the fact that we can. This is little more than the claim that there must be a theory of how we interpret P. The psychological claim points to a class of logics that take cognizance of that fact. A psychological claim that we cannot understand Q is followed by the claim that logic should not assume that we can or require us to do so. Some psychological claims can be expressed equally well as linguistic claims. There is a most intimate relation between claims about the structure of language and claims about linguistic behavior, which is to be explained by the mind's incorporation of linguistic properties. At the same time, natural languages have the properties they do only because those properties can be recognized by and manipulated by infants without the type of meta-linguistic assistance that second-language learners typically receive. In other words, there is a close fit between the mind's linguistic properties and the properties of natural languages.

We do not have infallible access to psychological facts. Although the claims I make are not particularly controversial and some are downright obvious, I recognize that seemingly obvious claims can be misleading, as Frege found to his dismay. I am fully prepared to accept the judgment of psychology (experimental or theoretical) or of logic on my putative psychological facts. For example, if my claims are shown to be inconsistent I will abandon some of them, because inconsistent sentences jointly express nothing comprehensible. I do not take pains to defend my psychological proposals fully, because my purpose is mainly to illustrate how psychology constrains logic rather than to establish once and for all a particular set of psychological constraints.

Nor do I suggest that a particular psychological claim guides us to a unique logic. I am not even sure that all the relevant psychological facts guide us to a unique logic. Naturally, however, the constraints increase as the number of facts increases. Finally, I fully acknowledge that there may be routes other than the ones I propose to the particular logic we arrived at. The relevance of these claims to the theory of language learning is, at least in a general way, obvious.

Psychological Claim 1.   If we are faithful to our linguistic intuition, we attach certain quantifiers (*a, many, few, another, one, two,* etc.) to count nouns only. On the universality of this claim across languages, see Emmon Bach (1994).

For example, we say "a dog," "another proof," but not *"two walkeds," *"many quickly," *"few hot." This means among other things that we can understand "a dog" but not "few hot."

Psychological Claim 2.   We cannot conceptually grasp an individual without the support of a count noun. An indexical, such as *this* will not do on its own. *This* applied to an individual person, for example, may draw attention to the person or to the person's clothes, or appearance or manners even. On its own it cannot unambiguously pick out any of those things. Neither can a predicable (adjectival or verb phrase) on its own. You cannot count whatever is blue in a room, because you do not know what to count as one blue—a whole blue shirt, or the sleeves separately on the grounds that they were sewn on, or the separate threads, or the fibers of the threads. It makes no difference that we would normally not think of counting blue fibers if we attempted to comply with an instruction "Count whatever is blue." It follows that a collection of predicables will not serve the purpose either. Neither will a proper name on its own. For one thing, most individuals do not have a proper name, so proper names could not be the general means for specifying an individual. When an individual is the bearer of a proper name, a count noun is needed to specify what the bearer is. Suppose you know who Steve is, you might be inclined to think that the name denotes the stuff in Steve's body, a certain mass of molecules. But that cannot be. Suppose Steve's body weighs 175 lbs; it is clear that such a mass of molecules was never born, although Steve was. By Leibniz's law it follows that Steve is not identical with the molecules of which his body is formed and hence that "Steve" does not denote the stuff in Steve's body. What does it denote? The answer is a certain person. What individuates the bearer of the name and traces its identity correctly is the count noun *person*. The bearer of a proper name always needs to be specified by a count noun. It follows that the learner of a proper name for a person needs to know a count noun synonymous with *person* to specify the bearer of the proper name.

The first two claims jointly point to a logic that recognizes count nouns as a logical category distinct from predicables. This is the major thesis of Gupta (1980). They also point to a logic in which any reference to an individual is typed by a count noun. This means that indexicals and proper names must be typed by a count noun. Referring definite descriptions wear their count noun visibly.

Psychological Claim 3. We cannot conceptually grasp an individual in a universal kind supposedly denoted by the count noun *thing* or *object*. The reasons are similar to those that reveal the inadequacy of a predicable for the purpose of specifying an individual. If asked to count the things in a room, I do not know whether to count persons separately from their organs, and their cells separately from their organs, because all might be characterized as things. (Later we will see that there is a clear notion of a thing, or entity, in a subcategory of kinds, but it has nothing to do with a universal category of things.) It follows that I cannot conceptually grasp an individual under the description "thing."

This fact supports the view that logic should not expect us to grasp an individual under the description "thing." Nor, what is almost the equivalent, should it suppose that we have a notion of a bare particular; that is, of an individual that is untyped by a bona fide count noun such as *bicycle*, *dog*, or *idea*. Now, on the Fregean approach, classical logic asks us to do just that. For that approach regiments "Some man is tall" as

$$\exists x(\text{Man } (x) \text{ and Tall } (x)) \tag{1}$$

The untyped variable is supposed to be interpreted into a universal kind *thing*. If one takes a more Peircean view, one may assume that the variable ranges over some more restricted domain of discourse. On that reading one must accuse logicians of being sloppy, because they have not so specified the domain of discourse as to make adequate provision for the individuation of the individual that has the properties of being a man and being tall. Both readings place the count noun *man* in subject position on equal logical footing with the predicable *tall*. We can correct both defects at once if we replace Equation 1 with

$$\exists(x{:}Man)\ Tall(x) \tag{2}$$

which reads: "Some individual in the kind *man* is tall." This is an example of restricted quantification, advocated by many logicians. There are no other reasons, also supported by psychological observation, for such quantification. Bach (1989) pointed out that such expressions as "most dogs" are uninterpretable in the way we naturally interpret them if quantification is unrestricted. The reason is that although it is true that most dogs have four legs, it is not true that most things are dogs and have four legs.

Notice the mutual determination of individual and kinds in the logic I am sketching. A kind is specified by its members; but the members are specified by the kind. This type of dialectical relation is familiar to psychologists from the writings of the gestalt school. Gestalt psychologists observed that perceptual figures or wholes are determined by their perceptual parts, whereas the perceptual role of the perceptual part is determined by the perceptual whole of which it is a part. Another familiar example is supplied by language. A sentence is determined grammatically and semantically by its constituents, and the grammatical function and semantic role of a constituent is determined by the sentence to which it belongs. I merely point out that logic should respect the dialectical relation between individuals and the kinds to which they belong. All this signals a special status in logic for count nouns, which refer to kinds.

This claim has particular relevance for developmental psychology. Typically, psychologists view babies as surrounded by a stock of individuals; the task they envisage for the babies is to discover the kinds to which the individuals belong. This is to posit at the outset a stock of individuals untyped by any kind less general than *thing*. An obvious contradiction! We can get around the contradiction and hold on to the psychologists' general idea if we allow babies access to individuals in a kind *perceptual entity*, corresponding to what the perceptual systems carve out as figures distinct from their (back)grounds. Unlearned access to such a kind makes our semantics psychologically well founded.

Psychological Claim 4. We employ the word *dog* to refer to the dogs of times past and to future dogs as well as to present-day dogs. In fact, we have no other means of referring to the whole kind *dog*. This suggests the logical principle that the reference of the count noun *dog* (i.e., the kind *DOG*) is independent of the time and circumstances of use, and so for all count nouns. We call this property of count nouns *modal constancy*, using the expression in a sense different from Gupta (1980). We mean by modal constancy that the reference of a count noun cannot in general be identified with the members that happen to exist at the moment the word is used. Instead it refers to a single immense object, a kind that embraces all the members that ever were, are, or will be. This suggests that a kind is an abstract object, and the simplest way to conceptualize it is as a set or more generally an object in a category. In fact, in the logic of kinds, a kind is presented as a set together with an existence relation on the set assigning to each member the situations, both factual and counterfactual, of which the member is a constituent.

This has certain implications for Piaget's general program. He hoped by biological means (adaptation) to explain the emergence of intentional states from initial states described solely in biological terms. We might call this the emergence of intentionality from biology. The trouble we now see is that any intentional state involves abstract entities. For example, if we say of a certain dog "Freddie is a pet," it is the kind *dog* that individuates and handles the identity of the bearer of the name "Freddie." In addition "to be a pet" denotes a predicate of *dog*, another abstract entity, and the sentence claims that Freddie is a member of the subset of dogs that have the property of being pets. Now it is simply false that biology can supply conceptual tools to elucidate the contact between the mind and abstract objects through reference. We need to introduce a nonbiological primitive *reference* to handle this. It follows that Piaget's program in such books as *Biologie et Connaissance* and *L'Équilibration des Structures* cannot work. I touch on these matters in Macnamara (1976). Similar strictures apply with little or no change to such neo-Piagetian projects as that outlined in Overton (1990), insofar as they follow the Piagetian lines in this matter.

We simply have to posit in children sufficient intentional resources to make reference possible. Among other things these must include logical resources to specify the meanings of the words they learn. Basic-level typing at the perceptual level plays a crucial role in specifying the kinds picked out by basic-level common nouns (like *dog* and *water*). Children also need logical resources sufficient to enable them to refer to words as words and to classify them in grammatical categories: proper name, mass noun, adjective, and so forth. Reference to a word is just as dependent on a linguistic kind as reference to a dog is on a biological kind. Macnamara and Reyes (1994a) elaborate on all this in detail.

Psychological Claim 5. We cannot directly express identity across different kinds. To illustrate, we may wish to claim that a boy is identical with the man he later became. But we cannot say that a certain boy is the same boy as a certain man, or that the boy is the same man as a certain man. What precisely the relation is becomes apparent when we see how to construct the notion of an entity in a subcategory of kinds.

A general theory that handles identity requires some sensitive regimentation of natural-language expressions. Sensitivity to the whole range of relevant intuition reveals that "=" is a typed predicable requiring that the referring expressions placed on its left and right to form a single sentence should both be typed by the same count noun. This is almost the same as Wiggin's (1980) Thesis D. I come back to another related logical provision after the next claim.

Psychological Claim 6.   We count passengers and persons differently (the example is from Gupta, 1980) and we can understand such ways of counting. If you travel three times with Air Canada in 1991 you will be counted as three passengers, although you are only one person. Similar distinctions are made in counting patients and persons in hospitals, diners and persons in a restaurant, majors and persons in a university (there being persons who take joint majors) and so on.

If we cannot directly express either identity or lack of identity over different kinds, such as *passenger* and *person*, how do we avoid a bloated ontology in which there are persons besides passengers crowded into airplanes? The first thing to notice is that the kind *passenger* is not included (set theoretically) in the kind *person*. Set-theoretic inclusion of A in B is one-one in this sense: For each member of A there is just one member of B that is identical with it and no member of B is identical with more than one member of A. It follows that the number of Bs cannot be less than the number of As. But the number of persons might well be less than the number of passengers. Set-theoretic inclusion cannot handle this. This observation tells against the numerous "class-inclusion" studies in the literature on the learning of hierarchies.

The logic of kinds handles it by positing an underlying map u between certain pairs of kinds—u: *passenger* $\rightarrow$ *person*. The map assigns to each passenger a person $u(p)$. The theory posits similar maps—u': *boy* $\rightarrow$ *person* and u'': *man* $\rightarrow$ *person*. We now express the relation between the boy and the man he later became as an identity of underlying persons. If b is the boy and m the man, we say $u'(b) = u''(m)$. Although respecting the typing of "=" the move is a first step towards avoiding the bloated ontology that threatened. I present a second step when discussing the notion of an entity in a subcategory of kinds.

Psychological Claim 7.   We can understand fairy-tale metamorphoses in which, contrary perhaps to the laws of nature, a prince is transformed into a frog and back into a prince. This was the point of departure for Marie La Palme Reyes (1988) to construct a logic that handles such understanding. She posited the existence in a counterfactual, fairy-tale world of counterparts of the kinds in the actual world with underlying morphisms between them. In La Palme Reyes (1994), she keeps the language of fairy tales the same as ordinary English and changes the interpretation. The intuition, a psychological one, is that the language of fiction and of nonfiction is the same; the difference is in the interpretation. She explained the understanding of the Frog-Prince and such stories by positing underlying maps between the fairy-tale kinds *frog'* and *prince'* on the one hand

and the fairy-tale kind *animal'*—*u*: *frog'* → *animal'* and *u'*: *prince'* → *animal'*. The identity of the frog-prince can then be understood as the identity of the underlying animal. The fact that we have to do, for example, with fairy-tale frogs and not real ones is signaled by the fact that the frogs in the story can talk. The storyteller invites us to posit new kinds appropriate for the story.

Psychological Claim 8.   We can understand systems whose logic is not classical. Evert Beth and Saul Kripke have proposed distinct models for intuitionistic logic. More impressive, however, is the fact that the logic of the open spaces in topology is naturally intuitionistic. I find this more impressive because the topology of open spaces is entirely uncontrived; rather, it is discovered.

More generally, I believe that ordinary semantic intuitions are local. They normally relate to small parts of the universe over short time intervals and have nothing very much to do with the rest of time and space. Coupling this with the discovery of intuitionist models in mathematics, I conclude that the logic of kinds should be classical (two-valued) only in special cases. It should make provision for intuitionism. In fact that logic of kinds developed by Gonzalo Reyes is category-theoretic, which is naturally intuitionist but also sufficiently general to embrace classical logic as a special case.

LOGICAL CONSTRAINTS ON PSYCHOLOGY

Lest I give the impression that the debt is all on one side, I would like to give one example from our experience in which mathematical developments led to psychological illumination.

In the early days of working on the logic of kinds we were puzzled about how to represent the "is a" of ordinary language, as in "A dog *is an* animal." We say that set-theoretic inclusion would not do. Gonzalo Reyes proposed that we employ the morphisms of which categorical logic is the study, in this case underlying maps between kinds. The stimulus, so to speak, was psychological; the response was to employ a well-established mathematical tool. The move, however, helped to clear up several other difficulties in an unforeseen manner.

One particular problem is related to the notion of an entity in a subcategory of kinds. (This is where I fulfill my promise to say something about the interpretation of the words *thing* and *object*.) Our solution as presented so far had the merit of keeping distinct what ought to be kept distinct—passengers from persons, patients from persons, and so on. Bill Lawvere suggested that the categorical notion of colimit of a functor could be used to construct the kind *entity* relative to a system of kinds. The colimit in question is obtained in two steps: First, take the disjoint union of all kinds in the system and then divide the disjoint union by an equivalence relation, namely the equivalence relation generated by pairs of members of kinds that are in the underlying relation. To see what this means, consider a party at which there are men and women, wives and husbands, students and professors, Canadians and Irish people. The disjoint union assembles the lot keeping wives distinct from women, from professors, and so on. The operation of dividing by the equivalence relation comes down to collapsing a particular woman, a particular wife, and a particular professor, for example, to a single entity in the given system. Thus, although the host appreciates that each woman, each wife, each professor, each Canadian, and each person at the party needs to be fed, he prepares only as many meals as there are entities at the party. In this case natural language supplies "person" to cover the notion of entity in the subcategory. Where, however, the higher order word is a mass noun, for example, *food*, one needs to construct the disjoint union in a way that does not readily fit linguistic intuition, collapsing, for example, over a particular fruit and a particular apple to obtain the notion of an entity or item in the system denoted by *food*. The mathematics led to a perfectly natural construal of the word *thing*, which has exercised the minds of several philosophers, Gibbard (1975) and Gupta (1980) for example, without previous resolution.

I am not saying that "thing" has no other uses. Obviously it sometimes functions as a variable over kinds, as in "I saw something blue in the bushes." In the notation already introduced we might regiment the critical part of that sentence as $(k:K)[\text{Blue}(k)]$, where K is a variable ranging over kinds and k is a variable ranging over individuals in K. There is, however, this other use of "thing" or "entity" that is revealed by the mathematical operations of taking the colimit of a system of kinds and dividing it by an appropriate equivalence relation.

We are now in a position to take the second step to avoid a bloated ontology. For certain purposes we collapse across certain individuals in a system of kinds and, for example, treat a certain passenger and a certain person as identical. The relation between a boy and the man he later became is that they form a single entity in the appropriate system. Thus we are entitled to treat a certain boy, a certain man, and a certain person as identical—as members of the single kind *entity* in the relevant system. The colimit of which I speak is the colimit of the functor that interprets a linguistic category N into the category K of kinds. At the linguistic level one has morphisms among count nouns of the type "dogs are animals," "passengers are persons." The functor that interprets such morphisms assigns to each a morphism of kinds: for example, $u:dog \rightarrow animal$, $u':passenger \rightarrow person$. If, however, the expressions in question occur in fiction, then following Marie La Palme Reyes's suggestion we posit a different interpretation into morphisms of the fictional world: for example, $u:dog' \rightarrow animal'$, $u':passenger' \rightarrow person'$. Category theory also gives us means to think of the relation between the category of kinds in the real world and that of kinds in the fictional world. If the fiction is realistic it seems that there is a functor relating the two categories. If the fiction is more fanciful there does not seem to be such a functor and even the linguistic category may need reconstruction. This gives us a glimpse of a theory that might explain what it is for fiction to be realistic. It also tempts us to theorize about how the mind switches from fact to fiction and back again.

The mathematics specifies precisely the operation that language learners must perform in learning a system of common nouns. There is no suggestion that children form the colimits of each system and then divide by an equivalence relation, any more than there is any suggestion on the part of a physicist that planets compute their orbits. Our logic characterizes the operations that children must perform; it does not specify the mechanisms that perform them.

INTUITION AS A SOURCE OF DATA
FOR PSYCHOLOGY

It is evident in the foregoing that the psychology I envisage is not exclusively experimental. It makes substantial use of intuition. We describe a proposition as being intuitive when it presents itself to us as true without benefit of conscious reasoning or proof. The word *intuition* comes from the Latin *intueri*, meaning to look at or gaze at. As used by psychologists and philosophers the word is a transparent metaphor. Just as we do not normally prove the existence of everyday objects that we can see with our eyes, so we say we do not normally prove the truth of certain propositions that we cannot verify directly by means of our senses. For example, I claimed that we so use the word *dog* as to embrace dogs past and dogs to come as well as present ones. I now claim that this psychological claim is intuitively obvious. By my intuition I know that I so employ the word. I can, of course, check other people's intuitions by asking them, and I can also study accepted practice. But even then the evidence has to be generously interpreted. The relation between a person's use of ''dog'' and dogs that have ceased to exist or not yet come into existence cannot be one that is directly verifiable by the senses. Admittedly, it is difficult to see how our senses verify that a person's use even of a dog's proper name denotes that dog when the dog is in full view of the speaker. Nevertheless, in whatever way our senses serve us in that case, they cannot serve us in the other where the dogs do not even exist at the time of speaking.

A lifetime as an experimental psychologist makes me edgy in this connection. Psychologists rightly insist on empirical evidence for psychological claims: They are leery of intuitions. They suspect that in appealing to intuition you are appealing to introspection under another name. So a few reassuring words are necessary.

To begin, intuitions are part of ordinary experience and therefore they are empirical in the ordinary sense of the word. They are not experimental, but that is another matter. When you see a cow, the cow enters the experience but so does the fact that you are seeing the cow, not touching or imagining her, and the fact that it is you and not some other person that is seeing her. Sometimes intuitions are obscure and it may help to check yours against those of others and even count heads, as psychologists frequently do. At others it may be important to check the intuition that you are seeing a cow, not imagining, by attempting to touch the cow. Other intuitions are so clear that such checking seems superfluous. Mathematics pays great heed to intuition and yet mathematics is the most surefooted of the sciences, never having had to retract any widely held theory, in the way that even physics has. Some psychological intuitions, such as that one cannot count whatever is white in a room, seem to me as sound as any in mathematics. Of course psychological intuition is not mathematical intuition. The content of one is psychology; that of the other is mathematics. Nevertheless there are important similarities. What I most object to in the division of labor between psychology and philosophy is that such obvious facts seem to be placed outside the purview of psychology. The only explanation that occurs to me is that psychologists are aping physicists, not as physicists really are, I fear, but as psychologists imagine them to be.

Franz Brentano (1874/1973) saw all this and, although his main source for psychological truth was intuition or "inner perception," he called his major book *Psychology from an Empirical Standpoint*. Another who sees it is Noam Chomsky, who all along has appealed to linguistic intuition as *empirical* evidence for linguistic theories.

Brentano was well aware of the pitfalls of introspection which he was at pains to distinguish from intuition. Because psychologists have wisely turned their back on introspection, after some bad experiences, it is worthwhile quoting Brentano (1874/1973) on the distinction between it and intuition or 'inner perception as he called it in the passage I cite:

> In observation, we direct our full attention to a phenomenon in order to apprehend it accurately. But with objects of inner perception this is absolutely impossible. This is especially clear with regard to certain mental phenomena such as anger. If someone is in a state in which he wants to observe his own anger raging within him, the anger must already be somewhat diminished, and so his original object of observation would have disappeared . . . It is only while our attention is turned toward a different object that we are able to perceive, incidentally [*nebenbei*], the mental processes that are directed toward that object. (pp. 29–30)

The trouble is that introspection was thought by some to reveal directly the mind's representations and processes. Owing, however, to intentionality, such representations and processes are never directly available to the mind, only their objects, the things that the representations and processes are about. That is why Brentano stressed that psychological intuition is incidental. When looking at the cow and attending to her, I am incidentally aware of my seeing. But if with introspective intent I attempt to study my seeing I cease to attend to the cow and my perception of her is altered.

Most important, Brentano's (1874/1973) appeal to intuition for psychological purposes is quite at odds with the Kantian division of labor that can be expressed in the equation

$$\frac{\text{Standards of perfection}}{\text{Philosophy}} = \frac{\text{Facts}}{\text{Psychology}}$$

What Brentano would most have objected to is the assumption that standards of perfection are irrelevant to the understanding of the human mind. As though access to such standards were not a psychological fact. For it is a psychological fact that the mind has access to standards of perfection that it can never fully realize in the extramental world; in measurement, in ease and grace of movement, in painting, sculpture, and the musical arts, in dress, in interhuman relations, in ethics and, of course, in reasoning. It is equally a fact that we cannot have direct access to these standards by means of our external senses. In fact, our main access to them is in intuition. So any psychology that eschews psychological intuition must be blind to perhaps the most important facts about the mind. And any psychology that ignores the mind's access to standards of perfection is not worthy of the name.

None of this is to deny that psychological surveys of intuition and psychological experiments have a place in the study of the mind in its logical aspects or a contribution to make to the development of a logic that is responsive to human thought processes. But it is not the purpose of this chapter to highlight the experimental approach.

FINAL STATEMENT

There has been much controversy in recent years about the role of sentences in intentional states. Fodor (1975, 1981) made sentences and propositional attitudes to sentences the essence of intentional states. This is in fact the natural stance for workers in artificial intelligence, as Pylyshyn (1984) pointed out. On the other hand, there are philosophers who go so far as to deny the reality of intentional states altogether, notably Patricia Churchland (1986) and Paul Churchland (1984), and so they have no important role for sentences in our mental lives. Others such as Dennett (1987), Stich (1983), and Putnam (1988) took a somewhat skeptical view about their role. Putnam in particular was impressed by what he referred to as the holism of the mental. By this he meant that it is in general impossible to specify one belief without appealing to or at least presupposing several others. I am sympathetic to his arguments, although like Fodor (1987) I would hope that the holism of the mental is local in the way that the meaning of the primitives in Hilbert's *Foundations of Geometry* is local.

Be all that as it may, I believe that we have to keep some place for sentences at the core of intentional states. Perhaps much more than sentences; but not less. The argument goes as follows. With the *major et sanior pars* of theoreticians I claim that intentional states are semantically evaluable. They specify to within some degree truth conditions in some domain of objects. But we have seen that to grasp an object or objects conceptually one has need of an appropriate count noun. A sentence is required to fix the grammatical category and reference of a particular linguistic form. It follows that to make the right type of conceptual contact with an individual there is need of a common noun in a sentence. It follows further that there is an essential role for sentences in intentional states.

Logic is the mathematical language with which to express and explore the interpretation of constituents of sentences and the implicational relations among sentences. It follows that logic is the appropriate mathematical language with which to characterize essential elements in intentional states, namely the interpretation of linguistic symbols and the ability to grasp implications among sentences. Not computation mind you. Computers in Dennett's apt phrase are syntactic engines not semantic ones. They are apt for modeling proof theory; less apt for modeling model theory. In human cognition the most basic work to be done is in relation to the interpretation of symbols. It would seem that in this connection the computer is not a helpful tool.

Neither does the methodological solipsism advocated by Fodor (1981), and essential for artificial intelligence, help. Fodor took the explanation of action in terms of beliefs and desires to be the core of cognitive psychology; and because beliefs and desires are logically opaque, he hoped that cognitive psychology can afford to ignore reference. This is a misconception. The main aim of cognitive psychology, as the name itself indicates, is to account for knowledge. Knowledge is a relation between the mind and the extramental world. Reference is the main ingredient in that relation. Reference is in fact logically prior to belief and belief-informed desire. It follows that Fodor's methodological solipsism is of little help. And with methodological solipsism must go the computer as an instrument for modelling cognitive states in their precisely cognitive respect.

Just as physics and mathematics mutually constrain each other (Galileo's insight), just as psycholinguistics and linguistics constrain each other (Chomsky's insight), so cognition and logic mutually constrain each other. We can express the relation as

$$\text{Cognition} \Leftrightarrow \text{Logic}$$

Perhaps it is only fair to attribute this insight to the father of logic, Aristotle.

Just as physics and mathematics do not collapse to a single subject, so cognition and logic do not collapse to a single subject. The basic mistake of the psychologistic logicians was to imagine that they do.

The logic of kinds of which I gave a thumbnail sketch is in some obvious sense of the word discovered by examining our interpretative practices. It is not a logic that one imposes in a brutal manner on the theory of cognition. It needs to be accommodated and expanded as one examines cognitive states and events. And although the logic of kinds takes on a mathematical life of its own, it retains a structural harmony with the basic facts of cognition. In one sense, then, the logic of kinds is objective; it is discovered by studying an area. The logic of kinds is also objective in another sense. It is the logic that appropriately mathematizes our conceptual grasp of objects.

I conclude with the expression of a growing conviction, that the mathematical tool best adapted to work in cognition is categorical logic. The logic of kinds is expressed in the terms of categorical logic. This is not an accident. Categorical logic is naturally intuitionist though it can also be classical when occasion arises. We saw that the natural logic of cognition needs to have this adaptability. Natural logic is many sorted and categorical logic, because it treats morphisms as basic seems specially adapted to deal with many-sorted systems. Natural logic involves the simultaneous handling of constancy and change, because change is conceivable only against a background of constancy. In the logic of kinds, the modally constant count nouns supply the background of constancy; predicables and modal connectives express change. Categorical logic with its sensitivity to functoriality is specially suited to handle such constancy and variability. For the same reason categorical logic is the appropriate mathematical tool for handling that functor between linguistic structures and the structure of the nonlinguistic that we call *interpretation*. Categorical logic has worked out a generalized theory of the structures of truth objects—against which classical logic's {0,1} appears as a special case. Its respect for functoriality makes categorical language the appropriate mathematical tool for mapping interpretations into truth values. Interested readers will find a sketch of categorical logic in Magnan and Reyes (1994) and a more general (although still tractable) introduction to category theory in Lawvere and Schanuel (1991).

I end by sharing with you a vision. It is that in cognition we are in the year 1690. Our calculus (categorical logic) has been invented—by Bill Lawvere. But it has only begun to be applied. My vision is of a deep and satisfying theory of the human mind developing and replacing tendencies in "cognitive studies" that strike me for the most part as unworthy of their subject.

ACKNOWLEDGMENTS

This chapter, a revised and abbreviated version of an article (Macnamara, 1994) presented at the Vancouver Conference on Logic and Cognition (February, 1991), was supported by a National Science and Engineering Research Council grant to the author. It benefited from conversations with David Davies, Eric Lewis, Michael Makkai, and Storrs McCall. I am indebted to David Davies for a careful reading of an earlier version and many useful comments. It has also benefited greatly from the critique of Hilary Putnam who was good enough to take on the task of commentator at the Vancouver Conference. It also reflects the comments and queries of many persons who took part in the conference. Its debt to Bill Lawvere became too acute at times to avoid particular mention in the text. Only categorical logicians will appreciate its overall indebtedness to him. I acknowledge my debt to Gonzalo and Marie Reyes in the text.

REFERENCES

Bach, E. (1989). *Informal lectures on formal semantics*. New York: State University of New York Press.

Bach, E. (1994). The semantics of linguistic categories: A cross linguistic perspective. In J. Macnamara & G. E. Reyes (Eds.), *The logical foundations of cognition* (pp. 264–281). New York: Oxford University Press.

Braine, M. D. S. (1978). On the relation between the natural logic of reasoning and standard logic. *Psychological Review, 85*, 1–21.

Braine, M. S. (1994). Mental logic and how to discover it. In J. Macnamara & G. E. Reyes (Eds.), *The logical foundations of cognition* (pp. 241–263). New York: Oxford University Press.

Brentano, F. (1973). *Psychology from an empirical standpoint*. London: Routledge & Kegan Paul. (Original work published 1874)

Bressan, A. (1972). *A general integrated modal calculus*. New Haven, CT: Yale University Press.

Churchland, P. M. (1986). *Neurophilosophy*. Cambridge, MA: Bradford/MIT Press.

Churchland, P. S. (1984). *Matter and consciousness*. Cambridge, MA: Bradford/MIT Press.

Cohen, L. J. (1981). Can human irrationality be experimentally demonstrated? *Behavioral and Brain Sciences, 4*, 317–370.

Davidson, D. (1980). *Essays on actions and events*. Oxford, England: Clarendon.

Dennett, D. (1987). *The intentional stance*. Cambridge, MA: Bradford/MIT Press.

Descartes, R. (1968). Meditations on first philosophy. In E. S. Haldane & G. R. T. Ross (Eds.), *The philosophical works of Descartes* (2 Vols.). New York: Cambridge University Press. (Original work published 1641)

Ennis, R. H. (1977). Conceptualization of children's logical competence: Piaget's propositional logic and alternative proposals. In L. S. Siegal & C. J. Brainerd (Eds.), *Alternatives to Piaget* (pp. 201–260). New York: Academic.

Fodor, J. A. (1975). *The language of thought*. New York: Crowell.

Fodor, J. A. (1981). *Representations*. Cambridge, MA: Bradford/MIT Press.

Fodor, J. A. (1987). *Psychosemantics*. Cambridge, MA: Bradford/MIT Press.

Frege, G. (1959). *The foundations of arithmetic*. Oxford, England: Basil Blackwell. (Original work published 1884)

Geach, P. T. (1957). *Mental acts*. London: Routledge & Kegan Paul.

Geach, P. T. (1961). Aquinas. In G. E. M. Anscombe & P. T. Geach (Eds.), *Three philosophers* (pp. 69–125). Ithaca, NY: Cornell University Press.

Geach, P. T. (1962). *Reference and generality*. Ithaca, NY: Cornell University Press.

Geach, P. T. (1972). *Logic matters*. Berkeley, CA: University of California Press.

Gibbard, A. (1975). Contingent identity. *Journal of Philosophical Logic, 4*, 187–221.

Gupta, A. K. (1980). *The logic of common nouns*. New Haven, CT: Yale University Press.

Haack, S. (1978). *Philosophy of logics*. New York: Cambridge University Press.

Henle, M. (1962). The relation between logic and thinking. *Psychological Review, 69*, 366–378.

Humphrey, G. (1951). *Thinking*. New York: Wiley.

Husserl, E. (1970). *Logical investigations*. London: Routledge & Kegan Paul. (Original work published 1900)

Inhelder, B., & Piaget, J. (1958). *The growth of logical thinking from childhood to adolescence*. New York: Basic.

Kant, I. (1974). *Logic* (R. S. Hartman & W. Schwarz, Trans.). New York: Bobbs-Merrill. (Original work published 1800)

Lakoff, G. (1988). Cognitive semantics. In U. Eco, M. Santambogio, & P. Violi (Eds.), *Meaning and mental representation* (pp. 119–154). Bloomington, IN: Indiana University Press.

La Palme Reyes, M. (1994). The referential structure of fictional texts. In J. Macnamara & G. E. Reyes (Eds.), *The logical foundations of cognition* (pp. 309–323). New York: Oxford University Press.

La Palme Reyes, M., Macnamara, J., & Reyes, G. E. (1994). Reference, kinds and predicates. In J. Macnamara & G. E. Reyes (Eds.), *The logical foundations of cognition* (pp. 90–143). New York: Oxford University Press.

Lawvere, F. W., & Schanuel, S. (1991). *Conceptual mathematics*. Buffalo, NY: Buffalo Workshop Press.

Macnamara, J. (1976). Stomachs assimilate and accommodate, don't they? *Canadian Psychological Review, 17*, 167–173.

Macnamara, J. (1986). *A border dispute: The place of logic in psychology*. Cambridge, MA: Bradford/MIT Press.

Macnamara, J. (1990). Ideals and psychology. *Canadian Psychology, 31*, 14–25.

Macnamara, J. (1994). Logic and cognition. In J. Macnamara & G. E. Reyes (Eds.), *The logical foundations of cognition* (pp. 9–32). New York: Oxford University Press.

Macnamara, J., & Reyes, G. E. (Eds.). (1994a). *The logical foundations of cognition*. New York: Oxford University Press.

Macnamara, J., & Reyes, G. E. (1994b). Foundational issues in the learning of proper names, count nouns and mass nouns. In J. Macnamara & G. E. Reyes (Eds.), *The logical foundations of cognition* (pp. 144–176). New York: Oxford University Press.

Magnan, F., & Reyes, G. E. (1994). Category theory as a conceptual tool in the study of cognition. In J. Macnamara & G. E. Reyes (Eds.), *The logical foundations of cognition* (pp. 55–89). New York: Oxford University Press.

Miller, G. A. (1951). Speech and language. In S. S. Stevens (Ed.), *Handbook of experimental psychology* (pp. 789–810). New York: Wiley.

Notturno, M. A. (1984). *Objectivity, rationality and the third realm: Justification and the grounds of psychologism*. The Hague, Netherlands: Nijhoff.

Overton, W. F. (1990). Competence and procedures: Constraints on the development of logical reasoning. In W. F. Overton (Ed.), *Reasoning, necessity and logic: Developmental perspectives* (pp. 1–32). Hillsdale, NJ: Lawrence Erlbaum Associates.

Piaget, J. (1953). *Logic and psychology*. Manchester, England: Manchester University Press.

Piaget, J., & Garcia, R. (1989). *Psychogenesis and the history of science*. New York: Columbia University Press.

Putnam, H. (1988). *Representation and reality*. Cambridge, MA: Bradford/MIT Press.

Pylyshyn, Z. (1972). Competence and psychological reality. *American Psychologist, 27*, 546–552.

Pylyshyn, Z. (1984). *Computation and cognition*. Cambridge, MA: Bradford/MIT Press.

Quine, W. V. (1970). *Philosophy of logic*. Englewood Cliffs, NJ: Prentice-Hall.

Reyes, M. (1988). *A semantics for literary texts*. Unpublished doctoral dissertation, Concordia University, Montreal.

Rips, L. J. (1984). Reasoning as a central intellective ability. In R. J. Sternberg (Ed.), *Advances in the psychology of human intelligence* (Vol. 2, pp. 105–147). Hillsdale, NJ: Lawrence Erlbaum Associates.

Smedslund, J. (1990). A critique of Tversky and Kahneman's distinction between fallacy and misunderstanding. *Scandinavian Journal of Psychology, 31,* 110–120.

Sober, E. (1978). Psychologism. *Journal for the Theory of Social Behavior, 8,* 165–192.

Stich, S. P. (1983). *From folk psychology to cognitive science.* Cambridge, MA: Bradford/MIT Press.

Wiggins, D. (1980). *Sameness and substance.* Oxford, England: Basil Blackwell.

8
Affective Dimensions of Meaning

Terrance Brown
University of Chicago

One day about 2 years into therapy, a young man, a boy really, who does not like to talk, brought me a poem.

a poem for Mr. Brown

In the day I sing a song
A song of myself I sing.
I sing for myself
and I sing for my friend
A song I've never heard.
To me it's
new each time,
At least a thousand times
it's new.
But he has a room
in which a thousand songs wait,
At least a thousand,
Maybe more,
Maybe many more.

In the night I sing a song
A song of myself I sing.

> *I sing for myself*
> *and I sing for my friend.*
> *It's a song I never hear*
> *as I glide between his arms*
> *and through his hair,*
> *Past his smile*
> *and by his eyes.*
> *It's a song he's heard a thousand times*
> *At least a thousand,*
> *Maybe more,*
> *Maybe many more.*
> *As I hold him the way*
> *they have held him,*
> *At least a thousand times,*
> *Maybe more.*
> *As I touch a thousand places,*
> *At least a thousand,*
> *Maybe more,*
> *Maybe many more.*[1]

I read it quickly and laid it on the small table beside my chair. I said nothing for a while, hoping that my distress could not be seen. Finally, he asked me if it was any good. I said, "Yes, it's very good," then changed the subject and stumbled through the session in some manner I do not recall.

When Dean returned later in the week, the first words out of his mouth were: "You didn't like my poem."

"Why do you say that?" I asked.
   "Because you didn't talk about it."
   "But I couldn't. I was too moved, too sad," I said to him.
   His manner changed. He was no longer accusatory but gently curious. "Why were you moved?"
   "Because you think I see you as a 'trick'. Because you think I'm like the nameless, faceless men you end up with, a 'one night stand' who's heard and done it all before. I was sad because you think you're just a mildly interesting 'affair' for me, one of many prey in a hunting game I play, nothing more to me than a way of getting my rocks off when I need to."
   He said, "Sometimes that's how I feel."

Dean's story is about a rich kid with a bitter critical mother and an absent father who grew up believing in some deep way that no one loved him and that it was his fault. As a freshman at the university, he found a graduate student

---

[1]The poem is used with the permission of the author.

whom he thought valued his physical beauty enough to forgive him, as he said, his "vile, disgusting" nature and his "lack of soul." As it turned out, his 6-week suitor was a notorious campus Casanova who had had a Kaposi's sarcoma removed from his neck some time before. Two months after he deserted Dean, Dean tested positive for HIV. Because of his poor relationship with his parents, he could not tell them, and the tale continues with long chapters on loneliness and despair. Full telling of how Dean has found some way to believe, however intermittently, in the possibility of love and to have some hope and aspiration for an almost certainly abbreviated future is not the purpose of this chapter. I relate these fragments because they introduce in terms of my realities the subject of this chapter.

WHAT IS AFFECTIVITY?

There is a certain irony in the fact that in discussing the affective aspects of meaning I claim that meaning precedes language and that words and sentences are subsidiary concepts in semantics, and yet I begin my discussion by making certain lexical distinctions. Still, the words on which I dwell are tools I need to carry out the intentions and promote the values that constitute the substance of my meanings, so there is no paradox after all.

As must be obvious, my topic takes us into areas I could only disingenuously pretend to understand and that, even if I did, I could only superficially treat in the space available. All that I can hope to do here is to identify some of the problems that must be solved if the affective dimensions of meaning are to be understood. As a first and exceedingly complex challenge, my title charges me with specifying what *affectivity* and *meaning* mean, or at least what I mean when I use those words. I begin with the sticky business of affectivity, and I do so in the curiously roundabout way of examining what is meant by the word *cognition*.

Affect and Cognition

Somewhere between Leibniz and Kant the mind was divided into three parts: cognition, affection, and conation (Hilgard, 1980). What got carved up originally was, of course, conscious experience. Classically, cognition was the name given to knowing in the broadest sense, affection referred to feelings and emotions, and conation to volition and the will. Although the fortunes of these terms have waxed and waned, they have been used repeatedly for 200 years and remain basic categories in psychology today. But a curious situation has arisen.

"Cognitive science" is the academic psychology currently in vogue, but it is no longer certain what cognition means. In fact, comparing the rhetoric with the practice of modern cognitivists leads to troubling conundrums. On the one hand, by holding onto the tripartite division of mind, cognitive psychologists have divorced the study of affection and conation from the study of knowing. With respect to affectivity, this trend has been so pervasive and so determined that in his history of the rise of cognitive psychology Howard Gardner (1985) listed *deemphasis on affect, context, culture, and history* as one of the defining features of cognitive science. With respect to conation, the subject is so far from cognitive scientists' thoughts that it has not even been graced with explicit exclusion, although it creeps in through the concept of intention. By dramatic contrast, the study of knowing has led ineluctably to the realization that knowledge is not something that exists apart from feeling (Blanchet, 1986; Brown, 1990; Brown & Weiss, 1987; Cellérier, 1979a, 1979b; Pugh, 1977), nor is it separate from volition and willing (Bullock, 1991; Nuttin, 1963/1968; Piaget, 1936/1952). As Darwin, Baldwin, Piaget, and others told us so very many years ago, knowledge is adaptation; as we are beginning to realize today, affection and conation are centrally involved in adaptation and constitute, therefore, crucial activities in the construction and use of knowledge. This leaves us in the strange position of asking, "What then is cognition?" because, by itself, it is not knowledge. "And what are cognitive psychologists?" because they ignore fundamental aspects of knowing.

Were there more time and were our topic not so complicated, I would attempt an answer. As it is, I must eschew the advice of Oscar Wilde to "resist all except temptation" and leave these queries open. Let me, then, proceed directly to the troubling question, "What is affectivity?" because that is central to our discussion.

The Evolutionary Perspective

What I want to do as quickly as I can is make clear the role that affectivity plays in mental adaptation, in the construction of knowledge, and then go on to differentiate affectivity from other categories such as emotion, arousal, and motivation with which it often is confused. That done, we can consider meaning and what affectivity contributes to it.

In *Morphisms and Categories* (Piaget, Henriques, & Ascher, 1990/1992), Piaget admitted that transformations are not all there is to mental life. Alongside transformations, there are comparisons and correspondences, categories and morphisms that play a central role in psychological construction. And it was his own creation of an isomorphism between genomic and intellectual processes that inspired everything that came thereafter. It was his realization that variation and selection had become psychologically possible that formed the essence of his theory and set his scientific program for life.[2]

---

[2]Lakoff's work on metaphor (chapter 3 of this volume) almost certainly explores one manifestation of the correspondences, morphisms, and categories that concerned Piaget in *Morphisms and Categories* (Piaget et al., 1990/1992). In particular, the prevalence of action metaphors described by Lakoff is strikingly similar to Piaget's notion of internalized schemes of action considered from the point of view of correspondences. The difficulty of the subject and space limitations do not allow me to develop the parallels here.

Certainly it is true that the analogy between organic evolution and knowledge did not originate with Piaget. In fact, in his review of evolutionary ideas in epistemology, Donald Campbell (1974/1987) found evidence of analogies between Lamarck's theory of organic adaptation and the construction of knowledge as early as Herbert Spencer (1862/1976) and analogies of a more Darwinian stripe in Alexander Bain (1874), Stanley Jevons (1874), and Paul Souriau (1881). But he identified Karl Popper as "the modern founder and leading advocate of a natural-selection epistemology" (p. 89), citing full expressions of these ideas in Popper's (1932/1979) first book published in 1932.

Now, you might ask, how does Piaget figure in Campbell's (1974/1987) reading of this history? Campbell referred to Piaget on two occasions only. One was to list him along with 28 other thinkers who have "considered some kind of an evolutionary interpretation of Kant's categories" (p. 83). The second reference is in a footnote concerning James Mark Baldwin. What he said is that if Baldwin's work "left any mark at all, it was in the French tradition out of which Jean Piaget's recent work on genetic epistemology emerges" (p. 77).

To me, Campbell's (1974/1987) estimation of Piaget's role in this history is disappointing. Because the burden of my thesis is that feelings somewhat less refined than necessity and truth play a major role even in our professional decisions, I digress briefly to set the record straight. Campbell's myopia may then be viewed as an illustration of my thesis.

Around 1912, when Piaget was 15 or 16, his godfather, worried about the boy's absorption with science, invited him for a visit, the purpose of which was to initiate him philosophically. About their conversations, Piaget (1976) had this to say:

> This was the first time that I had heard philosophy spoken of by anyone other than a theologian. I must admit that the shock was immense . . . The identification of God with life itself was an idea that moved me almost to ecstasy because it allowed me, from that moment onward, to see in biology the explanation of all things, even of the spirit . . . The problem of knowledge (properly speaking, the problem of epistemology) suddenly appeared to me in an entirely new perspective and as a fascinating subject for study. This made me decide to dedicate my life to explaining knowledge biologically. (pp. 7–8)

Six years later, Piaget (1918) published *Recherche*, the novel written when he was forbidden to work because of nervous exhaustion and in which he first laid out his "system." And true to his conviction that there is little worth in a philosophic system without some means of control, in the 1920s he began producing a nearly endless stream of publications supporting empirically his evolving conception of how knowledge is constructed. This, added to the fact that Piaget has been the author most cited in child development studies for almost 40 years (Wadsworth, 1989), settles the issue of priority in the modern era in favor of Piaget. One wonders, therefore, how a scholar so thorough as Campbell (1974/1987) could have made an error of this sort. No doubt it has to do with the isolation of philosophy of science from the empirical study of how knowledge is constructed, an isolation Piaget struggled to correct throughout his life (Piaget & Garcia, 1983/1989).

However history eventually decides these issues, neither Popper nor Piaget nor any of the scholars in Campbell's (1974/1987) long list of evolutionary epistemologists who have recognized "the existence of mental selectors, which vicariously represent the external environment . . ." (p. 66) have provided a convincing account of how such selectors work. For the most part, the authors on Campbell's list gesture vaguely in the directions of utility, success, or fit. Although I have not completed my examination of all 18 authors, my labors have, to date, not found a single thinker who makes a straightforward and explicit equation of mental selection with the affective system. In fact, the volume in which Campbell's article is reprinted, that is, Radnitzky and Bartley's (1987) *Evolutionary Epistemology, Theory of Rationality, and the Sociology of Knowledge*, although centrally concerned with the parallels between knowledge and organic adaptation, has not a single reference in the index to *affect, appraisal, arousal, drives, emotion, evaluation, intention, interest, motives, needs, preference, tendency, value, volition*, or *will*, although all of those words are used in the texts of the articles. And the same is true of Quine's (1969) "Epistemology Naturalized" and, except for *intention*, it is also true of Kornblith's (1985) *Naturalizing Epistemology*. So I conclude that epistemologists, Piaget included, are as confused about how affectivity contributes to the creation and fixation of beliefs as are the cognitive psychologists who would replace them.

Compare this failure to deal directly with affective issues with the following concerns of S. Chandrasekhar, one of the great scientists of history, discoverer of the upper limit of the mass a star can have and still evolve into a white dwarf, of the mathematical explanation for black holes, and of the possibility of negative ions of hydrogen, among much else. It is Chandrasekhar's thesis that what guides scientific search is an aesthetic, that scientific discovery is shaped by the scientist's idea of what is beautiful. Among the evidence he marshalled (Chandrasekhar, 1987) taken in the main from self-reports provided by great scientists, the following remark made by Hermann Weyl is representative: "My work [said Weyl] always tried to unite the true with the beautiful; but when I had to choose one or the other, I usually chose the beautiful" (p. 52).

And Chandrasekhar (1987) cited two examples showing that Weyl did exactly what he claimed. The first example concerns Weyl's gauge theory of gravitation. Weyl decided that the theory was not true but felt that it was beautiful, so he saved it anyway. Subsequently, the formalism of gauge invariance has been incorporated into quantum electrodynamics. The second example has to do with Weyl's two-component relativistic wave equation of the neutrino. This was rejected by physicists because it violated the invariance of parity, but Weyl retained it on aesthetic grounds. Thirty years later, physicists realized that Weyl was right, that there are situations in which parity is not conserved. So it is not "success," "utility," and "fit" alone that serve as criteria of psychological selection, and I am therefore puzzled as to why Campbell's (1974/1987) evolutionary epistemologists failed to consider feeling. Space permitting, I would look author-by-author at how each of them thought that psychological variation and selection are accomplished. In a brief discussion of this sort, all that I can do is to state baldly how I see this issue and hurry on to consider meaning. In laying out my thesis, there are two important distinctions that must be made. The first is the distinction between affectivity and emotion; the second between affectivity and arousal.

What Affectivity Is and What Affectivity Is Not

The identification of affectivity with emotion is relatively recent, and I do not know the reasons for it. Theorists from the 18th, 19th, and early 20th centuries felt it important to distinguish feelings from emotions (Alston, 1967), but by 1953 when Rapoport (1953/1967) wrote his influential article, "On the Psychoanalytic Theory of Affects," the distinction had dissolved. In his first footnote, Rapoport stated: "The term affect in this paper will be used to stand for the terms 'emotion' and 'feeling' also, since there is no clear distinction in the literature in the use of these terms" (p. 476). And I can find no recent reference that differentiates the three. Ortony, Clore, and Collins (1988) appear to have been on the brink of doing so, but they did not go over the brink in a convincing way. For my own part, I believe that affect (which I equate with feeling) must be distinguished from emotion for the simple reason that the two terms refer to different psychological functions and that the assignation of meaning cannot pretend to anything like authenticity or truth in the midst of such conceptual confusion.

As I suggested in my remarks on evolutionary epistemology, the purpose of affectivity is to *select* perceptions, ideas, and actions. In living systems, the ultimate basis of selection is thermodynamic stability. Through compensatory interaction, the causal mechanisms of which living systems are composed reverse disorganization resulting from thermodynamic equilibration. What is not generally appreciated is that the assessment of stability, adaptation, or what Piaget called "equilibrium" is extremely difficult by other than thermodynamic, causal means. Even at the highest reaches of human reason, adaptation cannot presently be modeled or calculated according to thermodynamic theory, and there is no evidence that psychological systems operate in that way (Brown, 1990; Brown & Weiss, 1987; Inhelder, Garcia, & Vonèche, 1976; Pugh, 1977).

Psychological selection depends, therefore, on evaluative criteria that are not direct measures of adaptation but that, with the possible exceptions of the values of truth and logical necessity, are *surrogates* for such measures (Pugh, 1977). Moreover, psychological evaluation or, more precisely, the results of our largely unconscious evaluative activities appear to consciousness in the form of feelings.

For that reason, I equate evaluation and affection. Concretely, we do not eat because we have in some way computed the adaptive value of eating; we eat because we are hungry. We do not attach to our mothers because we know that it increases our chances of survival; we do so because of feelings of calm, pleasure, and security in her presence that develop in myriad ways as we grow up. Nor are we, from very early on, bored by the familiar, interested in the somewhat unfamiliar, and scared by the truly new because we understand something about the importance of morphisms in developing rationality (Piaget et al., 1990/1992); we do so because thermodynamic processes beyond our ken have selected out these vague heuristics in order to orient activity adaptively. So whether feelings organized around physiological needs, around the adaptive advantages of cohesive populations, or around the development of intelligence are at issue, we are in every case dealing with heuristic estimations that serve as surrogates for thermodynamic selection and that, except perhaps at the highest levels of intellectual evaluation, never constitute true measures of it. But they do make it possible to estimate survival value in rapid and generally sufficing ways (Brown, 1990; Brown & Weiss, 1987; Pugh, 1977).

Now this is not what emotion does at all. In fact, the function of emotion, although it involves intense feeling, is not evaluation per se. Rather, the function of emotion is readaptation in the face of adaptive failure. Emotions are complex reactions that help higher animals and man reequilibrate in situations where their adaptive powers are overtaxed, where their assimilatory, accommodatory, and evaluative powers fail to produce adapted action. Fraisse (1968) made this point etymologically. Both motivation and emotion come from the Latin root *movere*, which means to move. However, the prefix *e-* in emotion means *out of* and indicates, therefore, a *going outside of motivation* or what, in older terms, might be called a loss of motivational set. So emotional reactions, far from being identical with the evaluative activities that play a part in all adaptive activity are what happens when adaptation fails.

There are at least five characteristics of emotion that I mention briefly. First is the *decrease in performance*. When emotional, animals and men exhibit increasing difficulty in maintaining and effectively pursuing goals, and this is as true of positive as it is of negative emotions. Have we not all been so excited or overjoyed that we could not think or pour champagne or that we knocked the teapot over?

The second characteristic of emotion is *feeling*, and this is a source of much confusion. Many of the words we use to label affects, as I use the term, are also words we use to label emotions. But evidence for a split between affectivity and emotion comes from the fact that the lists of words that name them do not match. In fact, the list used to label feelings is a good deal longer than and includes the list used to label emotions. There are no emotions that are not feelings, but there are many feelings that are not emotions. For example, one may be *interested* in something, *have a hunch that*, be *indifferent* to, *feel lazy, be inclined to*, and so forth, without being held to be emotional. But if I say that someone is angry, it is universally assumed that the person not only *feels* angry but that he is *emotional*, whereas in truth, it is possible to experience anger without exhibiting the other features of emotion. In common usage, these categories are degenerate.

The third characteristic of an emotional reaction is *intense arousal*. Arousal is both a psychological and a physiological category (Thayer, 1989). Psychologically, it has to do with the level of consciousness and the intensity of activity. With regard to emotional reactions, as various acts fail to produce progress toward a goal, arousal increases the intensity of both the positive value of succeeding and the negative value of failing. This motivates renewed efforts such as repetition of the means being tried, increases in the speed and force of what is done, institution of alternative methods, and so on. Physiologically, arousal has to do with increased neuroelectrical activity in the reticular core (Coyle, 1988), but that is not a level of analysis that I consider here.

The fourth characteristic of emotion is *involuntary expression*. Darwin was interested in the evolution of emotional expression, and it has received considerable attention since (e.g., Ekman & Friesen, 1975). There is little mystery in the fact that both within and between species, it is adaptively cogent for organisms to signal that they are highly aroused and disposed toward defensive behaviors. And certainly involuntary emotional expression is something of great use in establishing meaning. I do not, however, dwell on this matter, because other affective determinants of meaning are less obvious, less well understood, and require more attention.[3]

Finally, the fifth characteristic of emotion is *defense*. Defenses are low-level, generic readaptive procedures instituted when instrumental actions fail. Their major function is to reduce arousal and diminish the intensity of negative feelings. They occur on every level. The time-honored defenses of the sensorimotor level are fight and flight; Anna Freud (1946) provided the most widely accepted list of semiotic-operational defenses, the so-called ego defenses; and Piaget's (1974) empirically supported idea of "cognitive" repression based on the principle of *Prägnanz*[4] deserves more attention than it has received so far.

In sum then, the function of affectivity is evaluation, which is an aspect of all mental activity except the release of thermodynamically selected instincts,

---

[3]Bloom (chapter 10 of this volume) makes clear that affective states are readable in her subjects before and after they learn to speak in situations where they do not appear to be emotional. The claim here is not that involuntary expression is limited to emotional reactions, but that it is an invariable feature of them. That does not appear to be the case with feelings pure and simple. A great deal of evaluation is unaccompanied by particular expression, although in almost every situation we attribute affective qualities or states to people based on very general characteristics of their behavior. Specific expressions, however, appear to be peculiar to emotions, to be at least in part universal among humans, and even to be shared with other species.

[4] The English translation misses the technical reference to Gestalt psychology. My assertion can only be traced in the French edition.

and along with decreased performance, intense arousal, automatic expression, and defensiveness, it constitutes a component of emotion. By contrast, the function of emotion is readaptation. Although all emotional responses involve feeling, not all feelings are part of emotional reactions. For those reasons, I differentiate the two.

A similar conflation exists with respect to affectivity and arousal. As I hope I have made clear, the function of affectivity is psychological selection. In contrast, the function of arousal is to determine the level of consciousness and the intensity of activity. The crucial point is that arousal varies intensity but has no particular quality and that feelings vary quality but have no particular intensity. To equate affectivity and arousal leads, therefore, to serious problems that, were space available, I would illustrate with shocking psychiatric examples. Constraints being what they are, let me simply mention that conflating affectivity and arousal has led psychiatrists to misclassify *bipolar disorder* as a *mood disorder* when in fact it is a disorder of arousal.

There is a third distinction that should be made with respect to affectivity. This is the distinction between feelings and motivations. Because space is limited and because the issue of motivation devolves onto intention (Bullock, 1991; Nuttin, 1963/1968) and therefore onto meaning, I move on to the second aspect of our topic and deal, insofar as possible, with this third distinction there.

THE MEANING OF MEANING

At the beginning of his two-volume work *Semantics*, John Lyons (1977) examined 10 ways the words *meaning* and *to mean* are used:

1. What is the meaning of "sesquipedalian"?
2. I did not mean to hurt you.
3. He never says what he means.
4. She rarely means what she says.
5. Life without faith has no meaning.
6. What do you mean by the word "concept"?
7. He means well, but he's rather clumsy.
8. Fame and riches mean nothing to the true scholar.
9. Dark clouds mean rain.
10. It was John I meant and not Harry. (pp. 1–2)

In the ensuing discussion, Lyons (1977) indicated that the meaning of *meaning* seems to be closely related to *intending* in Sentences 2, 4, 6, 7, and 10 and that it seems to be closely related to *significance* or *value* in 5 and 8. Only in Sentences 1, 3, 4, and 10 does meaning have much to do with words. After further consideration, Lyons concluded, with respect to the meaning of meaning, that "Most linguists and some philosophers would be inclined to dismiss all but (1), and possibly (10), as exemplifying uses or senses of the words 'meaning' and 'mean' that are of no concern to the semanticist'' (p. 3). But he added: "It is arguable . . . that [even] this sense of 'meaning' cannot be explained or understood except in relation to the notions of intention, on the one hand, and significance (or value), on the other . . ." (p. 3).

For myself, I profoundly agree with Lyons that no theory of meaning can be formulated except in relation to the notions of value and intention. Because, as I insist, evaluation is the function of affectivity, it follows that I do not believe that meaning can be explained or understood except in relation to the notions of affectivity and intention. At the same time, I do not believe that even those concepts provide an adequate foundation for a theory of meaning. That edifice, if it is to last, must be built on the bedrock of a theory of mental adaptation, and that begins with the instinctual behaviors that appear before psychological evaluation or intention. Piaget's (1936/1952) principles of *functional invariance* and *structural continuity* between biological and psychological evolution acknowledge this requirement fully. Jonas Langer's cross-species studies (chapter 9 of this volume) also provide empirical concrete for constructing this foundation.

Explanation and Meaning

Consonant with that belief, I want to review ideas on structural attribution and psychological explanation that I have presented previously (Brown, 1989b). The essence of my argument is that all explanation, the explanation of the behavior of speaking animals as much as the explanation of the behavior of supernovae, has its origins in the subject's experience of himself as causal agent. Because that experience is intentionally structured from very early on (Piaget, 1936/1952), children begin by giving intentional explanations of all of the phenomena that they experience. This is the basis of the magico-phenomenalist causality inherent in sensorimotor reactions (Piaget, 1937/1954) and of the realism, animism, and artificialism that permeate the explanations of preschool children (Piaget, 1926/1972a, 1927/1972b). It is also what underlies many forms of illegitimate explanation exhibited by adults, perhaps the most striking being the teleological explanations so widespread in physics before Galileo and so widespread in biology up to and even after Darwin.

This reading was disputed by Carey (1985) who contended that mechanical and psychological causation are disjoint foundational concepts present, apparently, from birth and immutable thereafter. She therefore contested the conception promoted here, specifically that physical causation is differentiated out of the child's experience of himself as causal agent. Spatial constraints dictate that I make three points only. The first is that Carey's antagonism to Piaget's "*structures d'ensemble,*" that is, his notions of concrete and formal operational stages, and her argument in favor of domain specific construction is, in fact, based on a common misconception that Piaget's structures are constructed apart from domain-specific content and then applied to it. In reality, Piaget's position is that such structures are abstracted out of domain-specific constructions (Piaget, 1972) and depend crucially on them. Although it is true that his first models of formal operations indicated that such operations eventually are freed from all but the truth ''content'' of propositions, his revision of formal operational theory (Piaget & Garcia, 1987/1990) backs away from that extreme position by reintroducing semantic content.

My second point is that Carey's (1985) contention that "Piaget held that young children have no concept of mechanical causation'' (p. 193) is simply untrue. Consider, for example, the following excerpt from *The Child's Conception of Physical Causality* (Piaget, 1927/1972b): ''. . . during each [stage of mental development], the mind believes itself to be apprehending an external reality that is independent of the thinking subject . . . for the young child [that reality] is alive and permeated with finality, intentions, etc., whereas for the scientist, reality is characterized by its physical determinism. But the ontological function, so to speak, remains identical: each in his own way thinks that he has found the outer world in himself'' (p. 237). Carey's disjunction of psychological and physical theories is, on this view, untenable. All physical theories are contained within psychological theories, either in the form of pragmatic or in the form of logicomathematical structures.

My third and final point is that Carey (1985) herself produced no evidence on the nature of physical concepts or explanation. Her experiments center on the construction of biological concepts, and she concluded from them that children are ''endowed with the tools to build an intuitive psychology'' (p. 200) out of which their biological theories will be built. That contention, of course, affirms an important aspect of my own point of view. With regard to physical knowledge, the interpretations on which Carey based her primordial distinction of physical and biological-psychological causation are profoundly incoherent (Brown, 1989a).

Viewed from my perspective, the attribution of intentional frameworks is neither biologically inscribed nor is it illegitimate altogether. Rather, the child must learn when and how to make such attributions accurately. In explaining causal constellations that have come together by chance, that is, inorganic phenomena (Cellérier, 1976/1983; Cellérier & Ducret, 1990), it is not cricket to invoke organizing control of any sort. The only aspect of the child's phenomenal experience that may be attributed to the actions of inanimate objects are those aspects that have been freed from intentionality and feelings other than necessity. It is precisely this freeing from intentionality (Inhelder & Piaget, 1979) and this construction of a feeling of necessity (Piaget, 1981–1983/1987) that produces Piaget's operational structures. This eliminative procedure is what makes such structures the prime instruments for explaining physical events and provides the basis of Piaget's theory of causal explanation (Piaget & Garcia, 1971/1974).

When it comes to phenomena in which the causal constituents have not come together purely by chance (e.g., biological, psychological, or social phenomena), children's attributions need to include additional elements of their experience as causal agent. In biology, for example, they need to include some principle of selection corresponding to the affective evaluations that accomplish selection in thought and action. Because it hardly would have done to attribute feelings to the universe at large, Darwin invoked *selection by nature* as the basic explanatory principle of organic evolution, but he did not understand the mechanisms of selection in a profound way. Only recently have explicit theories of thermodynamic stabilization (Brooks & Wiley, 1986; Prigogine, 1980; Prigogine & Stengers, 1984) begun to give us some preliminary understanding of nature's "feelings," so to speak, of why nature "prefers" one highly organized constellation of causal mechanisms to another.

With psychology and sociology, of course, intentional attribution is on firmer ground and constitutes an essential element of many psychological and sociological explanations. Consider, for example, Richard II's (Shakespeare, 1593–1594/1936) interpretation of Northumberland's failure to kneel before him at Flint Castle:

> We are amazed; and thus long have we stood
> To watch the fearful bending of thy knee,
> Because we thought ourself thy lawful king:
> And if we be, how dare thy joints forget
> To pay their awful duty to our presence?
> If we be not, show us the hand of God
> That hath dismiss'd us from our stewardship;
> For well we know, no hand of blood and bone
> Can gripe the sacred handle of our sceptre,
> Unless he do profane, steal, or usurp.
> And though you think that all, as you have done,
> Have torn their souls by turning them from us,
> And we are barren and bereft of friends;
> Yet know, my master, God omnipotent,
> Is mustering in his clouds on our behalf
> Armies of pestilence; and they shall strike
> Your children yet unborn and unbegot,
> That lift their vassal hands against my head,
> And threat the glory of my precious crown. (p. 370)

If we look at what Richard is doing in explaining Northumberland's behavior, it is clear that it is something more than just attributing lexical semantic knowledge to him. In fact, Northumberland has not yet spoken. Nor is Richard just attributing feelings and emotions. The essence of Richard's interpretation is the attribution of an entire motivational structure determining Northumberland's refusal to kneel as protocol prescribes he should. In the beginning of the play,

Richard banishes Henry Bolingbroke for 6 years. Soon after, Bolingbroke's father, John of Gaunt, falls ill and dies after having reproached Richard for his dissolute life and irresponsible reign. Richard seizes Gaunt's holdings to support his Irish wars and thereby robs Bolingbroke of his inheritance. But Richard's fortunes turn. While he is in Ireland, Bolingbroke breaks exile, returns to England, and raises an army against him. Northumberland, a nobleman estranged from Richard, has joined forces with Bolingbroke and has been sent as his messenger to meet Richard at Flint Castle. When Richard appears on the castle wall, Northumberland fails to kneel, clearly denying that he recognizes Richard as king.

Richard's interpretation takes all of this into account by attributing a highly complicated model of intentionally organized teleonomic structure. The elements of that model have been constructed out of information of many sorts including but not limited to his knowledge of human feelings. There are facts about what etiquette requires, about the strength of his forces weakened by desertion, about Bolingbroke's alliances, about the probabilities of victory and escape, and about much else that go into Richard's explanation.

Alongside this factual information, affectivity enters Richard's understanding in two ways. First, there is the affective content of the model he attributes to Northumberland having to do with suppositions about the feelings that have shaped Northumberland's behavior. Second, there are Richard's own affective processes that have helped mold his interpretation. A less guilty, less vain, and less suspicious king might simply have inquired whether Northumberland had hurt his knee. Circumstances being what they are, such an explanation seems unlikely, and Richard affords it little value.

My point is that children are naturally inclined to make intentional attributions of this sort, albeit less complicated and in less elaborate language, but they have three kinds of difficulties to overcome before they can do so accurately. One difficulty arises from the fact that there are some, even many, psychological phenomena that are not intentional. The second difficulty arises from the fact that intentional attributions are not accurate a priori but must be controlled by evidence of many kinds to ensure that they really reflect the other person's meaning. The third difficulty arises from attempts to exclude intention; it arises from attempts to reduce psychological and sociological phenomena to biological or physical phenomena and nothing else. Let me illustrate these pitfalls with examples.

Pitfalls in Attributing Intentions

In our time, psychoanalysts have, I suppose, more than any other group carried intentional explanation to an extreme (Brown, 1991). I cannot tell you with what ferocity I, as a psychiatric resident, opposed supervisors' suggestions that I interpret every flat tire that made a patient late as some form of unconsciously motivated resistance. On one occasion I even refused to continue with a supervisor who explained a poor girl's reaction to having had an abortion in terms of motivated avoidance of a "fecal penis," whatever that was supposed to mean. And teaching of the idea that all behavior stems from unconscious motivation has not ended (Marmer, 1988; Nicholi, 1988) despite Grünbaum's (1984) devastating attack on Freud's theory of unconscious symbolization and Eagle's (1983) gentler insistence that when we frame explanations in terms of temperament, history, or environmental conditions we leave the realm of intentional or motivational explanation altogether. So one error that must be avoided in psychology is the attribution of intention where there is none; it is an error that Piaget (1967/1971, p. 38) referred to as reduction of the *lower* to the *higher*.

The second pitfall mentioned earlier, that is, the misattribution of intentions, takes two forms. The maxim "Don't judge others by yourself," gives solid evidence that the mistake of attributing one's own intentions to others is common. Who has not made or had to correct misattributions of this sort? The second kind of intentional misattribution, that is, attribution of a faulty model, is widespread also. Consider, for example, an experiment of Maratsos (1973). He tested children from 3 to 5 years of age on a task requiring them to communicate to another person which toy they wanted the person to put in a car and roll down a hill. Under one set of conditions the person could see the toys; under a second set, he could not. What Maratsos found was that children spontaneously differentiated the two sets of conditions. When the person rolling the cars down the hill could see, children usually indicated their choices by pointing and said little. When the person could not see, children spontaneously switched to verbal depictions. Responses in the second situation were scored as "adequate" or "inadequate" on the criterion that the response "would have been sufficient to specify the desired toy to a blindfolded person." What is strange about all this is that Maratsos considered statements like "the red duck" to be adequate responses. This means that if a child says to a blindfolded person, "Would you please send the red duck down the hill in the car," he is communicating adequately. Apparently both Maratsos and certain of his subjects believe that verbal communication about the visually perceptible properties of an object adequately accounts for the subjectivity of unsighted persons! Surely this is a misattribution.

In the same vein, Dean's feeling that I see him as a psychiatric "trick" constitutes an example of this second sort of error. It was the misattribution of his anonymous lovers' feelings and intentions to me that inspired him to write the poem. It was my evaluation of his misattribution that made me sad.

The third pitfall, that is, the error of refusing to attribute intentional finality even when dealing with intentionally organized phenomena, presents a curious situation because, unlike the two types of errors just mentioned, it is not universally recognized to be an error. Moreover, although it is occasionally seen in children, it is much more an error of children grown up. Under the rubric of reductionism, it has gained wide currency in our philosophic and scientific literatures, and it shapes our educational and research institutions in important ways.

In contemporary psychology there are two important and related movements that are organized around this sort of error. One centers on attempts to reduce mind to the biological mechanisms of the brain; the other centers on attempts to reduce mental phenomena to emergent effects arising from changes in the connectivity of networks composed of very large numbers of simple elements (Bunge & Ardila, 1987; Hanson & Burr, 1990; Smolensky, 1988). I use the first of these as my example of the third pitfall in attributing intentions.

Bunge (1990) provided a particularly bold statement of the neurophysiologic reductionist point of view: "Every explanation invokes some mechanism and every mechanism proper is material: There are no behavioral or mental mechanisms but only neuromuscular, neuroendocrine, or neuroimmune mechanisms" (p. 129). And similar or even stronger versions of the same basic position may be found in Coyle (1988), P. S. Churchland (1988), and P. M. Churchland (1981). At its worst, this form of reductionism even holds that mental entities, for example, perceptions, ideas, feelings, motivations, and so forth, are no more than neurophysiological entities and that once neurophysiological knowledge is sufficiently developed, there will be no further need to speak of mind (Wimsatt, 1976).

Space permitting, I would make the following points: (a) The word *mechanism* has multiple meanings; (b) even many physical explanations do not invoke mechanisms in the strict sense of the term; (c) mechanisms are not necessarily material; (d) mechanisms are not in themselves explanatory; and (e) neuromuscular, neuroendocrine, or neuroimmune mechanisms do not include and cannot explain psychological intention. (For a lengthier discussion, see Brown, 1991.) Under existing constraints, I can only provide two examples from the history of science which instruct us that explanations precede the discovery of physical instantiations and cannot, therefore, depend on mechanisms defined as material and, correlatively, that the mechanisms invoked in explanations may well be functional rather than material.

Consider first Darwin's explanation of the origin of species. The solution Darwin formulated was based on principles of variation, selection, and hereditary transmission; he knew nothing of the physical mechanisms by which these functions were accomplished. When 50 years later his principles were coupled with the laws of Mendelian inheritance, "neo-Darwinian" theory led to a search for the physical mechanisms by which the evolution of species was accomplished (Mayr, 1982). In what, researchers questioned, does Darwin's "inherited constitution" consist, how does it vary, and in what way is selection carried out? Eventually the first two questions were answered in terms of mutation, meiosis, mitosis, and certain other biophysical phenomena involving nucleic acid structures; the physical basis of selection remains a mystery. What is it then, that explains evolution? Is it Darwin's principles or is it nucleic acid chemistry? I come back to this question after a second example.

This has to do with Chandrasekhar's (1987) interpretation of Kerr's solution of the equations of general relativity as an explanation of black holes. Very early in his career Chandrasekhar calculated that if a star has a mass greater than about 1.4 times the mass of the sun, it cannot evolve into a white dwarf—the then-reigning notion of what happened to stars—"and one is left speculating on other possibilities." The idea was spurned by Eddington on affective grounds: "I think there should be a law of nature to prevent a star from behaving in this absurd way" (Tierney, 1991, p. 607) and was laid aside for 30 years. Eventually, however, Chandrasekhar's "limit" became the basis of the theory of black holes. When he was 63, Chandrasekhar again took up the subject. Let him describe the experience of discovery for himself: ". . . the most shattering experience [of my entire scientific life] has been the realization that an exact solution of Einstein's equations of general relativity, discovered by the New Zealand mathematician Roy Kerr, provides the *absolutely exact representation* of untold numbers of massive black holes that populate the universe" (Chandrasekhar, 1987, p. 54).

Now given that evidence for the existence of "black holes" is only recently discovered and not very certain (Penrose, 1974/1991), we again find ourselves in the somewhat startling position of having the explanation precede the physical instantiation of it. At least with Darwin, we had fossil evidence that species appear and disappear, but for a very long time black holes were only an inference from relativity theory. And even today, the best evidence we have is that every $5\frac{1}{2}$ days HDE 226868 in *Cygnus the Swan* circles about some sort of massive companion that we cannot see. So again, are we to conclude that material mechanisms are the stuff of which explanations are made or are we to conclude that they simply instantiate explanatory ideas? Even in this completely physical example, the parallel with the Darwin story cannot be denied.

What, then, may we conclude from these examples? First and foremost, as inferential models the elements of which are empirically established facts or laws (Piaget, 1963/1968), explanations invoke possibilities of action, possibilities that may be realized in various ways. In Darwin's case, variation and selection were modeled on the human choices practiced in animal husbandry, not on biological phenomena known to exist. In Chandrasekhar's case, his supposition of a limit to the size a star could have and still undergo white dwarf evolution was derived from quantitative considerations indicating that Pauli's exclusion principle could not resist the continued gravitational collapse of stars of sufficient mass; it was not derived from astronomical phenomena known to exist. So it appears that Bunge's formula must be turned around; that is, phenomena take on mechanistic meaning only within the context of explanatory theories and every explanation is psychological. Moreover, this reformulation implies that mechanisms need not be material but may well be functional constructs within biological, psychological, or sociological theories. (Overton, 1992, provided a particularly clean dissection of materialist and rationalist perspectives.)

On this view, Darwin's attribution to reality of a mental model of interacting biological functions—however realized physically—to organic evolution explains why chromosomes and nucleic acids are required; it gives them biological *meaning.* Without that, they would be mere biochemical curiosities. Conversely, the discovery of nucleic acids and the base-pair code shows how Darwin's theory is physically realized; it gives that theory biological *reality.* And similarly, Chandrasekhar's application of Kerr's solution to black holes explains or makes the observational phenomena meaningful, whereas the orbit of HDE 226868 gives Kerr's solution physical reality. In either case, the observational discoveries are only "the" or "a" mechanism by which Darwin's or Kerr's explanations are accomplished, instantiated, physically realized, or whatever other term is fitting. But both Darwin's and Kerr's theories are derivatives of their subjective experience scrubbed clean of inappropriate intentional, teleonomic elements. So it appears that all their lives and all their history people struggle to attribute aspects of their inner being accurately. And such attributions, their affective aspects included, are the source of meaning.

MEANING AND BEING

All that said, I ask myself whether I have told you anything interesting about the affective aspects of meaning. Perhaps a summary would help. The argument that I have been trying to sketch out goes as follows:

1. Intelligence is an adaptation, the function of which is to reproduce through internal resources of the organism the processes of organic evolution.
2. To do this, requires some sort of internal natural selection.
3. This internalized selection is the function of the affective system.
4. Psychological evaluation does not work through exact computation of adaptive value; rather it works through a surrogate system of heuristic estimations, the output of which is manifest in consciousness in the form of feelings.
5. The concerted action of affective evaluation approximates natural selection closely enough that ideas and actions selected in this way are generally effective in producing adaptation.
6. Feelings, although a component of emotion, are not emotions.
7. Feelings may produce arousal and thereby increase their own intensity; but intensity is the business of the arousal system. That system affects many components of mental activity and is not synonymous with feeling.
8. One is born with an undetermined number of affective schemes and these develop by processes not yet understood.
9. "Truth" and "necessity" are feelings and are, therefore, components of the affective system. They may have special status as true measures of adaptation, but the question remains unsettled.

10. The common language uses of meaning are intimately tied up with values and intentions.

11. Evaluation begins before intention.[5]

12. Intention begins before language.

13. Because of 11 and 12, semantics is not and can never be a purely linguistic discipline.

14. Theories of understanding are more fundamental to theories of meaning than are theories of language, of intention, or of affectivity.

15. All explanation consists in the attribution of semiotic-operational structure, whether axiologic, pragmatic, or logicomathematic.

16. Several types of explanation are differented out of the primordial subjective matrix of intentional causality, and we speak of each in terms of meaning.

17. Explanatory development involves keeping these different types of explanation and, therefore, these different meanings of meaning straight.

18. Physical explanations consist in the attribution of atemporal, operational structures to systems of causes that have come together by chance.

19. Biological explanations consist in the attribution of goal-directed, teleonomic structures to systems of causes that have been organized through external (thermodynamic) selection.

20. Except for instincts, psychological explanations consist in the attribution of goal-directed (habitual and intentional) or goal-corrected (intentional only) teleonomic structures to systems of causes that have been organized through internalized selection.

21. The affective dimensions of meaning are equivalent to and can only be understood from the point of view of the role that internal selection plays in psychological adaptation.

Reviewing this list of what I hope are entailed and entailing statements, I realize how far I have come up short in explicating fully the affective dimensions of meaning. I have said most of this before, and I have said nothing about how axiological knowledge is constructed—the problem that absorbs me currently. But I do not try to patch things up. Rather, I would like, in the few pages remaining, to point to a final feature of affectivity that Archibald MacLeish (1955) made clear with regard to poetry and that bears in an important way on all theories of meaning.

---

[5]What I have in mind is hedonic learning prior to the advent of intention. This involves selection of schemes of action whole rather than evaluation of means relative to ends. Although present throughout our lives in terms of habit formation, hedonic learning is overshadowed by more differentiated intentional evaluative structures very early in the infant's life. The exact age is unimportant.

A poem should be palpable and mute
As a globed fruit

Dumb
As old medallions to the thumb

Silent as the sleeve-worn stone
Of casement ledges where the moss has grown—

A poem should be wordless
As the flight of birds

A poem should be motionless in time
As the moon climbs

Leaving, as the moon releases
Twig by twig the night-entangled trees,

Leaving, as the moon behind the winter leaves,
Memory by memory the mind—

A poem should be motionless in time
As the moon climbs

A poem should be equal to:
Not true

For all the history of grief
An empty doorway and a maple leaf

For love
The leaning grasses and two lights above the sea—

A poem should not mean
But be.

MacLeish's (1955) focus in this poem is the distinction Aristotle (4th century B.C./1941) made between rhetoric and dialectic and that I believe relates to something fundamental about feelings. Recall in this respect, that feelings precede intention, that they are a constituent of what Piaget called "sensorimotor awareness" and what Jackendoff (1987; see also chapter 6 of this volume), if I understand him, referred to as "unreflected" or primary awareness. As such, they are akin to perceptions, and it is no more mysterious that interaction between affective structures and their inputs leads to the conscious experience of feelings than it is that interaction between perceptual structures and their inputs leads to the conscious experience of perceptions. Perhaps we know a bit more about lower level perceptual processes, but with regard to how they produce their conscious products, we understand them not one whit better than we understand affective processes. What we do know is that, moved to the semiotic-operational or reflective level, there is at least one great difference. It is this difference that underlies MacLeish's distinction between meaning and being.

Perhaps I can make myself clearer by indicating the way we communicate perceptual information. When we want a young child who does not speak or a deaf friend to see something, we point or turn their heads in the right direction. It is only by orienting their sensory organs that we can make them perceive the object of our interest. When the object is no longer present, we cannot make others perceive it, and we cannot ourselves perceive it either. We can, however, through mnemonic evocation bring back the image of, say, a tree, recall its form, its color, and its movement. And we can communicate these memories to enabled others using words, drawings, or symbols of other kinds. Although these memories and our communicative activity result in meanings reminiscent of the tree, the experience of those meanings is qualitatively different from the experience of perception.

Now it is not the same with feelings. True, it is possible to recall affective experience as well as perceptual experience using signs and symbols without actually reliving the experience. But in addition to dispassionate evocative recall of this kind, we can also use signs and symbols to create primary affective experience in another person. In fact, we can create such experience in many different ways. We may caress our fellows, shake them, stick out our tongues, or turn our backs. We may say beautiful or hurtful things. We may sing a song, put a sprig of rosemary beneath their noses, or paint a funny picture. The point is that, unlike perception, both sensorimotor and symbolic behaviors can cause indistinguishable experiences of feeling. The affective meaning of the statement "Tom is angry!" is not just the information it conveys about Tom's feelings or emotions but, when it is intended, it is also the feeling or emotion the speaker causes in the hearer. The look of fear or disgust or shame that crosses the hearer's face may well reflect the statement's affective meaning. At the same time, that is not necessarily the case. Feelings arise from the hearer's evaluation of the meaning he assigns the statement, but they constitute the statement's *affective meaning* only to the degree that they are effects intended by the speaker.[6] Intended or unintended, the experience of feeling is the distinctive feature of being in MacLeish's sense.

The importance that I ascribe to this distinction brings us back to Dean's poem and to the end of this long reminiscence. I think I understood Dean's metaphorical meaning when I restated it in terms of tricks and lovers. But I do not think that it was that interpretation or anything like it that has given him the courage to go on living. It was the value I assigned his metaphor; it was its effect on me, manifest in my sadness and my silence, that produced in him a feeling, finally, of being understood and loved. It was the being, not the meaning of his poem.

---

[6]When MacLeish (1955) said, "a poem should not mean," he was referring to lexical semantic meaning, not the affective meaning I am describing here.

REFERENCES

Alston, W. P. (1967). Emotion and feeling. In P. Edwards (Ed.), *Encyclopedia of philosophy* (Vol. 2, pp. 479–486). New York: Macmillan.

Aristotle. (1941). Rhetorica. In R. McKoen (Ed.), *The basic works of Aristotle* (pp. 1317–1451). New York: Random House. (Original work published 4th century B.C.)

Bain, A. (1874). *The senses and the intellect* (3rd ed.). New York: Appleton.

Blanchet, A. (1986). Rôle des valeurs et des systèmes de valeurs dans la cognition. *Archives de Psychologie, 54*, 251–270.

Brooks, D. R., & Wiley, E. O. (1986). *Evolution as entropy.* Chicago: University of Chicago Press.

Brown, T. (1990). The biological significance of affectivity. In N. L. Stein, B. L. Leventhal, & T. Trabasso (Eds.), *Biological and psychological approaches to emotion* (pp. 405–434). Hillsdale, NJ: Lawrence Erlbaum Associates.

Brown, T. (1991). Psychiatry's unholy marriage: Psychoanalysis and neuroscience. In D. Offer & M. Sabshin (Eds.), *The diversity of normal behavior* (pp. 305–355). New York: Basic.

Brown, T. (1989a, June). *Affective aspects of infants' cognitive abilities.* Paper presented at the 19th Annual Symposium of the J. Piaget Society, Philadelphia.

Brown, T. (1989b, June). *Structural attribution as a model for psychological explanation.* Paper presented at an international congress entitled "Piaget e os Novos Desafios nas Ciências e na Educaçao," Lisbon. (This paper is an expanded version of a paper entitled *A Piagetian Account of Psychological Explanation,* written with K. Ryan, and presented at the 18th Annual Symposium of the Jean Piaget Society held in Philadelphia on June 2, 1988.)

Brown, T., & Weiss, L. (1987). Structures, procedures, heuristics, and affectivity. *Archives de Psychologie, 55*, 59–94.

Bullock, M. (Ed.). (1991). The development of intentional action: Cognitive, motivational, and interactive processes. In D. Kuhn (Ed.), *Contributions to human development* (Vol. 22). Basel, Switzerland: Karger.

Bunge, M. (1990). What kind of discipline is psychology: Autonomous or dependent, humanistic or scientific, biological or sociological? *New Ideas in Psychology, 8*, 121–137.

Bunge, M., & Ardila, R. (1987). *Philosophy of psychology.* New York: Springer.

Campbell, D. (1987). Evolutionary epistemology. In G. Radnitzky & W. W. Bartley III (Eds.), *Evolutionary epistemology, theory of rationality, and the sociology of knowledge* (pp. 47–89). LaSalle, IL: Open Court. (Original work published 1974).

Carey, S. (1985). *Conceptual change in childhood.* Cambridge, MA: MIT Press.

Cellérier, G. (1983). The historical genesis of cybernetics: Is teleonomy a category of understanding? (T. Brown, Trans.). *Nature and System, 5*, 211–225. (Original work published 1976)

Cellérier, G. (1979a). Structures cognitives et schèmes d'action, I. *Archives de Psychologie, 47*, 87–106.

Cellérier, G. (1979b). Structures cognitives et schèmes d'action, II. *Archives de Psychologie, 47*, 107–122.

Cellérier, G., & Ducret, J.-J. (1990). Psychology and computation: A response to Bunge. *New Ideas in Psychology, 8*, 159–175.

Chandrasekhar, S. (1987). *Truth and beauty.* Chicago: University of Chicago Press.

Churchland, P. M. (1981). Eliminative materialism and the propositional attitudes. *The Journal of Philosophy, 78*, 67–90.

Churchland, P. S. (1988). *Neurophilosophy: Toward a unified science of mind/brain.* Cambridge, MA: MIT Press.

Coyle, J. T. (1988). Neuroscience and psychiatry. In J. A. Talbott, R. E. Hales, & S. C. Yudofsky (Eds.), *The American Psychiatric Press textbook of psychiatry* (pp. 3–32). Washington, DC: American Psychiatric Press.

Eagle, M. N. (1983). A critical examination of motivational explanation in psychoanalysis. In L. Laudan (Ed.), *Mind and medicine* (pp. 311–353). Berkeley: University of California Press.

Ekman, P., & Friesen, W. V. (1975). *Unmasking the face.* Englewood Cliffs, NJ: Prentice-Hall.

Fraisse, P. (1968). The emotions. In P. Fraisse & J. Piaget (Eds.), *Experimental psychology: Its scope and method. V. Motivation, emotion, and personality* (A. Spillmann, Trans.) (pp. 102–191). New York: Basic. (Original work published 1963)

Freud, A. (1946). *The ego and the mechanisms of defence.* New York: International Universities Press.

Gardner, H. (1985). *The mind's new science.* New York: Basic.

Grünbaum, A. (1984). *The foundations of psychoanalysis: A Philosophical critique.* Berkeley: University of California Press.

Hanson, S. J., & Burr, D. J. (1990). What connectionist models learn: Learning and representation in connectionist networks. *Behavioral and Brain Sciences, 13,* 471–518.

Hilgard, E. R. (1980). The trilogy of mind: Cognition, affection, and conation. *Journal of the History of the Behavioral Sciences, 16,* 107–117.

Inhelder, B., Garcia, R., & Vonèche, J. (Eds.). (1976). *Épistémologie génétique et équilibration.* Neuchâtel, Switzerland: Delachaux et Niestlé.

Inhelder, B., & Piaget, J. (1979). Procédures et structures. *Archives de Psychologie, 47,* 165–176.

Jackendoff, R. (1987). *Consciousness and the computational mind.* Cambridge, MA: MIT Press.

Jevons, S. (1874). *The principles of science* (1st ed.). London: Macmillan.

Kornblith, H. (Ed.). (1985). *Naturalizing epistemology.* Cambridge, MA: MIT Press.

Lyons, J. (1977). *Semantics: I & II.* Cambridge, England: Cambridge University Press.

MacLeish, A. (1955). Ars poetica. In L. Untermeyer with K. Shapiro & R. Wilbur (Eds.), *Modern American and modern British poetry* (pp. 272–273). New York: Harcourt Brace Jovanovich.

Maratsos, M. P. (1973). Nonegocentric communication abilities in preschool children. *Child Development, 44,* 697–700.

Marmer, S. S. (1988). Theories of the mind and psychopathology. In J. A. Talbott, R. E. Hales, & S. C. Yudofsky (Eds.), *The American Psychiatric Press textbook of psychiatry* (pp. 123–162). Washington, DC: American Psychiatric Press.

Mayr, E. (1982). *The growth of biological thought: Diversity, evolution, and inheritance.* Cambridge, MA: Harvard University Press.

Nicholi, A. M., Jr. (1988). *The new Harvard guide to psychiatry.* Cambridge, MA: Harvard University Press.

Nuttin, J. (1968). Motivation. In P. Fraisse & J. Piaget (Eds.), *Experimental psychology: Its scope and method. V. Motivation, emotion, and personality* (A. Spillmann, Trans.) (pp. 1–101). New York: Basic. (Original work published 1963)

Ortony, A., Clore, G. L., & Collins, A. (1988). *The cognitive structure of emotions.* Cambridge, England: Cambridge University Press.

Overton, W. F. (1992). The structure of developmental theory. In H. W. Reese (Ed.), *Advances in child development and behavior* (Vol. 23, pp. 1–37). New York: Academic.

Penrose, R. (1991). Black holes. In T. Ferris (Ed.), *The world treasury of physics, astronomy, and mathematics* (pp. 203–225). Boston: Little, Brown. (Original work published 1974)

Piaget, J. (1918). *Recherche.* Lausanne, Switzerland: Edition La Concorde.

Piaget, J. (1952). *The origins of intelligence in children* (M. Cook, Trans.). New York: International Universities Press. (Original work published 1936)

Piaget, J. (1954). *The construction of reality in the child* (M. Cook, Trans.). New York: Basic. (Original work published 1937)

Piaget, J. (1971). *Biology and knowledge.* Chicago: University of Chicago Press. (Original work published 1967)

Piaget, J. (1972a). *The child's conception of the world* (J. Tomlinson & A. Tomlinson, Trans.). Totowa, NJ: Littlefield, Adams. (Original work published 1926)

Piaget, J. (1972b). *The child's conception of physical causality* (M. Gabain, Trans.). Totowa, NJ: Littlefield, Adams. (Original work published 1927)

Piaget, J. (1972c). Intellectual evolution from adolescence to adulthood (J. Bliss & H. Furth, Trans.). *Human Development, 15,* 1–12.

Piaget, J. (1974). *La prise de conscience.* Paris: Presses Universitaires de France.

Piaget, J. (1976). Autobiographie. *Cahiers Vilfredo Pareto, 36–39,* 1–43.

Piaget, J. (1987). *Possibility and necessity* (Vols. 1 & 2) (H. Feider, Trans.). Minneapolis: University of Minnesota Press. (Original work published 1981–1983)

Piaget, J., Ascher, E., & Henriques, G. (1992). *Morphisms and categories: Comparing and transforming* (T. Brown, Ed. & Trans.). Hillsdale, NJ: Lawrence Erlbaum Associates. (Original work published 1990)

Piaget, J., & Garcia, R. (1974). *Understanding causality* (D. Miles & M. Miles, Trans.). New York: Norton. (Original work published 1971)

Piaget, J., & Garcia, R. (1989). *Psychogenesis and the history of science* (H. Feider, Trans.). New York: Columbia University Press. (Original work published 1983).

Piaget, J., & Garcia, R. (1990). *Toward a logic of meanings* (P. M. Davidson & J. Easley, Eds., P. M. Davidson & D. de Caprona, Trans.). Hillsdale, NJ: Lawrence Erlbaum Associates. (Original work published 1987)

Popper, K. (1979). *Die beiden grundprobleme der erkenntnistheorie.* Tübingen, Germany: J. C. B. Mohr Verlag. (Original work published 1932)

Prigogine, I. (1980). *From being to becoming.* San Francisco: Freeman.

Prigogine, I., & Stengers, I. (1984). *Order out of chaos.* Toronto: Bantam.

Pugh, G. E. (1977). *The biological origin of human values.* New York: Basic.

Quine, W. O. (1969). *Ontological relativity and other essays.* New York: Columbia University Press.

Radnitzky, G., & Bartley, W. W., III (Eds.). (1987). *Evolutionary epistemology, theory of rationality, and the sociology of knowledge.* LaSalle, IL: Open Court.

Rapoport, D. (1967). On the psychoanalytic theory of affects. In M. Gill (Ed.), *The collected papers of David Rapoport* (pp. 476–512). New York: Basic. (Original work published 1953)

Shakespeare, W. (1936). The tragedy of King Richard II. In W. A. Wright (Ed.), *The complete works of William Shakespeare* (pp. 351–383). Garden City, NY: Garden City Books. (Original work published 1593–1594)

Smolensky, P. (1988). On the proper treatment of connectionism. *Behavioral and Brain Sciences, 11,* 1–74.

Souriau, P. (1881). *Théorie de l'invention.* Paris: Hachette.

Spencer, H. (1976). *First principles.* Westport, CT: Greenwood. (Original work published 1862)

Thayer, R. E. (1989). *The biopsychology of mood and arousal.* New York: Oxford University Press.

Tierney, J. (1991). Quest for order. In T. Ferris (Ed.), *The world treasury of physics, astronomy, and mathematics* (pp. 605–613). New York: Little, Brown. (Original work published 1984)

Wadsworth, B. J. (1989). *Piaget's theory of cognitive and affective development* (4th ed.). New York: Longman.

Wimsatt, W. C. (1976). Reductionism, levels of organization, and the mind–body problem. In G. G. Globus, G. Maxwell, & I. Savodnik (Eds.), *Consciousness and the brain: A scientific and philosophic inquiry* (pp. 199–267). New York: Plenum.

9

From Acting to Understanding: The Comparative Development of Meaning

Jonas Langer
University of California at Berkeley

The roots of meaning are to be sought in subjects' constructive interactions with the environment. The initial case for this constructivist theory of the origins and nature of meaning in human ontogenesis was made a long time ago by Piaget (1936/1952). Piaget proposed that children's assimilations determine the significance of their actions and the objects of their actions. The meaning of actions and of objects to infants and young children is what they can do with them. Here is a recent capsule version of Piaget's conjecture: ''. . . there is no difference here between the meanings of objects and the meaning of actions . . . the meaning of actions consists of success or failure and is thus based on the outcomes of manipulations. The meaning of objects amount to 'what can be done with them,' thus referring in all cases to actions performed on them'' (Piaget & Garcia, 1987/1991, p. 41).

Accordingly, our comparative developmental research studies subjects' constructive interactions. Hence, it bears upon the origins, evolution, and development of meaning in primates in three ways. The first is by studying the actions that subjects map onto objects as a measure of what they can do with actions and objects. The findings tell us about the origins, evolution, and early development of instrumental meaning.

But meaning requires understanding if it is not to remain superficially tied to success and failure, if it is to go beyond its instrumental roots. Now, if understanding is a characteristic of cognizing then it is necessary to examine the cognitions constructed by subjects' interactions that lead to understanding. Studying subjects' original and early developing representational cognitions that lead to progressive understanding is therefore the second way that our research bears upon the nature and development of meaning.

I would further propose that meaningful understanding remains local unless it is informed by explanatory reasons. Explanation is an advanced development that requires a base of hierarchic conceptual integration. Conceptual integration is not truly possible without the hypotheticodeductive reasoning developed during adolescence (Inhelder & Piaget, 1955/1958). Its precursors, however, may reach back to earlier developments. Young children already begin to integrate their initial representational concepts. But their first efforts remain transductive; for example, young children confound the general with the particular (Piaget, 1945/1951).

To recapitulate, I am proposing three progressive stages of meaning that originate and develop as a function of subjects' constructive interactions: (a) *instrumental* meaning based on the success and failure of the actions subjects map onto objects, (b) *representational* meaning based upon subjects' local conceptual understanding, and (c) *reasoned* meaning based upon subjects' hierarchically integrated explanatory concepts.

Our current research has not yet advanced to the point that I can say much about reasoned meaning. The findings so far shed light mainly on the first two stages of meaning, instrumental and representational meaning. I therefore focus on our comparative developmental findings that are relevant to them, beginning with instrumental meaning.

INSTRUMENTAL MEANING
OR WHAT CAN BE DONE

It should be noted at the outset that when an action is mapped onto an object there are correlated transformative consequences for the instrumental meaning of both the action and the object. To illustrate what I mean by correlated transformative consequences I could, for example, demonstrate mapping a ''pick-up'' action on a ''glass-of-water'' object. In this interaction, the instrumental meaning of ''pick-up'' is not ''preparing for drinking.'' Rather, the action's significance is ''raising-for-demonstrating.'' So too, in this interaction, the instrumental meaning of ''glass-of-water'' is not ''a thing to quench my thirst with.'' Rather, the object's significance is ''a thing with which to demonstrate what I mean by mappings.''

Mappings are our unit of analysis for studying instrumental meaning. They capture the corresponding transformations in the significance of both the actions and the objects of the actions. Of course, as an adult I can transform my interactions pretty much at will. I can easily shift the instrumental meaning of both the actions and the objects, for example, by instead demonstrating drinking from the glass of water. The focus of our investigations, however, is to determine the nature and development of mappings when subjects first begin to generate them. In this way we are studying the constructive origins and early development of instrumental meaning. By studying mappings we are exploring what we might call, with Werner

TABLE 9.1
Six Most Frequent Mappings

Human Infants[a]	Cebus[b]	Macaques[b]
	BITE	BITE
HIT		
	HOLD AWAY TO LOOK AT	HOLD AWAY TO LOOK AT
HOLD IN HAND	HOLD IN HAND	
	HOLD IN MOUTH	HOLD IN MOUTH
MOUTH	MOUTH	MOUTH
PICKUP		
PUSH		
	ROTATE	ROTATE
TOUCH		TOUCH
6 months: 63%	16 to 48 months:	22 to 34 months:
12 months: 57%	58%	70%

[a]Data are from Ahl and Langer (in preparation).
[b]Data are from Natale (1989b).

(1926/1948) and von Uexküll (1934/1957), the thing-of-action Umwelt that is at the root of all meaning. In Werner's apt formulation, at this initial stage subjects' Umwelt comprises their lived "world-of-action" with its "signal-things."

Young human infants in our studies (observed in Langer, 1980) consistently map only about a half dozen actions onto objects. They hit, hold, mouth, pick up, push, and touch objects (see Table 9.1). In quantitative analyses currently underway we are finding that these six mappings comprise most of young infants' interactions when four discrete objects are presented. Regardless of their type, whether young infants are interacting with shapes or realistic objects, six mappings predominate (Ahl & Langer, in preparation). During their first year, the repertoire of infants' mappings and, therefore, their initial instrumental meanings are compact.

Remarkably, the phenomenon replicates in 2- to 4-year-old cebus (*Cebus apella*) and macaque (*Macaca fascicularis*) monkeys (Natale, 1989b). The mappings are not entirely alike. Still, six mappings also account for most of cebus' and most of macaques' interactions when presented with six objects (Table 9.1). The repertoire of monkeys' mappings and therefore their instrumental meanings are also compact.

Instrumental meaning develops further in humans. The main advance is that human infants begin to exploit the mappings they construct as a lexicon of instrumental meanings. Thus, older but not younger infants combine mappings with each other into sentencelike routines (Langer, 1986). Systematic combining of mappings induces a rapid and exponential expansion of instrumental meaning.

Three central features of infants' routines that transform their instrumental meaning and that originate early in infants' second year are:

1. *Anticipatory planning* of what to do; for example, preparing a cup to be a container by uprighting it, then picking up columns and containing them in the cup. Anticipation is crucial to constructing the instrumental meaning of the "future."

2. *Functional reciprocity*, which determines the complementary relations between what can be done; for example, using a spoon to stir in a cup and using a cup to be stirred in by a spoon.

3. *Imitation and pretend play*, which gives a symbolic and social dimension to what can be done; for example, pretending to go to sleep. Of course, this last feature of instrumental meaning immediately points to a major question that I try to address in a bit: What is the place of symbolization, including language, in the origins and early development of meaning?

Self-constructed routines are prerequisite to the acquisition of progressively conventional forms of combining mappings, such as scripts (Nelson, 1985).

Although humans make much more rapid and extensive progress, other primates also generate rudimentary routines that combine mappings (cf. Savage-Rumbaugh, 1991). For example, cebus (*Cebus apella*) generate routines in which they compose two short sticks in order to push a peanut out of a Plexiglas tube (Visalberghi, 1993; Visalberghi & Trinca, 1989). Cebus generate these routines in order to achieve success in getting the peanut.

But meaning requires understanding if it is not to remain superficially tied to success and failure of what can be done only. Meaning requires understanding if it is to go beyond purely instrumental routines to questions about what and how things work. Here even cebus, the seemingly most instrumentally advanced and prolific monkey species, already seem to be falling behind. Cebus' success is not characterized by any features that mark understanding of the instrumental routines they use; as indexed, for example, by profiting from a mixture of success and failure experience by eventually eliminating the failing routines (Visalberghi, 1993; Visalberghi & Trinca, 1989). Thus, after numerous successful routines in using appropriate sticks to get peanuts out of a Plexiglas tube, cebus' successful routines continue to be interspersed with many of the same failing routines they have used all along, even though they could simply reproduce their successful routines only. Success can not drive out failure in situations that require not only knowing what can be done with objects but also understanding how things work in order to know what works.

THE ORIGINS OF COGNITION IN PRIMATES

If understanding is a characteristic of knowledge, then an adequate cognitive base must develop for meaning to advance beyond its instrumental beginnings so as to include understanding. Since Piaget's (1937/1954) groundbreaking research on infant development, it has been increasingly acknowledged that the foundations of physical cognition, such as causality, are laid down by subjects' earliest actions (e.g., Spelke, 1991). Our research (Langer, 1980, 1986, 1990) is finding that the foundations of logicomathematical cognition, as well as physical cognition, are also being constructed by subjects' early actions. I review only those findings essential to illustrating the progress in meaning that becomes possible when it is informed by progressive understanding. Much of the findings on human infants that I review have already been replicated with both Aymara and Quecha Indian infants in Peru in a dissertation study by Terry Jacobsen (1984).

Part of our research method involves studying infants' spontaneous constructive interactions with four or eight objects. The range of objects span geometric shapes to realistic things such as cups (as illustrated in Figs. 9.1, 9.2, and 9.3). In this part of the research, no instruction of any kind is given and no problem of any kind is presented.

One other feature of our research method requires pointing out now in order to follow some of the findings I review. Class structures are embodied by some of the sets of objects with which subjects spontaneously interact. These sets of objects embody three different class conditions (i.e., additive, multiplicative, and disjoint). But there is nothing in the procedures used that requires subjects to do anything about them. As already mentioned, no instructions are given and no problems are presented for solution. It is important to note this feature. It marks the nondirective and nonverbal method we used with children, ages 6 months to 5 years, and the comparative developmental research with monkeys (*Cebus apella* and *Macaca fascicularis*) and chimpanzees (*Pan troglodytes*). For details on the class and object conditions, procedures, and analyses see Antinucci (1989) and Langer (1980, 1986).

Constructing the Elements of Cognition

Much of subjects' spontaneous constructive interactions with objects include composing sets with them by relating two or more objects to each other (as illustrated, e.g., in Figs. 9.1–9.3). These sets become elements for their logicomathematical cognitions, as well as for their physical cognitions that I get to in a while. All primate species are quite productive in their rate of composing sets of objects. Figure 9.4 shows this for the early ontogeny of human infants, cebus, and macaques (Langer, 1980, 1986, 1989; Poti & Antinucci, 1989).

Monkeys, young chimpanzees, and young human infants produce sets of objects one at a time (Langer, 1980, 1986; Poti & Antinucci, 1989; Spinozzi, 1993). Monkeys do not compose two temporally overlapping sets; human infants and chimpanzees do. Composing sets of objects in partial or total temporal overlap, two or more at a time, originates toward the end of human infants' first year. The frequency increases steadily with age (see Fig. 9.5). It originates a bit later in chimpanzees, toward the beginning of their second year (Fig. 9.5). Although it also

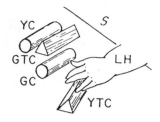

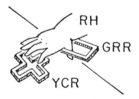

FIG. 9.1. Six-month-old subject composing a green cylinder with a yellow triangular column using left hand.

increases with age in chimpanzees, the frequency of production is lower and the rate of development is slower than in human infancy. Comparing the sets constructed in temporal overlap by chimpanzee and human children by their fifth year is a good index of their differential development in generating elements for their cognition. Only 18% of chimpanzees' sets overlap with each other (Spinozzi, 1993) whereas 52% of humans' sets overlap (Langer, in preparation).

Primates—monkeys, chimpanzees, and human infants—begin to construct logical, arithmetic, and physical cognitions with the sets they compose. Consider

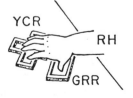

FIG. 9.2. Six-month-old subject composing a green rectangular ring with a yellow cross ring using right hand.

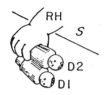

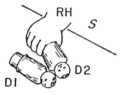

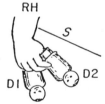

FIG 9.3. Six-month-old subject composing two dolls using right hand.

first a central logical cognition—classifying. Minimally, classifying produces relations of identity, similarity, and differences.

Classifying: A Logical Cognition

All primate species compose class-consistent sets of objects (Langer, 1980, 1986, 1990; Spinozzi, 1993; Spinozzi & Natale, 1989). But the sequence, extent, and rate of the classificatory development diverges between species. We begin with human infants.

Human Infants.   At first, human infants construct class-consistent single sets that do not overlap temporally with each other. The sequence of their development begins with infants consistently composing nonoverlapping single sets of *different*

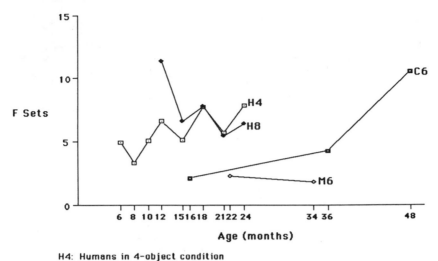

H4: Humans in 4-object condition
H8: Humans in 8-object condition
M6: Macaque in 6-object condition
C6: Cebus in 6-object condition

FIG. 9.4. Mean frequency of composing sets per minute.

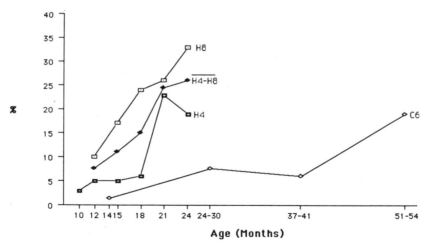

H4: Humans in 4-object conditions
H8: Humans in 8-object conditions
H4-H8: Humans in 4- and 8-object conditions
C6: Chimpanzees in 6-object conditions

FIG. 9.5. Percent of sets composed in temporal overlap.

198

objects at age 6 months (as illustrated in Figs. 9.1 and 9.2). This changes to *random* composing at ages 8 and 10 months: They are equally likely to compose sets of different, identical, and similar objects. The next change is the onset of composing *identical* objects at age 12 months (as illustrated in Fig. 9.3). The major change after this is the onset of composing *similar* objects into single sets at age 15 months (as illustrated in Fig. 9.6). Similarity is defined as identity in some properties (e.g., form) combined with differences in others (e.g., color).

In this entire developmental sequence, infants compose only one set with one class property at a time. I therefore call this *first-order classifying*. This structure is what differentiates these four sequential developments in first-order classifying from *second-order classifying*. Second-order classifying originates at age 18

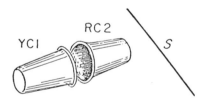

FIG. 9.6.   Three compositions of similar objects: an orange and a yellow spoon; a yellow and a red cup; and a green and yellow cylinder.

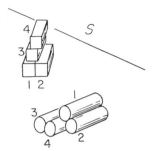

FIG. 9.7. Second-order classifying by a twenty-one-month old
subject.

months. Now infants begin to compose consistently two temporally overlapping sets—such that the objects comprising each set are identical, but the objects in the two sets are different (as illustrated in Fig. 9.7). Thus, second-order classifying means composing two sets and two class properties at the same time.

Monkeys. The sequence, extent, and rate of classificatory development is different in cebus and macaques. The extent does not progress beyond first-order classifying. Second-order classifying is precluded because monkeys do not compose two temporally overlapping sets. The limited elements that monkeys can construct—single sets—constrains the level of their cognitive development to first-order operations. Hence, monkeys do not develop second-order classifying.

Even within their more limited extent, the rate and sequence of developing first-order classifying is different in monkeys than in humans. In fact, it is different in different monkey species—that is, cebus and macaques—even though all primates end up by classifying by identities and similarities. Reviewing the rate and sequencing data would be too consuming, so I merely illustrate in perhaps oversimplified, broad comparative strokes for cebus monkeys (see Fig. 9.8). Cebus begin by mostly random classifying at age 16 months, change to mostly classifying by differences by age 36 months, and change to classifying by identities and similarities by age 48 months.

Chimpanzees. Classificatory development in chimpanzees is somewhere between that of monkeys and human infants in sequence, extent, and rate. Chimpanzees develop rudimentary second-order classifying. Their rate of classificatory development is markedly slower than that of human infants: The onset age for second-order classifying is the second year in human infants. The onset age is not until the fifth year in chimpanzees.

Correspondence and Exchange: Arithmetic Cognitions

Arithmetic constructions complement logical constructions, such as the just-described classifying, in all primate species (Langer, 1980, 1986, 1989, 1990; Poti & Antinucci, 1989, in preparation). For instance, all primates generate aspects

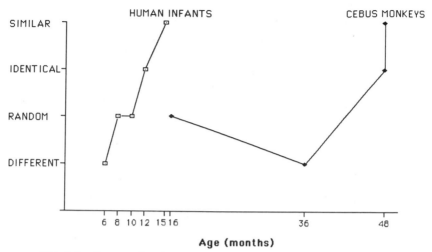

FIG. 9.8.   Comparative development of first-order classifying: Rate and sequence.

of exchange and correspondence constructions. The products are equivalence and nonequivalence relations. Exchange includes commuting, replacing, and substituting. I illustrate for substituting that produces equivalence relations.

Human Infants.   Not only do human infants consistently compose two objects into single sets by age 6 months, some already recompose these single sets by substituting objects. By taking away one object from a two-object set and then substituting another object in its place, infants recompose a two-object set—thereby producing equivalence within single sets. These are first-order cognitions. They comprise nothing more than one operation—substituting—to produce one relation—equivalence—in one element—a single set of objects only.

By age 10 months, all infants produce equivalence by substituting in single two-object sets. First-order substituting is expanded during infants' second year to produce equivalence in ever larger sets. For instance, by age 18 months half of the subjects already substitute in four-object sets. Yet all first-order proto-arithmetic operations, including substituting, are limited to producing relations, such as equivalence, within single sets that are not related to any of infants' other constructions.

The major development during infants' second year is the origins of second-order operations. Second-order operations integrate first-order operations with each other by mapping operations onto each other. Mapping operations onto each other produces a second level of more powerful cognitions, such as equivalences upon equivalences. By this recursive procedure, older infants begin to construct hierarchically integrated cognitive operations.

By age 24 months, all infants compose two very small sets in relation to each other and that overlap in time. All infants also match such compositions by one-to-one correspondence between the objects so that there is an equivalence relation between the two sets. For instance, infants may construct two stacks of three objects. Some infants transform these matched sets by substituting the top objects for each other. They preserve the equivalence relation between the two sets while transforming them. These infants are constructing equivalences upon equivalences by mapping substitution operations upon correspondence operations. By mapping their operations onto each other infants begin to construct second-order hierarchic arithmetic as well as logical cognitions.

The formation of second-order hierarchic cognition by mapping mappings onto mappings is a key feature of recursive cognitive development that I return to later. The mappings may be logicomathematical operations—as in the case of correspondence and substitution that are mapped onto each other. But we soon see that the mappings may be physical functions as well—as in the case of causal relations where the effect is a dependent function of the cause. So functions may also be mapped onto functions to form second-order hierarchic physical cognition.

Monkeys.   The comparative primate picture that is emerging on developing proto-arithmetic cognition is similar to that which I already outlined for protological cognition. Cebus and macaque monkeys develop first-order arithmetic cognitions. This includes producing equivalence relations in single sets by substituting. But the extent is limited; it rarely exceeds substituting in two-object sets. So even the extent of monkeys' first-order cognition is already less than that in human infants. Further, monkeys do not develop any second-order arithmetic cognition. As with logical cognition, this is not possible. They do not construct the requisite minimal elements, which are two temporally overlapping sets.

Chimpanzees.   Chimpanzees, we have already seen, do construct temporally overlapping sets. Unlike monkeys and like humans, chimpanzees also develop second-order arithmetic cognitions. Although the data are still being analyzed, it is becoming evident that the extent is relatively limited, approximating the level of second-order operations of 15- to 18-month-old human infants when chimpanzees are in their fifth year. So their rate of developing proto-arithmetic cognition is also much slower.

Causality: A Physical Cognition

Causality is a fundamental physical category, much like classes is a fundamental logical category. I therefore illustrate our findings on developing physical knowledge by briefly sketching some central features of primates' developing causal constructions (Langer, 1980, 1986, 1990; Natale, 1989a; Poti & Spinozzi, in preparation; Spinozzi & Poti, 1989). I also sketch some central findings on how primates' developing physical and logicomathematical cognitions relate to each other (Langer, 1989, 1992).

Human Infants.   Infants already construct first-order causal relations during their first year. They begin as early as age 6 months by constructing, minimally replicating, and observing effects that are direct functions of causes. To illustrate, 6-month-olds already use one object as a means with which to push another object several times in succession. Causal production is complemented by the origins of causal anticipation or prediction. To illustrate, 6-month-olds begin to use one object to block and stop another object that is rolling in front of them.

Infants make marked progress in constructing first-order causal relations during their second year. This includes generating effects that are ordered functions of causes. For instance, infants push objects harder and harder. These causal constructions may be formalized as one-way ratiolike relations, such as "Moving Farther is a dependent function of Pushing Harder." This is what differentiates first-order from second-order causal functions. The latter originate during infants' second year.

Second-order causal functions are integrative relations. They map first-order functions onto each other. This produces a second level of more powerful causal functions. The effects are directly dependent on the causes in first-order functions. In contrast, the effects begin to be proportional to the causes in second-order functions.

Older, like younger, infants use one object as an instrument with which to push a second dependent object. But beginning at age 18 months, when the effect is that the dependent object rolls away, then infants also transform the instrumental object into a means with which to block the dependent object. Infants thereby transform the end or goal from rolling to stopping. As soon as the dependent object stops rolling, infants transform the same instrumental object back into a means with which to make the dependent object roll away again. And so on.

Thus, older infants begin to covary their transformations of causes and effects. These covariations form proportionallike dependencies between causes and effects. By mapping previously constructed first-order functions onto each other, infants produce new second-order functions, such as "Moving is a function of Pushing as Stopping is a function of Blocking."

In general, infants begin to map their physical functions onto each other during their second year. Thereby infants begin to construct hierarchically integrated physical cognition in parallel with hierarchic logicomathematical cognition. Parallel development of logical, arithmetic, and physical cognition is the second key feature of recursive cognitive development that I return to later.

Monkeys.   Cebus and macaque monkeys develop first-order causal functions, but not second-order causality. Moreover, unlike human infants, monkeys' physical cognition, including causal cognition, does not develop in parallel with their logicomathematical cognition. Instead, most of their first-order physical cognition develops in their first year and a half whereas their development of logicomathematical cognition does not begin until that age. Thus, most of monkeys' developments of logicomathematical cognitions and physical cognitions do not overlap with each other in their ontogeny, whereas they do in human infants.

Although the order of mappings involved in monkeys' logicomathematical and physical cognition is the same—first-order—there is little temporal overlap in their development. This suggests a different form of linkage between logicomathematical and physical cognition than exists for humans, beginning already in infancy. In humans, contemporaneous development establishes conditions essential for recursive mappings of mappings extended laterally across cognitive categories in a manner I will discuss in the section Representational Meaning or Understanding How.

Chimpanzees.   The causal development of chimpanzees stands somewhere between that of monkeys and human infants, although I must again stress that the data are still being analyzed. Chimpanzees probably manifest some second-order physical cognition. And although their physical and logicomathematical cognitions do not develop in parallel as they do in human infants, there is greater ontogenetic overlap between their development than there is in monkeys. Chimpanzees' physical cognition begins to develop before their logicomathematical cognition does. But they also begin to develop logicomathematical cognition well before their development of physical cognition is completed.

REPRESENTATIONAL MEANING
OR UNDERSTANDING HOW

All these findings point to comparative differences in the sequence, extent, and rate of primate development at any one cognitive level. The findings also lead to three other comparative conclusions:

1. Cognitive development does not become recursive in monkeys: Their cognitions do not become hierarchic; and their cognitions do not develop in parallel. So on both counts their cognitions can not be directly integrated with each other.
2. Cognitive development becomes partially recursive in chimpanzees, although the analyses are not far enough along to determine the extent.
3. Cognitive development already begins to be recursive in human infants' second year as marked by two key integrative features: (a) lateral filiations between physical and logicomathematical cognition, and (b) the origins of second-order hierarchic cognition.

The development of recursive cognition ushers in understanding. Understanding already enables meaning to progress beyond its instrumental origins in human infancy. Monkeys do not progress beyond instrumental meaning because they lack recursive cognition. Chimpanzees develop some understanding because their cognition becomes partially recursive. But besides expecting that chimpanzees progress beyond instrumental meaning to meaning that is also marked by some understanding, it is premature to speculate. In a word, the idea is that recursiveness changes the rules of development (Langer, 1986, 1988, 1993).

Integration

Recursive cognitive development does at least two important things to foster understanding as early as infancy in humans. First, it provides the beginnings of an integrated conceptual base of relatively advanced logicomathematical and physical cognitions. As an illustration, recall that infants develop second-order classifying during their second year. This includes classifying simultaneously two sets of objects into two kinds. Then the objects comprising each set are identical but the objects in the two sets are different. Now, without the ability to classify simultaneously two kinds of objects into identities and differences, it is not possible to understand a host of phenomena. This includes understanding what can be done with objects. It is not possible to understand what is happening and how things work in these phenomena. For example, it is not possible to understand what is happening when some objects roll away when pushed whereas others do not. Being able to classify objects into two kinds, as infants begin to do in their second year, is prerequisite to any understanding of what is happening when some objects roll away if pushed whereas others do not. And indeed, we have found that when presented with cylinders and square-columns infants begin to do just this in their second year (Langer, 1986). They begin by pushing both kinds of objects, discover that only cylinders roll away, then continue pushing cylinders but not square-columns.

In effect these infants are applying a classifying operation to a causal function. This is a first step to understanding how these two kinds of objects work and, consequently, what kind of object will roll away when pushed and what kind will not. It requires integrating logicomathematical and physical cognition. Integrated conceptualizing begins to be possible in human infants because they develop logicomathematical and physical cognition in parallel. It is not possible in monkeys where the developmental trajectories are asynchronic. Note that this accounts for the finding that cebus develop instrumental success without understanding discussed in the section Instrumental Meaning or What Can Be Done (Visalberghi, 1993; Visalberghi & Trinca, 1989).

Asynchronic developmental trajectories in monkeys do not readily permit lateral integration between different conceptual structures because they are out of phase with each other. In contrast, from the start of human ontogeny, physical and logicomathematical cognition constitute contemporaneous developmental trajectories that become progressively interdependent. Contemporaneous developmental trajectories are subject to similar environmental influences and to each other's influence. This facilitates direct interaction or information flow between cognitive structures. Mutual and reciprocal influence between logicomathematical and physical cognition is possible because they develop in synchrony with each other. Thus, we have found that even in infancy, physical cognition introduces elements of contingency and uncertainty into logicomathematical cognition; at the same time, logicomathematical cognition introduces elements of necessity and certainty into physical cognition (Langer, 1985). Progressive cognizance of both contingency and necessity are fundamental to subjects' developing understanding of how things work.

Essential to this development is laterally integrated cognition because it facilitates progressively determining what is possible and what is impossible. In this way, infants progressively figure out not only what but how things work. Thus, we have found that by age 15 months infants already begin to experiment with what is possible and impossible (Langer, 1986). For example, they stand cylinders upright. Then they pick up a spoon and try to do the same thing but the spoon falls over.

By age 18 months infants successfully differentiate between such simple possible and impossible uses of cylinders and spoons. This enables them to undertake more advanced experimenting. For instance, infants take a cylindrical doll (such as those illustrated in Fig. 9.3) that they are used to standing upright on its base, turn it over, and try to stand it on its head. The result is disconfirmation of a new impossible condition.

So there is gradual progress in determining what is physically possible and what is impossible. This opens up novel opportunities for infants to figure out not only what works but how it works. One illustration from a 21-month-old subject should suffice. He stands a cylinder upright. Once it is standing he tilts the cylinder and lets go such that it falls over. Then he repeats the entire routine from uprighting to tilting the same cylinder. It appears that when infants become good at determining some possible and impossible conditions, such as what can stand up and what will fall over, they begin to figure out the possible and impossible parameters of these conditions in order to understand how they work.

At times, infants already accompany these second-order efforts at understanding with overt signs of cognizance and self-regulation. For instance, this same 21-month-old subject stacks two cylinders on top of each other, laughs, and acts pleased. After this he tries unsuccessfully to place two spoons on the cylindrical stack to build a T-shaped construction. But he does not release the spoons and let them fall as younger infants would. Instead, he takes the spoons off the stack when it does not work.

Efforts at understanding what is possible and how it works culminates by the end of infants' second year. Now they try to figure out what can be done with two objects so as to determine what can be done to a third object. This is well illustrated by part of the efforts of one 24-month-old subject (see Fig. 9.9).

Four important features of understanding mark this subject's efforts to figure out what works and how it works:

1. The subject creates his own goals or problems in order to figure out what can be done to a cylinder and how to do it.

2. The subject reciprocally coordinates two spoons with each other to form a larger and more complex means or solution in order to figure out what can be done with combinations of objects and how to do it.

3. The subject coordinates "what can be done with objects" and "what can be done to objects" in order to figure out what is possible and what is impossible. This procedure coordinates self-constructed problems with elaborate attempts at self-constructed solutions. Therefore, it is most likely to induce progressive understanding and cognizance of how things work. Understanding is becoming reflective.

4. No language accompanies this or any of the previously cited attempts beginning at age 15 months to understand. The origins and early development of representational meaning occurs without manifest language. Language is neither a necessary nor a sufficient condition for older human infants and chimpanzees to generate the understanding essential to the initial formation of representational meaning. Parisi (1991) came to a similar conclusion based upon his connectionist interpretation of sensorimotor development.

Hierarchization

This brings me to the other major advance brought about by recursive cognition that fosters progressive understanding. As already noted, in their second year infants begin to map their cognitions onto each other. By this recursive procedure, they generate the onset of more advanced cognition. Then the elements of their cognitive mappings are as much other cognitive mappings as actual things.

By mapping their mappings onto their own mappings as well as onto objects, infants begin to detach their logicomathematical operations and physical functions from their initial concrete objects of application. Operations begin to be applied to operations as well as to concrete objects; and functions begin to be applied to functions as well as to concrete objects. Detaching operations and functions from their concrete object referents and instead mapping them onto other operations and functions is pivotal. It provides the minimal necessary conditions for abstract reflection and the formation of representational concepts that are hierarchical as well as integrated. Recursive cognitive development, then, is prerequisite to any form of metacognition (such as that discussed in Flavell, 1979; Piaget, 1974/1976).

53. RH *holding Spoon 2 by handle pushes S2 such that bowl end of S2 is under Cylinder 1, pushing C1 against LH, while LH holds Spoon 1*

53a. *C1 lifts partly off table all the while touching LH*

54. *RH lifts S2 under C1 and lowers S2 again, while LH holds S1*

54a. *S2 pushes C1 about 2 inches toward subject*

55. *LH lifts S1 off table and withdraws S1 to the back of C1, while RH holds S2 under C1:*

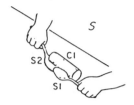

56.6. *RH pushes S2 against back of C1 toward subject*

56.5a. *C1 moves closer to subject*

56.5. *LH pushes S1 against back of C1 toward subject*

56.5a. *S1 pushes C1 to right a bit rotating C1 such that opposite (left) end rests on S2 as in Line 55:*

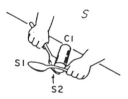

58.5. *RH lifts S2 out from under C1*

58.5. *LH lifts S1*

60. *LH immediately lowers handle part of S1 onto C1 and pushes handle against C1, also pushing LH thumb against C1, while RH holds S2*

60a. *C1 moves about 2 inches away from subject*

61.5. *RH raises S2 several inches in air*

61.5. *LH lifts C1 along with S1 such that S1 is on top of C1*

63.5. *RH lowers S2 a few inches in air*

63.5. *LH raises S1/C1 a little higher (above S2)*

65. *LH lowers S1/C1 on top of S2 (holding S1 on top of C1, so it doesn't contact S2) held by RH*

65a. *S1/C1 slowly pushes S2 down onto table*

FIG. 9.9.   Fragment from the protocol of a 24-month-old subject.

Conceptual Representation. Representation, on this proposal, begins with hierarchic mappings upon mappings. Its conceptual origins are subjects' mappings of operations onto operations and functions onto functions. A good illustration is the already cited development by infants during their second year of mapping substitutions onto correspondences to produce equivalences upon equivalences. Then the referents of the substitution operations are no longer limited to the concrete objects forming the two corresponding sets. The referents can become equivalence *relations*. But relations are more abstract than objects. So the referents are becoming abstract.

In general, with the formation of second-order hierarchic cognition, the referents of infants' operations and functions are no longer limited to objects. Cognition is no longer limited to the concrete. Progressively, the referents of infants' operations and functions are becoming relations, such as equivalence and dependency, that are the product of other operations and functions mapped onto objects. By mapping operations and functions onto relations, infants' cognition is becoming abstract and reflective or what we might call thoughtful. Then meaning, and certainly the significance of their representational logico-mathematical and physical concepts, can begin to become abstract and reflective (cf. Cassirer, 1910/1953). Reasons why or explanations for phenomena can begin to be constructed.

Symbolic Representation. There is, of course, another side to representational development that can not be neglected in any analysis of the development from acting to understanding. This is the development of symbolizing, particularly language. Symbolizing is crucial to communicating understanding in order to generate shared meaning. To do justice to this topic would take much more elaboration than is possible here. So I limit myself to two propositions (see Langer, 1986, for a fuller treatment).

Infants' developing representational concepts begin to provide them with the requisite knowledge base for understanding the meaning that others are trying to communicate to them. Reciprocally, without developing representational concepts, infants would have no conceptual understanding as a base for their own semantics to communicate to others. At most they could try to communicate instrumental meaning, as in playful pretense. Thus, shared meaning would be limited to the instrumental.

The first proposition, then, is that developing representational concepts is necessary for shared meaningful understanding. At most, very young infants and monkeys can communicate and share instrumental meaning. Older infants, and probably chimpanzees, begin to communicate and share representational meaning.

The second proposition is that recursive hierarchical cognition is necessary for the development of grammatical language (cf. Bickerton, 1990; Lieberman, 1991). Hierarchic cognition is necessary for infants to produce and comprehend arbitrary but conventional rules by which linguistic constructions stand for and communicate semantic referents in syntactic forms. Indeed, hierarchic second-order cognitions may well be axiomatic to grammatical formation in which linguistic symbols are progressively combinable and interchangeable yet meaningful. For example, this is not possible without the second-order operation of substituting elements within and between two constructions or sets that we have seen develops in infants' second year.

The hypothesis is that second-order hierarchical mappings of composing, matching, substituting, and other cognitive operations and functions I have not had time to review, provide the fundamental rewrite rules without which syntactic linguistic constructions are not possible. Therefore, grammatical language is not possible in monkeys and young infants but begins to be acquired by older infants. Chimpanzees develop rudimentary second-order cognition. So, on the present hypothesis, they do not develop language but can acquire some protogrammatical language. The data are confirmatory. At most, chimpanzees learn to connect two or three lexigrams into partially sentencelike forms (Greenfield & Savage-Rumbaugh, 1991). Because they can learn only protogrammatical language, chimpanzees' symbolic representations can play only a limited role in communicating and sharing meaning with others. When human children acquire grammatical language, then their symbolic representation can play a progressive role in communicating and sharing meaning with others.

Hierarchic Integration

Cognition constructs meaning. At first it does so by mappings and routines (i.e., combinations of mappings). They generate the instrumental significance of actions and objects, or what works. Recursive cognitive development of hierarchically and laterally integrated operations and functions generates understanding. Meaning progresses to a second, representational stage of significance. Recursive cognitive structures, we have shown, develop in late infancy by all humans (at least where there is no pathology). Universal development of recursive cognition is the guarantor of shared understanding or representational meaning by all humans. Our analyses are not far enough along to conclude with any serious confidence whether the recursive cognitive development we have found in chimpanzees is sufficient to ensure shared understanding between chimpanzees; but I would hazard the tentative hypothesis that it is adequate to rudimentary shared understanding.

Language does not construct or generate meaning. Language is a symbolic medium or vehicle for communicating meaning. Meaning, we have shown, antedates language in both the phylogeny and ontogeny of primates. Meaning precedes language during the instrumental stage in nonhuman as well as human primate species. Meaning also precedes syntactic language during the initial phase of its representational stage where it is already informed by some understanding.

Symbolic systems, such as language, are media for communicating meaning constructed by cognition. When they work well together, then cognition and language facilitate sharing meaning. Unfortunately, at times, language may also obscure. For example, ambiguous language use by young children obscures the representational meaning or understanding constructed by their recursive cognitive operations and functions. Then language interferes with shared understanding. Ambiguous language accounts, at least in part, for why young children's communications are so notoriously difficult to understand and are so misleading. Ambiguous language may even hinder progress to the next stage of reasoned explanatory meaning. Only progressive cognition or increased knowledge can overcome the distorting effects of obscurantist language usage and re-ensure shared meaning.

THE EVOLUTION OF MEANING

Meaning, I have been suggesting, is about what, how, and why—what works, understanding how, and explanatory reasons why. Meaning is constructed in evolution and development, at least in the evolution and development of primates.

At root, meaning is instrumental. Meaning is knowing what can be done with actions and objects. Instrumental meaning is developed by monkeys, chimpanzees, and very young human infants prior to any language.

The next stage of meaning comes from understanding how about phenomena. Understanding is a characteristic of conceptualization that begins with the development of representational cognition. Meaning informed by understanding originates in both chimpanzees and older human infants prior to grammatical language.

The most advanced stage of meaning develops when it is informed by reasons why for phenomena. Reasons why or explanations are characteristics of hierarchically integrated and reflective conceptualizations or theories. Their primitive precursors may be foreshadowed in the beginning hierarchically integrated cognitions that young children develop. On this hypothesis, precursory forms of reasoned meaning may originate in humans during early childhood.

Recursiveness changes the rules of development. Recursively mapping mappings onto mappings initiates hierarchically and laterally integrated cognition. The advanced stages of meaning are dependent on recursive cognitive development.

Recursive cognitive development seems absent in monkeys, is partially present in chimpanzees, and is fully instantiated in humans. As far as we know, the onset age of physical cognition is roughly the same, early infancy, in all primates. But we have seen that the onset age of logicomathematical cognition is later in monkeys, somewhat later in chimpanzees, and contemporaneous with physical cognition in human infants. Now, phylogenetic displacement in the ontogenetic onset or timing of one structural development relative to another causes a disruption in the repetition of phylogeny in ontogeny, or what Haeckel called heterochrony (cf. Gould, 1977; McKinney & McNamara, 1991). This is why I have proposed (Langer, 1989, 1993, in preparation) that heterochrony is a causal mechanism of cognitive evolution; and why I would now propose that heterochrony is a precondition to the evolution of representational and reasoned meaning.

REFERENCES

Ahl, V., & Langer, J. (in preparation). *The development of mappings by human infants.* Unpublished manuscript.

Antinucci, F. (Ed.). (1989). *Cognitive structure and development in nonhuman primates.* Hillsdale, NJ: Lawrence Erlbaum Associates.

Bickerton, D. (1990). *Language and species.* Chicago: University of Chicago Press.

Cassirer, E. (1953). *Substance and function.* New York: Dover. (Original work published 1910)

Flavell, J. (1979). Metacognition and cognitive monitoring. *American Psychologist, 34,* 906–911.

Gould, S. J. (1977). *Ontogeny and phylogeny.* Cambridge, MA: Harvard University Press.

Greenfield, P., & Savage-Rumbaugh, S. (1991). Grammatical combination in *Pan paniscus:* Processes of learning and invention. In S. Parker & K. Gibson (Eds.), *"Language" and intelligence in monkeys and apes: Comparative developmental perspectives* (pp. 540–578). Cambridge, England: Cambridge University Press.

Inhelder, B., & Piaget, J. (1958). *The growth of logical thinking from childhood to adolescence.* New York: Basic. (Original work published 1955)

Jacobsen, T. A. (1984). *The construction and regulation of early structures of logic: A cross-cultural study of infant cognitive development.* Unpublished doctoral dissertation, University of California, Berkeley.

Langer, J. (1980). *The origins of logic: Six to twelve months.* New York: Academic.

Langer, J. (1985). Necessity and possibility during infancy. *Archives de Psychologie, 53,* 61–75.

Langer, J. (1986). *The origins of logic: One to two years.* New York: Academic.

Langer, J. (1988). A note on the comparative psychology of mental development. In S. Strauss (Ed.), *Ontogeny, phylogeny, and historical development* (pp. 68–85). Norwood, NJ: Ablex.

Langer, J. (1989). Comparison with the human child. In F. Antinucci (Ed.), *Cognitive structure and development of nonhuman primates* (pp. 229–242). Hillsdale, NJ: Lawrence Erlbaum Associates.

Langer, J. (1990). Early cognitive development: Basic functions. In C. A. Hauert (Ed.), *Developmental psychology: Cognitive, perceptuo-motor, and neuropsychological perspectives* (pp. 19–42). Amsterdam: North Holland.

Langer, J. (1993). Comparative cognitive development. In K. Gibson & T. Ingold (Eds.), *Tools language and cognition in human evolution* (pp. 300–313). New York: Cambridge University Press.

Langer, J. (in preparation). *The origins and early development of cognition in comparative perspective.* Unpublished manuscript.

Lieberman, P. (1991). *Uniquely human.* Cambridge, MA: Harvard University Press.

McKinney, M. L., & McNamara, J. K. (1991). *Heterochrony: The evolution of ontogeny.* New York: Plenum.

Natale, F. (1989a). Causality II: The stick problem. In F. Antinucci (Ed.), *Cognitive structure and development in nonhuman primates* (pp. 121–133). Hillsdale, NJ: Lawrence Erlbaum Associates.

Natale, F. (1989b). Patterns of object manipulation. In F. Antinucci (Ed.), *Cognitive structure and development in nonhuman primates* (pp. 145–161). Hillsdale, NJ: Lawrence Erlbaum Associates.

Nelson, K. (1985). *Making sense: The acquisition of shared meaning.* New York: Academic.

Parisi, D. (1991). *Take Piaget as guide.* Paper presented at the MacArthur Workshop on Connectionism and Developmental Psychology, San Diego.

Piaget, J. (1952). *The origins of intelligence in children.* New York: International Universities Press. (Original work published 1936)

Piaget, J. (1954). *The construction of reality in the child.* New York: Basic. (Original work published 1937)

Piaget, J. (1951). *Play, dreams and imitation in childhood.* New York: Norton. (Original work published 1945)

Piaget, J. (1976). *The grasp of consciousness.* Cambridge, MA: Harvard University Press. (Original work published 1974)

Piaget, J., & Garcia, R. (1991). *Toward a logic of meaning.* Hillsdale, NJ: Lawrence Erlbaum Associates. (Original work published 1987)

Poti, P., & Antinucci, F. (1989). Logical operations. In F. Antinucci (Ed.), *Cognitive structure and development of nonhuman primates* (pp. 189–228). Hillsdale, NJ: Lawrence Erlbaum Associates.

Poti, P., & Antinucci, F. (in preparation). *Chimpanzee's logical development: Main results.* Unpublished manuscript.

Poti, P., & Spinozzi, G. (in preparation). *Early sensorimotor development in chimpanzees* (Pan troglodytes). Unpublished manuscript.

Savage-Rumbaugh, E. S. (1991). Language learning in the Bonobo: How and why they learn. In N. A. Krasnegor, D. M. Rumbaugh, R. L. Schiefelbusch, & M. Studdert-Kennedy (Eds.), *Biological and behavioral determinants of language development* (pp. 209–233). Hillsdale, NJ: Lawrence Erlbaum Associates.

Spelke, E. E. (1991). Physical knowledge in infancy: Reflections on Piaget's theory. In S. Carey & R. Gelman (Eds.), *The epigenesis of mind: Essays on biology and cognition* (pp. 133–169). Hillsdale, NJ: Lawrence Erlbaum Associates.

Spinozzi, G. (1993). The development of spontaneous classificatory behavior in chimpanzees (*Pan troglodytes*). *Journal of Comparative Psychology, 107*, 193–200.

Spinozzi, G., & Natale, F. (1989). Classification. In F. Antinucci (Ed.), *Cognitive structure and development of nonhuman primates* (pp. 163–188). Hillsdale, NJ: Lawrence Erlbaum Associates.

Spinozzi, G., & Poti, P. (1989). Causality I: The support problem. In F. Antinucci (Ed.), *Cognitive structure and development of nonhuman primates* (pp. 113–120). Hillsdale, NJ: Lawrence Erlbaum Associates.

Visalberghi, E. (1993). Capuchin monkeys. A window into tool use activities by apes and humans. In K. Gibson & T. Ingold (Eds.), *Tools, language and cognition in human evolution* (pp. 138–150). New York: Cambridge University Press.

Visalberghi, E., & Trinca, L. (1989). Tool use in capuchin monkeys: Distinguishing between performing and understanding. *Primates, 30*(4), 511–521.

von Uexküll, J. (1957). A stroll through the world of animals and men. In C. H. Schiller (Ed.), *Instinctive behavior* (pp. 000–000). New York: International Universities Press. (Original work published 1934)

Werner, H. (1948). *Comparative psychology of mental development.* New York: International Universities Press. (Original work published 1926)

10
Meaning and Expression

Lois Bloom
Teachers College, Columbia University

This chapter has three goals. The first is to draw attention to the distinction between meaning that is public, shared, and conventionally constructed in language, on the one hand, and meaning that is private, personal, and mentally constructed, on the other hand. The second goal is to show how private, personal, mentally constructed meanings exist before language is acquired. And the third goal is to argue that infants acquire language in the effort to express and articulate these private meanings so as to make them public.

Two principles drive the acquisition of language and they follow from the cognitive developments in the first 2 years of life that are responsible for the meanings a child can hold in mind. The first is the *principle of discrepancy*: Children will acquire words and language structures because the contents of mentally constructed meanings become increasingly discrepant from the data of perception. This discrepancy between things as they are, and things as they are expected or remembered to be, requires expression for shared understanding with other persons, and creates the demand for language. The second is the *principle of elaboration*: With acquisition of information about the world, mentally constructed meanings become increasingly elaborated. The more elements and relations between them that are constructed in mind, the more the child will need to know of the words and structures of language for their expression. Understanding language development, therefore, requires that we understand the mental meanings for which a child acquires the conventional forms and meaning in language.

MEANING IN CHILD LANGUAGE

In the 1960s, when I first started thinking of the importance of meaning for language development, meaning was not a popular topic. Because meaning in language comes from what we know about the world, it is potentially limitless. For this reason, and in addition to problems of multiple interpretation, meaning was not considered a reasonable subject for linguistic inquiry. This assumption had a long history in structural and transformational linguistics, at least since Bloomfield (1933) through Chomsky (1965). Correspondingly, meaning was ignored as well in studies of syntax acquisition in the child language renaissance of the 1960s. In this context, I was invited to make a presentation to a Columbia University faculty seminar based on what was, at that time, my dissertation research (eventually published in L. Bloom, 1970). They were a distinguished group of men: linguists, philosophers, sociologists, psychologists. They listened politely, smiled a bit condescendingly, and finally let go with: "We don't even know what adults mean half the time, how could you possibly pretend to know what a *child* means?" I answered: "It isn't so terribly complicated; one cannot know the abstract semantic structure of a child's utterance but can have little or no difficulty knowing what that utterance *is about*. Very little children talk about what they are doing or about to do or want someone else to do and those things are usually evident from the context. In fact, parents depend on it and routinely interpret children's messages all the time. Knowing what a child's message is about, one can attribute something of what the child assumes the words and relations between words in the message mean." That was in 1968. We have been studying meaning in child language ever since—in particular, acquisition of the *linguistic* meanings invested in the words and grammatical forms of language.

Children Acquire Linguistic Meanings That Are Public, Shared, and Conventionally Constructed

The main point of my original study was that children use the meanings of words and the relational meanings between words to discover categories and rules for syntax (L. Bloom, 1970). Meaning, therefore, could not be ignored in the effort to understand syntax acquisition. Children learn the syntax of simple sentences for expressing a core of basic meanings. Later, they learn the syntax of complex sentences to express other meanings that connect the basic meanings of two or more simple sentences. Today, the importance of semantics for syntax acquisition has been extended and formalized in contemporary learnability research as "semantic bootstrapping" (Grimshaw, 1981; Pinker, 1984). The idea is now virtually taken for granted, not only for child grammar but in research on thematic roles and relations in adult grammar that provide the input children receive.

The meanings in children's simple sentences are of two kinds. Certain meanings come from the particular words that children use often in their early phrases, words like *more* and *no*. For example, "more juice" *means* recurrence because *more* means recurrence; the meanings of negation in little sentences like "no fit" and "no dirty soap" (nonexistence, rejection, denial) come from the meaning of *no*. More important, however, are the grammatical meanings in sentences with two or more constituents of verbs (whether the verb itself is actually said or not): the little sentences children say like "Mommy pigtail," "read book," "Baby do it," "this go there." The meanings in the majority of early sentences come from categories of verbs that most often name actions and their thematic relations. These typically include inanimate objects that are affected by an action (the grammatical theme or what we called "affected object" in our studies in the 1970s), animate nouns as actor or agent, and the places to which actors or objects move (L. Bloom, 1991).

Complex sentences connect the structures underlying simple sentences, and the meanings of early complex sentences are acquired sequentially; they are also semantically cumulative. The earliest learned is a simple *additive* meaning, when two simple sentences are connected with no other meaning relation between them. An example is "Maybe you can carry that and I can carry this." Subsequently, complex sentences appear with *temporal* meaning, which is also additive, for example, "I going this way and then come back." Children eventually learn more semantically complex meanings when a *causal* relation is combined with additive and temporal meanings. The meanings of such sentences as "Maybe you can bend him so he can sit" express a causal connection that is necessarily both additive and temporal as well (L. Bloom, Lahey, Hood, Lifter, & Fiess, 1980).

The point is that these meanings of simple and complex sentences belong to the language: To learn the forms of the language is to learn their meanings. Learning a language is learning the conventional, shared, and public connections between sound and meaning.

The Syntax of Early Sentences Is Determined by the Meaning of Verbs and Their Arguments

Children learn syntax and semantics together by learning the verbs of the language and the configurations in which the arguments of the verb can appear. The semantics of simple sentences is in the thematic relations between verbs and nouns; the syntax of simple sentences is in the formal configurations of these thematic relations. The verbs children learn are subcategorized for different noun arguments; for example, the subcategory of action verbs like *make* requires an agent argument, and subcategories of locative verbs like *put* and *go* require a place argument. These subcategories of verbs license the different syntactic arrangements in which they can appear in sentences with other syntactic and inflectional categories (L. Bloom, 1981, 1991).

In a succession of studies in the 1970s and 1980s, we identified subcategories of verb meaning in early sentences that determined the subsequent acquisition of the syntax of simple sentences, verb morphology, and complex sentences. The first subcategorization distinguished between verbs that did and did not name a movement: *action* and *state* verbs, and the second subcategorization was whether the goal of the action or the focus of the state was the location of an object: *locative action* and *locative state* verbs. These different subcategories of verbs licensed different arguments in the same syntactic (*subject*) position: subject in children's sentences differs according to its thematic role with action and locative action verbs. Sentence subjects could be agents of action verbs as in "Kathryn make a bridge." Or, with intransitive locative verbs, sentence subjects could be either patients ("*lamb* go here" as the child puts the lamb in a block) or movers (where agent and patient are the same, as in "*Mommy* go work").

In sum, linguistic meanings we identified in simple sentences were *action*, *state*, and *location* and subcategories of verbs with these meanings guided subsequent discovery of the forms of language. Between the ages of 2 and 3 years, the meanings of simple sentences are eventually combined to form complex sentences with new meanings. The meanings of complex sentences included *additivity*, *time*, *causality*, and, eventually, the psychological attitudes named by state verbs of *volition*, *directedness*, *perception*, and *certainty*. In yet another study, we showed how shared meaning between successive sentences, by different speakers, developed with the acquisition of procedures for creating and maintaining contingent discourse. All these studies, now brought together in the book, *Language Development from Two to Three* (L. Bloom, 1991), document the meanings children acquire when they learn the words and the structures for their early simple and complex sentences. An underlying thread in these studies of the acquisition of grammar and linguistic meanings was an appreciation for the developments in other aspects of cognition that contribute to language.

COGNITION AND CHILD LANGUAGE

Children learn the meanings of words and structures of the language in the context of their conceptual development as they learn about objects and events in the world.

Early Syntactic Meanings Build on Concepts of Movement and Location

It was not difficult to see the connection between meanings in early sentences and the cognitive developmental history of the young language-learning child (Bates, 1976; L. Bloom, 1973; Brown, 1973; and many others since). In particular, the semantic roles in early sentences build on what the child already knows about movement and location. The importance of the two conceptual notions of movement and location has longstanding precedence in developmental psychology and has since assumed credibility in theoretical linguistics as well. Piaget, in his several infant books, stressed again and again that children learn about objects in the world by acting on them and perceiving them in different places (Piaget 1936/1952, 1937/1954, 1951/1962). Young infants move objects from place to place, watch other persons moving objects, and discover things anew in different places. Through these perceptions and actions in the first 2 years of life, children come to appreciate the effects of movement and location for constructing a theory of objects and space. The semantics of their early sentences builds on the conceptual knowledge acquired through these appreciations in infancy.

In linguistics, Ray Jackendoff proposed a theory of adult semantics in which the meaning expressed through the lexical and grammatical systems of language are closely tied to conceptual structure: In particular, "the semantics of motion and location provide the key to a wide range of further semantic fields" (Jackendoff, 1983, p. 188, citing Gruber, 1970; see also chapter 6 of this volume). The ontological categories in his conceptual structure for adult grammar included *action*, *thing*, and *place*. The action and locative categories we had identified in children's early sentences are essentially their nascent form. More recently, George Lakoff and his colleagues have pointed to the importance of movement and location for the structure and function of metaphor in the adult language (see chapter 3 of this volume).

In sum, movement and location are prominent in the meanings children acquire when they learn grammar, and their understanding begins with the conceptual developments of early infancy. Correspondingly, the meaning and conceptual structure of adult language, building as they do on movement and location, have their origins in these very early developments. However, language and cognition are connected in still other ways in their acquisition.

Developments in Other Aspects of Cognition Contribute to the Linguistic Meanings Children Acquire

It does little good to hear words and sentences spoken in relation to events if these events are not themselves recognized and understood. Linguistic and nonlinguistic inputs are data for a child only when their appraisal is within the child's perceptual and cognitive abilities. Young children express a small core of meanings and some of these are expressed more frequently than others. Moreover, certain meanings in adult language occur infrequently or not at all in early child sentences, for example, comparative constructions, conditionals, and the instrumental role of an object in an action. Semantic relations in early sentences, therefore, are not just a random sampling of possible meanings in the language. More likely, children select from the meanings available to them in the speech they hear only those which fall within their cognitive understanding (L. Bloom, 1970). This semantic selection no doubt goes hand in hand with input frequency and, indeed, frequency in the input is probably guided by what people talking to children believe that a child knows about and can, therefore, understand.

A major fallout from introducing meaning into the study of syntax acquisition was the question: How do developments in other aspects of cognition contribute to learning language? Much research has been directed at answering this question in order to understand the origins of the words and sentences children learn. This inquiry into cognitive developments and language has had, by and large, two thrusts. One is the focus on the child's knowledge base and one or another version of the traditional child language "mapping problem": how children attach the forms of language to what they know about objects, events, and relations in the world (see, e.g., L. Bloom, 1970, 1973; Gopnik & Meltzoff, 1987; Mervis, 1984; Nelson, 1974, 1985; and many others). The importance for language of concepts of objects and events is, by now, virtually self-evident. Most simply, children learn to talk about what they know at least something about. The second cognitive focus in child language research has been on development of the structures of thought that make possible the acquisition of concepts, event knowledge, and language itself (see, e.g., Bates, 1976; L. Bloom, 1973; L. Bloom, Lifter, & Broughton, 1985; Brown, 1973; Gopnik & Meltzoff, 1984; Kelly & Dale, 1989; Lifter & Bloom, 1989; McCune-Nicolich, 1981; Tomasello & Farrar, 1984). These have included, at least, development of the symbolic capacity and such Piagetian constructs as object permanence and means–end relations.

We have, then, these two cognitive perspectives in child language research. One is on the mapping relation between the conventional forms of language and concepts of objects, events, and relations in the world. The other is on development of the processes and structures of thought needed to acquire this knowledge. The result of this research is that we now have some idea of how cognitive developments contribute to the acquisition of words and the structures of language in the period from 1 to 3 years of age.

Yet another perspective is offered by Hirsh-Pasek, Golinkoff, and Reeves (chapter 11 of this volume), who suggest that something more than development in general cognition is required for learning words. They approach the mapping problem with the assumption that children would be unable to begin to learn words in the first place unless they were equipped with certain *language-specific* principles that provide the foundation for building a language. They allow that such principles are developmental to the extent that they "are acquired in a sequence and build upon one another . . . as they emerge." Nevertheless, they make clear that they believe the principles have precedence and make word learning possible—that a child could not begin to learn words without them.

Thus far, however, the argument advanced for language-specific principles is primarily a logical one, building as it does on the dilemma of "radical translation" posed by Quine (1960), rather than an empirical one. This is because the data cited in support of linguistic principles typically come from children who are at least 2 years old. I am puzzled, for example, how demonstrating that children use lexical principles after a vocabulary spurt can explain the vocabulary spurt, as they claim. More likely, 2-year-olds perform as they do on experimental word-learning tasks because of what they already know from 2 years worth of language learning (Nelson, 1988). Further, resorting to lexical principles for explaining word learning underestimates the relevance of words in the typical language-learning scenario: Children learn words when they hear them in connection with the mental meanings they already have in mind, as a consequence of focus of attention, motivation, and affect (L. Bloom, 1993; Nelson, 1988).

The lexical principles proposed by Hirsh-Pasek, Golinkoff, and Reeves (and others they cite) do, in fact, make sense because they are *descriptive* of what happens in the course of development. And they are language-specific because it is language learning they describe. Two-year-old children do what the principles say they do: make reference, extend words to new exemplars, label objects that form basic-level categories, assume that a new word is the name for a nameless object, and use the words that they hear other persons use. But they do all these things because it is language they are learning. Learning a language means to acquire this sort of domain-specific knowledge, and as such knowledge is acquired, it can be used in the service of learning more about the domain. Learning one thing about the linguistic system boosts the child into another linguistic problem space; solving that problem gives a leg up on the next one, and so forth. Having learned a lexical principle by learning something about what words are and what they do, a child would be expected to use the principle to learn more words.

Once a child learns something about objects and events, and about words qua words, word learning consists of good old-fashioned associative learning. In the beginning, the data for learning the meanings of language are in the circumstances of use in which children hear words and sentences. The meanings of early words like *cookie*, *gone*, *more*, and *mama*, or little sentences like "eat meat," or "throw ball," can be gotten from the connections between the words and their corresponding events. Eventually, meaning in language becomes increasingly arbitrary and is no longer transparent in circumstances of use. Words like *citizen*, *honor*, and *trust* are learned indirectly, through the other words a child already knows. Associative learning has now reappeared in contemporary theory as "connectionism" and has come a long way since the days of E. L. Thorndike (who was the original connectionist; see the 1949 anthology of his articles, *Selected Writings from a Connectionist's Psychology*). Connectionism will continue to be debated in the realm of syntax for some time, but so far it offers a more parsimonious account of lexical learning than a theory based on a priori lexical principles (see Harris, 1989).

The emphasis on the mapping problem and the cognitive developments that contribute to solving it has, at least so far, been more product oriented than process oriented. The products we have emphasized in our research and theory are concepts, the forms of language, and connections between concepts and language forms. In fact, I think it fair to say that most linguistic inquiry, with adults as well as children, is not ordinarily concerned with the on-line thinking that goes into actually saying and understanding words and sentences. And yet the dynamic processes involved in acts of expression and interpretation have everything to do with how children learn language.

Do we have any evidence of such on-line processing? In fact we do. From our studies of early word and syntax learning, we know that demands on a child's thinking influence what the child is able to say. Also, we know from still other studies in my laboratory that thinking for language influences and is influenced by behaviors in other domains, like emotional expression and play with objects. This is because the on-line processing for emotion and actions, just as with learning language and using language for expression and interpretation, put demands on the resources of the young language-learning child.

Language, Along with Other Aspects of Cognition, Requires the Distribution of Cognitive Resources

In our studies of early syntax, we had shown that on-line processing demands for expression influence the length and relative completeness of the sentences children say (L. Bloom, 1970; L. Bloom, Miller, & Hood, 1975). The effects were quite systematic and predictable in a way that errors from strictly performance factors, like fatigue and distractions (such as Chomsky described, e.g., 1965), are not. Saying sentences puts certain demands on the young child's cognitive resources. There is, first of all, the need to access the syntactic procedures themselves and execute the plan for saying a sentence. In addition, the child needs to recall the words, maintain discourse contingency by sharing the topic of what someone else has said, and might also need to add such syntactic complexity as negation or prepositions to an otherwise simple sentence.

Thus, having learned something of the words and syntax of the language does not mean that accessing them for expression is automatic; far from it. Access may be more or less facile according to whether different linguistic subsystems compete for the child's essentially limited resources. Thus, recalling words that are newly learned and infrequent, or adding negation or prepositions to a sentence, or answering a question unrelated to what the child is thinking can add to the cognitive load of the child sentence so that something has to give. For example, we see such sentences as "Mommy read book" and "no read book" early on but we do not see sentences like "Mommy no read book." Negative sentences or sentences with newly learned verbs are shorter than are affirmative sentences with well-known verbs, because negation and using new words in a sentence "costs" the child extra cognitive effort. But the distribution of cognitive resources also means that the subsystems of language can also complement and facilitate one another. Thus, a sentence is more likely to be complete when a child can use old, relatively well-known words, has support from the discourse, and does not add complexity (L. Bloom, 1970; L. Bloom et al., 1975; see also, P. Bloom, 1989). Findings like these are evidence of on-line processing taking place in acts of expression, within the domain of language.

In addition to effects within the domain of language, we also have other sorts of evidence of the effects from other domains, such as emotional expression and play with objects, when children need to access words for expression. This evidence comes from our more recent studies of vocabulary acquisition by 1-year-old children in the single-word period before syntax. When children begin to acquire a vocabulary of words, affect expression is already in place for communication and has been for some time. Early words are tentative and imprecise, but children's displays of affect—the whole gamut of smiles, chortles, laughs, frowns, whines, and cries—are readily interpreted as meaningful by caregivers. And the 1-year-old child, in turn, is adept at reading similar signals from other persons. They appear to be effortless and automatic. However, Richard Beckwith and I have shown that the cognitive activity for constructing a plan to say a word can inhibit expression of emotion (L. Bloom & Beckwith, 1989).

When we plotted the frequency of emotional expressions in the moments before and after words were said, we found that a peak in emotional expression occurred immediately after a word. We interpreted this to mean that, as one might expect, the children were learning words to talk about what their feelings were about. However, emotional expression was below baseline levels in the moments before words were said at the beginning of word learning. This preword decrease in emotional expression was taken to mean that the mental activity associated with the experience and expression of emotion had been preempted by the cognitive processes required for constructing a mental meaning and saying a word. But the effects were mutual: Saying words was also influenced by emotional expression. These children did not say words when they were expressing heightened levels of affect, and were more likely to say words with positive affect than with negative affect.

In another study, we looked at the likelihood that children would be saying words or expressing emotion as they played with objects. When the children were intent on constructing thematic relations between objects (like putting nesting cups together, stringing beads, giving a baby doll a ride in a truck, and the like), the frequencies of expressive behaviors—saying words and expressing emotion—fell substantially below their respective baseline rates (Beckwith, Tinker, & L. Bloom, 1993). This result, although evidence of the competition for cognitive resources between developmental domains, has yet another contributing factor. When the children played with objects in a goal-directed way—to construct a thematic relation between them—they were less likely to be attending to their mothers at the same time. This lack of social-directedness no doubt contributed as well to the relative decrease in talking and expressing emotion, both of which have a strong social component.

These results from our more recent studies of early word learning relate to the earlier work on syntax acquisition in the following way. In the syntax studies, the meaning of the children's sentences was usually transparent but the form of their sentences was incomplete. We had proposed a probability model to capture the likelihood that child sentences would be complete or not (L. Bloom et al., 1975). The probabilities in such a model were determined by the relative on-line accessibility of words and syntactic structures, and relative support from accompanying discourse events. However, we now have evidence that linguistic processing can also be influenced by demands on the child's cognitive resources from other directions, notably action with objects and emotional expression. The probabilities for saying words in the single-word period in the second year, and the probability of saying a whole sentence when children are using multiword speech in the third year, could be expected to change with developments that influence the distribution of social, affective, and cognitive resources.

In addition, learning and using language require distribution of resources for an aspect of on-line processing that is not ordinarily considered in language acquisition research: the thinking that is required for constructing the representations in consciousness that are the mental meanings expressed by language.

MENTAL MEANINGS IN CHILD LANGUAGE

An important part of the mental plans we construct when saying words and sentences is the representation we have in mind for the word or sentence to express. These representations are the mental meanings that underly acts of expression and result from acts of interpretation. They are private, personal meanings in contrast to the conventional meanings in language we have been talking about so far, which are public and shared. Constructing the representations in these mental meanings also requires cognitive effort.

Public, Shared, Conventional Meanings of Language Express and Articulate Private, Personal Mental Meanings

Plans for expressing and interpreting include procedures for language and also such representations as Fauconnier (1985) described: representations "that we set up as we talk or listen and that we structure with elements, roles, strategies, and relations" (p. 1). These representations are set up in the part of the mind that has traditionally been called "working memory" or "consciousness." They are the mental meanings that individuals express when they talk and that they construct when they interpret the speech of other persons.

A focus on these underlying representations connects a theory of language development to theories of intentional states in philosophy (in the sense, in particular, of Danto, 1973, 1983; Fodor, 1979; Searle, 1983; Taylor, 1985, among others). Intentional states are momentary beliefs, desires, and feelings "about something"; they are states of mind directed at an object, event, or set of circumstances in the world. These internal, personal representations contribute to the mental meanings made external and public by language. Constructing intentional states as we talk and listen are the critical aspect of thinking for language and for the process of language acquisition. In linguistics and psychology, they have appeared in the "mental models" of Johnson-Laird (1983), the "mental spaces" of Fauconnier (1985), the "complex mental attitudes" of Pollack (1990), and the products in consciousness of the "computational mind" in Jackendoff (1987). These representations are *cognitive* not linguistic constructions, but "language does not come without them" (Fauconnier, 1985, p. 1).

The acquisition of language depends, then, on changes in the representations a child can hold in mind. Two principles follow from this assumption. The first is the principle of discrepancy: Children will acquire words and the grammar of a language as representations in intentional states become increasingly discrepant from the data of perception. In earliest infancy, what young infants are seeing is, to a large extent, what they are thinking. With developments in the capacity for representation and in procedures for retrieval and recall, infants come to access objects and events from memory that do not match the data of perception. This recall of past events is needed for interpreting what others do and, eventually, what they say. The corollary is that expression through acting and, eventually, through acts of speaking, becomes necessary in order for other persons to know what the child has in mind. The second principle is the principle of elaboration. The consequence of learning more about the world is that the child has an increasing store of past experiences and knowledge of objects and events in memory. This allows for increasingly elaborated representations in intentional states. If the capacity to generate expressions is to keep up with changes in the contents of a child's mental meanings, then the child must acquire the semantics and syntax of language.

What this means is that other developments are needed for language in addition to acquiring concepts of objects and events, and mapping conventional forms and meaning to those concepts in long-term memory. These would be cognitive developments that contribute to the thinking for language taking place in consciousness, in particular, developments in the symbolic capacity and in the cues a child can use for retrieval and recall. These and other aspects of mental activity, such as computational procedures and capacity, contribute to the resources the infant uses for all sorts of thinking and problem solving (e.g., Benson, 1990; Case, 1978, 1985; Pascual-Leone, 1987). They have received a good amount of attention in psychological theory and research with somewhat older children, particularly in neo-Piagetian accounts of cognitive development cast in terms of "information processing" and cognitive "resource models" (see, e.g., the articles in Demetriou, 1988, and Bjorklund, 1990, respectively). However, their importance for language development and the on-line processes contributing to acts of expression and interpretation has not generally been acknowledged.[1]

---

[1]For exceptions, see Campbell (1979, 1986), Golinkoff (1986), Gopnik (1982), Hamburger and Crain (1987). The distinction drawn here between representations in consciousness (intentional states or mental meanings) and knowledge in memory correspond, respectively, to Campbell's (1979) distinction between a "domain of the organism, the contents of which are constantly changing and available to awareness and whose dynamic is rational ... [and another] domain, the contents of which change only slowly, are not available to awareness, and whose dynamic is causal" (p. 420).

To sum up so far, I am suggesting that we look beyond the child language-mapping problem, which I have characterized as being directed at the products of language acquisition, for evidence of how the child's thinking contributes to acquisition. A focus on on-line processing leads us to how children set up representations in intentional states and the cognitive developments that enable them. These representations are the private, personal mental meanings for which the child learns the public, conventional meanings of language. Language expresses and articulates these representations in acts of expression and sets up such representations in acts of interpretation.

The focus in this perspective is on the mind of the child, to be sure, but that is not to deny the critical part played in all of this by the social world. The public meanings constructed between persons absolutely depend on the private meanings constructed within persons. This fact was recognized by Fritz Heider, the founder of attribution theory in social psychology, who proposed that the psychology of persons guides the psychology of the interpersonal (Heider, 1958). Attribution theory made clear that the beliefs, feelings, and desires of individuals must be taken into account in the effort to understand and explain coordinated social activity. Social contexts depend on what is in the minds of the participants and acts of expression and interpretation are central in all social activity. A large part of why languages began in the first place was no doubt the need in a society for individuals to have expressive power: to make external and public to other persons what is otherwise internal and private to themselves. Languages are social products but they depend on what is in the minds of the participants.

Private and Personal Mental Meanings Exist Before
Language Is Acquired for Their Expression

Attributing meaning to children's speech has been a relatively conservative enterprise so far. This is because attributions based on what children say are ordinarily restricted to attributing public, conventional linguistic meaning to words and combinations of words. More recently in our research, we have begun to extend the practice of rich interpretation to make attributions of intentional states—the representations in states of mind that give rise to children's expressions (L. Bloom, Beckwith, Capatides, & Hafitz, 1988).

I do not have the space here to go into the full rationale and the procedures we used for coding intentional states. We are certainly aware that doing so involved many pitfalls and we no doubt fell into our share of these. We also know that any attempt at capturing the full content and structure of states of consciousness is doomed to failure: We could never verify the units, with their roles and the relations between them, in a child's mental construction at any one point in time. But we could make attributions of what the contents of a child's momentary beliefs and desires were about, which is what parents and caregivers do routinely. When a baby whimpers, the parent might attribute hunger or discomfort or an inability to reach a toy. We made the same sorts of attributions of what children were thinking about when they said words in the single-word period. In coding these attributions we used the kinds of cues that parents use: what the child says, what the child does, what has been said or what is subsequently said, what is observable in the context, and what we know of the child from past experience. Moreover, we could do what a parent could not do. We used our videotapes to watch and listen, over and over, in the moments that surrounded an expression, and we could look ahead as well as backwards for relevant cues.

I can only present the highlights of the results of our studies of 1-year-old children in the period when they progressed from saying First Words (FW, at a mean age of about 14 months) to a Vocabulary Spurt (VS, when mean age was about 19 months). In these studies we focused on several aspects of the mental meanings underlying their single-word expressions and I talk about two of them here. First, if the principle of discrepancy is correct, then development in the personal and private meanings attributed to a child's words will be in what children *anticipate* in the context. This is, indeed, what we found. Development in the single-word period of a group of 14 infants whom we have studied was in the expression of anticipated events. Previous research that has looked for evidence of "displaced speech" has typically focused on talk about relatively distant past events with somewhat older children (e.g., Sachs, 1983), but talk about the past was relatively rare by the 1-year-olds whom we studied.

This first analysis consisted of attributing mental meanings to what a child had in mind when saying a word, with two categories of attribution: *evident* and *anticipated* meanings. An attributed mental meaning was considered evident when it was directed at something in the context that either had already taken place or was in progress. For example, a child looked at the toy cow and said "cow." When, in contrast, the attributed meaning was *anticipated*, the expression preceded an imminent event in the context that the expression was about. An example with the same word was the same child who, turning to his mother for help in putting the cow into a block, said "cow." In the first instance, he saw the cow as he named it, and his meaning was evident; in the second, he wanted some action with the cow from his mother, and the meaning was anticipative. In such anticipated meanings, mental contents were derived from knowledge in memory, being more or less cued by perceptual data.

Evident expression was always more frequent and, at FW, *evident* meaning was twice as frequent as *anticipated* meaning. However, development occurred in the relative frequency of *anticipated* expression at VS, chi square $(1, N = 14)$ = 5.273, $p = .022$ (see Fig. 10.1). One development in word learning in the single-word period, then, came with the increased ability to talk about something the child had in mind that was imminent but not yet evident in the context, and provided support for the principle of discrepancy.

Second, if the principle of elaboration is correct, then development in the period would also occur in the expression of mental meanings with a focus on

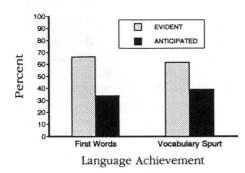

FIG. 10.1. Percentage of *evident* and *anticipated* meanings attributed to words at First Words and Vocabulary Spurt (from L. Bloom, 1993).

more than one element and relations between elements. And this too is what we found: Development occurred in the increasing expression of mental meanings directed at an action, with multiple elements and different roles and relations between them.

We identified two categories of meaning that we called *see* and *act*. The category *see* included predicates of presentation in intentional states; these were *point*, *see*, *show*, *give*, and *have*. An example was a child turning to her mother and showing her a cup, for her to see it. The category *act* consisted of the dynamic predicates *do* and *go* in intentional states. An example was a child saying "up" as she climbed onto a chair. When the children first began to say words at FW, these two categories of meaning content were similar in their relative frequencies of attribution. However, in the interval in which they progressed from their first words to a vocabulary spurt, words that expressed *act* meaning increased relative to the frequency of expression of *see* meaning with chi square $(1, N = 14) = 47.889$, $p < .001$ (see Fig. 10.2). At the time of the vocabulary spurt, *act* was attributed to mental meaning far more frequently than *see*, with a ratio of more than 2 to 1, $t(13) = 6.717$, $p < .001$.

These results mean that when the children began to learn words, their early words expressed presentational mental meanings about as often as action meanings. The development that occurred was in the greater increase in expression of dynamic *act* meaning, which came to predominate at VS, relative to stative *see* meaning. Mental meanings with stative *see* events were directed

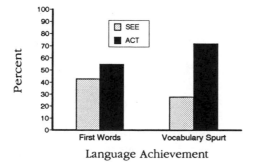

FIG. 10.2. Percentage of *see* and *act* meanings attributed to words at First Words and Vocabulary Spurt (from L. Bloom, 1993).

at a single element that the child had in mind while showing, giving, pointing, or otherwise presenting. However, dynamic meanings directed at actions have several elements with different roles and relations between them, according to the dynamics of the action. Thus, the second development in the single-word period was this increase in number of elements with different roles and relations in mental meanings, and provided support for the principle of elaboration.

Moreover, the increase in *anticipated* expression was greater for *act* than for *see* meanings. An example of an anticipation with *see* content was when a child held out a cup for her mother to see it, saying "cup." Although *anticipated* expression was more frequent with *see* meaning at FW, *anticipated* expression was far more frequent for *act* meaning at VS, chi square $(3, N = 14) = 104.23$, $p < .001$ (see Fig. 10.3). Thus, the two developments relevant to discrepancy and elaboration were coextensive. Development in the single-word period was in the children's ability to use words to express their private, mental meanings that could not otherwise be known to their listeners because they were anticipated by the child and not yet evident in the context. These mental meanings were, moreover, increasingly elaborated because they entailed action events with multiple objects, roles, and relations. Expression of anticipated mental meanings may appear at first to be inconsistent with the often cited "here and now" character of children's early speech. However, anticipated events were here and now events because they almost always concerned the objects and persons in the playroom; they were imminent, as in the previous examples. Development, therefore, was in a shift from immediate to imminent here and now content.

In sum, the development that occurred in the single-word period of the children whom we studied was in learning conventional word meanings for the expression of mental meanings with anticipated, action-oriented content. This was clearly not a "plateau" in development, which is how the single-word period has sometimes been described (Bates, Benigni, Bretherton, Camaioni, & Volterra, 1979; Nelson, 1979). Moreover, these analyses were more revealing of developments in the period than were analyses based on the kinds of words the children were learning (reported in L. Bloom, 1993).

These results support the claim that mental meanings exist before children acquire the conventional meanings of the forms of language for expression. First,

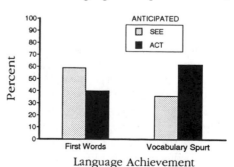

FIG. 10.3. Percentage of *antici-pated see* and *act* meanings attributed to words at First Words and Vocabulary Spurt (from L. Bloom, 1993).

these children were expressing anticipated content with their single-word speech long before they acquired the relevant forms "wanna," "gonna," and "will." Second, they were expressing *act* content with multiple elements and relations between elements before they were using verbs and combining verbs with nouns and pronouns to express thematic relations in multiword utterances.

This ability to talk about what can be anticipated has its origins in early infancy. As young as 3.5 months of age, infants have shown they can form expectations for visual events that are presented to them in a series, providing very early evidence of future-oriented behavior (Haith, Hazan, & Goodman, 1988). In addition, children are used to hearing speech in anticipation of the imminent events the speech is about. In a study of early verb learning, children in the single-word period (ages 15 and 21 months) most often heard their mothers use verbs before the action named by the verb actually occurred (Tomasello & Kruger, 1992). Moreover, they tended to learn these verbs, in particular, when they were relevant, by virtue of mothers saying them during episodes of joint attention. Attending to an object, a child can anticipate a relevant action with the object and have that action in mind as the mother names it.

The Internal and External Contexts for Acquiring a Language Are Rich and Building a Language Does *Not* Recapitulate Evolution

The assumption that language-specific principles are necessary for word learning has led Hirsh-Pasek, Golinkoff, and Reeves (chapter 11 of this volume) to also assume that a constructivist explanation without them is analogous to an evolutionary theory. We all agree that a newborn infant today is a far different creature from persons in that long ago world in which languages, as we know them, did not exist. However, the question is whether that difference takes the form of "lexical and grammatical biases."

Certain basic capacities for building a language are, indeed, already in place at the beginning of life, and a newborn infant is exquisitely prepared to acquire a language. Socially, in the first few hours of life a human infant can tell the difference between its own mother's voice and a strange female voice (DeCasper & Fifer, 1980). Acoustically, an infant as young as a few weeks olds can hear the difference between categories of speech sounds, such as the difference between /p/ and /b/ (Eimas, Siqueland, Jusczyk, & Vigorito, 1971). And, semantically, infants produce cries, whines, and whimpers to which their caregivers attribute meaning (Trevarthen, 1979). Although these capacities serve language, they are not specific to language. Even the discrimination of the sounds of speech, for example, is an acoustic, psychophysical capacity that will make the perceptual analysis of speech possible (Aslin, Pisoni, & Jusczyk, 1983; Kuhl, 1988). It is not a phonetic, linguistic capacity as was originally believed.

Given these and other basic capacities, an infant proceeds to build a language by analyzing speech in relation to the contexts in which it occurs. These contexts for analyzing speech embrace both the external circumstances in an event and the internal condition of the baby in the event: what the baby is attending to and believes, feels, and desires about an object of attention. This analysis is linguistic because language is its target and, also, because the analysis is informed by the language in the process of its learning.

We can begin to see the effects of a baby's efforts at linguistic analysis very early, in both infant perception and production of sounds. With respect to perception, infants show the effects of linguistic experience in their perception of vowel sounds by at least 6 months of age (Kuhl, 1991). With respect to production, 3-month-old infants vocalize with more speechlike, syllabic sounds when an adult responds to them contingently than when the adult responds randomly (K. Bloom, Russell, & Wassenberg, 1987) and when the adult uses speech rather than nonspeech sounds (K. Bloom, 1988). By the time they are 12–14 months old, most infants have begun to appreciate the connections between words and their circumstances of use (Golinkoff & Hirsh-Pasek, 1987; Oviatt, 1980) and may have begun to say words as well. By the end of the third year, the construction of language is well underway. Clearly, the human infant is not a preevolutionary creature. The linguistic analysis by which a baby acquires language exploits all of the baby's cognitive, social, and affective resources (L. Bloom, 1993), and these have been influenced by the evolution of language without necessarily being specific to it.

CONCLUSIONS

The essential claim of this chapter is that infants acquire the public conventional meanings of language in the effort to express and articulate the private personal meanings they have in mind. The contents of mind underlying acts of expression and interpretation are the unobservable facts in language acquisition but they determine that knowledge of language—lexicon, semantics, syntax, and discourse procedures—will be acquired.

The two conclusions we drew from the results of our effort to tap the personal meanings of our 1-year-old subjects relate to the principles of discrepancy and elaboration. According to the principle of discrepancy, children acquire words and linguistic structures in order to express what cannot otherwise be known to other persons. We found that the children whom we studied increased in the relative frequency with which they expressed anticipated (imminent) meanings. The discrepancy between the world as it is and the world as the child expects, wants, or imagines it to be was reflected in the increasing expression of anticipated content. The second conclusion concerns the principle of elaboration. We take the developmental increase in expression of action meaning as evidence of the representation of multiple elements with different roles and relations between them in mental meanings. Thus, the increase in expression of *act* meaning in the single-word period would provide the impetus to learn verbs of movement and location for simple sentences. And we know that the vocabulary spurt is often followed by the emergence of multiword speech and the beginning of a simple sentence grammar.

By the end of the first year of life, infants have discovered quite a lot about the world. As they enter the second year, all they have learned about objects, persons, and the self inform their beliefs, desires, and feelings and these can no longer be expressed, much less articulated, by the displays of affect that served the younger infant so well. Other modes of expression are required and, waiting in the wings, is language. Language has evolved in societies for expressing and interpreting personal meanings as we relate to one another in everyday events. It is the preeminent mode of expression provided in a society to embody and make public what is otherwise internal and private to the individual: the goals and plans, beliefs and desires, and the feelings we have that are, themselves, unobservable (L. Bloom, 1993).

But language does not replace affect expression and children continue to express their feelings through affect as they learn language (L. Bloom et al., 1988). And, indeed, language too has limitations with respect to how much and how well we can express what we mean in everyday conversation. Language can express many aspects of the objects, circumstances, and feelings in our everyday lives but by no means all their aspects. For example, words fail us altogether when our feelings are most intense and we fall silent, waiting for the feelings to abate and the words to come. Terrance Brown (chapter 8 of this volume) has shown, with eloquence, how the complexity and intensity of meaning might be expressed in private by writing a poem, before being shared when another person reads the poem.

Our 1-year-olds were on the very threshold of language and the words they were learning were small words, with extensions limited to the persons, objects, and events of their first 2 years. They were learning more about themselves and more about the world and they were acquiring the power of expression: first, by saying a word or two, and then a sentence or two, and, eventually perhaps, by writing a poem.

ACKNOWLEDGMENT

Much of the material in the second half of this chapter is from L. Bloom (1993).

REFERENCES

Aslin, R., Pisoni, D., & Jusczyk, P. (1983). Auditory development and speech perception in infancy. In M. Haith & J. Campos (Eds.), P. Mussen (Series Ed.), *Handbook of child psychology: Vol. 2. Infancy and developmental psychobiology* (pp. 573–688). New York: Wiley.

Bates, E. (1976). *Language in context.* New York: Academic.

Bates, E., Benigni, L., Bretherton, I., Camaioni, L., & Volterra, V. (1979). *The emergence of symbols: Communication and cognition in infancy.* New York: Academic.

Beckwith, R., Tinker, E., & Bloom, L. (1993, March). *The integration of expressive behaviors and object play.* Poster presented at a meeting of the Society of Research in Child Development, New Orleans.

Benson, N. (1990). *Mental capacity constraints on early symbolic processing: The origin of language from a cognitive perspective.* Unpublished doctoral dissertation, York University, Ontario.

Bjorklund, D. (Ed.). (1990). *Children's strategies: Contemporary views of cognitive development.* Hillsdale, NJ: Lawrence Erlbaum Associates.

Bloom, K. (1988). Quality of adult vocalizations affects the quality of infant vocalizations. *Journal of Child Language, 15,* 469–480.

Bloom, K., Russell, A., & Wassenberg, K. (1987). Turn taking affects the quality of infant vocalizations. *Journal of Child Language, 14,* 211–227.

Bloom, L. (1970). *Language development: Form and function in emerging grammars.* Cambridge, MA: MIT Press.

Bloom, L. (1973). *One word at a time: The use of single-word utterances before syntax.* The Hague, Netherlands: Mouton.

Bloom, L. (1981). The importance of language for language development: Linguistic determinism in the 1980s. In H. Winitz (Ed.), *Native language and foreign language acquisition* (pp. 160–171). New York: New York Academy of Sciences.

Bloom, L. (1991). *Language development from two to three.* New York: Cambridge University Press.

Bloom, L. (1993). *The transition from infancy to language: Acquiring the power of expression.* New York: Cambridge University Press.

Bloom, L., & Beckwith, R. (1989). Talking with feeling: Integrating affective and linguistic expression. *Cognition and Emotion, 3,* 313–342.

Bloom, L., Beckwith, R., Capatides, J., & Hafitz, J. (1988). Expression through affect and words in the transition from infancy to language. In P. Baltes, D. Featherman, & R. Lerner (Eds.), *Life-span development and behavior* (Vol. 8, pp. 99–127). Hillsdale, NJ: Lawrence Erlbaum Associates.

Bloom, L., Lahey, M., Hood, L., Lifter, K., & Fiess, K. (1980). Complex sentences: Acquisition of syntactic connectives and the semantic relations they encode. *Journal of Child Language, 7,* 235–261.

Bloom, L., Lifter, K., & Broughton, J. (1985). The convergence of early cognition and language in the second year of life: Problems in conceptualization and measurement. In M. Barrett (Ed.), *Single word speech* (pp. 149–180). London: Wiley.

Bloom, L., Miller, P., & Hood, L. (1975). Variation and reduction as aspects of competence in language development. In A. Pick (Ed.), *Minnesota symposia on child psychology* (Vol. 9, pp. 3–55). Minneapolis: University of Minnesota Press.

Bloom, P. (1989). Subjectless sentences in child language. *Linguistic Inquiry, 21,* 491–504.

Bloomfield, L. (1933). *Language.* New York: Holt, Rinehart & Winston.

Brown, R. (1973). *A first language, the early stages.* Cambridge, MA: Harvard University Press.

Campbell, R. (1979). Cognitive development and child language. In P. Fletcher & M. Garman (Eds.), *Language acquisition* (2nd ed., pp. 419–436). Cambridge, England: Cambridge University Press.

Campbell, R. (1986). Language acquisition and cognition. In P. Fletcher & M. Garman (Eds.), *Language acquisition: Studies in first language development* (2nd ed., pp. 30–48). Cambridge, England: Cambridge University Press.

Case, R. (1978). Intellectual development from birth to adulthood: A neo-Piagetian interpretation. In R. Siegler (Ed.), *Children's thinking: What develops?* (pp. 37–72). Hillsdale, NJ: Lawrence Erlbaum Associates.

Case, R. (1985). *Intellectual development: Birth to adulthood.* New York: Academic.

Chomsky, N. (1965). *Aspects of the theory of syntax.* Cambridge, MA: MIT Press.

Danto, A. (1973). *Analytical philosophy of action.* Cambridge, England: Cambridge University Press.

Danto, A. (1983). Toward a retentive materialism. In L. Cauman, I. Levi, C. Parsons, & R. Schwartz (Eds.), *How many questions? Essays in honor of Sidney Morgenbesser* (pp. 243–255). Indianapolis: Hackett Publishing.

DeCasper, A., & Fifer, W. (1980). Of human bonding: Newborns prefer their mothers' voices. *Science, 208*, 1174–1176.

Demetriou, A. (Ed.). (1988). *The neo-Piagetian theories of cognitive development: Toward an integration.* North-Holland: Elsevier Science.

Eimas, P., Siqueland, E., Jusczyk, P., & Vigorito, J. (1971). Speech perception in infants. *Science, 171*, 303–306.

Fauconnier, G. (1985). *Mental spaces: Aspects of meaning construction in natural language.* Cambridge, MA: MIT Press.

Fodor, J. (1979). *The language of thought.* Cambridge, MA: Harvard University Press.

Golinkoff, R. (1986). "I beg your pardon?": The preverbal negotiation of failed messages. *Journal of Child Language, 13*, 455–476.

Golinkoff, R., & Hirsh-Pasek, K. (1987, October). *A new picture of language development: Evidence from comprehension.* Paper presented at the Boston University Child Language Conference, Boston.

Gopnik, A. (1982). Words and plans: Early language and the development of intelligent action. *Journal of Child Language, 9*, 303–318.

Gopnik, A., & Meltzoff, A. (1984). Semantic and cognitive development in 15- to 21-month-old children. *Journal of Child Language, 11*, 495–513.

Gopnik, A., & Meltzoff, A. (1987). The development of categorization in the second year and its relation to other cognitive and linguistic developments. *Child Development, 58*, 1523–1531.

Grimshaw, J. (1981). Form, function, and the language acquisition device. In C. Baker & J. McCarthy (Eds.), *The logical problem of language acquisition* (pp. 165–182). Cambridge, MA: MIT Press.

Gruber, J. (1970). *Studies in lexical relations.* Bloomington, IN: Indiana University Linguistics Club.

Haith, M., Hazan, C., & Goodman, G. (1988). Expectation and anticipation of dynamic visual events by 3.5-month-old babies. *Child Development, 59*, 467–479.

Hamburger, H., & Crain, S. (1987). Plans and semantics in human processing of language. *Cognitive Science, 11*, 101–136.

Harris, C. (1989). *Connectionist explorations in cognitive linguistics.* Unpublished manuscript.

Heider, F. (1958). *The psychology of interpersonal relations.* Hillsdale, NJ: Lawrence Erlbaum Associates.

Jackendoff, R. (1983). *Semantics and cognition.* Cambridge, MA: MIT Press.

Jackendoff, R. (1987). *Consciousness and the computational mind.* Cambridge, MA: MIT Press.

Johnson-Laird, P. (1983). *Mental models: Towards a cognitive science of language, inference, and consciousness.* Cambridge, MA: Harvard University Press.

Kelly, C., & Dale, P. (1989). Cognitive skills associated with the onset of multiword utterances. *Journal of Speech and Hearing Research, 32*, 645–656.

Kuhl, P. (1988). Auditory perception and the evolution of speech. *Human Evolution, 3*, 19–43.

Kuhl, P. (1991). Human adults and human infants show a "perceptual magnet effect" for the prototypes of speech categories, monkeys do not. *Perception and Psychophysics, 50*, 93–107.

Lifter, K., & Bloom, L. (1989). Object play and the emergence of language. *Infant Behavior and Development, 12*, 395–423.

McCune-Nicolich, L. (1981). The cognitive basis of relational words in the single word period. *Journal of Child Language, 8*, 15–34.

Mervis, C. (1984). Early lexical development: The contributions of mother and child. In C. Sophian (Ed.), Origins of cognitive skills (pp. 339–370). Hillsdale, NJ: Lawrence Erlbaum Associates.

Nelson, K. (1974). Concept, word and sentence: Interrelations in acquisition and development. *Psychological Review, 81*, 267–285.

Nelson, K. (1979). The role of language in infant development. In M. Bornstein & W. Kessen (Eds.), *Psychological development from infancy: Image to intention* (pp. 307–337). Hillsdale, NJ: Lawrence Erlbaum Associates.

Nelson, K. (1985). *Making sense: The acquisition of shared meaning.* New York: Academic.

Nelson, K. (1988). Constraints on word learning. *Cognitive Development, 3*, 221–246.

Oviatt, S. (1980). The emerging ability to comprehend language: An experimental approach. *Child Development, 51*, 97–106.

Pascual-Leone, J. (1987). Organismic processes for neo-Piagetian theories: A dialectical causal account of cognitive development. *International Journal of Psychology, 22*, 531–570.

Piaget, J. (1952). *The origins of intelligence in children.* New York: International Universities Press. (Original work published 1936)

Piaget, J. (1954). *The construction of reality in the child.* New York: Basic. (Original work published 1937)

Piaget, J. (1962). *Play, dreams and imitation in childhood.* New York: Norton. (Original work published 1951)

Pinker, S. (1984). *Language learnability and language development.* Cambridge, MA: Harvard University Press.

Pollack, M. (1990). Plans as complex mental attitudes. In P. Cohen, J. Morgan, & M. Pollack (Eds.), *Intentions in communication* (pp. 77–103). Cambridge, MA: MIT Press.

Quine, W. (1960). *Word and object.* Cambridge, MA: MIT Press.

Sachs, J. (1983). Talking about the then and there: The emergence of displaced reference in adult–child discourse. In K. Nelson (Ed.), *Children's language* (Vol. 4, pp. 1–28). Hillsdale, NJ: Lawrence Erlbaum Associates.

Searle, J. (1983). *Intentionality: An essay in the philosophy of mind.* Cambridge, England: Cambridge University Press.

Taylor, C. (1985). *Philosophy and the human sciences: Philosophical papers.* Cambridge, England: Cambridge University Press.

Thorndike, E. L. (1949). *Selected writings from a connectionist's psychology.* New York: Appleton–Century–Crofts.

Tomasello, M., & Farrar, M. (1984). Cognitive bases of lexical development: Object permanence and relational words. *Journal of Child Language, 11*, 477–493.

Tomasello, M., & Kruger, A. (1992). Joint attention on actions: Acquiring verbs in ostensive and non-ostensive contexts. *Journal of Child Language, 19*, 311–333.

Trevarthen, C. (1979). Communication and cooperation in early infancy: A description of primary intersubjectivity. In M. Bullowa (Ed.), *Before speech: The beginning of interpersonal communication* (pp. 321–347). Cambridge, England: Cambridge University Press.

11

Constructivist Explanations for Language Acquisition May Be Insufficient: The Case for Language-Specific Principles

Kathy. Hirsh-Pasek
Temple University

Roberta Michnick Golinkoff
University of Delaware

Lauretta Reeves
Temple University

In a recent article, George Miller (1990) wrote that human language is the joint product of a rich representational system and of a communication system that permits the public expression of internal meanings. It was not evolutionarily necessary for the representational and communications systems to be combined; other species have survived and adapted to their environment without the advantages conferred by a linguistic system. Rather, it is an "evolutionary peculiarity" of humans that these two systems get subsumed by language. Language, according to this view, is an emergent property of other processes and is therefore analogous to the case of the elephant's trunk (to borrow Sperber & Wilson's [1986] analogy): The elephant's appendage did not evolve in order to facilitate picking things up, but once the trunk did develop (to serve other survival purposes), there was no reason not to use it for grabbing objects.

Thus, Miller's (1990) account of language evolution explicitly assumes that language arose out of general cognitive capacities, such as the semantic and communication systems. The language system did not begin as a modular one but as a general cognitive one (see also Greenfield, 1991). For language to have emerged at all, the species must (a) have already developed a highly elaborated representational system (including operations that could be performed on those representations, such as mapping back and forth between sounds and meanings), and (b) have been actively communicating via some more elementary technique.

The advantages of language in furthering both representational and communicative goals are self-evident. As a representational system, human language allows us to distance ourselves from the immediacy of our environment, and to represent (and convey) to others the past, present, and future. It permits social discourse about events as filtered through the prior knowledge, or feelings of the speaker, including inferences and interpretations of those events. As a communication system, language must be able to deliver these private representations into the public realm in a quick and efficient way, so that meanings are expressed before the signal fades. The syntactic system will help to determine the form of these expressions. Thus, the cognitively unique set of hierarchical, context-dependent rules and relations that characterizes human grammar is the design product of one system that fulfills two functions.

Theories of grammar acquisition have long been sensitive to each ´of the functions of language as ways of explaining how children acquire their native tongue. There are those who take one side or the other of Miller's (1990) bifurcation of linguistic function and argue that language is the result of either the representational system alone, or of the communication system alone. At one extreme are theories like Bickerton's (1990), which argue that the need for a rich representational system rules the day. To serve the representational requirements, humans developed a bioprogram for language and grammar that enabled them to create extensive representations early in life. On this view, humans come preequipped with a grammatical program that aids in the representation of actions, objects, and events, and communication plays a secondary role in language development. At the other extreme are theorists such as Bates, Benigni, Bretherton, Camaioni, and Volterra (1979) and Greenfield and Smith (1976), for whom the desire to communicate serves as the motive for the ontogenetically evolving language system. According to them, our grammar is an emergent property of the child's growing ability to communicate efficiently, first through gesture (e.g., pointing at a spoon), then through symbol (e.g., the act of stirring stands for the "spoon"), and then through words (e.g., using the word *spoon*).

The main theorist to bridge these two aspects of language, and to reconcile them under a unitary system, is Lois Bloom (1991a, 1991b). Her theory is one in which the first words, and eventually grammar, spring forth from both a developing, increasingly complex, internal system of meaning and a desire to communicate with others about those private meanings (see chapter 10 of this volume). The key point is that Bloom's theory is the ontogenetic equivalent of Miller's (1990) evolutionary perspective, as grammar in the young child evolves jointly from semantic or representational capacities, and the desire to communicate the meanings of inner representations. Bloom's current theory, and the bulk of her empirical work in the past, has been concerned with syntactic acquisition. How do children acquire a grammatical system that allows them to give form to expression of their internal representations? Bloom eschewed the existence of a set of genetically based syntactic structures that are merely activated via environmental input; her theory is decidedly bottom-up. Unlike evolutionary theories that posit that individuals of a species are the passive recipients of their genetic endowments, Bloom's tale of the ontogenetic development of language is one in which children are active constructors of their linguistic systems. Language arises from the dynamic interaction between children's growing cognitive abilities and their encounters with the social world. Bloom's theory is fundamentally constructivist in that the interplay between representation and communication forms the impetus for the construction of grammar (see chapter 10 of this volume).

In this chapter, we briefly review Bloom's theory and evaluate whether it can adequately explain how language gets off the ground. Although the interplay between meaning and communication can take us a long way toward explaining the emergence of grammar, we argue that it is not sufficient. Especially in early language learning, children may rely on a set of language-specific principles to guide them in lexical and syntactic attainment. For example, Bloom's theory says nothing about how initial mappings between words and meaning take place. Yet, if the child does not make these initial mappings between the words heard and the meanings represented, the entire learning process is thwarted. We argue that early word learning and early grammar learning would be impossible without language-specific principles or constraints. A flurry of recent research on this topic suggests that such principles might be used to "hook up" the first words and meaning.

In this chapter, then, we briefly review Bloom's theory and philosophy. The review is then followed by a discussion of the types of language-specific principles (here lexical principles) that can be used to supplement Bloom's position. Together, a "Bloom-plus-principles" account of language acquisition can provide a powerful constructivist model of how children acquire their native tongue.

BLOOM'S THEORY OF LANGUAGE ACQUISITION

As we interpret it, Bloom's story is a dialectic one in which the development of private meaning drives the acquisition of language so that the child can make this meaning public. Complementarily, the increasing expressive and interpretive power of language affords the development of ever enriched meanings. Under this view, children begin the language process by building up a dynamic storehouse of knowledge based on their understanding of the perceptual world. Equipped with memory and selective attention, however, each child's mental world becomes increasingly removed from the perceptual one. Children become able to construct "mental models" of the world, and to manipulate what takes place in those models. In other words, children come to be able to think thoughts and formulate intentions that are one step removed from "what is," to "what might be."

As this mental world begins to take shape, children attempt to express parts of that inner world. Whereas other communication systems, such as affect or gesture, were sufficient at an earlier time to express the contents of mental space, by 9 or 10 months of age, affective commentaries and pointing are no longer specific enough to allow children to make their inner meanings public. To give an example, showing that you are unhappy will not assist your caretaker in detecting the source of your malaise. Affective expressions can only go so far in expressing your internal mental state; the pin that is sticking in your bottom cries out to be labeled with a word. This is Bloom's principle of "discrepancy" (see chapter 10 of this volume); children's inability to share the contents of their increasingly elaborated mental constructions is what propels them to learn language.

The principle of discrepancy, according to Bloom, captures the motivation for learning language, and leads to affective expression giving way to linguistic expression. Bloom and Capatides (1987) claimed that affect and language abilities are initially independent. In the second year, word production and affect will come together gradually and with some difficulty. Eventually, however, single words will also prove insufficient for making the child's increasingly complex inner world public. What happens with single words is analogous to what happens with affect: The expressive power of single words begins to lag behind the contents of internally constructed mental space just as affect began to lag behind privately constructed, internal meaning. According to Bloom (1991a, 1991b), around the end of the second year, the mental world becomes replete with not only elements, but with relations between those elements. Single words (or even two- or three-word utterances) do not allow the child to express these relations unambiguously. So, the need for grammar is born from the principle of "elaboration." In sum, the public expression of internal meaning becomes the raison d'être for language development.

It should be noted that Bloom's theory is not an instrumental one. Children's motive in learning language is not to obtain some good or service; children are not operating on "market principles." Rather, they learn language in order to share the contents of their mental states, including their beliefs, feelings, and desires. This contention has empirical support: Golinkoff (1986, in press; Golinkoff & Gordon, 1988) found that a large portion of children's utterances, even during mealtime when instrumental requests would be expected to dominate conversation, were designed simply to share the contents of mental space, and not to achieve a material goal.

Having discussed the motives for why children develop language, the question remains how language is acquired. It is necessary but not sufficient that children have a rich representational life. They must also have some means of expressing the complexity of their representations. First words, and then words organized by syntax, serve this function by providing the conventional forms in which internal thoughts become publicly manifest. The content of an utterance is based on children's representation of the event they wish to convey; how it is expressed depends on knowledge of words and syntax.

As previously stated, Bloom's major emphasis is on how children learn grammar in language acquisition. To further elucidate her view, it may be useful here to provide a comparison of Bloom's theory with more traditional theories of how syntactic knowledge is attained. One such traditional perspective is what Bloom (1991a) termed the "learning-theoretic" approach. Based on the Chomskian view that language is a modular faculty, independent from other aspects of cognition, the learning-theoretic perspective posits that the child comes to the task of language learning with a strong biological endowment of language-specific grammatical knowledge that need only be "triggered" through appropriate environmental input. The child is considered a passive recipient of this input, and does not *construct*, only *activates* preexisting representational structures. At birth, then, the principles of grammar are already scripted and hard-wired. In this respect, the process is predominantly top-down, in comparison to Bloom's staunch bottom-up stance. Furthermore, the syntactic system is distinct from, and independent of, the semantic system. Cognitive advances in other domains do not determine linguistic advances, nor vice versa, under this pure linguistic explanation of language acquisition.

Bloom's view, on the other hand, is a developmental one with roots in the Piagetian tradition. She does not believe that language in general, nor grammar in specific, is a modular system unto itself, but a result of changes in and development of the child's overall cognitive capacities. As Piaget first postulated, developments in different domains can influence each other. Furthermore, children are active participants in their own linguistic achievements, not being granted innate grammatical knowledge with which to guide their language learning. The learning-theoretic view, claims Bloom, underestimates how hard children work at language learning. Children construct their own grammars in a series of stages as appropriate to their current cognitive capacities, each of which increasingly approximates that of the adult, rather than merely "discovering" adult grammar as the learning-theoretic tradition implies.

Syntax in children arises out of their general conceptual knowledge and their increasing symbolic capabilities. Lois Bloom (1970) and Roger Brown (1973) were among the first researchers to suggest that meaning and grammatical subsystems of language are interconnected. This position is aptly captured in Bloom's (1991a) statement, "meaning is the thread that [leads] children to discover the forms of language" (p. 17). Children, in other words, learn to talk about what they know and are able to represent. Especially important are the concepts of action, state, and location, which are acquired by acting on and observation of objects during the sensorimotor stage of development. These concepts also happen to correspond to the types of verbs found in children's early sentences. Developments that lead to representation of the meaning of such concepts lay the foundation for language acquisition.

Specifically, then, once children acquire early words and are motivated through the principles of discrepancy and elaboration to go beyond the single word, they discover syntax via verbs. The verb is, as Bloom (1991a) wrote, the hero of the sentence and the learning of individual and classes of verbs is critical to a child's development of language: The "child learn[s] grammar by learning semantic categories of verbs that determine the argument structure of sentences" (pp. 16–17). Several examples help to make the verb-centered approach clear. Locative verbs have a place as an argument ("go *home*") whereas action verbs have an object ("tie *shoe*"). For children to learn these verbs, they must first learn to represent certain semantic relations between objects. This is a representational task. They then learn the appropriate verbs to express these relations, which in turn permits grammatical expression of these more complex representations: "[L]earning the semantic relations actor-action and action-affected object and the constituents subject-verb-object in simple sentences depends on knowing the corresponding roles and relationships in action events" (Bloom, 1991a, p. 23). The learning of action verbs leads to the production of active sentences ("Gia [ride] bike"); locative-action verbs drive production of such sentences ("Put [cup] there"); and so on for state sentences ("Caroline sick"), and locative-state utterances ("Sit chair"). As children come to produce the arguments required by the individual verbs, they come to cross-classify these arguments and verb types on more abstract syntactic grounds rather than just on meaning relations. Indeed, this ability to derive and store meaning about these subcategories of acts or states of being, and thus learn about verb subcategories, predicts the grammatical structure of children's spoken sentences better than counting the number of times they hear each category of sentence (Bloom, Lightbrown, & Hood, 1975). That is, children do not merely reproduce the forms they hear else they would use Wh-questions (which are quite prevalent in speech to young children—see Bloom et al., 1975; Newport, Gleitman, & Gleitman, 1977) early on in their speech. Rather, they work out certain meaning-form relations as they construct the grammar. Bloom's data provide us with a glimpse of that construction process.

In sum, then, Bloom offers us a theory of acquisition in which the interplay between meaning and communication can be used to explain grammatical learning. To the "why" of language development, Bloom suggests that children learn to talk because they want to make their increasingly complex internal meaning system, public. Language is a vehicle for both the expression of internal meaning and for an expansion of these internal meanings through interpretation of others' language (see chapter 10 of this volume). This dialectic process is fueled by the processes of discrepancy and elaboration. To the question of "how" language is learned, Bloom sets us on a course of acquisition that is verb centered. At the same time that children are constructing complex nonlinguistic relations, they are learning verb labels and predicate-argument structure. Thus, the verb becomes the centerpiece of syntactic acquisition. Bloom was among the first to suggest the now popular assumption that verb structure holds the key to the understanding of grammar. Not only does Bloom's theory offer a theory of how and why, but she also accompanies her explanations with exquisite data on how the child moves through the process (see Bloom, 1991a, for a review). Thus, for Bloom, we might argue that ontogeny recapitulates phylogeny as each child constructs grammar anew from a growing cognitive system.

IS A PURELY CONSTRUCTIVIST ACCOUNT OF LANGUAGE ACQUISITION SUFFICIENT?

The question before us is whether Bloom's ontogenetic account holds—whether early language acquisition can truly be seen as emerging from an expanding cognitive system or whether there are additional assumptions, specifically linguistic in nature, required to make the story go through. These assumptions become evident when we examine one critical difference in what happens when a species develops language as opposed to when young children develop a language. The child, but not the species, is surrounded by input language of an already highly developed sort. For Bloom's theory to work, the child must somehow analyze that input and map it onto the internal representation. But what mechanisms enable the child to do this? How does the child extract words from the perceptual flux? What assumptions does the child make about a word—that it refers, that it denotes categories? What makes children attend to the order of the words around the verb or the inflections on the nouns as cues to relationships? Why do children make what appear to be linguistically sensible assumptions like those previously discussed rather than bizarre ones—for example, why should children not assume that all nouns refer to proper names or that relationships are denoted by the fifth syllable in every sentence?

Our guess (Hirsh-Pasek & Golinkoff, 1993) is that infants make reasonable assumptions about how to "read" the input because they are predisposed to note certain language relevant properties in the input over others. That is, at this point in the course of human history, humans have evolved in ways that enable them to find words and phrases, to map words onto meanings, and to prefer word order rather than number of syllables as relevant to language processing. Without these language relevant assumptions, children might not learn their language in the normal developmental timetable and would be expected to show much more individual variability in the course of development. Thus, we propose that children construct language as Bloom argues, but that they are assisted in their efforts by a small and as yet undetermined set of language-specific principles. The language-specific principles form a kind of skeleton (as Gelman & Greeno [1989] argued for the development of number concepts) for the language-learning system that biases it toward the right kind of data in the input. Together a "Bloom-plus-language-principles" approach would provide us with a fuller account of how the child could learn language from what Feldman and Gelman (1987) and Gelman (1991) called a "rational/constructivist" perspective. In other words, a Bloom-plus-language-principles theory would still be fundamentally constructivist but would incorporate an element that grants the existence of language-specific processes prepared by evolution.

Our own work (see Golinkoff & Hirsh-Pasek, 1990; Golinkoff, Hirsh-Pasek, Cauley, & Gordon, 1987; Golinkoff, Mervis, & Hirsh-Pasek, in press; Hirsh-Pasek & Golinkoff, 1991, in press) has been largely devoted to explaining the language-specific assumptions that young children make in very early word and grammatical acquisition. As a case in point, the following section of the chapter describes a set of assumptions children might entertain in the area of word learning—an area critical to Bloom's theory. Throughout, we suggest how Bloom's theory could be expanded to include these language-relevant principles.

PRINCIPLES OF WORD LEARNING: ONE EXAMPLE OF LANGUAGE-SPECIFIC ASSUMPTIONS

How does language get off the ground to begin with? If, as Bloom (1974) claimed, the mappings between speech and underlying representations are neither transparent nor isomorphic, what aids children in the initial tentative mappings that establish their toehold in language learning? Intuitively, it seems an insurmountable task for children to acquire language from the cacophony of linguistic input that confronts them without some guiding principles. Without such principles, how would the child know what even counts as a word, much less what a word means or maps onto? There are an infinite number of random possibilities for children to choose from; without some direction, how are children to know with which to start?

Apropos to the current discussion is Quine's (1960) classic Gavagai dilemma: Imagine a linguist hoping to decipher a previously untranslated tongue. She hears a native speaker of this tongue utter "Gavagai!" as a rabbit scurries by. The linguist assiduously notes in her journal, "Gavagai" = "rabbit." How does she know this? Could not the speaker have meant "animal" or "white" instead of rabbit? Or what about "hopping" or "moving object"? Rightly or wrongly, the linguist's first hypotheses will probably be biased toward the hypothesis that a single term such as "gavagai" refers to a single object. If, through subsequent exposure to the term as used in given contexts, this hypothesis turns out to be erroneous, the linguist can precede to another hypothesis. For example, perhaps she will conclude that this term refers to an attribute of the object (e.g., white or fluffy), or to an action being performed by the object (e.g., hopping). Thus, the linguist imports biases into her task of translation that have the effect of constraining the infinite number of hypotheses with which she might contend. We contend (Golinkoff et al., in press), along with others, that infants learning a language may operate as the linguist does, using guiding principles to learn their first words.

A number of researchers in recent years, such as Clark (1987) and Markman (1989), have come to the conclusion that young language learners start out with certain "biases" or "constraints" or "principles" of lexical acquisition, which guide children in mapping words to objects, attributes, and actions, and so forth. This idea is consistent with research in animal learning that has found that some learning tasks are easier to master than others, due to biological predispositions (Gallistel, Brown, Carey, Gelman, & Keil, 1991; Seligman & Hager, 1972).

The principles view, as it is conceived by most researchers, assumes that children may have certain biases that increase the likelihood that some hypotheses will be favored over others. Far from tunneling the child into a deterministic path, linguistic constraints may potentiate learning by limiting the hypotheses considered by an early language learner (Carey & Gelman, 1990), without preventing the child from exercising other options.

Consistent with Bloom's position, the lexical principles framework as conceived by Golinkoff et al. (in press) is developmental. Lexical principles are acquired in a sequence and build upon one another, altering the character of the acquisition process as they emerge. In Golinkoff et al.'s view, lexical principles are themselves a partial product of children's increasing sensitivity to the input.

Golinkoff et al. (in press) reviewed the literature in this tradition and set forth a tentative proposal for a set of principles children appear to use to guide lexical acquisition. These consist of a set of six language-specific heuristics, some of which have been suggested by others, that children use to learn words—especially words for objects. Some of the six principles already have some empirical support, others merely have promissory notes. Although the majority of research has been conducted on learning object labels, these lexical principles are assumed to be relevant for learning words from other early-appearing form classes as well.

The first principle posited by Golinkoff et al. (in press) is that of *reference*—the idea that words denote objects out there in the perceptual world or in mental space, and that the meaning of a term is the object that it denotes. It is difficult to see how we could acquire language without a certain prejudice to map acoustic sounds with items in the (often) visual world. As Brown (1958) noted, "The use of language to make reference is the central language function which is prerequisite to all else" (p. 7). If Bloomian children did not have reference they would be unable to even begin to share the contents of their mental spaces with others.

Accordingly, Golinkoff et al. (in press) proposed that reference serves as the first of a set of foundational principles upon which language acquisition is based. For example, a principle of reference could guide the child in determining that a word "attaches" to something within a given context. If language-specific, this mapping should occur more readily to human-produced acoustic signals than to other sounds, such as music, and so on. Although research has shown that labeled objects are looked at more by 10-month-olds than are unlabeled objects (Baldwin & Markman, 1989), the same advantage may occur when the objects are paired with music as an auditory stimulus (Roberts & Jacobs, 1992). The issue of when linguistic sounds are afforded special status with regard to reference begs for further research and exploration.

Simply knowing that a word denotes an object, person, or event would allow for very limited language development, as words could possibly only be understood as applying to the original exemplar to which they were first used. The child needs in addition a principle that allows words to *extend* to nonidentical exemplars. Golinkoff et al. (in press) called this the principle of *extendability*. For example, Bloom (1974) described how her daughter Allison understood the word *birds* only when it applied to the bird mobile over her changing table. Later, Allison understood the word *birds* to apply more widely. As with Allison, children must come to realize that words can extend to like objects; that is, *dog* applies not only to scruffy Rover, but also to the sleek Doberman down the road, and to the cartoon characters Snoopy and Scooby Doo. The bases upon which word extension occurs need not initially be accurate (the child may mistakenly call a cat "doggie"); it is sufficient that the child realize that a single term can denote multiple objects. This is necessary for language learning to progress. One should thus be able to find a developmental shift from underextension (where a child uses a term to refer only to a specific exemplar—see Bloom, 1974; Dromi, 1987, for examples), to overextension (e.g., Lewis' [1963] example of a child who used "quack" to refer to ducks, water, other birds, insects, etc.).

Empirical support for a principle of extendability comes from reports that from $10\frac{1}{2}$ months, children extend terms to similar although nonidentical objects (Mervis, 1984; Mervis & Canada, 1983), and that the greatest number of indeterminate extensions take place early in linguistic acquisition (Dromi, 1987; Rescorla, 1980).

A third lexical principle, first proposed by Macnamara (1982; also see Markman & Wachtel, 1988), predicts that the child will assume that words apply to whole objects rather than to parts or attributes of that object. Golinkoff et al. (Golinkoff, Hirsh-Pasek, Baduini, & Lavallee, 1985; Golinkoff et al., in press) termed this *object scope*. A principle that biased the child to assume that words labeled whole objects (as opposed to their parts, attributes, or the surface upon which they rest) would significantly reduce the number of hypotheses the child need consider for what a new word might mean. For Bloomian children, who construct representations of objects and their relations and who are eager to talk about these representations, there is an advantage to assuming that words label whole objects. Thus, if *cow* is uttered as a mother points to a cow in a picture book, the child will take the label to refer to the cow, and not to its tail or udder, nor to its brown color. Word scope is not specific to learning object labels; *jump* will be recognized by the child (we contend) as referring to the whole act of jumping, not merely to the preliminary crouch, or to the time the person is suspended in air.

Evidence for object scope as a strategy children use to acquire lexical information is that the child's first words are usually names for objects (Gentner,

1983, 1988), and that names of object parts are rare (Mervis, 1991; also Mervis, personal communication, May 1993). This may in part be due to their parents' direction; while reading picture books, parents tended to label whole objects before labeling parts or attributes of those objects (Ninio, 1980; Ninio & Bruner, 1978). Furthermore, labels for parts of an object are often mistaken as a label for the object itself (Mervis, 1987; Mervis & Long, 1987); the same is true for attribute labels (Hoffman as cited in Macnamara, 1982). And when a previously labeled object reappears with a similar salient part but different overall shape, it is typically rejected by children as a member of the original lexical category (Mervis & Long, 1987).

Object scope appears not to be based on perceptual abilities but on the saliency of linguistic data. In other words, it is not that this principle is due to whole objects being better perceived than parts. Research shows that infants are able not only to recognize the perceptual boundaries of objects (Spelke, 1990), but also the properties and parts of objects (Bornstein, 1988; Gibson & Spelke, 1983; Younger & Cohen, 1986). Thus there is no perceptual reason why object wholes should receive more attention; it must be that linguistic input serves to direct a child's attention to whole objects over parts or attributes.

An outgrowth of the principles of extendability (that words refer to more than the original exemplar) and object scope (that words tend to refer to whole objects) is that object words refer to *categories* of objects. This is the principle of *categorical scope* (Golinkoff et al., in press). That is, it is not enough to know that words refer, extend to other than the original exemplar, or label whole objects. The child must also know that words typically label items in the same taxonomic category. This was first introduced by Markman and Hutchinson (1984) as the "taxonomic principle." Golinkoff et al. reconfigured that principle to state more precisely that words label "basic-level" categories for young children and not categories formed on a myriad of other bases such as thematic relations. A principle such as categorical scope would work well for Bloomian children who are constructing various nonlinguistic categories at the same time that they are acquiring language. Bloom needs this language-specific principle to enable her children to discuss language- relevant, taxonomic categories as opposed to any of the other categories research has shown children are capable of constructing (e.g., Suchman & Trabasso, 1966). Categorical scope, emphasizing as it does extension at the basic level, refers to the fact that words refer mainly to objects that share shape and function. Thus the principle of categorical scope predicts that early in lexical development, children's word extensions will occur primarily to other items in the same basic-level category.

Research bears this out: Golinkoff, Shuff-Bailey, Olguin, and Ruan (1991) showed that children prefer to extend words to items in the same basic-level category as opposed to items in the same superordinate-level category. That is, children prefer to extend a novel term for a cow to another type of cow (an item in the same basic-level category) rather than to a pig (an item in the same superordinate-category, namely, that of "animal"). Golinkoff, Shuff-Bailey et al. showed this in a series of studies utilizing a modified version of a design used originally by Markman and Hutchinson (1984) and Waxman and Kosowski (1990). In the original Markman and Hutchinson study, 3- and 4-year-old children were shown a picture of a familiar object (e.g., a cow), and then asked to "Find another one" or "Find another *nonsense label*" in a forced-choice task from among two pictures. One of the choices was a picture of an item in the same taxonomic category as the original object (e.g., a pig); the other picture showed a thematic associate (e.g., a container of milk). When children were asked to, "Find another one" (i.e., the original object was not asked for by a novel name), either taxonomic and thematic responses were equally likely or, in later studies, thematic responses predominated. However, when the original object was given a novel label (e.g., the cow was called a "fep") by a puppet serving as teacher, subjects were more likely to select the pig than the milk when asked to find another "fep." Markman and Hutchinson and Waxman and Kosowski claimed that these results indicated that children prefer to respond to thematic relations without a label and to taxonomic relations (at the superordinate level) once a label was heard.

Golinkoff et al. (in press) and Golinkoff, Shuff-Bailey et al. (1991) pointed out that these conclusions were premature and that both studies suffered from the same two problems. First, children could simply have been operating with an "anti-thematic bias" for the extension of novel words, selecting anything but the thematic item once they heard a label. This problem could have been avoided if a third response choice had been included. The second problem was that the perceptual similarity of the taxonomic item and the target was not controlled. Thus, the pig looked a lot more like the cow than did a container of milk. If children were responding merely on the basis of perceptual similarity—and not on the basis of taxonomic category membership—they may well have selected the taxonomic choice. Golinkoff et al. corrected these problems and found that young children extend novel names only on the basis of basic-level category membership. Evidence for extension on the basis of superordinate- category membership (even in the absence of perceptual similarity) was first clearly seen in this task in 7-year-olds.

The fact that using words to label objects seems to cause young children to attend to taxonomic relations at the basic level, suggests that categorical scope is a principle specific to language. This hypothesis is reminiscent of that by Whorf (1956), which argued that language alters the way people perceive the world. Categorical scope is weaker in that it only claims that language influences the formation of conceptual "cuts" but not perceptual abilities. Once children realize that words label categories of objects, they attempt to fix new labels they hear to categories of previously unnamed objects. To capture this fact, Golinkoff et al. (in press) introduced the principle of *novel name-nameless category* or

"N3C," which proposes that upon hearing a new word, a child will assume that it applies to an unnamed, basic-level object. Such a principle would allow the Bloomian child to readily increase her storehouse of words and enable the phenomenon known as the "vocabulary spurt" where the child suddenly acquires many new words.

N3C has links to Clark's (1983, 1987, 1988, 1990) principle of contrast (new words are expected to contrast with established meanings) and Markman's (1987, 1989) principle of mutual exclusivity (children are biased to assume that an object can have only one name). Where N3C differs from each of the aforementioned principles is that it makes fewer assumptions than either contrast or mutual exclusivity. It assumes only that children are motivated to find labels for unnamed categories. Thus, the child's motivation is not jointly to affix a new label to an unnamed object *and* to reject a second label for a previously named object, but rather the former motive alone.

What is the evidence for the existence of the N3C principle? Golinkoff, Hirsh-Pasek, Bailey, and Wenger (1992) found that 28-month-olds handed over a familiar object from a set of four when it was requested by name, but delivered a novel object when a novel word was used in the same trial. Various experimental controls and a separate control experiment ruled out the possibility that the child was simply responding to the novelty of the object. This experiment demonstrates that children are motivated to affix novel names to novel objects (see also Markman & Wachtel, 1988; Merriman & Bowman, 1989). Golinkoff, Jacquet, and Hirsh-Pasek (1991) found that the principle also extends to verb learning. That N3C is instrumental in promoting rapid vocabulary growth is documented in a study by Mervis and Bertrand (1991) who tested 19-month-olds who either had or had not experienced a vocabulary spurt. Only children who had experienced a vocabulary spurt showed evidence of the N3C principle. Further, when the children who had not had a vocabulary spurt were retested after their spurt occurred, they then showed evidence of having attained the N3C principle. N3C allows Bloomian children to enrich their internal representations by learning many new words rapidly.

For Bloomian children to efficiently communicate the contents of their mental space, they must learn to do so in conventional ways. For example, if they call a dog "ruff," they may not be understood outside their immediate family. Thus, the use of conventional terms opens up the communicative horizons and reduces ambiguity. Clark (1983) suggested the lexical principle of *conventionality* to serve this role. Conventionality, as Clark conceived it, predicts that terms coined by the child should decrease in usage, to be replaced by more standard terms used by the community at large.

The emergence of this principle is evident when a child uses one term to refer to an object in the presence of his family (e.g., "pops" for "pacifier"), and the more commonly accepted term (pacifier) in the presence of outsiders (Mervis, in Golinkoff et al., in press). A corollary to the conventionality principle is that given that language and meanings exist in the public domain, names are not changed from day to day. What is called a "dog" one day will be called a dog the next.

Although much empirical work needs to be done to show that these principles are valid assumptions by which the child works to understand language, they at least suggest a possible course for the development of linguistic skills. They also have the advantage of being able to account for the vocabulary spurt that occurs around 18 months. If it is found that language-specific principles help to tell the story of lexical acquisition, it is possible that a set of principles may also exist to aid the child in syntactic acquisition.

CONCLUSIONS

Given that language evolved through the twin pressures for rich representation and effective communication, it makes sense to posit that children learning language should draw upon the interplay between these same systems in their construction of language. Though she might not draw the analogy between her theory and an evolutionary one, Bloom has provided us with just such an account of the child's grammatical acquisition. Indeed, hers is among the most detailed and cogent theories of language from a cognitive, developmental perspective. In her writing she offers a description of why children talk—motivating language through the child's desire to make internal meanings public. She also offers an explanation of how children acquire their language—detailing a limited resource model of language expression and a verb-centered theory of grammatical learning.

Although her theory is fairly complete, there are prerequisite skills that Bloomian children must have if they are to succeed at the task. These prerequisite abilities (such as finding the words in the input, mapping the words onto their referents, and discovering the structure surrounding the verbs) are the major supports upon which the theory rests. Yet, the problem of how children acquire these rudimentary skills comprise a problem space that Bloom does not address.

Our own solution to the problem of how infants come to analyze the language input around them is to suppose that years of evolutionary history have left their mark. The child is primed for language with certain lexical and grammatical biases. Equipped with language-specific biases, the number of hypotheses that the child must entertain for word learning and grammatical learning is much reduced. Although biases do not constrain development in a negative way, they provide a kind of skeletal framework on which future development can rest (see Hirsh-Pasek & Golinkoff, 1993, for a review of this position).

In this chapter, we put forth one set of biases in the form of lexical principles for early word learning. Some of these principles have been suggested by

Markman (e.g., 1989) and by Clark (e.g., 1983) and some by Golinkoff et al. (in press), who organized them in a developmental framework. To summarize, Golinkoff et al. contended that children hypothesize that words refer (the principle of reference); that words can be extended to nonidentical exemplars (the principle of extendability); that words usually label whole objects rather than their parts or attributes (the principle of object scope); that words label taxonomic categories—especially those at the basic level (the principle of categorical scope); that novel words label unnamed basic-level categories (the principle of novel name-nameless category or N3C); and that words are shared widely and used consistently within a language community (the principle of conventionality). Without these fundamental hypotheses for word learning, the child would forever be lost in a Quinean quagmire. Without these initial, language-specific biases about how words work, the Bloomian child could never begin the process of language learning.

Though it offers food for thought, ontogeny probably does not recapitulate phylogeny for the language learner. Rather, children probably construct their language (still a fundamentally developmental claim) with a little bit of guidance from systems specialized for language processing.

ACKNOWLEDGMENT

For her invaluable assistance with this chapter the authors wish to thank Vickie Porch.

REFERENCES

Baldwin, D. A., & Markman, E. M. (1989). Establishing word–object relations: A first step. *Child Development, 60*, 381–389.

Bates, E., Benigni, L., Bretherton, I., Camaioni, I., & Volterra, V. (1979). *The emergence of symbols: Cognition and communication in infancy.* New York: Academic.

Bickerton, D. (1990). *Language and species.* Chicago: Chicago University Press.

Bloom, L. (1970). *Language development: Form and function in emerging grammars.* Cambridge, MA: MIT Press.

Bloom, L. (1974). Talking, understanding and thinking: Developmental relationship between receptive and expressive language. In R. L. Schiefelbusch & L. Lloyd (Eds.), *Language perspectives—Acquisition, retardation and intervention* (pp. 295–312). Baltimore: University Park Press.

Bloom, L. (1991a). *Language development from two to three.* New York: Cambridge University Press.

Bloom, L. (1991b). Representation and expression. In N. Krasnegor, D. M. Rumbaugh, R. L. Schiefelbusch, & M. Studdert-Kennedy (Eds.), *Biological and behavioral determinants of language development* (pp. 117–140). Hillsdale, NJ: Lawrence Erlbaum Associates.

Bloom, L., & Capatides, J. (1987). Expression of affect and the emergence of language. *Child Development, 58*, 1513–1522.

Bloom, L., Lightbrown, P., & Hood, L. (1975). Structure and variation in child language. *Monographs of the Society for Research in Child Development, 40,* 2.

Bornstein, M. H. (1988). Perceptual development across the life cycle. In M. H. Bornstein & M. E. Lamb (Eds.), *Developmental psychology: An advanced textbook* (pp. 151–204). Hillsdale, NJ: Lawrence Erlbaum Associates.

Brown, R. (1958). How shall a thing be called? *Psychological Review, 65,* 14–21.

Brown, R. (1973). *A first language, the early stages.* Cambridge, MA: Harvard University Press.

Carey, S., & Gelman, R. (1990). Description of their forthcoming edited book, *The epigenesis of mind: Essays on biology and cognition. The Genetic Epistemologist,* Fall issue, p. 7.

Clark, E. V. (1983). Convention and contrast in acquiring the lexicon. In T. B. Seiler & W. Wannenmacher (Eds.), *Concept development and the development of word meaning* (pp. 67–89). Berlin: Springer-Verlag.

Clark, E. V. (1987). The principle of contrast: A constraint on language acquisition. In B. MacWhinney (Ed.), *Mechanisms of language acquisition* (pp. 1–34). Hillsdale, NJ: Lawrence Erlbaum Associates.

Clark, E. V. (1988). On the logic of contrast. *Journal of Child Language, 15,* 317–337.

Clark, E. V. (1990). On the pragmatics of contrast. *Journal of Child Language, 17,* 417–431.

Dromi, E. (1987). *Early lexical development.* Cambridge, England: Cambridge University Press.

Feldman, H., & Gelman, R. (1987). Otitis media and cognitive development. In J. F. Kavanagh (Eds.), *Otitis media and child development* (pp. 27–41). Parkton, MD: York Press.

Gallistel, C. R., Brown, A. L., Carey, S., Gelman, R., & Keil, F. C. (1991). Lessons from animal learning for the study of cognitive development. In S. Carey & R. Gelman (Eds.), *The epigenesis of mind: Essays on biology and cognition* (pp. 3–36). Hillsdale, NJ: Lawrence Erlbaum Associates.

Gelman, R. (1991). Epigenetic foundations of knowledge structures: Initial and transcendent constructions. In S. Carey & R. Gelman (Eds.), *The epigenesis of mind: Essays on biology and cognition* (pp. 293–322). Hillsdale, NJ: Lawrence Erlbaum Associates.

Gelman, R., & Greeno, J. G. (1989). On the nature of competence: Principles for understanding in a domain. In L. B. Resnick (Eds.), *Knowing and learning: Issues for a cognitive science of instruction* (pp. 125–186). Hillsdale, NJ: Lawrence Erlbaum Associates.

Gentner, D. (1983). Why nouns are learned before verbs: Linguistic relativity versus natural partitioning. In S. Kuczaj (Ed.), *Language development. Vol. 2: Language, cognition, and culture* (pp. 301–334). Hillsdale, NJ: Lawrence Erlbaum Associates.

Gentner, D. (1988, October). *Cognitive and linguistic determinism: Object reference and relational reference.* Paper presented at the Boston Child Language Meetings, Boston.

Gibson, E. J., & Spelke, E. (1983). The development of perception. In P. H. Mussen (Series Ed.) and J. H. Flavell & E. Markman (Vol. Eds.), *Handbook of child psychology: Vol. 3. Cognitive development* (pp. 1–76). New York: Wiley.

Golinkoff, R. M. (1986). "I beg your pardon?": The preverbal negotiation of failed messages. *Journal of Child Language, 13,* 455–476.

Golinkoff, R. M. (in press). When is communication a meeting of minds? *Journal of Child Language.*

Golinkoff, R. M., & Gordon, L. (1988). What makes communication run? Characteristics of immediate successes. *First Language, 8,* 103–124.

Golinkoff, R., & Hirsh-Pasek, K. (1990). Let the mute speak: What infants can tell us about language acquisition. *Merrill–Palmer Quarterly, 36,* 67–93.

Golinkoff, R. M., Hirsh-Pasek, K., Baduini, C., & Lavallee, A. (1985). *What's in a word?: The young child's predisposition to use lexical contrast.* Paper presented at the Boston Child Language Conference, Boston.

Golinkoff, R. M., Hirsh-Pasek, K., Bailey, L. M., & Wenger, R. N. (1992). Young children and adults use lexical principles to learn new nouns. *Developmental Psychology, 28,* 99–108.

Golinkoff, R. M., Hirsh-Pasek, K., Cauley, K. M., & Gordon, L. (1987). The eyes have it: Lexical and syntactic comprehension in a new paradigm. *Journal of Child Language, 14,* 23–46.

Golinkoff, R. M., Jacquet, R., & Hirsh-Pasek, K. (1991). *Lexical principles underlie verb learning.* Unpublished manuscript.

Golinkoff, R., Mervis, C. B., & Hirsh-Pasek, K. (in press). Early object labels: The case for lexical principles. *Journal of Child Language.*

Golinkoff, R. M., Shuff-Bailey, M., Olguin, K., & Ruan, W. (1991). *Young children extend novel words at the basic level: Evidence for the principle of categorical scope.* Unpublished manuscript.

Greenfield, P. (1991). Language, tools, and brain: The ontogeny and phylogeny of hierarchically organized sequential behavior. *Behavioral and Brain Sciences, 14,* 531–595.

Greenfield, P., & Smith, J. (1976). *The structure of communication in early language development.* New York: Academic.

Hirsh-Pasek, K., & Golinkoff, R. M. (1991). Language comprehension: A new look at some old themes. In N. Krasnegor, D. Rumbaugh, M. Studdert-Kennedy, & R. Schiefelbusch (Eds.), *Biological and behavioral aspects of language acquisition* (pp. 301–321). Hillsdale, NJ: Lawrence Erlbaum Associates.

Hirsh-Pasek, K., & Golinkoff, R. (1993). Skeletal supports for grammatical learning: What the infant brings to the language learning task. In C. Rovee-Collier & L. Lipsitt (Eds.), *Advances in infancy research.* New Jersey: Ablex.

Lewis, M. M. (1963). *Language, thought, and personality in infancy and childhood.* New York: Basic.

Macnamara, J. (1982). *Names for things.* Cambridge, MA: MIT Press.

Markman, E. M. (1987). How children constrain the possible meanings of words. In U. Neisser (Ed.), *Concepts and conceptual development: Ecological and intellectual factors in categorization* (pp. 255–287). Cambridge, England: Cambridge University Press.

Markman, E. M. (1989). *Categorization and naming in children.* Cambridge, MA: MIT Press.

Markman, E. M., & Hutchinson, J. E. (1984). Children's sensitivity to constraints on word meaning: Taxonomic vs. thematic relations. *Cognitive Psychology, 16,* 1–27.

Markman, E. M., & Wachtel, G. F. (1988). Children's use of mutual exclusivity to constrain the meaning of words. *Cognitive Psychology, 20,* 121–157.

Merriman, W. E., & Bowman, L. (1989). The mutual exclusivity bias in children's word learning. *Monographs of the Society for Research in Child Development, 54*(Serial No. 220).

Mervis, C. B. (1984). Early lexical development: The contributions of mother and child. In C. Sophian (Ed.), *Origins of cognitive skills* (pp. 339–370). Hillsdale, NJ: Lawrence Erlbaum Associates.

Mervis, C. B. (1987). Child-basic object categories and early lexical development. In U. Neisser (Ed.), *Concepts and conceptual development: Ecological and intellectual factors in categorization* (pp. 201–233). Cambridge, England: Cambridge University Press.

Mervis, C. B. (1991). Operating principles, input, and early lexical development. *Comunicazioni Scientifiche di Psicologia Generale* [Special Issue].

Mervis, C. B., & Bertrand, J. (1991, May). *Acquisition of new words by children with Down syndrome.* Paper presented at the Gatlinburg Conference on Research on Mental Retardation/Developmental Disabilities, Key Biscayne, FL.

Mervis, C. B., & Canada, K. (1983). On the existence of competence errors in early comprehension: A reply to Fremgen & Fay and Chapman & Thomson. *Journal of Child Language, 10,* 431–440.

Mervis, C. B., & Long, L. M. (1987). *Words refer to whole objects: Young children's interpretation of the referent of a novel word.* Paper presented at the biennial meeting of the Society for Research in Child Development, Baltimore.

Miller, G. A. (1990). The place of language in a scientific psychology. *Psychological Science, 1,* 7–14.

Newport, E. L., Gleitman, H., & Gleitman, L. R. (1977). Mother, I'd rather do it myself: Some effects and noneffects of maternal speech style. In C. E. Snow & C. A. Ferguson (Eds.), *Talking to children: Language input and acquisition.* Cambridge, MA: Cambridge University Press.

Ninio, A. (1980). Ostensive definition in vocabulary teaching. *Journal of Child Language, 7,* 565–573.

Ninio, A., & Bruner, J. (1978). The achievement and antecedents of labelling. *Journal of Child Language, 5,* 1–15.

Quine, W. V. O. (1960). *Word and object.* Cambridge, England: Cambridge University Press.

Rescorla, L. A. (1980). Overextension in early language development. *Journal of Child Language, 7*, 321–335.

Roberts, K., & Jacobs, M. (1992). Linguistic versus attentional influences on nonlinguistic categorization in 15-month-old infants. *Cognitive Development, 6*, 355–375.

Seligman, M. E. P., & Hager, J. L. (Eds.). (1972). *The biological boundaries of learning.* New York: Appleton Press.

Spelke, E. S. (1990). Principles of object perception. *Cognitive Science, 14*, 29–56.

Sperber, D., & Wilson, D. (1986). *Relevance: Communication and cognition.* Oxford, England: Blackwell.

Suchman, R. G., & Trabasso, T. (1966). Color and form preference in young children. *Journal of Experimental Child Psychology, 37*, 439–451.

Waxman, S. R., & Kosowski, T. D. (1990). Nouns mark category relations: Toddlers' and preschoolers' word-learning biases. *Child Development, 61*, 1461–1490.

Whorf, B. L. (1956). *Language, thought and reality.* New York: Wiley; and Cambridge, MA: MIT Press.

Younger, B. A., & Cohen, L. B. (1986). Developmental change in infants' perception of correlations among attributes. *Child Development, 57*, 803–815.

12

Plot, Plight, and Dramatism: Interpretation at Three Ages

Carol Feldman
Jerome Bruner
David Kalmar
Bobbi Renderer
New York University

In a recent volume, *Acts of Meaning*, Bruner (1990) urged that a culturally based cognitive psychology must focus upon meaning—upon the processes and tools by which human beings construct meanings that are viable within a system of cultural conventions. The central argument of that book is that the important cognitive processes of our species lie in the interpretive processes by which events are given meaning through the use of semiotic systems.

In this view, human cognitive processing is strongly specialized toward the use of culturally shared semiotic systems, systems comprising not only a lexicon and a grammar but also larger scale rule structures for constructing representations more extended than sentences, speech acts, and the like. For meaning making, after all, is not simply a moment-to-moment, or event-by-event, or even line-by-line exercise in reality construction, but rather is a more extended effort at what Nelson Goodman (1978) called "worldmaking." One of the principal vehicles of worldmaking, in his sense, is the making of narratives. Like so many other culturally significant semiotic activities, narrative construction depends on both intrinsic cognitive operations and culturally canonical forms that "exist" in a culture's tool kit. This focus has seemed to many in our field to be attractive as a theoretical commitment. At the same time, it has not been easy to see what form empirical research would take within a cultural cognitive psychology focused on meaning-making processes. This chapter is intended as a token offering in exemplification of an *empirical* cognitive psychology focused on processes of interpretation. Our specific aim within that compass is to explore how the making of narratives changes in the course of development.

The studies to be reported here explored how literate people of three different ages interpret the same short story, with a view to discovering any systematic changes in the forms of interpretation distinctive to each age. The youngest group comprised 12 children (ages 10;5–12;8 years), with an average age just over 11½ years (11;8 years). A second group of 14 adolescents (15–19 years) averaged age 16;6. The 12 adults (26–49 years) averaged age 32;6. All three groups were evenly distributed by gender. They were all drawn from the literate middle class. The first short story, Brendan Gill's (1961) "Truth and Consequences" is about a young man who, on the eve of entering a seminary to train for the priesthood, goes off to a summer resort for a holiday with his mother, who has from the beginning wanted him to enter the profession. At the resort he is drawn to an attractive and bold young woman with a lame leg and a penchant for swearing. He and the girl talk about their plans—his to be a priest, and hers to get married. She asks him whether he really has a calling. The story ends as his mother approaches them heavily in the gathering dusk.

The story leaves a good deal of room for interpretation—it is "writerly" in Barthes' (1974) sense. Readers at every age extract a variety of main themes when they are asked for the story's "gist." Some readers see the story as being principally about issues of personal individuation: "You have to do what you really want to do and not what other people tell you." Others focus on its epistemological equivalent: "Sometimes you think you know what you want, but then someone helps you realize you don't really know." In contrast to this "be your own person" theme, there is a boy-discovers-girl theme: Eventually even the most sheltered boy discovers there is a world out there and wants to be part of it; or, a boy is torn between the priesthood and his attraction to a girl and he's going to have to decide. And, rather interestingly, one also meets the theme of the young man intending to be a priest who wants to help a girl who is lame. There is also a wide range of genres that subjects attribute to the story. Some see it as fiction, even a fable, others as a morality tale designed to teach the reader a principle to live by, and still others see it as a slice of life, or a story about a young man's development. This variability in theme and genre is seen not only between, but also within, age groups.

And yet, notwithstanding the variability in theme and in genre within them, each of the three age groups has a form or pattern of interpretation distinctive to the group. Together, the three age-specific interpretive patterns constitute a developmental sequence for constructing the meaning of text according to different plans. We now turn to the data that formed the basis for inferring these age-specific patterns.

The story was read aloud to each subject, interrupted at fixed points with questions like "What's the most important thing I've told you so far?" "Why?" and "What are the directions this could be going?" "Why?" Several further questions were asked at the end, and subjects were asked to retell the story. The interview schedule is given in Appendix A. The transcribed responses were then subjected to various forms of thematic and stylistic coding (for an early report of these codes, see Feldman, Bruner, Renderer, & Spitzer, 1990).

Though we could only glimpse the overall pattern in snatches by that means, the codes nonetheless suggested certain features of the age-specific differences in interpretation. Two of these findings are of special interest for what follows. The first is the suggestion that kids have a different inference pattern than older subjects do. For kids, "the most important thing" was usually a psychological fact—indeed, usually a desire or want of some sort. However, their answer to the question "Which way do you think it will go?" usually took the form of specifying an action—doing or telling. Psychological states apparently lead directly to action in the children's way of conceiving of things. In contrast, teens and adults usually specify some action as "the most important thing," but when you ask them about which way the story will go, they answer by naming some psychological state. In a word, the causal link that goes directly from desire to action in kids no longer operates among adolescents and adults. They see the link between action and psychological states as a problematic link, to be understood only by interpretation.

The second finding was the discovery of a changing basis of interpretation with age—roughly from *plot*, to *plight*, to *dramatism*, terms we more fully explain shortly. When we asked why they thought the story would go as they said, kids gave reasons of plot and mental state in about equal measure. In contrast, far more of the teen answers were about mental state, with plot and dramatism of minor, but equal, importance. In adults, the three were given equal weight. A final observation from the earlier analysis bears mention here—that the retelling of the bare events in the story changed very little with age. What changed, then, is the system of interpretation used at different ages. However inconclusive they were, having these earlier analyses in hand served well as a rough road map through unknown terrain when we came to the word-frequency analyses, to which we now turn.

The bulk of the evidence to be reported here rests on an analysis of the actual words used in the text of the subjects' responses: word-frequency analysis for all single words using Brian MacWhinney's (1989) CLAN program; phrase-frequency analysis for certain interesting phrases; a series of univariate analyses of variance (ANOVAs) comparing the three age groups on all the words used; pairwise contrasts between age groups for words whose usage was found significantly different across groups in the ANOVAs; and finally, an examination of usage in context for all words distinctive to an age group on the basis of the relevant pairwise contrasts. (See Appendix B for details.) Unless otherwise noted, the words, word clusters, and phrases reported as distinctive to each group are significant across groups at at least $p < .05$, and show distinctive pairwise contrasts between that group and both of the other age groups. These provide us with our major clues about the differences in interpretive procedures at the three ages. All significant words, those mentioned in the text that follows and those not mentioned, are listed with their contrasts in Table 12.1.

TABLE 12.1
Significant Words for the Gill Story

Word	F	Mean for Kids	Mean for Teens	Mean for Adults	Kids vs. Teens	Kids vs. Adults	Teens vs. Adults
after +[a] before + now	3.65*	1.99	4.18	2.24	T > K		T > A
approached	7.68**	.00	.00	.40		A > K	A > T
are	3.30*	1.46	1.20	2.85			A > T
asked	3.85*	2.25	.90	.34		K > A	
away[a]	5.68**	.31	1.44	.69	T > K		T > A
basically[a]	3.86*	.50	.08	.09	K > T	K > A	
because[a]	11.76****	10.60	4.54	4.39	K > T	K > A	
being[a]	5.29**	.69	2.45	1.98	K < T	K < A	
between	3.87*	.05	.79	.99	K < T	K < A	
by	7.49**	.88	4.33	2.81	K < T	K < A	
coming	4.09*	.12	.80	.48	T > K		
conflict[a]	6.34**	.07	.04	.53		A > K	A > T
direction	3.38*	.00	.38	.65		A > K	
do[a]	14.76****	8.78	3.48	2.66	K > T	K > A	
doesn't[a]	6.28**	4.57	1.89	2.17	K > T	K > A	
enough	3.61*	.00	.41	.73		A > K	
everything[a]	5.42**	1.57	.45	.28	K > T	K > A	
for	6.27**	2.15	5.14	5.85	K < T	K < A	
from	4.32*	.94	2.72	2.36	K < T	K < A	
gist	4.44*	.00	.33	.66		A > K	
gonna	3.39*	.35	2.64	1.06	T > K		
hanging	4.78*	.00	.42	.00	T > K		T > A
happens[a]	4.13*	.06	.16	.45		A > K	A > T
have to[a]	3.53*	.38	1.34	.69	K < T		
he[a]	7.13**	40.21	24.73	22.22	K > T	K > A	
heading[a]	4.91*	.00	.00	.28		A > K	A > T
his	7.97**	6.80	15.28	13.87	K < T	K < A	
if	3.81*	4.41	2.60	1.52		K > A	
important	4.53*	.89	.30	1.27			A > T
in	8.30**	5.55	9.45	10.07	K < T	K < A	
is	3.72*	5.47	7.77	11.94		A > K	
knowing[a]	5.85**	.00	.00	.41		A > K	A > T
lame	3.45*	.10	1.69	1.57	K < T	K < A	
language[a]	3.38*	.66	.00	.22	K > T		
leg[a]	3.52*	1.85	.73	.45	K > T	K > A	
life[a]	5.60**	.58	2.17	3.42		A > K	
like	7.32**	16.80	6.73	5.88	K > T	K > A	
man + woman[a]	4.02*	.05	.84	1.45		A > K	
mother[a]	3.71*	5.89	8.89	5.45	T > K	T > A	
named	3.51*	.52	.00	.41	K > T		
obviously	3.66*	.00	.81	.27	T > K		
of	5.76**	13.51	18.82	26.41		A > K	A > T
people[a]	7.03**	4.62	1.96	.91	K > T	K > A	
point[a]	5.25*	.17	1.90	.40	T > K		T > A

(Continued)

TABLE 12.1
(Continued)

Word	F	Mean for Kids	Mean for Teens	Mean for Adults	Kids vs. Teens	Kids vs. Adults	Teens vs. Adults
possible[a]	3.46*	.00	.07	.37		A > K	A > T
priest[a]	7.72**	10.57	4.94	3.95	K > T	K > A	
question	5.41**	.29	.17	1.24		A > K	A > T
reaction[a]	3.57*	.00	.43	.00	T > K		T > A
relation	3.40*	.11	.98	1.32		A > K	
set[a]	4.48*	.13	.09	.84		A > K	A > T
sexual[a]	11.23***	.00	.04	.76		A > K	A > T
she[a]	9.22***	24.22	11.77	10.96	K > T	K > A	
she's	4.20*	3.64	4.64	2.00			T > A
show	3.27*	.17	.00	.34			A > T
so	3.42*	6.84	3.70	4.79	K > T		
sure	4.79*	2.83	1.13	.71	K > T	K > A	
swimming	3.92*	.64	.08	.26	K > T		
taken	4.93*	.00	.07	.33		A > K	A > T
tells[a]	4.67*	1.19	.23	.09	K > T	K > A	
there's[a]	8.27**	.55	2.66	1.30	T > K		T > A
thinks[a]	5.42**	1.05	.15	.31	K > T	K > A	
told[a]	5.57**	3.03	.56	.42	K > T	K > A	
towards[a]	4.50*	.10	.32	.76		A > K	A > T
uh	3.64*	5.47	8.78	26.41		A > K	A > T
vulnerable[a]	5.69**	.00	.00	.29		A > K	A > T
walk	4.49*	.25	.86	.21	T > K		T > A
walking	6.44**	1.05	.00	.17	K > T	K > A	
want[a]	7.16**	5.79	2.05	1.46	K > T	K > A	
wanted[a]	7.37**	2.43	.71	.99	K > T	K > A	
wants[a]	3.32*	2.65	1.16	1.24	K > T	K > A	
well	3.91*	8.26	4.26	5.09	K > T	K > A	
where[a]	4.00*	.16	1.15	1.17	K < T	K < A	
which	4.35*	.46	1.24	2.04		A > K	
without[a]	4.07*	.00	.04	.78		A > K	A > T
woman	4.24*	.05	.19	.82		A > K	A > T
would	3.30*	5.33	2.81	2.94	K > T	K > A	
you	6.14**	14.35	8.59	7.03	K > T	K > A	
young[a]	5.71**	.20	.98	2.58		A > K	A > T

Note. K = kids; T = teens; A = adults.
[a]Discussed in text.
* = $p < .05$. ** = $p < .01$. *** = $p < .001$. **** = $p < .0001$.

THE YOUNGEST GROUP—WANTS AND ACTIONS
OF PLOT FIGURES

The youngest group gives an account that is organized around categories that correspond to the functions of the plot. A plot, inter alia, has to have at least one protagonist (main character) who undertakes some action. For these young subjects, the protagonist is simply "he who acts"—it is not important who he is or how he is situated in the culture. Consistent with this, they typically refer to the two main characters in the story simply as *he* and *she*, and to everyone else just as *people*. The protagonists, then, are seen as figures rather than as persons, a distinction discussed more generally in Rorty (1988, chapter 4). As figures, they are completely defined by their place in a plot that is composed as a categorial system, as we see as we turn now to the protagonists' defining traits.

The major descriptor word for the boy, *he*, is *priest*, which identifies his categorical role within the story as one who cannot go out with the girl, *she*. The principal lexical descriptors for the girl are also plot functions—*leg* and *language*. *Leg* identifies the girl as someone who could get a would-be priest's attention by virtue of her disability and his sympathy. *Language*, as in "she uses bad language," identifies the kind of girl a would-be priest ought not to hang around with. (*Language* is used more often by kids than teens, but the kid–adult contrast is not significant.) The engine that gives this form of construal its dramatic interest is the categorical oppositionality between the figures (nice boy, bad girl) and between the courses of action open to each of them (priesthood vs. marriage). It is vividly exemplified by this set of contrastive, noncombinable terms.

The protagonists are endowed with little by way of intentional states or consciousness; mainly, theirs is a tale of actions and motives to act. The subject-positioned pronouns take three principal verbs—*do* (and *doesn't*), *tells* (and *told*), and three versions of *to want*—*want*, *wanted*, and *wants*. For children, wants constitute mental life, a mental life that is nothing more than a motive to action. Thus, for these youngsters, what each character wants (or does not want) is tightly coupled to what they do and say. Their usage strongly presupposes that stories consist of plots where protagonists do (or don't) do things because they want (or don't want) to do them. The only suggestion of any separation of these landscapes of consciousness, on the one hand, and of action on the other, is the presence of the age-distinctive mental verb *thinks*, positioned before variants of *want*, as in "He thinks he wants to be a priest." Here *thinks* hedges the desire and questions its implications for action.

This leads directly to how the age-specific word *because* is used, signaling a direct, indeed causal, link between wants and actions, as in "He says he can't because he wants to be a priest." It is a pattern that virtually disappears at later ages. Indeed, when we ask them what will happen next, adult subjects actually tell us that there is no knowing what our protagonist will actually do even when you know what he wants, or, as protagonists' inner states are more elaborated by adults, even when you know what exactly he thinks and feels.

So now we have *he* and *she* as protagonists in the categorial roles of *priest* and bad *leg*, who *do* and *tell(s) because* of *wants* in the midst of others who are simply *people*. This gives the basic style of the children's story. But, at times, even at this age, children mark something interpretive they say *as being an interpretation*. In these remarks we can see something of their working model of narrative structure. They use two words—*basically* and *everything* (especially, when this is used in the phrase *and everything*)—to indicate that the particular aspect that they are talking about merely exemplifies or stands in for a structurally necessary element. These expressions are used to mark the categorial identity of the protagonists as well as the categorial relationship between them. Categorial identity of protagonists is marked in the following examples: "She swears and everything" and "He was very set on being a priest and everything." The categorial kind of their relationship is marked in the following example: "Since they're basically opposites."

The narrative for these young subjects, then, is the structural-functional elaboration of coupled wants and actions of two rather bare figures defined by their opposed categorical positions in a plot. They are not so much in a human conflict, or even in a relationship, as they are in figural identities that create opposing requirements for subsequent action. If their personalities seem thin, it is because their identities as characters are determined and restricted by the role they take in the plot. Their muted drama is one of icons rather than of flesh and blood.

When we ask children what will happen next, they tell us of an action, and the basis for the course of future action they predict in the story is given by the requirements of the plot created by these figures. In contrast, adolescents tell us of feelings the protagonist will have, and their basis for predicting those feelings is the psychology of the characters, who have, at that age, a rich inner landscape. Thus, prediction itself takes on a different meaning here. And actions themselves take on a new importance for they permit the reader to draw inferences about the inner landscape of characters. We turn to the adolescent data now, but just to look ahead a bit, this system too will be displaced in adulthood when subjects add authorial intention to the considerations in their pattern of construal. For adults, dramatistic requirements on well-wrought works of narrative art displace, or rather reconfigure, characters' psychology, and dramatism comes to serve as the basis for understanding the tale.

THE TEENAGERS—TIME-BOUND, FATALISTIC PLIGHT

To summarize what has not yet been told, it can be said that the teenagers use an interpretive system that is organized around a human plight. Characters are encountered at a difficult moment in their development. The plight-like quality comes from the fact that in this form of interpretation, the character's present situation has grown inexorably out of earlier states of being, and must inevitably move to a future moment when it is put in the past, but its knotty complexity can never really be unraveled. Their interpretations are thus time-bound and fatalistic.

The language of their interpretations is saturated with age-distinctive mentions of narrative time. The words *after*, *before*, and *now*, not taken singly but as a cluster as if they constituted a single time word, are distinctive for them. This only suggests that theirs is a temporally organized pattern. But time is also conveyed by other markers. The temporal *where*, as in "And during a moment where the mother isn't aware of what . . ." occurs more often in teens than kids, though not than adults. Finally, the word *point* is distinctive to them. It is used temporally as in "at this point," very often to mark the moment of the realization of plight. And its augmented form also flowers as well: "And during a *point where* the mother isn't aware of . . ." or "will reach a *point where* they have to make a decision for themselves." The point where plight is realized is a crossroads on a linear path where the road to the future forks.

In the adolescent view, one path leads ahead in a straight line from the past, whereas the other fork is a new possibility not so obviously determined by the whole sequence of what went before (here are traces of the child's causality subsumed into a more complex pattern). This picture of a time line with paths taken and not taken is conveyed by the use of *reaction* as in a "reaction toward (or away from) the girl," and in the use of *away* as in "break away from his mother." Indeed the word *mother* itself, particularly when used in the phrase *his mother*, perhaps belongs in this group, for this is an essential historical element in the constitution of his present plight, a moment when the protagonist reacts to (or away from) the girl and breaks away (or not) from the historical path that his mother represents.

This time line does not describe a world passed through but rather the essential state of being of the character. It is a developmental account of character, rather like the Bildungsroman. The protagonist of the adolescent then has an enduring state of being that forms the basis of his plight. The essential quality of character for adolescents is revealed in the use of another of their terms, the word *being*, as in such expressions as "the coming-outness of being eighteen" or "he would end up being, like, less entwined with his mother," and "he has this way of being." Teens use *being* more than do kids. They do not use it significantly more often than do adults, but adults do not tend to use it in this teen distinctive way.

But, even more than *being*, the expression that gives this pattern of construal its distinctive flavor as plight-like, rather than being merely about a decision point, is the age distinctive marker *have to*, as in "To go out into the world he would *have to* break ties with his mother." Teens use *have to* more than do kids, but not than do adults. It is because there is an obligation to deal with the entire forked road, because no erasure is possible, that the boy's status is a plight—a fated state that one cannot fundamentally escape or resolve. That is to say, both the road taken and the road not taken will have consequences that are part of one's next state of being. Indeed, if one wanted to be extravagant about it, one could herald this achievement of the sense of plight as the birth of tragedy.

That the adolescents have a narrative model in mind, a model with obligatory features, is suggested by their age-distinctive use of the expression *there's*, used to note important elements that constitute the boy's situation as a plight. "Well, there's a girl," or "There's a chance he starts resenting his mother." Through its use, the dramatic elements of the plight are being decomposed, and although the adolescents do not exploit this analytic possibility as much as do adults, one sees its beginnings here.

THE ADULTS—DRAMATISM

The shift from adolescent to adult narrative construal is a shift from the dominance of plight to the growth of what Kenneth Burke (1945) called dramatism. Adult interpretations tend to decompose the story into something like Burke's well-known Pentad. There is an Agent, an Act, a Goal (his Purpose), a Scene, and an Instrument (his Agency). According to Burke, narrative is created by an imbalance between some or all of these, which is the source of trouble. Accordingly, to his five features, we add Trouble as an emergent sixth. Age-specific words mark this shift to dramatism. The first is *set*, which marks Burke's Scene, as in "they're all set to X." The second is *conflict*, which is just exactly Burkean Trouble. The third is *heading*, as in "He's heading toward a relationship with the girl," a term that portends movement in the direction of Trouble.

The fourth is *towards* which, when used without *heading*, tends to describe the protagonist's Goal, and the fifth is *sexual* which is Instrumental in creating the trouble.

The sixth and seventh words are used to mark imbalances between elements of the Pentad. Adults use the word *without* to mark some version of imbalance, as in "a lot of inner conflict without being seduced by her" or "just wind up growing old without having a wife, really." Another word is also used to capture imbalance, this time between the landscape of action and the landscape of consciousness that in adult narratives assumes its full role as an equal and balancing domain to the unfolding tale of action. The word is *knowing*, usually used with the negative *not*, as in the following examples: "He's trying to do the right thing without really knowing why he's trying to do it," or, commenting about the young man's intended profession, "about the priesthood and not really knowing about other people." So now the dissonance between hopes for the priesthood and attraction to the flamboyant girl need not be interpreted as either a criterial violation as in childhood or a time-bound plight as in adolescence, but rather as an imbalance creating a story that can variously be viewed as touching, typical, or perhaps even a little amusing.

The eighth and final key word is perhaps the most interesting for the way it suggests that the Burkean Pentad (Burke, 1945) may have some structural necessity for the subjects, offering a canonical pattern with obligatory slots: It is the word *happens*, and it carries with it the sense of movement in the drama as a whole—as in "Everything happens," and "What happens is . . ." or, most tellingly, "That has to happen before anything else happens." For these subjects, the construed story must be a dramatistically structured sequence of events where an overall structure dictates that certain kinds of events must occur at certain points. These dramatistic necessities are what is marked with *happens*, at a point in the interpretation when the particular details of how the necessary action will occur are not yet clear. *Happens*, then, like *basically* and *everything* in the kids' transcripts, and *there's* in the teens, is a marker that suggests subjects have a narrative model in mind.

Dramatism not only decomposes the teenagers' plight into its constituents, but it also leads to a more situated characterization of the story, and especially of the protagonists. Transcending the figural and psychological characterizations of younger groups to arrive at a view of the character as situated in a world, adults describe the boy as *young* and as *vulnerable*. Indeed, adults actually talk about his *life*. For example, "finding out things about life," "and removed from that kind of life," and "all he had known, really, his entire life." In fact, the figural protagonists *he* and *she* of childhood become a *man* and a *woman*, which taken together as a cluster appear significantly more often among adults. (But for *life*, and for *man* plus *woman*, the adjacent group contrast is not significant: There is a significant overall F and the only significant contrast is adults vs. kids.)

Dramatism permits the adult to transcend the teenager's dependence on an unfolding plight by decomposing a would-be plight into a set of constituent elements that can be recomposed in terms of culturally canonical balances and imbalances. The locked-in characterization of plight can be loosened by dramatism, and, in fact, this open quality of adult interpretations is confirmed by our subjects' word usage, particularly words used when speculating about the protagonist's future course of action. Specifically, the adolescent's use of the interpretive marker *have to* is replaced in adults by their distinctive interpretive marker *possible*. The shift from *have to* to *possible* is a singular and vivid exemplification of the more general shift from the adolescents' model of plight to the adults' model of dramatism. And interestingly, on those relatively few occasions when adults use the expression *have to*, they tend to use it in the negated form that denies any necessity others may see, as in "She *doesn't have to* play this game of swearing," or they weaken it with a hedge: "He *may have to* confront his mother," that has the effect of turning the necessary into the merely possible.

DISCUSSION

Those are the three distinctive patterns of narrative interpretation we have found. The first, of the kids, rests on categorial plot elements and figural characters. The second, of the teens, is based upon development over time and its creation of knotty plights. And the third, of the adults, is based upon dramatistic patterns. Each of these forms of narrative interpretation must exist, as it were, in the minds of readers, however much they may all in some sense coexist in the story itself, for the same story was read to all of the subjects.

On the other hand, at any age, many specific narrative genres may serve as interpretive mental models. Feldman (1991a) discussed the possibility that literary genres may serve as mental models used for interpretation. The interpretive patterns we have described here are more abstract. Each pattern could embrace many genres and give to each of those genres a distinctive stamp.

In fact, even very young children know several genres. Paley (1988), for example, described a preschool classroom with two distinct genres: stories with bad guys that cannot have birthdays, and stories with babies that cannot have guns. What the present results suggest is that all of the genre-like models typical of a single age must obey the constraints imposed by the more general age-dependent interpretive patterns of narrative construal described here.

Why would they develop in this direction—from plot functions, to plight-like, to dramatistically composable? It must be a matter not only of cognitive but also of cultural development, the two being inextricably connected in the act of interpretive cognition. Though we have used lexical usage as our index for tracking change, it seems reasonably clear that the changes we have chronicled derive not entirely from the lexicon, or even from culture more generally (though this must play an important role), but also from capabilities for experiencing the social world in childhood, adolescence, and adulthood.

One arrives at this point, wondering whether the patterns found here would actually have any empirical generality—would we have obtained the same findings had we told another story? Even if this developmental sequence were obtained only for a single story, it might provide a theory that psychologists would find useful in their own thinking about the interpretive aspect of cognitive development. But the problem is different if we are trying to establish that people may actually have certain ways of knowing at certain ages—in this case, ways of knowing that take the form of distinctive patterns for interpretation. As cognitive psychologists, and particularly as cognitive developmentalists, it is very much in the tradition of the last 40 years to want to address this harder question, of what is actually going on in the mind of the child rather than how we can formalize this from outside as theoretical psychologists. (For an extended discussion of this distinction in the Piagetian context, see Feldman & Toulmin, 1976.)

To approach an answer to this question is, at very least, to search for some evidence of *pervasiveness*, to look for a generalized application of a way of interpreting. With generality goes the cognitive economy that is widely shared by cognitive structures in many domains, and that seems such a fundamental feature of human intelligence. In the present case, it is to search for the same patterns in a different story. But now a new question arises. If a new story has new content, as it must, it is bound to have different words used, but somehow these words would share the same or a similar function as those found in the first story. We turned to a new story, then, wondering what we would find. A story was chosen in which another young man reaches a crisis point and has to make choices—but, the two stories differed in virtually every other way.

THE SECOND STORY: IN SEARCH
OF CONFIRMATION

A second story was read, in counterbalanced order, to the same subjects in the same session—"Grease Spots" by Heinrich Böll (1986). As the story begins, our nameless protagonist is going to visit his old friend Walter on the eve of Walter's marriage to our protagonist's former girlfriend, Erica. They had all lived together when, as poor boys, Walter and his friend earned engineering degrees by night and paid their way by working construction jobs by day. Both have risen in the world from the grease spots on the kitchen table of those days. The protagonist has married, badly—a cold, rich woman named Francesca. He sets out for the hotel, planning to talk Walter out of marrying this socially unsuitable woman. Walter, who is having a bubble bath when our protagonist arrives, mocks his attempts to foil his plans for marriage. The protagonist gives up and leaves, shedding a tear in the elevator on his way down. It is a very different style of story than the first: more understated, more sophisticated, and with more of a landscape of consciousness than the first.

Because this story would have been too difficult for the children, we presented it only to the teenagers and the adults, asking them the same interpretive questions as before. The same techniques of data analysis were used, with minor changes to accommodate for the fact that we were now comparing only two groups. Each word commonly used was tested for a significant difference between the two age groups. This time, only 31 words differentiated significantly between the groups, fewer than the 75 lexical items in the first study. These significant words were considered distinctive for the group that used them more often. Eleven such words were used significantly more often by the teens, 20 by the adults. The full set of significant words, with their contrasts, is given in Table 12.2. We inspected each word's usage in context to see whether it had a functional correspondence to any of the distinctive words of the first study for the corresponding group.

TABLE 12.2
Significant Words for the Böll Story

Word	F	Mean for Teens	Mean for Adults
an	4.97*	1.79	3.17
anymore[a]	4.40*	.63	.08
behind[a]	4.63*	.50	.04
cut	5.25*	.00	.44
early	4.64*	.00	.46
educated[a]	5.70*	.61	.00
feelings[a]	4.34*	.14	1.34
gets	4.64*	.42	.08
had	13.37**	1.66	4.24
he's	5.70*	11.89	7.03
himself	5.56*	.70	2.37
I'd	4.34*	.70	.04
if[a]	6.57*	1.46	3.04
of	7.60*	18.77	28.46
particular	4.26*	.00	.28
problem[a]	5.46*	.00	.30
rest	5.06*	.43	.00
same[a]	10.18**	1.48	.26
self	7.49*	.00	.37
situation[a]	4.78*	.03	.35
social[a]	6.24*	.00	.62
socially	5.52*	.00	.16
somehow[a]	6.66*	.00	1.02
they're	5.03*	2.29	.85
things[a]	5.45*	1.72	3.47
try[a]	9.12**	.11	1.24
Walter's	5.28*	1.13	.22
warn	5.18*	.05	.81
what	4.94*	4.47	8.48
world[a]	6.71*	.05	.53
younger[a]	5.37*	.38	.00

[a]Discussed in text.
* = $p < .05$. ** = $p < .01$.

THE SECOND STORY—TEENS

Did the teenagers use a plight-like interpretive model in the second story as they had in the first? In the first story, this was seen first in markers of time and development. In the second story, teenagers again focused on time and development. But not surprisingly, given the shift in surface content, they used different words to do so. There were three of these. One was *anymore* (as in "They weren't friends anymore," "Erica is not part of his life anymore," and "He's not constructing anything anymore"). Another was *behind* ("he's always wanted to put that behind him," and "leaving her behind"). And the third was *younger* ("involved with a woman during his younger period," and "A man he had known back when they were younger, when they were less educated"). All served to mark the impoverished situation in the past that the protagonist has left behind.

But, the protagonist has regrets not only about his past but also about leaving it, longings that are rather plaintively marked by these far from neutral or objective markers of time. In the first story, the time words were more neutral. In contrast with them, *anymore, behind*, and *younger* suggest a loss, indeed, the loss of a still much desired golden age. In this way, these time words mark not only time, but also the knottiness of the present situation as an historical/developmental plight, a further inference that had to be supported in the first story by additional words, especially *have to*. If anything, the integration of time and fate into plight is more vividly expressed here.

Moreover, the teens plainly saw this story, as they had the first, as being about how character is formed along a developmental path, in the manner of the Bildungsroman. In the first story, the main indicators of straight and branching roads on the way to maturity were the words *reaction* and *away*. And the focus on the character's essential self was conveyed by *being*. In the interpretation of the Böll (1986) story, a single word carries both of these ideas. It is the distinctive word *same*. It is used to characterize common origins before developmental trajectories diverged: "They both came from the same level," and "they weren't going to be the same anymore."

The teens are also interested in events along the path that led to the present plight. They lay the blame for divergence on education, an education that though shared, nevertheless led the protagonist, but not Walter, into a foreign social milieu with an accompanying alienation from past, from old friends, and indeed from self. Indeed, *educated* is used in this story (as having created the protagonist's regretful bourgeois stance) with much the same function as *mother* in the first one (she having contributed to Charles's regretful commitment as would-be priest). And whereas at the surface, *educated* and *mother* are very different words, in fact both of them function alike to identify an essential historical fact that creates the knotty plight in the two stories.

Our distinction is analogous to the one that Vladimir Propp (1968) made when he differentiated between the *function* played by a character or situation in a folk tale, and the actual character or situation used for fulfilling that function. So, for example, an empowering gift given to the hero can be as varied as clairvoyance in one story, a tireless horse in another, and an endless gold thread in a third. All serve to get the task done by means of a supernatural gift received by the hero from a donor. And, by the same token, the hero and donor can also differ from story to story so long as they fill the functional roles required by the plot structure.

THE SECOND STORY—ADULTS

Did our adults reveal the distinctive dramatistic pattern that characterized their interpretations of the first story? Recall that relative to the teens, adults had nearly twice as many distinctive words. This fact alone greatly improved the possibility of finding some correspondence between their interpretations of the two stories. That much said, it is still striking that we find so many of the same dramatistic functions, though served by different words.

We turn first to the augmented list of elements in the Burkean Pentad). Scene, which was captured in the first story by the word *set*, is caught this time by the comparable word *situation*. Some examples are, "an early love kind of situation," and "he can kind of control this situation." The extra element Trouble, marked in the first story by the use of the word *conflict*, has its counterpart here in the use of *problem*—as in "getting married; and there's a problem," and "he's neurotic about his grease problem." Goal, represented in "Grease Spots" by the protagonist's objective of getting Walter to call off the wedding, is now marked by the distinctive adult word *try*. Examples are, "going to talk to his friend to try to discourage him from getting married" and "male chauvinistic duty to try to get his friend to realize."

There is also elaboration of the Instrument of Trouble. In the first story it was captured by the word *sexual*. In the second, its exact counterpart is found in the use of the word *social*, in the sense of social class. For example, "her old ethnic and social background," and "involved with someone beneath his social class," and "he has sort of changed social classes." The girl's sexuality in the first story creates trouble for Charles' plans for the priesthood. In the second story, the social standing of the protagonists, or perhaps the protagonist's anxiety about it, is instrumental to the Trouble.

In the first story, we said that the use of *happens* was interesting for the way it suggested that the Burkean pattern may have had some structural necessity for the subjects, that it indicated that some events were seen as dramatistic necessities even at an early point when the particular details of how the necessary action will occur are not yet known. In the interpretations of the second story, two words, *somehow* and *things*, are used similarly in a fashion that suggests that subjects do have a narrative model in mind. Examples of the first are: "Going to talk to the groom to somehow call off the wedding" and "The narrator was somehow connected with the woman." The plain spirit of these is that the generic goal (in the first) must be present even though we do not know what specifically he will do to achieve it, or, in the second, that a breached relationship—of some kind—must be the psychological engine that is driving our protagonist toward his ill-conceived goal. Examples of the use of *things* are: "The narrator can keep things from getting out of hand," "It seems like things are turning on ambivalence," "And realizing that things could have been different if his life. . . ." *Things*, too, is used to mark dramatic elements so evidently part of the canonical dramatistic pattern that they can be discussed even though they lack specificity.

The open-endedness of dramatism is caught in the first story by the word *possible*, a word that distinguishes adult dramatistic interpretation from the teenagers' locked in fatalism. It has its counterpart in the second story in the distinctive adult marker *if*. Examples are "His life could be different if he was different," "what would it be like if I saw her again." In sum, then, there is strong confirmation that the dramatistic model that characterizes adults' interpretive thinking about the first story also characterizes interpretation of the second.

And the situatedness of adult thinking that we saw before also appeared again, as we see later. In the analysis of the first story, we discovered that subjects using the dramatistic narrative model not only decompose a story into its dramatic elements but also situate the tale in an imagined world. Situatedness, recall, is imagining the characters and action as existing in some lifelike context. This contrasts with both the rather barren landscape of the children's plots, and with the teens' narrow and plight-bound definitions of characters, both of which transcend the particulars of setting.

We also noted before that adult subjects are aware of the author and of constraints on the story as a constructed work of art. But situated fictional realism, on the one hand, and constructivism on the other, seem to pose a contradiction in adult interpretation. Yet, we found these same interesting patterns again. Along with a dramatistic pattern of awareness of authorial option, the second story also evoked situated responses from the adults. Recall that in the first story, situatedness was conveyed inter alia by the word *life*. This has a very close counterpart in the second story in the distinctive adult word *world*. Examples are "firmly grounded in the working world," "he too has gone further in the world," "what it takes now to live in this new world," and "enter another world." A second word was also used that helps to situate action in a more lifelike, imagined world—*feelings*. The use of this word reflects the adults' exploration of characters' inner lives, making them more like real (though invented) people rather than figures or beings caught in a plight. Examples are, "narrator has some unresolved feelings about Erica," and "This recognition of his feelings for the woman in the elevator," and "tight examination of what his feelings are at that particular moment."

Evidently, these two developments—toward realism and constructivism—are synergistic in the adult narrative model, however much it seems that they would be contradictory in an undramatized account. We can speculate that imagining characters as real people in a world suggests possibilities for dramatic construction of text, and, conversely, that developing those dramatic possibilities deepens the characters, making them more like "real" people. This finding, that two elements that might be contradictory in noninterpretive cognition function in interpretation in a synergistic pattern, gives a tantalizing whiff of the possible surprises that are bound to come from further investigation of interpretive thinking. It suggests that there are rules, perhaps even a logic, of narrative thinking that are both distinct from those we know in more analytic domains, rules that are also well formed.

Indeed, the dual pull toward realism and constructivism may reflect a deeper, indeed defining, duality in drama—that it is enacted simultaneously on a landscape of action and a landscape of consciousness, in the world and in the mind (Bruner, 1986). This duality has no counterpart in the organization of our computational knowledge. It could be responsible, once its elaborations were understood, for entirely different kinds of rule systems for regulating interpretive thinking.

CONCLUSION

The present studies strongly suggest that narrative models are an important and ubiquitous part of the cognitive tool kit available to people in our culture, and indeed in any culture with narrative artifacts. And because narrative art is about as ubiquitous a cultural product as one can find, found even in oral cultures, the mastery of narrative models must be one of the central tasks of cognitive development in any culture. In our culture, these models, like other important cognitive models, seem to undergo interesting and rather systematic reorganization with age and development.

And we might conjecture that there would be developmental changes in these models in other cultures, even though adult genres elsewhere may be entirely different from ours. In any culture, we would expect recognizably childlike and adultlike renditions of the same "tale." Not only could genres differ, but we should also expect that the dual landscape of subjectivity and action might not be universal, even though it is known to be widespread (Feldman, 1991b). Recent research on the "primary attribution error" (Markus & Kitayama, 1991), for example, seems to suggest that in Far Eastern cultures there is less of a tendency to attribute action to the motives and traits of protagonists, and more emphasis on obligation, reflecting more general emphases in the culture. This might lead to quite different developmental changes.

The three deep questions for an interpretive cognitive psychology are:

1. How are narrative models constructed by human groups as part of their culture?
2. What form do these models take in various cultures?
3. How do individual members of the culture acquire its narrative forms, and how does their understanding of them alter in the course of development?

In the previous pages, we have tried to illustrate how one might go about studying the third question, but all three questions pose similar challenges to empiricism, for to ask any of them in a scientific way is to take on a more interpretive role oneself. And this poses many interesting problems, some of which we have tried to grapple with in the earlier discussion. So we offer our present findings not so much as conclusions about fixed "stages" of development in narrative interpretation, though they may later prove to be that, but rather as illustrations of how to get on with the difficult task of constructing an interpretive cultural psychology.

Though our focus here has been developmental, we believe that the present study also illustrates more general questions about the forms of knowing that are applied to narration. We know now that the patterns that have turned up—interpretation by plot, plight, and dramatism—are distinctive and not to be found in studies of cognitive development using other, nonnarrative material. The task now is to formulate ways of understanding such interpretive activity, in whatever domains it may happen to express itself.

We propose consequently that interpretive cognition may be taken on as an important part of any human being's epistemological equipment, for it has all the earmarks of a powerful epistemological system, for two reasons. First, we now must take it as likely that interpretive forms of knowing fall into patterns that have a generality that transcends particular stories or situations. And, second, we have seen that models have an internal coherence that is suggestive of a rule-governed system.

Studies of interpretive cognition can be done within a scientific psychology, and without losing the scientifically essential distance between the investigator and the object of study, for transcripts of people's actual talk give us a chance to look at what they are saying in a manner that separates the observer from the observed. Of course, we then have to interpret what they say, and scientific interpretation plays an essential role here. But, this is not unique, for such interpretation always plays a role in a cognitive psychology that seeks to interpret action in a fashion that will reveal what the acting person thinks or means by their acts. The present study suggests that what people think, and what we think, can be kept apart sufficiently to make discovery possible.

ACKNOWLEDGMENTS

This chapter, and the analysis contained therein, were made possible by an ongoing grant from the Spencer Foundation, "Inquiries in Cultural Psychology," to Jerome Bruner. The data were originally collected under a grant from NICHHD, 5PO1 HD20807. An earlier version of this chapter was presented at the Twenty-First Annual Symposium of the Piaget Society in Philadelphia on May 30, 1991, at a special session on "Meaning and Intentionality." Reprinted from "Plot, plight, and dramatism: Interpretation at three ages" by C. Feldman, J. Bruner, D. Kalmar, and B. Renderer, 1993, *Human Development, 36*(6), 327–342 (with small modifications).

REFERENCES

Barthes, R. (1974). *S/Z: An essay*. New York: Hill & Wang.

Böll, H. (1986). Nostalgia or: Grease spots. In H. Böll (Ed.), *The stories of Heinrich Böll* (pp. 677–680). New York: Knopf.

Bruner, J. (1986). *Actual minds, possible worlds*. Cambridge, MA: Harvard University Press.

Bruner, J. (1990). *Acts of meaning*. Cambridge, MA: Harvard University Press.

Burke, K. (1945). *A grammar of motives*. New York: Prentice-Hall.

Feldman, C. (1991a). Genres as mental models (Italian translation). In M. Ammaniti & D. N. Stern (Eds.), *Rappresentazioni e narrazioni* (pp. 113–131). Rome: Laterza.

Feldman, C. (1991b). Oral metalanguage. In D. Olson & N. Torrance (Eds.), *Literacy and orality* (pp. 47–65). Cambridge, England: Cambridge University Press.

Feldman, C., Bruner, J., Renderer, B., & Spitzer, S. (1990). Narrative comprehension. In B. Britton & A. Pellegrini (Eds.), *Narrative thought and narrative language* (pp. 1–78). New York: Lawrence Erlbaum Associates.

Feldman, C., & Toulmin, S. (1976). Logic and the theory of mind. In W. J. Arnold (Ed.), *Nebraska symposium on motivation, 1975* (pp. 409–476). Lincoln: University of Nebraska Press.

Gill, B. (1961). Truth and consequences. In R. B. Goodman (Ed.), *75 short masterpieces: Stories from the world's literature* (pp. 93–96). New York: Bantam.

Goodman, N. (1978). *Ways of worldmaking*. Indianapolis: Hackett Publishing.

MacWhinney, B. (1989). Manual for the use of the CLAN programs of the child language data exchange system [Computer program]. Pittsburgh: Carnegie Mellon University, Department of Psychology.

Markus, H., & Kitayama, S. (1991). Cultural imperatives. In R. E. Nisbett & H. Markus (Eds.), Culture, cognition, and social conflict [Unpublished memorandum]. Ann Arbor: University of Michigan.

Paley, V. G. (1988). *Bad guys don't have birthdays: Fantasy play at four*. Chicago: University of Chicago Press.

Propp, V. (1968). *Morphology of the folktale*. Austin: University of Texas Press.

Rorty, A. (1988). *Mind in action: Essays in the philosophy of mind*. Boston: Beacon Press.

APPENDIX A

The following two questions were asked twice—after the first fourth and the first third of the story had been read:

1. What is the most important thing I've told you so far?
2. Why?

The following three questions were asked twice—after half and three fourths of the story had been read:

1. What are the directions this could be going?
2. Which way do you think it will go?
3. Why?

Each of the following six questions was asked once, in the order presented, after the whole story had been read:

1. What happened in the end?
2. Tell me some things about [give the name of the main character] that I haven't told you. What's he like?
3. This is a hard question, but I'd like you to give it a try. What was the author trying to say?
4. What kind of story is this? It's not a mystery; it's not a folk tale. What would you call it?
5. I'd like you to tell me the story now—the same story I told you, but in your own words.
6. What was the gist of your story?

APPENDIX B

The ultimate goal in this data analysis is to determine whether there are any statistically reliable differences among any of the words that the different groups of subjects used. Achieving this goal, however, is a computationally daunting task. Among all of the subjects in a typical experiment, hundreds to thousands of unique words might be used. The process of reading through each transcript and counting by hand the frequency of word usage for each subject for even a single word is labor-intensive; to count hundreds of words and compute the relevant ANOVAs would be labor-prohibitive. The challenge, then, is to develop a set of procedures that would automate the analysis of our transcripts for word-frequency usage. We have developed such a set of procedures by using a series of computer programs and routines to analyze our transcripts.

To understand the procedure we follow, keep in mind the following critical points. We begin with transcripts of our interview tapes, prepared on a computer. From these transcripts, we need to know for each subject what words that particular subject uses, and for each of those words, how frequently that subject used it. With this information, we then know all of the words used in the experiment. We also know, for each subject, which of those words he or she used, and how frequently he or she used each word. This information can be placed in the form of a word-by-subject matrix. This matrix can be analyzed using any of a number of major statistical analysis packages. When analyzing such a large dataset, a statistical package might generate on the order of sometimes thousands of pages of output. This volume of output needs to be reduced to manageable proportions. The point of this reduction is to highlight words that are candidates for representing interpretive differences between subjects. With the reduced set of analysis results, we can then return to the original transcripts and interpret the ways in which subjects use these highlighted words.

The tape recordings of the interviews were transcribed by a professional transcription service. The service used the WordPerfect 4.2 software for the IBM. We then compared sections of these transcripts with the original recordings for accuracy of transcription. Then began the task of getting from these transcription files to the completed analyses.

1. *Converting files to ASCII format:* Files in the WordPerfect 4.2 format contain hidden control codes that must be eliminated before analysis begins. We accomplish this by converting the WordPerfect 4.2 files to a basic ASCII (text) format, using the CONVERT program that is part of the WordPerfect 5.0 package.

2. *Giving all of the files a uniform structure:* The original files tended to vary slightly from each other when they arrived from the transcriber. For example, sometimes a marker for the beginning of a question might have been entered as "Q.1," sometimes as "Q1" (without the period). Such inconsistencies need to be corrected. We also needed to add additional structure to the files for later analysis. For example, we wanted the subject number to appear with each question asked by an experimenter, so that there would be no ambiguity over which response went with which subject. Accordingly, we converted all files to a common format.

To do this, a series of transformations was applied to each transcript, treated as a data file. WordPerfect's Program Editor was useful for this task because it supports the use of macros. We wrote a macro for each transformation. A typical macro would be something like, "for each instance of '.c:' in the file, replace it with '.C:'." The complete set of macros was then chained together to be run one after the other without intervention. The number of such macros required varied from 21 to 52. The macros were not only chained, but the full set of macros were set up to loop so that, once invoked, the full set could operate successively upon all of the data files.

3. *Remove the experimenter's utterances from the files:* Our counts were intended to include only the subject's and not the experimenter's utterances. All of the experimenter's utterances and the transcriber annotations were removed from the transcripts. Again, we used macros written for the Program Editor.

4. *Compute word frequency for each subject:* Once the transcript files are cleaned up and uniformly structured, we can determine the word-frequency usage for each subject. For this we used the FREQ program from the 1989 version of the CLAN package (MacWhinney, 1989), directing the output from each analysis to an output file.

5. *Clean up the output files for further analysis:* Along with the basic information concerning the frequency with which each word was used by a subject, the output files also contained a few summary statistics, such as a count

of the total number of words the subject used (tokens) and the total number of different words the subject used (types). This summary information was written down for use later, and was then edited out of the file. After this editing, the files contained only the words and the associated frequencies, so that these files could be used as input files for the next step in the analysis.

6. *Creating a word-by-subject matrix:* Our goal in this step was to create a word-by-subject matrix. All of the words in the entire corpus were used. For each of the subjects, the number of times that subject used each word would be contained in the matrix. Not all subjects use all of the words, so some cells in this matrix would represent zero entries. Creating this matrix is conceptually simple but computationally difficult for a large vocabulary. It would have been prohibitively expensive for us to conduct this step on the mainframe computer. We had access to a Macintosh IIci computer, thanks to a gift from Alan Kay and Apple Computer, and transferred the files to that computer, using the Apple File Exchange 1.1.4 program. We then used the data manipulation module in the Systat 5.0 program to create the large word-by-subject matrix. For this particular study, there were a total of 38 subjects and 2,665 different words, yielding over 100,000 data points. The matrix was then sent to an output file. This final data matrix could then be used for the mainframe data analysis.

7. *Getting the data to the mainframe:* This output matrix was edited with the QUED/M 2.07 editor in order to reduce blank spaces (and hence reduce the amount of text to be transferred), and was then transferred back to the IBM. Using the ProComm 2.4.2 program on the IBM, the file was then uploaded to an IBM mainframe running the Wylbur 8.1 operating system.

8. *Preparing the data set for analysis:* The target format for these data was to be a subject-by-words matrix, where the variable names correspond to the actual words. In SAS (the only mainframe package that we know of that will support the data analysis procedure outlined next), variable names are limited to eight characters—a shorter length than that of many words. Hence, special names must be created by truncating the actual words, and care must be taken to avoid assigning identical truncation to different words, like the eight-letter "twenty-f" for both "twenty-four" and "twenty-five." As a final twist, the FREQ program will sometimes capitalize words, sometimes not, and the SYSTAT program treats upper-case and lower-case letters as distinct, causing many words to appear twice in the word-by-subject matrix. These must be summed together. The core of the SAS program to handle these types of problems is around 150 lines long.

The matrix file was then read into SAS 5.18. For each subject, the frequency value for each word represented the actual number of times the subject used the word. These have next to be converted into relative frequencies based on each subject's total number of words used. In this study, a subset of words with their relative word frequencies were selected for further analysis. These were a set of words such that at least four subjects in one of the three age groups used a given word at least once. A total of 458 words were thereby retained by this selection criterion.

9. *The ANOVA step:* Using the ANOVA procedure in SAS 5.18, an ANOVA using a single MODEL statement was performed for each word in the subset. We used SAS 5.18 because it would allow us to run hundreds of ANOVAs at a time. This analysis could not be completed in SAS 6.06 (or in, e.g., SPSS-X), because the ANOVA module was rewritten in such a fashion that one can only include roughly 10 words in a single model statement, rather than the several hundred at a time permitted by SAS 5.18.

10. *Analyzing the analysis:* At this point, we had hundreds of pages of output. To make sense of the results in this format would be a Herculean task. So, the goal here was to reduce the volume of results to manageable proportions. The target format would have, inter alia, the overall ANOVA significance levels, means, and post hoc *t* tests between means for each word all on 1 line, with 50 lines on a page, so that the words could be examined more easily. To this end, the output from the ANOVA analysis was then edited and used as input to a further SAS analysis, in order to consolidate these results. In this new analysis, the printout data was read in using variables such as "mean square," "*F* value," and "*p* value." This new dataset was then used as the basis for further analysis.

With this dataset in hand, a criterion must be established for what words should be considered further. In our case, the words were all sorted according to their significance level (the equivalent of effect size in this case), and the words were pulled for further analysis that had an overall ANOVA with a *p* value less than .05. For the first story, 75 words met this criterion.

11. *Interpreting the results:* Returning with this set of words to the IBM, the Micro Oxford Concordance Program was then used to find and print out each use of each word, along with its surrounding context. This permitted us to determine usage for each word—and thereby to infer in what way any word or class of words might be "special" to a particular age group.

13

Semantic Naturalism: The Problem of Meaning and Naturalistic Psychology

Richard F. Kitchener
Colorado State University

The problem of meaning is (arguably) the central problem in 20th century philosophy. Whether it takes the linguistic form of an inquiry into semantics, a mentalistic form of an inquiry into intentionality, or a cultural-historical form of an inquiry into the meaning of a text or an action, the problem of meaning has been at the center of philosophical discussion both in Anglo-Saxon analytic philosophy and in European phenomenology, structuralism, hermeneutics, and poststructuralism. With only a little exaggeration could one say that both philosophical traditions have been primarily concerned with *semiotics*—the theory of signs[1]—even though their respective theories of meaning and their conceptualizations of the problem seem divergent.

A similar situation can be said to characterize 20th-century psychology: a preoccupation with the nature and existence of mental representation with little consensus about a correct solution. This problem is exacerbated by the fact that "semantic theory" includes a variety of quite different fields in which semantics is conceptualized in quite different way.[2] Consequently, my coverage of different

---

[1]Semiotics, which is traditionally divided into *syntax* (the formal-structural relations of signs to other signs), *semantics* (the relation of signs to objects signified), and *pragmatics* (the relation of signs to sign users), has a long history, and includes the key figures C. S. Pierce, Ferdinand de Saussure, and Charles Morris. One issue that arises here is whether meaning is primarily linguistic in nature or whether it is primarily psychological in nature. The dominant tradition in 20th-century philosophy and cognitive science has favored the former.

[2]For general surveys dealing with semantics within the context of philosophy of language, see Harrison (1980), Martin (1987), and Devitt and Sterelny (1987). For linguistics, see Chierchia and McConnell-Ginet (1990), J. D. Fodor (1977), and Kempson (1977). For semantics and artificial intelligence, see Boden (1988), and for semantics and cognitive science, see Barwise & Etchemendy (1989), Johnson-Laird (1983), Larson (1990), and Stillings et al. (1987).

theories of meaning is restrictive, focusing on the problem of meaning within cognitive science. After briefly examining the problem of "naturalizing semantics," I briefly discuss four major theories of meaning and how they attempt to naturalize meaning. I conclude that although the project of naturalizing semantics is difficult, it is unavoidable.

THE PROBLEM OF SEMANTIC NATURALISM

The Problem of Meaning

Several psychologists (Skinner, 1957, 1974; Watson, 1958) and philosophers (P. M. Churchland, 1981; P. S. Churchland, 1986; Quine, 1960; Stich, 1983) have wanted to eliminate meaning from the realm of intelligible scientific discourse. Why? What is so problematic about meaning?

The central motive behind this move seems to be the commitment of most 20th-century psychologists and philosophers to *naturalism* and to the thesis that naturalism is incompatible with meaning (Katz, 1990; Mohanty, 1981).

A word or sentence is something physical in nature. How then can something physical be about something else—the meaning of the word or sentence? This is the problem of the "aboutness" relation and none of the natural relations present within the scientific image of the world seem sufficiently like this aboutness relation.

Secondly, a physical token is about something—its meaning or signification. But the meaning of the sign does not seem to be something natural either: Although the meaning of some signs may be natural objects, it is not true of many other signs, for example, abstract ideas.

If linguistic meaning has problematic features, the related psychological notion of *intentionality*—the notion that mental states (propositional attitudes) are about nonmentalistic states of affairs—seems equally problematic. Although Ponce de Leon sought the fountain of youth, this intentional state is problematic for naturalistic psychology because the underlying intentional relation between the mental state and the state of affairs to which it is directed seems to be nonnaturalistic and the sought after state of affairs may be nonexistent.[3] If the intended state of affairs is nonexistent, how can one's mental states be about it?[4]

It is because concepts involving meaning seem to be resistant to a naturalistic analysis that many psychologists and philosophers have suggested they simply be eliminated from scientific discourse (*eliminativism*). Another option would be

---

[3]This led Brentano (1874/1973) to argue that psychology was an autonomous "science," radically unlike the physical sciences.

[4]Of course, one might try to solve this problem by saying that it is not the actual but nonexistent state of affairs F that is causally relevant here, but instead the underlying belief (desire, etc.) that is the cause of the subsequent behavior. But now we have the same problem as before—the belief in question is "about" some state of affairs. But how can we explain this particular relation naturalistically?

to define or translate meaning-concepts into, say, behavioristic terms (Morris, 1946; Osgood, 1964; Skinner, 1957, 1974). But if *eliminativism* and *definism* are not plausible, then how can we retain semantic concepts and also have a naturalistic psychology? Is it possible, in short, to have a *semantic naturalism*?

Naturalism

What is meant by naturalism (Bhaskar, 1979; Hatfield, 1990)? The most general account is that of *generic naturalism*: only the natural world exists; the only things that can be known are known by naturalistic methods; norms and values reside in nature. Generic naturalism thus denies the existence of the *super*natural, the possibility of any supernaturalistic ways of knowing, and the possibility of any supernatural values or norms. Hence, it would be opposed to certain kinds of ontologies (Platonism, Cartesian dualism, and Kantian noumenal entities— God, the soul), epistemologies and methodologies (intuitionism, transcendental-ism, mysticism), and certain theories of value (intuitionism, moral sense theory, certain versions of deontology). But it takes no ontological stance on the nature of the natural and is consistent with physicalism, materialism, empiricism, positivism, and pragmatism. It is also consistent with the methodologies of inductivism, hypothetico-deductivism, inference to the best explanation, and so forth, and with a wide variety of ethical theories.

If one were to equate "natural" with "physical" one would have what is termed *physicalistic naturalism*: nothing exists except the physical realm—the realm of space and time—and nothing is knowable except via the methods of the physical sciences. Hence, all values must ultimately be physical in nature (or supervenient upon the physical).[5] If nothing exists outside the space-time nexus, then everything knowable must occur within this nexus and must be knowable in virtue of its *causal effects* (Ellis, 1990). (Of course, now the issue turns on what is meant by *causality* and *space-time*.)

Finally, nothing about physicalistic naturalism requires it to be reductionistic (definism or eliminativism). One can countenance emergent entities by virtue of believing in the doctrine of *supervenience*; that is, every existent property must have an underlying naturalistic (physicalistic) base that "generates" the property in question. According to semantic supervenience, therefore, meaning supervenes on the natural (physical) realm. It thus appears possible to be a physicalistic naturalistic and also a nonreductionistic.

Extension Versus Intension

Traditionally, meaning has been understood in relation to the distinction between the extension (denotation, reference) of terms versus the intension (connotation, sense) of terms. In fact, the basic issue dividing the different theories of meaning

---

[5]This is *weak physicalism* and should be distinguished from *strong physicalism*, which is the view that everything is reducible to the physical where by "physical" is meant the entities and processes adequate to explain the *inorganic realm* (Meehl & Sellars, 1956).

concerns the question of whether meaning is just extensional—this is usually thought to be a reductionistic approach—or must be intensional.

The *extension* of a term consists of those particular objects to which the term in question is correctly ascribed. Thus, the extension of "Socrates" is a particular man, and the extension of "philosopher" is a set of objects.

On the other hand, the *intension* of a term consists of those properties possessed by all and only members of the denotation of that term. Thus, the intension of "philosopher" is the set of properties: rational, animal, lover of wisdom, speaker of a language, and so forth.

The distinction between a term's extension and its intension thus divides theories of meaning into three camps: *extensionalism*, the thesis that meanings are fundamentally extensions (referents, denotations), *objective intensionalism*, the thesis that meanings are objective intensions, and *subjective intensionalism*, the thesis that meanings are subjective intensions. (These three theories of meaning coincide, roughly, with the three traditional solutions to the problem of universals: nominalism, Platonic realism, and conceptualism.)

Extensionalism can easily accommodate naturalism because an extensionalist needs only a set of particular spatio-temporal concrete objects for his theory of meaning (together with sets and truth-values). By contrast, an intensionalist will have a more difficult time because she will have to countenance not only sets of objects and instantiated properties, but either Platonic-like entities—Frege's (1960) senses, abstract ideas, or Platonic Forms—or concepts in the mind. Both kinds of entities seem to be problematic for naturalism.

AN OVERVIEW OF THEORIES OF MEANING

In this section I present a rough overview of four major theories of meaning: truth-conditional semantics (TCS), conceptual-role semantics (CRS), ecological semantics (ES), and intention-based semantics (IBS) and how they attempt to solve the problem of semantic naturalism.[6]

Truth-Conditional Semantics (TCS)

The fundamental thesis of TCS is the following: The meaning of a symbol "p" is the set of conditions p under which p is true. The meaning of "snow is white" consists of those conditions in the world under which this proposition is true, namely, when snow is white.

---

[6]It should be pointed out that these theories of meaning are not mutually exclusive and are combinable in various ways (e.g., Barwise & Perry, 1983; Block, 1986; Searle, 1983). In fact, dual-role semantics, a combination of TCS and CRS, has become something of the received view concerning the nature of meaning.

Davidsonian Semantics. Perhaps the most widely discussed version of TCS is that of Davidson (1984), who claimed (following Quine, 1960) that one can avoid talk of meanings as intensions and instead have a completely extensional theory of meaning. For Davidson, therefore, the only semantic notions required are those of truth, denotation, and satisfaction—all of which, it is claimed, are extensional in nature. Davidson's particular version of TCS employs Tarski's (1956) model-theoretic notion of truth—the semantic conception of truth—which results in the following claim: "Snow is white" is true if and only if snow is white. This is cashed in in terms of the extensional notions of *denotation* and *satisfaction.*[7]

Verificationist Semantics. TCS can also be used to answer the question, "Under what conditions does a person understand or know the meaning of some symbol?" The answer is that one knows or understands the meaning of "*p*" when one knows or understands those very conditions under which "*p*" is true. Hence, if one knows the conditions under which "snow is white" is true, namely, when snow is white, then one understands its meaning. But when does one know these conditions?: when she can explicitly *state* the conditions?, when he can *recognize* the conditions when they obtain?, when she can specify the conditions that must be satisfied in order for such a proposition to be *verified* or confirmed? The latter option led Dummett (1975, 1976) to propose a verificationist semantics (VS): The meaning of a proposition *p* consists of those conditions that would verify *p*. This in turn involves a specification of a set of procedures such that carrying out these procedures results in the recognition that *p* is true. The meaning of a sentence, therefore, ceases to be related to a realist conception of meaning and instead is translated into an epistemic or cognitive concept, one in terms of one's evidential grounds for asserting the sentence.[8]

Possible World Semantics (PWS). PWS, game-theoretic semantics, Montague semantics, and situation semantics are further variations of TCS. TCS is often characterized in terms of *model theory* in which one is concerned with offering *interpretations* of strings of symbols, that is, assignment of truth-values in some domain.[9] In this process, individual constants ("Socrates") are mapped

---

[7]As Field (1972) argued, part of the motivation behind Tarski's (1956) semantic theory of truth was his desire to be a strict physicalist and hence to reduce all semantic notions to physicalistic o nes.

[8]Few individuals have pointed out the implications of Dummett's (1976) verificationism for cognitive psychology. Although Dummett (1976) denied a theory of meaning is a psychological hypothesis, he frequently reiterated the point that meaning (sense) is directly connected with knowledge, hence presumably representation, and admitted he is offering a psychological account. Indeed, his stress on verification procedures puts him clearly in the camp of procedural semantics (Johnson-Laird, 1977, 1983; Woods, 1981).

[9]In the 1960s, model theory was developed into PWS, largely as an attempt to deal with intensional logic, modal logic, the logic of counterfactual conditionals, and propositional attitudes.

onto individuals, predicates ("philosopher") are mapped onto sets of individuals, and propositions are mapped onto truth values. If one maps predicates onto individual objects—such mappings being termed *functions*—one can speak of the set of objects satisfying the predicate as the "meaning" of the predicate.[10]

Situation Semantics. PWS is a mapping of propositions onto possible worlds. Several technical problems with such an approach led to an increasing emphasis on context in determining meaning. In the situation semantics of Barwise and Perry (1983), sentences denote entities in particular situations. In fact, they explicitly adopted what I call an ecological theory of meaning, modeled after the work of Gibson (1979), in which the meaning of an utterance is a relation between the situation in which the sentence is uttered and the situation described by the sentence. In such a model, internal cognitive representations understood computationally are thought to be otiose: Meanings are "more in the world and less in the head than the traditional view of meaning assumed" (Barwise & Perry, 1983, p. x). Here TCS becomes merged with ecological semantics.

Conceptual Role Semantics (CRS)

CRS has been closely associated with a philosophical view concerning the nature of mental states—*functionalism* (Block, 1986, 1987; Peacocke, 1981)—and in cognitive science/artificial intelligence with *procedural semantics* (Johnson-Laird, 1977, 1983; Woods, 1981).[11] Roughly, functionalism is the view that mental states are to be understood in terms of their functional role, that is, the role they play in the sequence of psychological states from stimulus input, through inferential processing, to behavioral output.

What is distinctive about CRS is the notion that the meaning of a term consists not in the relevant truth conditions, but of the role the symbol plays in the larger conceptual system: The meaning of a symbol "p" consists of the entire set of conceptual relations into which "p" enters. This is an example of semantic-holism—a coherence theory of meaning. As Harman (1974) put it:

> The meaning of a sentence is determined by the role in a conceptual scheme of the thoughts that the sentence would normally be used to express . . . meaning has

---

[10]How is PWS relevant to cognitive psychology? One answer is that the representation of meaning via PWS can occur via internal modeling of possible words, for example, mental models (Johnson-Laird, 1983) or mental spaces (Fauconnier, 1985).

[11]Although I do not discuss procedural semantics in this chapter it is not for want of importance. According to procedural semantics, the meaning of a symbol consists of a set of procedures that operate on it (e.g., procedures for deciding its truth value). This obviously brings to mind Piaget's operational theory of meaning. No one I know of has attempted an examination of procedural semantics in relation to Piaget.

to do with evidence, inference, and reasoning, including the impact sensory experiences has on what one believes, the way in which inference and reasoning modify one's beliefs and plans, and the way beliefs and plans are reflected in action. (p. 11)

But because one's conceptual scheme consists of the speaker's "beliefs, plans, hopes, fears, and so on" and because these mental states are typically thought to involve meaning already, it remains unclear what CRS really is.

There are two versions of CRS, a purely syntactical version and a semantic version—two-factor theory. According to the syntactical version, sometimes called *the representational theory of mind* (*computationalism*) (J. A. Fodor, 1981; Lycan, 1988; Pylyshyn, 1980): The meaning of a symbol "p" consists of all the syntactical-computational relations into which "p" enters. For example, functionalism was initially explicated in terms of Ramsey sentence clauses, and Ramsey sentences are purely syntactical (formal) in nature (Block, 1980; Lewis, 1970) and assimilated to Turing machine states (Putnam, 1980). These syntactical relations sometimes were also thought to be causal in nature, in the sense that a sequence of syntactical forms could also be a causal sequence involving input, mediating states, and output in a computational format.

It is an essential feature of syntactical CRS that all semantic features of mental states can be mirrored by syntactical relations or expressed in a syntactical meta-language (*translational semantics*). If this is combined with semantic compositionality, then all semantic features of mental states are purely compositional. Of course, eventually one's decomposition must stop somewhere and one then encounters *semantic primitives*. What cannot be accounted for by compositional semantics, however, is the meaning of these primitive concepts themselves—*the problem of original meaning* (Haugeland, 1985). Because such an approach cuts off word meaning from the external, public world and from communication, the *semantic markers* approach often associated with syntactical CRS has faltered as a semantic theory (Chierchia & McConnell-Ginet, 1990; J. D. Fodor, 1977; Kempson, 1977).

Syntactical CRS is thus a version of *solipsistic semantics* (LePore & Loewer, 1986) and accordingly inadequate. Consequently, virtually no one today advocates syntactical CRS. (See, however, Jackendoff, 1983.) Instead, those who continue to advocate CRS adopt a second version of CRS—*dual-aspect CRS*, which has become something of the received view concerning meaning. It is as follows: The meaning of a symbol "p" consists of (a) all the syntactical-computational relations into which "p" enters, and (b) its relations with the external objects in the environment. Dual-aspect CRS is thus a combination of syntactical CRS and a TCS and/or an ES (Block, 1986, 1987; Field, 1977; J. A. Fodor, 1987; Harman, 1987; Loar, 1981; Lycan, 1988). But if so, then syntactical CRS is inadequate by itself and in need of supplementation. Hence, the issue surrounding CRS becomes the question of whether the more liberal version of CRS can still be entitled CRS at all or whether CRS is essentially committed to syntactical CRS. Although I do not have the time to complete the argument, I have suggested that CRS is committed to a syntactical form if one interprets functionalism in a purely internalist way involving narrow content; that is, if one interprets the "inputs" and "outputs" as being essentially internal, describable in formalist terms, and thus limited to narrow content. If I am right, then no version of CRS is adequate and a dual-aspect CRS is an oxymoron.[12]

Ecological Semantics (ES)

A third kind of semantics is what can be called ecological semantics (ES). Unlike CRS, which seems committed to a purely internalist conception—a first-person point of view—typified by methodological solipsism, ES takes an externalist perspective—a third-person point of view—the organism in relation to its environment.[13] ES has several varieties.

Causal ES.   First, there is a cluster of theories that are committed, in one way or another, to a *causal* theory of semantics, for example, a causal theory of reference (Devitt, 1981; Kripke, 1980; Putnam, 1975). According to this view, the meaning of some internal symbol "p" is the corresponding object in the environment—p—that causally initiates a chain of events eventuating in the symbolic representation "p." The model here is that of an external object, say, snow causally initiating a series of events that result in a person's internal mental representation—"snow." "Snow" thus means (denotes) snow, just as "smoke" means fire.

There are numerous refinements and qualifications such a causal notion requires, including the idea, for example, that the distal object must *reliably cause* the resulting mental representation, that there must be *counterfactual support* of the aforementioned causal generalization, that such connections between causes and effects must be *nomological*, and so forth. Furthermore, to avoid certain kinds of problems with such a theory, it may be necessary to have several different causal stages intervening between the distal object and the mental

---

[12]If this is correct, then the computational theory of mind (methodological solipsism) is also inadequate and so is "cognitivism" (Haugeland, 1978).

[13]Internalism in epistemology is the view that what is known (justified) must be known (justified) from the individual's subjective point of view and not just from the external, third-person point of view (Goldman, 1980). Both versions derive from a radical cognitivism, which ultimately goes back to Descartes. Instead of Berkeley's idealism—"to be is to be perceived" (*esse ist percipi*)—the idealism of the modern cognitivist and constructivist is "to be is to be represented" (*esse ist concipi*).

representation (J. A. Fodor, 1987). The basic idea, however, is that a reliable effect is a good indicator of its corresponding cause and hence its meaning.

Teleological ES. Causal ES has taken a variety of forms and evolved in different directions. One development was toward an information-theoretic approach (Dretske, 1981) in which the meaning of a symbol "*p*" is its informational content, the information contained in "*p*" about the corresponding state of affairs *p*. But such an approach had to face the problem of misrepresentation or false representations, which soon led to a line of development I call *teleological ES.*

The problem that teleological ES attempts to solve is the problem of the improper functioning of the system, whether causal or informational, by addressing the issue of what it means for a system to be functioning normally or properly. Hence it was suggested: The function of the mental representation "*p*" is to indicate the status of its correlative cause. Here, function was understood in a biological (teleological) sense; namely, it was somehow part of the "design" of "*p*"—its design via natural selection—to be a representation (see also Lycan, 1988). Thus functioning gave way to *proper functioning* understood as "biologically proper." This in turn ruled out a merely statistical sense of "normal" and in turn led individuals to look at the history of the system in relation to its environment to understand proper function (Millikan, 1984).

Millikan's (1984) adaptationist account is clearly a naturalistic account, not a straightforward causal account, but a teleological (biological) account. Clearly, it is also an externalist account with a prominent ecological dimension. But not only is a stress placed on the system in its environment, the account is historical in a way that standard cognitive (computational) psychology cannot countenance (Cummins, 1989). Hence, if Millikan's ES is even close to being right, computationalism and those cognitive psychologies based upon it must be wrong.

Gibsonian ES. Talk of ecological naturally brings to mind the work of Gibson (1979), who can also be said to have been committed to an ES (Reed, 1987). According to this account, natural objects in the environment possess affordances, which are directly picked up by our sensory organs; for example, a large rock affords us sit-ability. Such affordances can be said to constitute an object's meaning—what can be done with it. A Gibsonian ES is a theory involving the primacy of knowing-how, not knowing-that, of procedural knowledge, not declarative knowledge, of praxis, not theory. Here too belong what can be called *motor theories of the mind* (Weimer, 1977; Winograd & Flores, 1986), theories of meaning that claim that meaning is originally to be found in an organism's action on environmental objects (Bickhard, 1980). This original and primitive meaning based upon praxis provides the basis for a later stage in which meaning is internalized and symbolically represented as in Piagetian semantics.

Like its causal counterpart, this type of ES is wedded to a naturalistic semantics (although it eschews computationalism, the representational theory of mind, and associated cognitive theories). Indeed, some version of ES seems to be the only visible candidate for a theory of original meaning (although what such a theory would look like remains unclear and very sketchy).

Intention-Based Semantics (IBS)

A fourth type of semantic theory represents a kind of extension of the third category, an extension of meaning into the social arena of the public use of language and a consequent stress on the pragmatic dimensions of language. Although some individuals in this group would disavow the Wittgensteinian dictum that "meaning is use" (Wittgenstein, 1953), it seems to be clear that the movement termed *speech-act theory* (Austin, 1975; Searle, 1969) was, at least originally, inspired by something like Wittgenstein's later views on the pragmatic and social nature of language. Although speech-act theory was never touted as a complete theory of meaning, it has been extended and developed in this direction by the work of Grice (1989).[14]

The central thesis of Grice's (1989) work is that (a) the linguistic meaning (semantic meaning) of symbols is reducible to the speaker's meaning in using these symbols, and (b) speaker meaning in turn is reducible to psychological meaning (the subject's intention), where intention does not involve anything linguistically semantic. Hence, semantic meaning is reduced to psychological meaning. The fundamental perspective of IBS, therefore, is the notion of a speaker who is communicating to an audience by means of some kind of speech act, that is, who is using language to produce some effect in the audience. Because it is an act of linguistic communication, such a social action has a certain goal, can be said to be conformable to certain kinds of cooperative rules (rules of conversational implication), and hence is essentially rational in nature.[15]

IBS is typically construed as having (at least) two stages: first, an account of what an utterer means on a particular occasion, and second, an account of "timeless meaning," that is, an account of the generality and social dimension of meaning independent of particular occasions and individual speakers. This later stage thus involves the attempt to explicate the notion of what an utterance of a particular type means; such an explication employs the notion of social conventions.

The first stage of IBS involves the following claim:

(IBS₁) When a speaker S utters a statement u to an audience A, S means that p if S utters u (a) intending to produce in A a certain response, viz., the belief that p,

---

[14]Bennett (1976), Lewis (1969), Loar (1981), and Schiffer (1972, 1987) represent important extensions, modifications, and criticisms of some of the basic ideas of Gricean IBS.

[15]Although I do not have time to discuss Grice's (1989) logic of conversation, I do want to point out its importance for Habermas' (1979) theory of communicative competence and its striking similarity to Piaget's (1979) logic of social cooperation (Kitchener, 1991).

(b) intending that A should recognize that S intends to do this, and (c) intending that A's belief that p should result from A's recognition that S intends to do this.

For example, when a teacher, giving an examination, utters the statement "I'm afraid time is up," the teacher means "the examination period is over; cease writing": (a) if the teacher intends to produce in the class the belief that the examination period is over; cease writing; (b) the teacher intends that the class should recognize that he intended to do this; and (c) the teacher intends that this belief of the class should be the effect of the class's recognition of the teacher's intention.

A second stage has been added on to this to accommodate what most individuals take to be the public nature of linguistic meaning. Here, the more ordinary meaning of a linguistic symbol is reducible to social conventions, namely:

(IBS$_2$) The utterance of u to A means p if there exists in a social community (including S and A), a set of conventions (correlations) between the utterance of u and acts of speaker intentions.

Hence, permanent meaning is an emergent phenomenon: It emerges from the social communicative relations between individuals and the key component here is to explain how social conventions can emerge from behavioral regularities (Bennett, 1976; Lewis, 1969).

If IBS is to produce a semantic naturalism, both phases must be completed in a thoroughly naturalistic way. First, although (let us assume) linguistic meaning can be defined in terms of speakers' intentions, can intentions be explicated in a naturalistic way? Grice's (1989) own views on this subject seem to be less than helpful because he viewed intention as (somehow) naturalistic but he did not say how.

Secondly, a naturalism would have to be able to handle conventions in a purely naturalistic (nonsemantic) way, for example, in terms of regularities of behavior (uttering sentences) in relation to underlying intentions. This would involve an analysis of conventions that did not rely on semantic meaning or psychological meaning. Hence, in addition to the necessity of providing a naturalistic interpretation of intention, action, and so on, one would also have to provide a naturalistic account of *convention*, as, say, a set of purely empirical, natural regularities connecting intentions and actions. Whether one can give a completely naturalistic account of such rule-following behavior is currently not clear.

CONCLUSION

Each of the four theories of meaning discussed can be interpreted as being versions of semantic naturalism: TCS is naturalistic because it only employs extensional concepts; CRS purports to be naturalistic and has been tied very closely to the syntactical approaches of artificial intelligence, computer simulation, methodological solipsism, and radical cognitivism; ES is clearly a version of semantic naturalism because it employs something like a causal relation between environmental objects and mental states; IBS is naturalistic because it ultimately reduces meaning to social and psychological dispositions. But although these various theories of meaning may be interpreted in naturalistic terms, their relevance to contemporary psychology and to its task of incorporating a theory of meaning into a naturalistic psychological framework remains unclear; indeed, the entire relation between a theory of meaning and psychology has been hotly debated. But what is clear is that, insofar as contemporary psychology must employ a naturalistic theory of meaning, one (or more) of the aforementioned seem to be the most likely candidates.

Any adequate psychology seems committed to semantics whether linguistic or psychological; but modern psychology is also firmly committed to naturalism. These two positions appear to be incompatible, however. One could give up semantics altogether. But given the central importance of meaning in our lives, this seems to be an implausible alternative.[16] One could also give up naturalism. But what the abandonment of naturalism would mean remains unclear, just as it is unclear what alternative to naturalism is currently available. Most individuals would not take seriously a *metaphysical nonnaturalism*, whereas *methodological nonnaturalism* remains undeveloped at best. Contemporary psychology, like the other sciences, seems fundamentally committed to some version of naturalism.

The task for contemporary psychology, therefore, appears to involve the construction of a naturalist psychological semantics: a theory of (psychological) meaning that countenances only naturalistic entities knowable by naturalistic methods. This would seem to involve adopting an "external" point of view and abandoning a purely "internal" point of view (cognitivism). This opens up the possibility that contemporary psychology needs to consider less cognitive approaches to the mind (e.g., Piagetian, Gibsonian, social-constructivist, Vygotskyian semantics). But even if it does not, the task of finding a place for meaning in a naturalistic psychology seems unavoidable.

ACKNOWLEDGMENTS

An earlier version of this chapter was presented at the 21st annual symposium of the Jean Piaget Society. I wish to thank Michael Chandler for the invitation to participate in an invited symposium. I also wish to thank Michael Losonsky

---

[16]Another option would be to retain meaning but give up cognitivism, or at least the dominant interpretation of it—the representational theory of mind. This seems to be the option of Gergen (1982) and other social constructionists (e.g., Coulter, 1979; Harre, 1986) who are attempting to construct a noncognitivist theory of meaning.

and Bernie Rollin for numerous conversations on many of these topics, and Karen Kitchener for reading and improving an earlier version of this manuscript.

REFERENCES

Austin, J. (1975). *How to do things with words* (rev. ed.). Oxford, England: Oxford University Press.

Barwise, J., & Etchemendy, J. (1989). Model-theoretic semantics. In M. I. Posner (Ed.), *Foundations of cognitive science* (pp. 207–244). Cambridge, MA: MIT Press.

Barwise, J., & Perry, J. (1983). *Situations and attitudes*. Cambridge, MA: MIT Press.

Bennett, J. (1976). *Linguistic behavior*. Cambridge, England: Cambridge University Press.

Bhaskar, R. (1979). *The possibility of naturalism*. Atlantic Highlands, NJ: Humanities Press.

Bickhard, M. (1980). *Cognition, convention, and communication*. New York: Praeger.

Block, N. (1980). Troubles with functionalism. In N. Block (Ed.), *Readings in the philosophy of psychology* (Vol. 1, pp. 268–305). Cambridge, MA: Harvard University Press.

Block, N. (1986). Advertisement for a semantics for psychology. In P. A. French et al. (Eds.), *Midwest studies in philosophy: Vol. 10. Studies in the philosophy of mind* (pp. 615–678). Minneapolis: University of Minnesota Press.

Block, N. (1987). Functional role and truth conditions. *The Aristotelian Society, Supplementary Volume lxi*, 157–182.

Boden, M. (1988). *Computer models of mind*. Cambridge, England: Cambridge University Press.

Brentano, F. (1973). *Psychology from an empirical standpoint* (A. C. Pancurello, D. B. Terrell, & L. L. McAlister, Trans.). New York: Humanities. (Original work published 1874)

Chierchia, G., & McConnell-Ginet, S. (1990). *Meaning and grammar: An introduction to semantics*. Cambridge, MA: MIT Press.

Churchland, P. M. (1981). Eliminative materialism and propositional attitudes. *Journal of Philosophy, 78*, 67–89.

Churchland, P. S. (1986). *Neurophilosophy: Toward a unified science of the mind/brain*. Cambridge, MA: MIT Press.

Coulter, J. (1979). *The social construction of mind*. London: Macmillan.

Cummins, R. (1989). *Meaning and mental representation*. Cambridge, MA: MIT Press.

Davidson, D. (1984). *Inquiries into truth and interpretation*. Oxford, England: Clarendon Press.

Devitt, M. (1981). *Designation*. New York: Columbia University Press.

Devitt, M., & Sterelny, K. (1987). *Language and reality: An introduction to the philosophy of language*. Cambridge, MA: MIT Press.

Dretske, F. (1981). *Knowledge and the flow of information*. Cambridge, MA: MIT Press.

Dummett, M. (1975). What is a theory of meaning? In S. Guttenplan (Ed.), *Mind and language* (pp. 97–138). Oxford, England: Clarendon Press.

Dummett, M. (1976). What is a theory of meaning? II. In G. Evans & J. McDowell (Eds.), *Truth and meaning: Essays in semantics* (pp. 67–137). Oxford, England: Clarendon Press.

Ellis, B. (1990). *Truth and objectivity*. Oxford, England: Basil Blackwell.

Fauconnier, G. (1985). *Mental spaces*. Cambridge, MA: MIT Press.

Field, H. (1972). Tarski's theory of truth. *Journal of Philosophy, 69*, 347–375.

Field, H. (1977). Logic, meaning, and conceptual role. *Journal of Philosophy, 74*, 379–408.

Fodor, J. A. (1981). Methodological solipsism considered as a research strategy in cognitive psychology. In J. Fodor (Ed.), *Representations: Philosophical essays on the foundations of cognitive science* (pp. 225–256). Cambridge, MA: MIT Press.

Fodor, J. A. (1987). *Psychosemantics: The problems of meaning in the philosophy of mind*. Cambridge, MA: MIT Press.

Fodor, J. D. (1977). *Semantics: Theories of meaning and generative grammar*. New York: Crowell.

Frege, G. (1960). On sense and reference (M. Black, Trans.). In P. Geach & M. Black (Eds.), *Translations from the philosophical writings of Frege* (pp. 56–78). Oxford, England: Basil Blackwell. (Original work published 1892)

Gergen, K. (1982). *The transformation of social knowledge.* New York: Springer-Verlag.

Gibson, J. J. (1979). *The ecological approach to visual perception.* Boston: Houghton-Mifflin.

Goldman, A. (1980). The internalist conception of justification. In P. A. French et al. (Eds.), *Midwest studies in philosophy: Vol. V. Studies in epistemology* (pp. 27–51). Minneapolis: University of Minnesota Press.

Grice, P. (1989). *Studies in the way of words.* Cambridge, MA: Harvard University Press.

Habermas, J. (1979). *Communication and the evolution of society* (T. McCarthy, Trans.). Boston: Beacon Press.

Harman, G. (1974). Meaning and semantics. In M. K. Munitz & P. Unger (Eds.), *Semantics and philosophy* (pp. 1–16). New York: New York University Press.

Harman, G. (1987). (Nonsolipsistic) conceptual role semantics. In E. Lepore (Ed.), *New directions in semantics* (pp. 55–82). New York: Academic.

Harre, R. (Ed.). (1986). *The social construction of emotion.* Oxford, England: Basil Blackwell.

Harrison, B. (1980). *An introduction to the philosophy of language.* New York: St. Martin's Press.

Hatfield, G. (1990). *The natural and the normative: Theories of spatial perception from Kant to Helmholtz.* Cambridge, MA: MIT Press.

Haugeland, J. (1978). The nature and plausibility of cognitivism. *The Behavioral and Brain Sciences, 2,* 215–260.

Haugeland, J. (1985). *Artificial intelligence: The very idea.* Cambridge, MA: MIT Press.

Jackendoff, R. (1983). *Semantics and cognition.* Cambridge, MA: MIT Press.

Johnson-Laird, P. (1977). Procedural semantics. *Cognition, 5,* 189–214.

Johnson-Laird, P. (1983). *Mental models.* Cambridge, MA: Harvard University Press.

Katz, J. J. (1990). *The metaphysics of meaning.* Cambridge, MA: MIT Press.

Kempson, R. M. (1977). *Semantic theory.* Cambridge, England: Cambridge University Press.

Kitchener, R. F. (1991). Jean Piaget: The unknown sociologist. *British Journal of Sociology, 42,* 421–442.

Kripke, S. (1980). *Naming and necessity.* Cambridge, MA: Harvard University Press.

Larson, R. K. (1990). Semantics. In D. N. Osherson & H. Lasnik (Eds.), *An invitation to cognitive science: Vol. 1. Language* (pp. 23–42). Cambridge, MA: MIT Press.

LePore, E., & Loewer, B. (1986). Solipsistic semantics. In P. A. French et al. (Eds.), *Midwest studies in philosophy. Vol. 10. Studies in the philosophy of mind* (pp. 595–614). Minneapolis: University of Minnesota Press.

Lewis, D. (1969). *Convention.* Cambridge, MA: Harvard University Press.

Lewis, D. (1970). How to define theoretical terms. *Journal of Philosophy, 67,* 427–446.

Loar, B. (1981). *Mind and meaning.* Cambridge, England: Cambridge University Press.

Lycan, W. G. (1988). *Judgment and justification.* Cambridge, England: Cambridge University Press.

Martin, R. M. (1987). *The meaning of language.* Cambridge, MA: MIT Press.

Meehl, P., & Sellars, W. (1956). The concept of emergence. In H. Feigl & M. Scriven (Eds.), *Minnesota studies in the philosophy of science: Vol. 1. The foundations of science and the concepts of psychoanalysis* (pp. 239–252). Minneapolis: University of Minnesota Press.

Millikan, R. G. (1984). *Language, thought, and other biological categories.* Cambridge, MA: MIT Press.

Mohanty, J. N. (1981). Intentionality and noema. *Journal of Philosophy, 78,* 706–717.

Morris, C. W. (1946). *Signs, language and behavior.* Englewood Cliffs, NJ: Prentice-Hall.

Osgood, C. (1964). A behavioristic analysis of perception and language as cognitive phenomena. In R. Harper et al. (Eds.), *The cognitive processes* (pp. 184–210). Englewood Cliffs, NJ: Prentice-Hall.

Peacocke, C. (1981). The theory of meaning in analytic philosophy. In G. Floistad (Ed.), *Contemporary philosophy: A new survey. Vol. 1. Philosophy of language* (pp. 57–82). The Hague, Netherlands: Martinus Nijhoff.

Piaget, J. (1979). *Etudes sociologiques* [Sociological studies] (2nd ed.). Geneva, Switzerland: Droz.

Putnam, H. (1975). The meaning of "meaning." In H. Putnam, *Philosophical Papers. Vol. 2: Mind, language and reality* (pp. 215–271). Cambridge, England: Cambridge University Press.

Putnam, H. (1980). The nature of mental states. In N. Block (Ed.), *Readings in the philosophy of psychology* (Vol. 1, pp. 223–231). Cambridge, MA: Harvard University Press.

Pylyshyn, Z. (1980). Computation and cognition. *The Behavioral and Brain Sciences, 3*, 111–132.

Quine, W. V. O. (1960). *Word and object.* Cambridge, MA: MIT Press.

Reed, E. (1987). James Gibson's ecological approach to cognition. In A. Costall & A. Still (Eds.), *Cognitive psychology in question* (pp. 142–175). New York: St. Martin's Press.

Schiffer, S. (1972). *Meaning.* Oxford, England: Oxford University Press.

Schiffer, S. (1987). *Remnants of meaning.* Cambridge, MA: MIT Press.

Searle, J. (1969). *Speech acts.* Cambridge, England: Cambridge University Press.

Searle, J. (1983). *Intentionality: An essay in the philosophy of mind.* New York: Cambridge University Press.

Skinner, B. F. (1957). *Verbal behavior.* New York: Appleton–Century–Crofts.

Skinner, B. F. (1974). *About behaviorism.* New York: Knopf.

Stich, S. P. (1983). *From folk psychology to cognitive science: The case against belief.* Cambridge, MA: MIT Press.

Stillings, N. A., Feinstein, M. H., Garfield, J. L., Rissland, E. L., Rosenbaum, D. A., Weisler, S. E., & Baker-Ward, L. (1987). *Cognitive science: An introduction.* Cambridge, MA: MIT Press.

Tarski, A. (1956). The concept of truth in formalized languages (J. H. Woodger, Trans.). In A. Tarski (Ed.), *Logic, semantics, and metamathematics* (pp. 152–278). Oxford, England: Clarendon Press.

Watson, J. B. (1958). *Behaviorism.* Chicago: University of Chicago Press.

Weimer, W. (1977). A conceptual framework for cognitive psychology: Motor theories of the mind. In R. Shaw & J. Bransford (Eds.), *Perceiving, acting and knowing: Toward an ecological psychology* (pp. 267–311). Hillsdale, NJ: Lawrence Erlbaum Associates.

Winograd, T., & Flores, F. (1986). *Understanding computers and cognition.* Reading, MA: Addison-Wesley.

Wittgenstein, L. (1953). *Philosophical investigations.* Oxford, England: Basil Blackwell.

Woods, W. A. (1981). Procedural semantics. In A. Joshi, B. N. Webber, & I. Sag (Eds.), *Elements of discourse understanding* (pp. 300–334). Cambridge, England: Cambridge University Press.

Author Index

Subject Index